Excel®
for Scientists
and Engineers

Numerical Methods

D1088564

THE WILEY BICENTENNIAL—KNOWLEDGE FOR GENERATIONS

$\mathcal{E}$ach generation has its unique needs and aspirations. When Charles Wiley first opened his small printing shop in lower Manhattan in 1807, it was a generation of boundless potential searching for an identity. And we were there, helping to define a new American literary tradition. Over half a century later, in the midst of the Second Industrial Revolution, it was a generation focused on building the future. Once again, we were there, supplying the critical scientific, technical, and engineering knowledge that helped frame the world. Throughout the 20th Century, and into the new millennium, nations began to reach out beyond their own borders and a new international community was born. Wiley was there, expanding its operations around the world to enable a global exchange of ideas, opinions, and know-how.

For 200 years, Wiley has been an integral part of each generation's journey, enabling the flow of information and understanding necessary to meet their needs and fulfill their aspirations. Today, bold new technologies are changing the way we live and learn. Wiley will be there, providing you the must-have knowledge you need to imagine new worlds, new possibilities, and new opportunities.

Generations come and go, but you can always count on Wiley to provide you the knowledge you need, when and where you need it!

WILLIAM J. PESCE
PRESIDENT AND CHIEF EXECUTIVE OFFICER

PETER BOOTH WILEY
CHAIRMAN OF THE BOARD

Excel® for Scientists and Engineers

Numerical Methods

E. Joseph Billo

WILEY-INTERSCIENCE
A John Wiley & Sons, Inc., Publication

Published by John Wiley & Sons, Inc., Hoboken, New Jersey.
Published simultaneously in Canada.

For general information on our other products and services or for technical support, please contact our Customer Care Department within the United States at (800) 762-2974, outside the United States at (317) 572-3993 or fax (317) 572-4002.

Wiley also publishes its books in a variety of electronic formats. Some content that appears in print may not be available in electronic format. For information about Wiley products, visit our web site at www.wiley.com.

Wiley Bicentennial Logo: Richard J. Pacifico

Library of Congress Cataloging-in-Publication Data is available.

ISBN: 978-0-471-38734-3

Printed in the United States of America.

10 9 8 7 6 5 4

Summary of Contents

Contents

Preface

The solutions to mathematical problems in science and engineering can be obtained by using either analytical or numerical methods. Analytical (or direct) methods involve the use of closed-form equations to obtain an exact solution, in a nonrepetitive fashion; obtaining the roots of a quadratic equation by application of the quadratic formula is an example of an analytical solution. Numerical (or indirect) methods involve the use of an algorithm to obtain an approximate solution; results of a high level of accuracy can usually be obtained by applying the algorithm in a series of successive approximations.

As the complexity of a scientific problem increases, it may no longer be possible to obtain an exact mathematical expression as a solution to the problem. Such problems can usually be solved by numerical methods.

The Objective of This Book

Numerical methods require extensive calculation, which is easily accomplished using today's desktop computers. A number of books have been written in which numerical methods are implemented using a specific programming language, such as FORTRAN or C++. Most scientists and engineers received some training in computer programming in their college days, but they (or their computer) may no longer have the capability to write or run programs in, for example, FORTRAN. This book shows how to implement numerical methods using Microsoft Excel®, the most widely used spreadsheet software package. Excel® provides at least three ways for the scientist or engineer to apply numerical methods to problems:

- by implementing the methods on a worksheet, using worksheet formulas

- by using the built-in tools that are provided within Excel

- by writing programs, sometimes loosely referred to as macros, in Excel's Visual Basic for Applications (VBA) programming language.

All of these approaches are illustrated in this book.

This is a book about numerical *methods*. I have emphasized the methods and have kept the mathematical theory behind the methods to a minimum. In many cases, formulas are introduced with little or no description of the underlying theory. (I assume that the reader will be familiar with linear interpolation, simple calculus, regression, etc.) Other topics, such as cubic interpolation, methods for solving differential equations, and so on, are covered in more detail, and a few topics, such as Bairstow's method for obtaining the roots of a regular polynomial, are discussed in detail.

In this book I have provided a wide range of Excel solutions to problems. In many cases I provide a series of examples that progress from a very simple implementation of the problem (useful for understanding the logic and construction of the spreadsheet or VBA code) to a more sophisticated one that is more general. Some of the VBA macros are simple "starting points" and I encourage the reader to modify them; others are (or at least I intended them to be) "finished products" that I hope users can employ on a regular basis.

Nearly 100% of the material in this book applies equally to the PC or Macintosh versions of Excel. In a few cases I have pointed out the different keystrokes requires for the Macintosh version.

A Note About Visual Basic Programming

Visual Basic for Applications, or VBA, is a "dialect" of Microsoft's Visual Basic programming language. VBA has keywords that allow the programmer to work with Excel's workbooks, worksheets, cells, charts, etc.

I expect that although many readers of this book will be proficient VBA programmers, others may not be familiar with VBA but would like to learn to program in VBA. The first two chapters of this book provide an introduction to VBA programming – not enough to become proficient, but enough to understand and perhaps modify the VBA code in this book. For readers who have no familiarity with VBA, and who do not wish to learn it, do not despair. Much of the book (perhaps 50%) does not involve VBA. In addition, you can still use the VBA custom functions that have been provided.

Appendix 1 provides a list of VBA keywords that are used in this book. The appendix provides a description of the keyword, its syntax, one or more examples of its use, and reference to related keywords. The information is similar to what can be found in Excel's On-Line Help, but readers may find it helpful at those times when they are reading the book without simultaneous access to a PC.

A Note About Typographic Conventions

The typographic conventions used in this book are the following:

Menu Commands. Excel's menu commands appear in bold, as in the following examples: "choose **Add Trendline...** from the **Chart** menu...," or "**Insert→Function...**"

Excel's Worksheet Functions and Their Arguments. Worksheet functions are in Arial font; the arguments are italicized. Following Microsoft's convention, required arguments are in bold font, while optional arguments are in nonbold, as in the following:

VLOOKUP(*lookup_value, table_array, column_index_num*, range_lookup)

The syntax of custom functions follows the same convention.

Excel Formulas. Excel formulas usually appear in a separate line, for example,

=1+1/FACT(1)+1/FACT(2)+1/FACT(3)+1/FACT(4)+1/FACT(5)

Named ranges used in formulas or in the text are not italicized, to distinguish them from Excel's argument names, for example,

=VLOOKUP(Temp,Table,MATCH(Percent,P_Row,1)+1,1)

VBA Procedures. Visual Basic code is in Arial font. Complete VBA procedures are displayed in a box, as in the following. For ease in understanding the code, VBA keywords are in bold.

```
Private Function Deriv1(x)
'User codes the expression for the derivative here.
Deriv1 = 9 * x ^ 2 + 10 * x - 5
End Function
```

Problems and Solutions

There are over 100 end-of-chapter problems. Spreadsheet solutions for the problems are on the CD-ROM that accompanies this book. Answers and explanatory notes for most of the problems are provided in Appendix 8.

The Contents of the CD

The CD-ROM that accompanies this book contains a number of folders or other documents:

- an "Examples" folder. The Examples folder contains a folder for each chapter, e.g., 'Ch. 05 (Interpolation) Examples.' The examples folder for each chapter contains all of the examples discussed in that chapter: spreadsheets, charts and VBA code. The location of the Excel file pertinent to each example is specified in the chapter text, usually in the caption of a figure, e.g.,

Figure 5-5. Using VLOOKUP and MATCH to obtain a value from a two-way table. (folder 'Chapter 05 Interpolation,' workbook 'Interpolation I,' sheet 'Viscosity')

- a "Problems" folder. The Problems folder contains a folder for each chapter, e.g., 'Ch. 06 (Differentiation) problems.' The problems folder for each chapter contains solutions to (almost) all of the end-of-chapter problems in that chapter. VBA code required for the solution of any of the problems is provided in each workbook that requires it; the VBA code will be identical to the code found in the 'Examples' folder.

- an Excel workbook, "Numerical Methods Toolbox," that contains all of the important custom functions in this book.

- a copy of "Numerical Methods Toolbox" saved as an Add-In workbook (an .xla file). If you open this Add-In, the custom functions will be available for use in any Excel workbook.

- Two Excel workbooks containing the utilities Solver Statistics and Trendline to Cell.

Comments Are Welcomed

I welcome comments and suggestions from readers. I can be contacted at numerical_methods.billo@verizon.net.

E. Joseph Billo

Acknowledgments

Dr. Richard N. Fell, Department of Physics, Brandeis University, Waltham, MA; Prof. Michele Mandrioli, Department of Chemistry and Biochemistry, University of Massachusetts–Dartmouth, North Dartmouth, MA; and Prof. Christopher King, Department of Chemistry, Troy University, Troy, AL, who read the complete manuscript and provided valuable comments and corrections.

Prof. Lev Zompa, University of Massachusetts–Boston, and Dr. Peter Gans, Protonic Software, for UV-vis spectral data.

Edwin Straver and Nicole Steidel, Frontline Systems Inc., for information about the inner workings of the Solver.

The Dow Chemical Company for permission to use tables of physical properties of heat transfer fluids.

About the Author

E. Joseph Billo retired in 2006 as Associate Professor of Chemistry at Boston College, Chestnut Hill, Massachusetts. He is the author of *Excel for Chemists: A Comprehensive Guide*, 2nd edition, Wiley-VCH, New York, 2001. He has presented the 2-day short courses "Advanced Excel for Scientists and Engineers" and "Excel Visual Basic Macros for Scientists and Engineers" to over 2000 scientists at corporate clients in the United States, Canada and Europe.

Chapter 1

Introducing
Visual Basic for Applications

In addition to Excel's extensive list of worksheet functions and array of calculation tools for scientific and engineering calculations, Excel contains a programming language that allows users to create procedures, sometimes referred to as macros, that can perform even more advanced calculations or that can automate repetitive calculations.

Excel's first programming language, Excel 4 Macro Language (XLM) was introduced with version 4 of Excel. It was a rather cumbersome language, but it did provide most of the capabilities of a programming language, such as looping, branching and so on. This first programming language was quickly superseded by Excel's current programming language, Visual Basic for Applications, introduced with version 5 of Excel. Visual Basic for Applications, or VBA, is a "dialect" of Microsoft's Visual Basic programming language, a dialect that has keywords to allow the programmer to work with Excel's workbooks, worksheets, cells, charts, etc. At the same time, Microsoft introduced a version of Visual Basic for Word; it was called WordBasic and had keywords for characters, paragraphs, line breaks, etc. But even at the beginning, Microsoft's stated intention was to have one version of Visual Basic that could work with all its applications: Excel, Word, Access and PowerPoint. Each version of Microsoft Office has moved closer to this goal.

The Visual Basic Editor

To create VBA code, or to examine existing code, you will need to use the Visual Basic Editor. To access the Visual Basic Editor, choose **Macro** from the **Tools** menu and then **Visual Basic Editor** from the submenu.

The Visual Basic Editor screen usually contains three important windows: the Project Explorer window, the Properties window and the Code window, as shown in Figure 1-1. (What you see may not look exactly like this.)

The Code window displays the active module sheet; each module sheet can contain one or several VBA procedures. If the workbook you are using does not

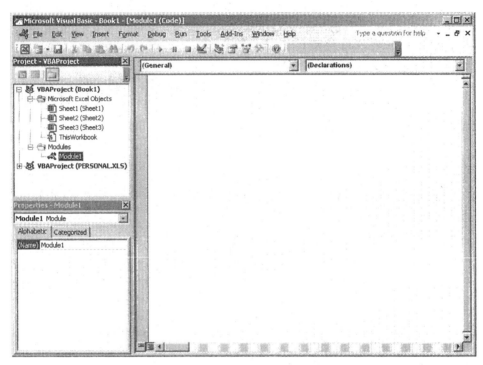

Figure 1-1. The Visual Basic Editor window.

contain any module sheets, the Code window will be empty. To insert a module sheet, choose **Module** from the **Insert** menu. A folder icon labeled Modules will be inserted; if you click on this icon, the module sheet Module1 will bedisplayed. Excel gives these module sheets the default names Module1, Module2 and so on.

Use the Project window to select a particular code module from all the available modules in open workbooks. These are displayed in the Project window (Figure 1-2), which is usually located on the left side of the screen. If the Project window is not visible, choose **Project Explorer** from the **View** menu, or click on the Project Explorer toolbutton 🖳 to display it. The Project Explorer toolbutton is the fifth button from the right in the VBA toolbar.

In the Project Explorer window you will see a hierarchy tree with a node for each open workbook. In the example illustrated in Figure 1-2, a new workbook, Book1, has been opened. The node for Book1 has a node (a folder icon) labeled Microsoft Excel Objects; click on the folder icon to display the nodes it contains— an icon for each sheet in the workbook and an additional one labeled ThisWorkbook. If you double-click on any one of these nodes you will display the code sheet for it. These code sheets are for special types of procedures called automatic procedures or event-handler procedures, which are not covered in this

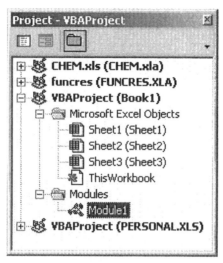

Figure 1-2. The VBE Project Explorer window.

book. Do not use any of these sheets to create the VBA procedures described in this book. The hierarchy tree in Figure 1-2 also shows a Modules folder, containing one module sheet, Module1.

The Properties window will be discussed later. Right now, you can press the Close button to get rid of it if you wish.

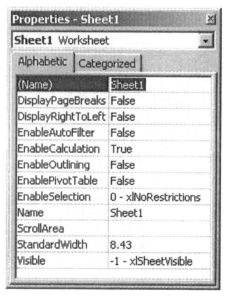

Figure 1-3. The Properties window.

Visual Basic Procedures

VBA macros are usually referred to as *procedures*. They are written or recorded on a *module* sheet. A single module sheet can contain many procedures.

There Are Two Kinds of Macros

There are two different kinds of procedures: **Sub** procedures, called command macros in the older XLM macro language, and **Function** procedures, called function macros in the XLM macro language and often referred to as custom functions or user-defined functions.

Although these procedures can use many of the same set of VBA commands, they are distinctly different. **Sub** procedures can automate any Excel action. For example, a **Sub** procedure might be used to create a report by opening a new worksheet, copying selected ranges of cells from other worksheets and pasting them into the new worksheet, formatting the data in the new worksheet, providing headings, and printing the new worksheet. **Sub** procedures are usually "run" by selecting **Macro** from the **Tools** menu. They can also be run by means of an assigned shortcut key, by being called from another procedure, or in several other ways.

Function procedures augment Excel's library of built-in functions by adding user-defined functions. A custom or user-defined function is used in a worksheet in the same way as a built-in function like, for example, Excel's SQRT function. It is entered in a formula in a worksheet cell, performs a calculation, and returns a result to the cell in which it is located. For example, a custom function named FtoC could be used to convert Fahrenheit temperatures to Celsius.

Custom functions can't incorporate any of VBA's "action" commands. No experienced user of Excel would try to use the SQRT function in a worksheet cell to calculate the square root of a number and also open a new workbook and insert the result there; custom functions are no different.

However, both kinds of macro can incorporate decision-making, branching, looping, subroutines and many other aspects of programming languages.

The Structure of a Sub Procedure

The structure of a **Sub** procedure is shown in Figure 1-4. The procedure begins with the keyword **Sub** and ends with **End Sub**. It has a ProcedureName, a unique identifier that you assign to it. The name should indicate the purpose of the function. The name can be long, since after you type it once you will probably not have to type it again. A **Sub** procedure has the possibility of using one or more arguments, Argument1, etc, but for now we will not create **Sub** procedures with arguments. Empty parentheses are still required even if a **Sub** procedure uses no arguments.

```
Sub ProcedureName(Argument1, ...)
    VBA statements
End Sub
```

Figure 1- 4. Structure of a **Sub** procedure.

The Structure of a Function Procedure

The structure of a **Function** procedure is shown in Figure 1-5. The procedure begins with the keyword **Function** and ends with **End Function**. It has a FunctionName, a unique identifier that you assign to it. The name should be long enough to indicate the purpose of the function, but not too long, since you will probably be typing it in your worksheet formulas. A **Function** procedure usually takes one or more arguments; the names of the arguments should also be descriptive. Empty parentheses are required even if a **Function** procedure takes no arguments.

```
Function FunctionName(Argument1, ...)
    VBA statements
    FunctionName = result
End Function
```

Figure 1-5. Structure of a user-defined function.

The function's *return statement* directs the procedure to return the result to the caller (usually the cell in which the function was entered). The return statement consists of an assignment statement in which the name of the function is equated to a value, for example,

```
FunctionName = result
```

Using the Recorder to Create a Sub Procedure

Excel provides the Recorder, a useful tool for creating command macros. When you choose **Macro** from the **Tools** menu and **Record New Macro...** from the submenu, all subsequent menu and keyboard actions will be recorded until you press the Stop Macro button or choose **Stop Recording** from the **Macro** submenu. The Recorder is convenient for creating simple macros that involve only the use of menu or keyboard commands, but you can't use it to incorporate logic, branching or looping.

The Recorder creates Visual Basic commands. You don't have to know anything about Visual Basic to record a command macro in Visual Basic. This provides a good way to gain some familiarity with Visual Basic.

To illustrate the use of the Recorder, let's record the action of applying scientific number formatting to a number in a cell. First, select a cell in a worksheet and enter a number. Now choose **Macro** from the **Tools** menu, then **Record New Macro...** from the submenu. The Record Macro dialog box (Figure 1-6) will be displayed.

The Record Macro dialog box displays the default name that Excel has assigned to this macro: Macro1, Macro2, etc. Change the name in the Macro Name box to ScientificFormat (no spaces are allowed in a name). The "Store Macro In" box should display This Workbook (the default location); if not, choose This Workbook. Enter "e" in the box for the shortcut key, then press OK.

Record Macro

Macro name:

Macro1

Shortcut key: Store macro in:

Ctrl+   This Workbook

Description:

Macro recorded 8/27/2000 by Billo

OK   Cancel

Figure 1-6. The Record Macro dialog box.

The Stop Recording toolbar will appear (Figure 1-7), indicating that a macro is being recorded. If the Stop Recording toolbar doesn't appear, you can always stop recording by using the **Tools** menu (in the Macro submenu the **Record New Macro...** command will be replaced by **Stop Recording**).

Figure 1-7. The Stop Recording toolbar.

Now choose **Cells...** from the **Format** menu, choose the Number tab and choose Scientific number format, then press OK. Finally, press the Stop Recording button.

To examine the macro code that you have just recorded, choose **Macro** from the **Tools** menu and **Visual Basic Editor** from the submenu. Click on the node for the module in the active workbook. This will display the code module sheet containing the Visual Basic code. The macro should look like the example shown in Figure 1-8.

```
Sub ScientificFormat()
'
' ScientificFormat Macro
' Macro recorded 6/22/2004 by Boston College
'
' Keyboard Shortcut: Ctrl+e
'
    Selection.NumberFormat = "0.00E+00"
End Sub
```

Figure 1-8. Macro for scientific number-formatting, recorded in VBA.

This macro consists of a single line of VBA code. You'll learn about Visual Basic code in the chapters that follow.

To run the macro, enter a number in a cell, select the cell, then choose **Macro** from the **Tools** menu, choose **Macros...** from the submenu, select the ScientificFormat macro from the Macro Name list box, and press Run. Or you can simply press the shortcut key combination that you designated when you recorded the macro (CONTROL+e in the example above). The number should be displayed in the cell in scientific format.

The Personal Macro Workbook

The Record Macro dialog box allows you to choose where the recorded macro will be stored. There are three possibilities in the "Store Macro In" list box: This Workbook, New Workbook and Personal Macro Workbook. The Personal Macro Workbook (PERSONAL.XLS in Excel for Windows, or Personal Macro Workbook in Excel for the Macintosh) is a workbook that is automatically opened when you start Excel. Since only macros in open workbooks are available for use, the Personal Macro Workbook is the ideal location for macros that you want to have available all the time.

Normally the Personal Macro Workbook is hidden (choose **Unhide...** from the **Window** menu to view it). If you don't yet have a Personal Macro Workbook, you can create one by recording a macro as described earlier, choosing Personal Macro Workbook from the "Store Macro In" list box.

As you begin to create more advanced Sub procedures, you'll find that the Recorder is a useful tool to create fragments of macro code for incorporation into your procedure. Instead of poring through a VBA reference, or searching through the On-Line VBA Help, looking for the correct command syntax, simply turn on the Recorder, perform the action, and look at the code produced. You may find that the Recorder doesn't always produce exactly what you want, or perhaps the most elegant code, but it is almost always useful.

Note that, since the Recorder only records actions, and **Function** procedures can't perform actions, the Recorder won't be useful for creating **Function** procedures.

Running a Sub Procedure

In the preceding example, the macro was run by using a shortcut key. There are a number of other ways to run a macro. One way is to use the Macro dialog box. Again, enter a number in a cell, select the cell, then choose **Macro** from the **Tools** menu and **Macros...** from the submenu. The Macro dialog box will be displayed (Figure 1-9). This dialog box lists all macros in open workbooks (right now we only have one macro available). To run the macro, select it from the list, then press the Run button.

Assigning a Shortcut Key to a Sub Procedure

If you didn't assign a shortcut key to the macro when you recorded it, but would like to do so "after the fact," choose **Macro** from the **Tools** menu and **Macros...** from the submenu. Highlight the name of the macro in the Macro Name list box, and press the Options... button. You can now enter a letter for the shortcut key: CONTROL+<key> or SHIFT+CONTROL+<key> in Excel for

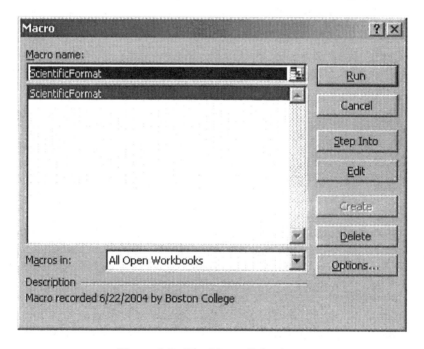

Figure 1-9. The Macro dialog box.

Windows, OPTION+COMMAND+<key> or SHIFT+OPTION+COMMAND+<key> in Excel for the Macintosh.

Entering VBA Code

Of course, most of the VBA code you create will not be recorded, but instead entered at the keyboard. As you type your VBA code, the Visual Basic Editor checks each line for syntax errors. A line that contains one or more errors will be displayed in red, the default color for errors. Variables usually appear in black. Other colors are also used; comments (see later) are usually green and some VBA keywords (**Function**, **Range**, etc.) usually appear in blue. (These default colors can be changed if you wish.)

If you type a long line of code, it will not automatically wrap to the next line but will simply disappear off the screen. You need to insert a *line-continuation character* (the underscore character, but you must type a space followed by the underscore character followed by ENTER) to cause a line break in a line of VBA code, as in the following example:

```
Worksheets("Sheet1").Range("A2:B7").Copy _
    (Worksheets("Sheet2").Range("C2"))
```

The line-continuation character can't be used within a string, i.e., within quotes.

I recommend that you type the module-level declaration **Option Explicit** at the top of each module sheet, before any procedures. **Option Explicit** forces you to declare all variables using **Dim** statements; undeclared variables produce an error at compile time.

When you type VBA code in a module, it's good programming practice to use TAB to indent related lines for easier reading, as shown in the following procedure.

```
Sub Initialize()
For J = 1 To N
    P(J) = 0
Next J
End Sub
```

Figure 1-10. A simple VBA **Sub** procedure.

In order to produce a more compact display of a procedure, several lines of code can be combined in one line by separating them with colons. For example, the procedure in Figure 1-10 can be replaced by the more compact one in Figure 1-11 or even by the one in Figure 1-12.

```
Sub Initialize()
For J = 1 To N: P(J) = 0: Next J
End Sub
```

Figure 1-11. A **Sub** procedure with several statements combined.

```
Sub Initialize(): For J = 1 To N: P(J) = 0: Next J: End Sub
```

Figure 1-12. A **Sub** procedure in one line.

Creating a Simple Custom Function

As a simple first example of a **Function** procedure, we'll create a custom function to convert temperatures in degrees Fahrenheit to degrees Celsius.

Function procedures can't be recorded; you must type them on a module sheet. You can have several macros on the same module sheet, so if you recorded the ScientificFormat macro earlier in this chapter, you can type this custom function procedure on the same module sheet. If you do not have a module sheet available, insert one by choosing **Module** from the **Insert** menu.

Type the macro as shown in Figure 1-13. DegF is the argument passed by the function from the worksheet to the module (the Fahrenheit temperature); the single line of VBA code evaluates the Celsius temperature and returns the result to the *caller* (in this case, the worksheet cell in which the function is entered).

```
Function FtoC(DegF)
   FtoC = (DegF − 32) * 5 / 9
End Function
```

Figure 1-13. Fahrenheit to Celsius custom function.

A note about naming functions and arguments: function names should be short, since you will be typing them in Excel formulas (that's why Excel's square-root worksheet function is SQRT) but long enough to convey information about what the function does. In contrast, command macro names can be long, since command macros are run by choosing the name of the macro from the list of macros in the Macro Run dialog box, for example.

Argument names can be long, since you don't type them. Longer names can convey more information, and thus provide a bit of self-documentation. (If you look at the arguments used in Excel's worksheet functions, you'll see that single letters are usually not used as argument names.)

Using a Function Macro

A custom function is used in a worksheet formula in exactly the same way as any of Excel's built-in functions. The workbook containing the custom function must be open.

Figure 1-14 shows how the FtoC custom function is used. Cell A2 contains 212, the argument that the custom function will use. Cell B2 contains the formula with the custom function. You can enter the function in cell B2 by typing it (Figure 1-14). When you press enter, the result calculated by the function appears in the cell (Figure 1-15).

	A	B
1	T, °F	T, °C
2	212	=FtoC(A2)

Figure 1-14. Entering the custom function.

	A	B
1	T, °F	T, °C
2	212	100

Figure 1-15. The function result.

You can also enter a function by using the Insert Function dialog box. Select the worksheet cell or the point in a worksheet formula where you want to enter the function, in this example cell B2. Choose **Function...** from the **Insert** menu or press the Insert Function toolbutton f_x to display the Insert Function dialog box. Scroll through the Function Category list and select the User Defined category. The FtoC function will appear in the Insert Function list box (Figure 1-16).

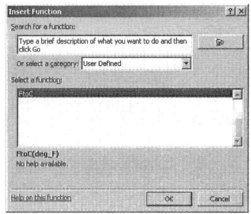

Figure 1-16. The Paste Function dialog box.

When you press OK, the Function Arguments dialog box (Figure 1-17) will be displayed. Enter the argument, or click on the cell containing the argument to enter the reference (cell A2 in Figure 1-14), then press the OK button.

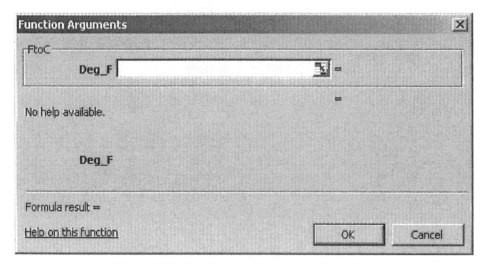

Figure 1-17. The Function Arguments dialog box.

A Shortcut to Enter a Function

You can enter a function without using Insert Function, but still receive the benefit provided by the Function Arguments screen. This is useful if the function takes several (perhaps unfamiliar) arguments. Simply type "=" followed by the function name, with or without the opening parenthesis, and then press CONTROL+A to bypass the Insert Function dialog box and go directly to the Function Arguments dialog box.

If you press CONTROL+SHIFT+A, you bypass both the Insert Function dialog box and the Function Arguments. The function will be displayed with its placeholder argument(s). The first argument is highlighted so that you can enter a value or reference (Figure 1-18).

	A	B	C
1	T, °F	T, °C	
2	212	=FtoC(deg_F)	

Figure 1-18. Entering a custom function by using CONTROL+SHIFT+A.

Unfortunately, if you're entering the custom function in a different workbook than the one that contains the custom function, the function name must be entered as an external reference (e.g., Book1.XLS!FtoC). This can make typing the function rather cumbersome, and it means that you'll probably enter the function by using Excel's Insert Function. But, see "Creating Add-In Function Macros" in Chapter 2.

Some FAQs

Here are answers to some Frequently Asked Questions about macros.

I Recorded a Command Macro. Where Did It Go? If you have trouble locating the code module containing your macro, here's what to do "when all else fails": choose **Macro** from the **Tools** menu and **Macros...** from the submenu. Highlight the name of the macro in the Macro Name list box, and press the Edit button. This will display the code module sheet containing the Visual Basic code.

I Can't Find My Function Macro. Where Did It Go? If you're looking in the list of macros in the Macro Name list box, you won't find it there. Only command macros (macros that can be **Run**) are listed. Function macros are found in a different place: in the list of user-defined functions in the Insert Function dialog box. (Choose **Function...** from the **Insert** menu and scroll through the Function Category list and select the User Defined category.)

How Do I Rename a Macro? To rename a **Sub** or **Function** procedure, access the Visual Basic Editor and click on the module containing the procedure. The name of the macro is in the first line of code, immediately following the **Sub** or **Function** keyword. Simply edit the name. Again, no spaces are allowed in the name.

How Do I Rename a Module Sheet? You use the Properties window to change the name of a module. The module sheet whose name you want to change must be the active sheet. If the Properties window is not visible, choose **Properties Window** from the **View** menu, or click on the Properties Window toolbutton to display it. The Properties Window toolbutton is the fourth button from the right in the VBA toolbar.

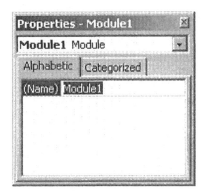

Figure 1-19. Changing the name of a module by using the Properties window.

When you display the Properties window, you will see the single property of a module sheet, namely its name, displayed in the window. Simply double-click on the name (here, Module1), edit the name, and press Enter. No spaces are allowed in the name.

How Do I Add a Shortcut Key? If you decide to add a shortcut key to a command macro "after the fact," choose **Tools→Macro→Macros...**. In the Macro Name list box, click on the name of the macro to which you want to add a shortcut key, then press the Options button. In the Shortcut Key box, enter a letter, either lower- or uppercase. To run the macro, use CTRL+<letter> for a lowercase shortcut key, or CTRL+SHIFT+<letter> for uppercase.

Warning: The shortcut key will override a built-in shortcut key that uses the same letter. For example, if you use CTRL+s for the ScientificFormat macro, you won't be able to use CTRL+s for "Save." This will be in effect as long as the workbook that contains the macro is open.

How Do I Save a Macro? A macro is part of a workbook, just like a worksheet or a chart. To save the macro, you simply **Save** the workbook.

Are There Some Shortcut Keys for VBA? Yes, there are several. Here's a useful one: you can toggle between the Excel spreadsheet and the VBA Editor by pressing ALT+F11. A list of shortcut keys for VBA programming is found in Appendix 2.

Chapter 2

Fundamentals of Programming with VBA

This chapter provides an overview of Excel's VBA programming language. Because of the specialized nature of the programming in this book, the material is organized in a way that is different from other books on the subject. This book deals almost exclusively with creating custom or user-defined functions, and a significant fraction of VBA's keywords cannot be used in custom functions. (For example, custom functions can't open or close workbooks, print documents, sort lists on worksheets, etc. — these are actions that are performed by command macros.) Therefore, that portion of the VBA language that can be used in custom functions is introduced in the first part of this chapter, and programming concepts that are applicable in command macros appear in the latter part of the chapter.

If you are familiar with programming in other versions of BASIC or in FORTRAN, many of the programming techniques described in this chapter will be familiar.

Components of Visual Basic Statements

VBA macro code consists of *statements*. Statements are constructed by using VBA commands, operators, variables, functions, objects, properties, methods, or other VBA keywords. (VBA Help refers to keywords such as **Loop** or **Exit** as statements, but here they'll be referred to as commands, and we'll use "statement" in a general way to refer to a line of VBA code.)

Much of the VBA code that you will create will consist of *assignment statements*. An assignment statement assigns the result of an expression to a variable or object; the form of an assignment statement is

variable = expression

for example,

increment = 0.00000001*XValue

or

K = K + 1

which, in the second example, says "Store, in the memory location to which the user has assigned the label 'K', the value corresponding to the expression K + 1."

Operators

VBA operators include the arithmetic operators (+, −, *, /, ^), the text concatenation operator (&), the comparison operators (=, <, >, <=, >=, <>) and the logical operators (**And**, **Or**, **Not**)

Variables

Variables are the names you create to indicate the storage locations of values or references. There are a few rules for naming variables or arguments:

- You can't use any of the VBA reserved words, such as **Formula**, **Function**, **Range** or **Value**.
- The first character must be a letter.
- A name cannot contain a space or a period.
- The characters %, $, #, !, & cannot be embedded in a name. If one of these characters is the last character of a variable name, the character serves as a type-declaration character (see later).
- You can use upper- and lowercase letters. If you declare a variable type by using the **Dim** statement (see "VBA Data Types" later in this chapter), the capitalization of the variable name will be "fixed" — no matter how you type it in the procedure, the variable name will revert to the capitalization as originally declared. In contrast, if you have not declared a variable by using **Dim**, changing the case of a variable name in any line of code (e.g., from formulastring to FormulaString) will cause all instances of the old form of the variable to change to the new form.

You should make variable names as descriptive as possible, but avoid overly long names which are tedious to type. You can use the underscore character to indicate a space between words (e.g., formula_string). You can't use a period to indicate a space, since VBA reserves the period character for use with objects. The most popular form for variable names uses upper- and lowercase letters (e.g., FormulaString).

Long variable names like FormulaString provide valuable self-documentation; months later, if you examine your code in order to make changes, you'll probably be more able to understand it if you used (for example) FormulaString as a variable name instead of F. But typing long variable names is time-consuming and prone to errors. I like to use short names like F when I'm developing the code. Once I'm done, I use the Visual Basic Editor's **Replace...** menu command to convert all those F's to FormulaString.

To avoid inadvertently using a VBA keyword as a variable name (there are hundreds of VBA keywords, so this is easy to do), I suggest that you type the variable name in all lowercase letters. If the variable name becomes capitalized, this indicates that it is a reserved word. For example, you may decide to use FV as a variable name. If you type the variable name "fv" in a VBA statement, then press Enter, you will see the variable become "FV," a sign to you that FV is a reserved word in VBA (the FV function calculates the future value of an annuity based on periodic, fixed payments and a fixed interest rate.)

In fact, it's also a good idea to type words that you know are reserved words in VBA in lowercase also. If you type "activecell," the word will become "ActiveCell" when you press the Enter key. If it doesn't, you have typed it incorrectly.

Objects, Properties and Methods

VBA is an *object-oriented* programming language. *Objects* in Microsoft Excel are the familiar components of Excel, such as a worksheet, a chart, a toolbar, or a range. Objects have *properties* and *methods* associated with them. Objects are the nouns of the VBA language, properties are the adjectives that modify the nouns and methods are the verbs (the action words). Objects are used almost exclusively in **Sub** procedures, while properties and some methods can be used in **Function** procedures. A discussion of objects and methods can be found in the section "VBA Code for Command Macros" later in this chapter.

Objects

Some examples of VBA objects are the **Workbook** object, the **Worksheet** object, the **Chart** object and the **Range** object. It's very unlikely that a custom function would include any of these keywords. But if a custom function takes as an argument a cell or range of cells, the argument is a **Range** object and has all of the properties of a **Range** object.

Properties

Objects have *properties* that can be set or read. Some properties of the **Range** object are the **ColumnWidth** property, the **NumberFormat** property, the **Font** property and the **Value** property. A property is connected to the object it modifies by a period, for example

    CelFmt = **Range**("E5").**NumberFormat**

returns the number format of cell E5 and assigns it to the variable CelFmt, and

    Range("E5").**NumberFormat** = "0.000"

sets the number formatting of cell E5.

Some properties, such as **Column** or **Count**, are read-only. The **Column** property of a **Range** object is the column number of the leftmost cell in the specified range; it should be clear that this property can be read, but not changed. The **Count** property of a **Range** object is the number of cells in the range; again, it can be read, but not changed.

Properties can also modify properties. The following example

Range("A1").Font.Bold = True

makes the contents of cell A1 bold.

There is a large and confusing number of properties, a different list for each object. For example, as of this writing (Excel 2003), the list of properties pertaining to the **Range** object contains 93 entries:

AddIndent	Font	MergeArea	Row
Address	FormatConditions	MergeCells	RowHeight
AddressLocal	Formula	Name	Rows
AllowEdit	FormulaArray	Next	ShowDetail
Application	FormulaHidden	NumberFormat	ShrinkToFit
Areas	FormulaLabel	NumberFormatLocal	SmartTags
Borders	FormulaLocal	Offset	SoundNote
Cells	FormulaR1C1	Orientation	Style
Characters	FormulaR1C1Local	OutlineLevel	Summary
Column	HasArray	PageBreak	Text
Columns	HasFormula	Parent	Top
ColumnWidth	Height	Phonetic	UseStandardHeight
Comment	Hidden	Phonetics	UseStandardWidth
Count	HorizontalAlignment	PivotCell	Validation
Creator	Hyperlinks	PivotField	Value
CurrentArray	ID	PivotItem	Value2
CurrentRegion	IndentLevel	PivotTable	VerticalAlignment
Dependents	Interior	Precedents	Width
DirectDependents	Item	PrefixCharacter	Worksheet
DirectPrecedents	Left	Previous	WrapText
End	ListHeaderRows	QueryTable	XPath
EntireColumn	ListObject	Range	
EntireRow	LocationInTable	ReadingOrder	
Errors	Locked	Resize	

This large number of properties, just for the **Range** object, is what makes VBA so difficult for the beginner. You must find out what properties are associated with a particular object, and what you can do with them. For our purposes (creating custom functions), only a limited number of these properties of the **Range** object can be used. Some of the properties of the **Range** object that can be used in a custom function are listed in Table 2-1. Note that, when used in a custom function, these properties can only be read, not set.

Table 2-1. Some Properties of the **Range** Object

Column	Returns a number corresponding to the first column in the range.
ColumnWidth	Returns or sets the width of all columns in the range.
Count	Returns the number of items in the range.
Font	Returns or sets the font of the range.
Formula	Returns or sets the formula.
Name	Returns or sets the name of the range.
NumberFormat	Returns or sets the format code for the range.
Row	Returns a number corresponding to the first row in the range.
RowHeight	Returns or sets the height of all rows in the range.
Text	Returns or sets the text displayed by the cell.
Value	Returns or sets the contents of the cell or range.

Using Properties

In a **Sub** procedure, properties can be set or read. In a **Function** procedure, properties can only be read, not changed. To return an object's property, use the following syntax:

VariableName = ObjectName.PropertyName

For example, to obtain the number of cells in a range of cells passed to a function procedure as the argument rng, and store it in the variable NCells, use the following:

NCells = rng.**Count**

Properties can have values that are numeric, string, or logical.

Functions

Many of the functions available in VBA are similar to the functions available in Excel itself. There are 187 VBA functions listed in Excel 2003 VBA Help. Tables 2-2 through 2-4 list some of the more useful ones for mathematical or scientific calculations.

If you are reasonably familiar with Excel's worksheet functions, you will have little trouble using VBA's functions. The names of many VBA functions, such as **Abs, Exp, Int, Len, Left, Mid** and **Right**, are identical to the corresponding worksheet functions (ABS, EXP, INT, LEN, LEFT, MID AND RIGHT, respectively). Others, such as **Asc, Chr** and **Sqr,** are spelled a little differently (the corresponding worksheet functions are CODE, CHAR and SQRT, respectively) or completely differently (**LCase** and **UCase** correspond to LOWER and UPPER). These VBA functions are used in exactly the same way that they are used in worksheet formulas; they take the same type of arguments and return the same type of values.

Note that although Excel has three worksheet functions that return logarithms (LN returns the natural or base-e logarithm, LOG10 returns the base-10 logarithm, and LOG returns a logarithm to a specified base), VBA has only one logarithmic function, **Log**, that returns the base-e logarithm. If you need to work with base-10 logarithms in your VBA code, use the relationship $\log_{10}(a) = \log_e(a)/ \log_e(10)$.

VBA does not provide a function to evaluate π, but you can calculate it in a function by using the expression **4*Atn(1)**. Or, you can use the worksheet function PI(), in the manner described in the following section.

Table 2-2. Some VBA Mathematical Functions

Abs	Returns the absolute value of a number.
Atn	Returns the arctangent of a number. The result is an angle in radians.
Cos	Returns the cosine of an angle in radians.
Exp	Returns *e* raised to a power.
Int	Returns the integer part of a number (rounds down).
Log	Returns the natural (base-*e*) logarithm of a number.
Rnd	Returns a random number equal to or greater than 0 and less than 1.
Sin	Returns the sine of an angle in radians.
Sqr	Returns the square root of a number.
Tan	Returns the tangent of an angle in radians.

The above mathematical functions, except for **Rnd**, have the syntax *FunctionName(argument)*. **Rnd** takes no argument, but requires the empty parentheses.

VBA provides functions for working with text; some of the more useful ones are listed in Table 2-3. Most of these are identical to Excel's text worksheet functions. If you are unfamiliar with the use of text functions, see the syntax and examples in Appendix 1.

Table 2-3. Some VBA Text Functions

Asc	Returns the ASCII character code of a character.
Chr	Returns the character corresponding to an ASCII code.
Format	Formats a number according to a built-in or user-defined number format expression. The result is a string.
Instr	Returns the first occurrence of a substring within a string. Similar to Excel's FIND worksheet function.
Len	Returns the length (number of characters) in a string.
Left	Returns the leftmost characters of a string.
Right	Returns the rightmost characters of a string.
Mid	Returns a specified number of characters from a string.
LTrim	Returns a string without leading spaces.
RTrim	Returns a string without trailing spaces.
Trim	Returns a string without leading or trailing spaces.
Str	Converts a number to a string. A leading space is reserved for the sign of the number; if the number is positive, the string will contain a leading space.
LCase	Converts a string into lowercase letters.
UCase	Converts a string into uppercase letters.

VBA also provides a number of information functions, including eight **"Is"** functions, shown in Table 2-4.

Table 2-4. VBA Information Functions

IsArray	Returns **True** if the variable is an array.
IsDate	Returns **True** if the expression is a date.
IsEmpty	Returns **True** if the variable is uninitialized.
IsError	Returns **True** if the expression returns an error.
IsMissing	Returns **True** if an optional value has not been passed to a **Function** procedure.
IsNull	Returns **True** if the expression is null (i.e., contains no valid data).
IsNumeric	Returns **True** if the expression can be evaluated to a number.
IsObject	Returns **True** if the expression references a valid object.
LBound	Returns the lower limit of an array dimension.
UBound	Returns the upper limit of an array dimension.

All the above **Is** functions have the syntax **FunctionName**(argument) and return either **True** or **False.**

Using Worksheet Functions with VBA

In addition to the 187 VBA functions, you can make use of any of Excel's worksheet functions in your VBA code. To use one of Excel's worksheet functions, simply use the syntax

Application. WorksheetFunctionName(argument1,...)

and supply arguments for the function just as you would in a worksheet. For example, to use the SUBSTITUTE function in VBA, use the code

FormulaString **= Application.Substitute(**FormulaString, XRef, NewX**)**

to replace all occurrences, in the string contained in the variable FormulaString, of the variable XRef with the variable NewX.

Some Useful Methods

Although most methods can only be used within **Sub** procedures, there are a few methods that can be used within **Function** procedures. Only methods that do not "change the appearance of the screen" can be used in **Function** procedures; it should be obvious that methods like **Cut**, **Paste**, **Open**, **Close** etc., cannot be used in a custom function.

Table 2-5. Some Methods Applicable to the **Range** Object
That Can Be Used in a **Function** Procedure

Address	Returns the reference of a cell or range, as text.
Columns	Returns a Range object that represents a single column or multiple columns.
ConvertFormula	Converts cell references in a formula between A1- and R1C1-style, and between relative and absolute.
Evaluate	Converts a formula to a value.
Intersect	Returns the reference that is the intersection of two ranges.
Rows	Returns a Range object that represents a single row or multiple rows.
Volatile	Marks a user-defined function as volatile. The function recalculates whenever calculation occurs in any cell of the worksheet.

Other Keywords

In addition to VBA's objects, properties, methods and functions, there are additional keywords that deal with program control: looping, branching and so on. These keywords are described in detail in the following sections.

VBA keywords that will *not* be discussed in this book include objects such as menu bars, menus and menu commands, toolbars and toolbuttons and the many properties and methods pertaining to them.

Program Control

If you are familiar with computer languages such as BASIC or FORTRAN, you will find yourself quite comfortable with most of the material in this section.

Branching

VBA supports **If...Then** statements very similar to the Excel worksheet function IF. The syntax of **If...Then** is

If *LogicalExpression* **Then** *statement1* **Else** *statement2*

The **If...Then** statement can be a Simple If statement, for example:

If (x >0) **Then** numerator **=** 10 ^ x

If *LogicalExpression* (in this example x > 0) is **True**, *statement1* is carried out; if *LogicalExpression* is **False**, nothing is done (program execution moves to the next line).

If...Then...Else structures are also possible. For example:

If Err.Number = 13 Then Resume pt1 **Else End**

In a Block If statement, **If** *LogicalExpression* **Then** is followed by multiple statement lines and is terminated by **End If**, as in Figure 2-1.

```
If Err.Number = 13 Then
    On Error GoTo 0    'Disable the error handler.
    Resume pt1      'and continue execution.
End If
```

Figure 2-1. Example of VBA Block If structure.

You can also create a Block-If-type structure in a single line, as in the following statement.

If *LogicalExpression* **Then** *statement1* **:** *statement2* **Else** *statement3*

If...Then... ElseIf structures are also possible, as illustrated in Figure 2-2.

```
If reference.Rows.Count > 1 Then
    R = equation.Row
ElseIf reference.Columns.Count > 1 Then
    C = equation.Column
End If
```

Figure 2-2. Example of the VBA **If...ElseIf...End If** structure.

Logical Operators

The logical operators **And**, **Or** and **Not** can be used in *LogicalExpression*, as in the following example.

If C >= 0 **And** C <= 9 **Then**

Select Case

VBA also provides the **Select Case** decision structure, similar to the ON *value* GOTO statement in BASIC. The **Select Case** statement provides an efficient alternative to the series of **ElseIf** *conditionN* statements when *conditionN* is a single expression that can take various values. The syntax of the **Select Case** statement is illustrated in Figure 2-3.

```
Select Case TestExpression
    Case ExpressionList1
        statements
    Case ExpressionList2
        statements
    Case ExpressionList3
        statements
    Case Else
        statements
End Select
```

Figure 2-3. The VBA **Select Case** structure.

TestExpression is evaluated and used to direct program flow to the appropriate **Case**. ExpressionListN can be a single value (e.g., **Case 0**), a list of values separated by commas (e.g., **Case 1, 3, 5**), or a range of values using the **To** keyword (e.g., **Case 6 To 9**). The optional **Case Else** statement is executed if *TestExpression* doesn't match any of the values in any of ExpressionListN.

Looping

Loop structures in VBA are similar to those available in other programming languages.

For...Next Loop

The syntax of the **For...Next** loop is given in Figure 2-4.

```
For Counter = Start To End Step Increment
    statements
Next Counter
```

Figure 2-4. The VBA **For...Next** structure.

For example,

```
For J = 1 To 100
    statements
Next J
```

Figure 2-5. Example of a **For...Next** loop.

The **Step** *Increment* part of the **For** statement is optional. If *Increment* is omitted, it is set equal to 1. *Increment* can be negative or nonintegral, for example

For J = 100 **To** 0 **Step** -1

Do While... Loop

The **Do...Loop** is used when you don't know beforehand how many times the loop will need to be executed. You can loop **While** a condition is **True** or **Until** a condition becomes **True.** The two possibilities are shown in Figures 2-6 and 2-7.

```
Do While LogicalExpression
    statements
Loop
```

Figure 2-6. The **Do While...Loop** structure.

```
Do
    statements
Loop While LogicalExpression
```

Figure 2-7. Alternate form of the **Do...Loop While** structure.

Note that this second form of the **Do While** structure executes the loop at least once.

For Each...Next Loop

The **For Each...Next** loop is a loop structure peculiar to an object-oriented language. The **For Each...Next** loop executes the statements within the loop for each *object* in a group of objects. Figure 2-8 illustrates the syntax of the statement.

```
For Each Element In Group
    statements
Next Element
```

Figure 2-8. The VBA **For Each...Next** structure.

The **For Each...Next** loop returns an object variable in each pass through the loop. You can access or use all of the properties or methods that apply to Element. For example, in a loop such as the one shown in Figure 2-9, the variable cel is an object that has all the properties of a cell (a **Range** object): **Value**, **Formula**, **NumberFormat**, etc.

```
For Each cel In Selection
    FormulaText = cel.Value
    statements
Next cel
```

Figure 2-9. Example of a **For Each...Next** loop.

Note that there is no integer loop counter, as in the **For** Counter = Start **To** End type of loop structure. If an integer counter is needed, you will have to initialize one outside the loop, and increment it inside the loop.

Nested Loops

Often one loop must be nested inside another, as illustrated in the following example.

```
For I = 1 To N1
    statements
    For J = 1 To N2
        statements
    Next J
Next I
```

Figure 2-10. Example of nested loops.

Exiting from a Loop or from a Procedure

Often you use a loop structure to search through an array or collection of objects, looking for a certain value or property. Once you find a match, you don't need to cycle through the rest of the loops. You can exit from the loop using the **Exit For** (from a **For...Next** loop or **For Each...Next** loop) or **Exit Do** (from a **Do While...** loop). The **Exit** statement will normally be located within an **If** statement. For example,

If CellContents.**Value** <= 0 **Then Exit For**

Use the **Exit Sub** or **Exit Function** to exit from a procedure. Again, the **Exit** statement will normally be located within an **If** statement.

Exit statements can appear as many times as needed within a procedure.

VBA Data Types

VBA uses a range of different data types. Table 2-6 lists the built-in data types. Unless you declare a variable's type, VBA will use the **Variant** type. You can save memory space if your procedure deals only with integers, for example, by declaring the variable as **Integer**. The keyword **Dim** is used to declare a variable's data type, as will be described in a following section.

Table 2-6. VBA's Built-in Data Types

Data Type	Storage Required	Range of Values
Boolean (Logical)	2 bytes	**True** or **False**
Integer	2 bytes	–32,768 to 32,767
Long integer	4 bytes	–2,147,483,648 to 2,147,483,647
Single precision	4 bytes	–3.402823E+38 to –1.401298E-45 for negative values; 1.401298E-45 to 3.402823E+38 for positive values
Double precision	8 bytes	–1.79769313486232E+308 to –4.94065645841247E-324 for negative values; 4.94065645841247E-324 to 1.79769313486232E+308 for positive values
Currency	8 bytes	–922,337,203,685,477.5808 to 922,337,203,685,477.5807
Date	8 bytes	
Object	4 bytes	Any Object reference
String	1 byte/character	
Variant	16 bytes + 1 byte/character	Any numeric value up to the range of a **Double** or any text

The Variant Data Type

The **Variant** data type is the default data type in VBA. Like Excel itself, the **Variant** data type handles and interconverts between many different kinds of data: integer, floating point, string, etc. The **Variant** data type automatically chooses the most compact representation. But if your procedure deals with only one kind of data, it will be more efficient and usually faster to declare the variables as, for example, **Integer**.

Subroutines

By "subroutine" we mean a **Sub** procedure that is "called" by another VBA program. In writing a VBA procedure, it may be necessary to repeat the same instructions several times within the procedure. Instead of repeating the same lines of code over and over in your procedure, you can place this code in a separate **Sub** program; this subroutine or subprogram is then executed by the main program each time it is required.

There are several ways to execute a subroutine within a main program. The two most common are by using the **Call** command, or by using the name of the subroutine. These are illustrated in Figure 2-11. MainProgram calls subroutines Task1 and Task2, each of which requires arguments that are passed from the main program to the subroutine and/or are returned from the subroutine to the main program.

```
Sub MainProgram()
    etc.
Call Task1(argument1,argument2)
    etc
Task2 argument3,argument4
    etc
End Sub

Sub Task1(ArgName1,ArgName2)
    etc
End Sub

Sub Task2(ArgName3,ArgName4)
    etc
End Sub
```

Figure 2-11. A main program illustrating the different syntax of subroutine calls.

The two methods use different syntax if the subroutine requires arguments. If the **Call** command is used, the arguments must be enclosed in parentheses. If only the subroutine name is used, the parentheses must be omitted. Note that the variable names of the arguments in the calling statement and in the subroutine do not have to be the same.

There are several advantages to using subroutines: you eliminate the repetition of code, and you make the programming clearer by adopting a modular approach. Perhaps most important, a subroutine that is of general usefulness can be called by several different procedures.

Scoping a Subroutine

A **Sub** procedure can be **Public** or **Private**. Public subroutines can be called by any subroutine in any module. The default for any **Sub** procedure is **Public**. A **Private** subroutine can be called only by other subroutines in the same module. To declare the subroutine Task3 as a private subroutine, use the statement

Private Sub Task3**()**

A **Sub** procedure that is declared **Private** will not appear in the list of macros that can be run in the Macro dialog box. The name of a **Sub** procedure that takes arguments (i.e., a subroutine), will also not appear in the Macro dialog box; only **Sub** procedures without arguments, that is, with empty parentheses following the procedure name, appear in the Macro dialog box.

VBA Code for Command Macros

Command macros (**Sub** procedures) are "action" macros: they can enter or modify data on a spreadsheet, create a report, display a dialog box and so on. The CD that accompanies this book includes some examples of **Sub** procedures, so the material in the following sections will be useful in understanding the VBA code in these procedures.

Objects and Collections of Objects

Some examples of VBA objects are the **Workbook** object, the **Worksheet** object, the **Chart** object and the **Range** object. Note that the **Range** object can specify a single cell, such as E5 in the preceding example, or a range of cells, for example, **Range**("A1:E101"). There is no "cell" keyword in VBA to refer to a single cell; that would be redundant.

You can also refer to *collections* of objects. A collection is a group of objects of the same kind. A collection has the plural form of the object's name (e.g., **Worksheets** instead of **Worksheet**). **Worksheets** refers to all worksheets in a particular workbook.

To reference a particular worksheet in a collection, you can use either **Worksheets**(*NameText*) or **Worksheets**(*index*), For example, you can refer to a specific worksheet by using either **Worksheets**("Book1") or **Worksheets**(3). The latter form is useful, for example, if you want to examine all the worksheets in a workbook, without having to know what text is on each sheet tab.

There is a *hierarchy* of objects. A **Range** object is contained within a **Worksheet** object, which is contained within a **Workbook** object. You specify an object by specifying its location in a hierarchy, separated by periods, for example,

>   **Workbooks**("Book1")**.Worksheets**("Sheet3")**.Range**("E5")

In the above example, if you don't specify a workbook, but just use

>   **Worksheets**("Sheet3")**.Range**("E5")

you are referring to the active workbook. If you don't specify either workbook or worksheet, e.g.,

>   **Range**("E5")

you are referring to cell E5 in the active sheet.

Instead of the keyword **Worksheets**, you may sometimes need to use the keyword **Sheets**. **Sheets** is the collection that includes all sheets in a workbook, both worksheets and chart sheets.

A complete list of objects in Microsoft Excel is listed in Excel's On-line Help. You can also use the Object Browser to see the complete list of objects. To display the Object Browser dialog box, choose **Object Browser** from the **View** menu in the VBE.

"Objects" That Are Really Properties

Although **ActiveCell** and **Selection** are properties, not objects, you can treat them like objects. (**ActiveCell** is a property of the **Application** object, or the **ActiveWindow** property of the **Application** object.) The **Application** object has the following properties that you can treat just as though they were objects: the **ActiveWindow**, **ActiveWorkbook**, **ActiveSheet**, **ActiveCell**, **Selection** and **ThisWorkbook** properties. Since there is only one **Application** object, you can omit the reference to **Application** and simply use **ActiveCell**.

You Can Define Your Own Objects

The **Set** keyword lets you define a variable as an object, so that you can use the variable name in your code, rather than the expression for the object. Most often this is done simply for convenience; it's easier to type or remember a variable name rather than the (perhaps) long expression for the object. The variable will have all of the properties of the object type.

Note the difference between identical expressions with and without the use of the **Set** keyword. In the expression

XValues = **Workbooks**("Book1").**Worksheets**("Sheet3").**Range**("E2:E32")

the variable XValues contains only the values in cells E2:E32, while the expression

Set MyRange = **Workbooks**("Book1").**Worksheets**("Sheet3").**Range**("E2:E32")

creates an object variable MyRange, a Range object that allows you to read (or set) any of the properties of this object. For example, in addition to the value of any cell in the range E2:E32, you can obtain its number format, column width, row height, font and so on.

Remember, VBA will allow you to equate a variable to an object in an assignment statement, but the variable does not automatically become an object. If you then attempt to use the variable in an expression that requires an object, you'll get an "Object required" error message. You must use the **Set** keyword in order to create an object variable.

Methods

Objects also have *methods*. The Excel 2003 VBA Help lists 71 methods, listed below, that apply to the **Range** object. Many of these methods correspond to familiar menu commands.

Activate	ClearNotes	FindNext	RowDifferences
AddComment	ClearOutline	FindPrevious	Run
AdvancedFilter	ColumnDifferences	FunctionWizard	Select
ApplyNames	Consolidate	GoalSeek	SetPhonetic
ApplyOutlineStyles	Copy	Group	Show
AutoComplete	CopyFromRecordset	Insert	ShowDependents
AutoFill	CopyPicture	InsertIndent	ShowErrors
AutoFilter	CreateNames	Justify	ShowPrecedents
AutoFit	Cut	ListNames	Sort
AutoFormat	DataSeries	Merge	SortSpecial
AutoOutline	Delete	NavigateArrow	Speak
BorderAround	DialogBox	NoteText	SpecialCells
Calculate	Dirty	Parse	Subtotal
CheckSpelling	FillDown	PasteSpecial	Table
Clear	FillLeft	PrintOut	TextToColumns
ClearComments	FillRight	PrintPreview	Ungroup
ClearContents	FillUp	RemoveSubtotal	UnMerge
ClearFormats	Find	Replace	

Some Useful Methods

Methods can operate on an object or on a property of an object. Some methods that can be applied to the **Range** object are the **Copy** method, the **Cut** method, the **FillDown** method or the **Sort** method. Statements involving methods usually do not appear in an assignment statement (that is, no equal sign is required). For example,

Range("A1:E1").**Clear**

clears the formulas and formatting in the range A1:E1.

Some useful VBA methods are listed in Table 2-7.

Table 2-7. Some Useful VBA Methods

Activate	Activates an object (sheet, etc.).
Clear	Clears an entire range.
Close	Closes an object.
Copy	Copies an object to a specified range or to the Clipboard.
Cut	Cuts an object to a specified range or to the Clipboard.
FillDown	Copies the cell(s) in the top row into the rest of the range.
Select	Selects an object.

Two Ways to Specify Arguments of Methods

VBA methods usually take one or more arguments. The **Sort** method, for example, takes 10 arguments. The syntax of the **Sort** method is

*object.***Sort***(key1, order1, key2, order2, key3, order3, header, orderCustom, matchCase, orientation)*

The *object* argument is required; all other arguments are optional.

You can specify the arguments of a method in two ways. One way is to list the arguments in order as they are specified in the preceding syntax, i.e.,

Range("A1:E150").**Sort** "Last Name", xlAscending

which sorts the data contained in the range A1:E150 in ascending order, using as the sortkey the values in the column headed by the label Last Name. xlAscending is one of many built-in constants. You can look them up in the On-line Help or use the Recorder to provide the correct one.

In the preceding example, only the arguments *key1* and *order1* were specified; the remaining arguments are optional and are not required.

The second way is to use the name of the argument as it appears in the preceding syntax, with the := operator, to specify the value of the argument, as in the following:

Selection.**Sort** Key1:=**Range**("A2"), Order1:=xlAscending, _
Key2:=**Range**("B2"), Order2:=xlAscending, Key3:=**Range**("C2"), _
Order3:=xlDescending, Header:=xlGuess, OrderCustom:=1, _
MatchCase:=**False**, Orientation:=xlTopToBottom

When using this method, the arguments can appear in any order, and optional ones can be omitted if you do not need to specify a value.

Arguments with or without Parentheses

The arguments of a method sometimes appear within parentheses, sometimes without parentheses (see the examples immediately preceding). Sometimes either syntax will work, sometimes one or the other fails. Why is this?

As well as performing an action, methods create a return value. The return value can be either **True** or **False: True** means the method worked, **False** means that it failed. Even the **ChartWizard** method creates a return value: **True** if the chart was created successfully, **False** if the method failed. Usually you aren't interested in these return values; if your procedure executed successfully, you are happy. But occasionally the return value is important.

An example of a method that creates a useful return value is the **CheckSpelling** method. The **CheckSpelling** method has the following syntax:

Application.CheckSpelling(word)

If you use this method, you'll need the return value (either **True** or **False**) to determine whether the word is spelled correctly.

If you want to use the return value of a method, you must enclose the arguments of the method in parentheses. If the arguments are not enclosed in parentheses, then the return value will not be available for use. Put another way, the expression

result = **Application.CheckSpelling(ActiveCell.Value)**

does not produce a syntax error, while the expression

result = **Application.CheckSpelling ActiveCell.Value**

does give a syntax error.

Making a Reference to a Cell or a Range

One of the most important skills you'll need in order to create **Sub** procedures that manipulate data in workbooks is the ability to make a reference to a cell or range of cells. You'll need to be able to send values from a worksheet to a module sheet so that you can perform operations on the worksheet data, and you'll need to be able to send the results back from the module sheet to the worksheet.

A Reference to the Active Cell or a Selected Range

Often a macro will be designed to operate on a user-selected cell or range.

To refer to the active cell or a selected range of cells, use the **ActiveCell** or **Selection** keywords. The **ActiveCell** keyword is usually used when the user has selected a single cell, whereas the **Selection** keyword is used when the user has selected a range of cells. However, **Selection** can refer to a single cell or a range.

A Reference to a Cell Other than the Active Cell

Sometime a macro will be designed to operate on values from specified rows and columns in a worksheet, independent of where the cursor has been "parked" by the user. To refer to a cell or range other than the selection, use either the **Range** keyword or the **Cells** keyword. The syntax of the latter is **Cells(***RowIndex, ColumnIndex***)**.

The following references both refer to cell B3:

Range("B3"**)**

Cells(3,2**)**

The preceding are "absolute" references, since they always refer to, in this example, cell B3. You can also use what could be called a "computed" reference, in which the reference depends on the value of a variable. The **Cells** keyword is conveniently used in this way. For example, the expression

Cells(x,2**)**

allows you to select any cell in column B, depending on the value assigned to the variable x. The **Range** keyword can be used in a similar way by using the concatenation operator, e.g.,

Range("B" & x**)**

It's usually good programming practice not to use the **Select** keyword unless you actually need to select cells in a worksheet. For example, to copy a range of cells from one worksheet to another, you could use the statements shown in Figure 2-12, and in fact this is exactly the code you would generate using the Recorder. But you can do the same thing much more efficiently, and without switching from one worksheet to another, by using the code shown in Figure 2-13.

```
Range("D1:D20").Select
Selection.Copy
Sheets("Sheet15").Select
Range("A1").Select
ActiveSheet.Paste
```

Figure 2-12. VBA code fragment by the Recorder.

Range("D1:D20").**Copy** (**Sheets**("Sheet15").**Range**("A1"))

Figure 2-13. A more efficient way to accomplish the same thing, without selecting cells.

References Using the Union or Intersect Method

VBA can create references by using methods that are the equivalents of the *union operator* (the comma) or the *intersection operator* (the space character) that can be used in worksheet formulas. The worksheet union operator creates a reference that includes multiple selections, for example, SUM(A1,B2,C3,D4,E5). The syntax of the corresponding VBA **Union** method is **Union**(*range1*, *range2*,...). The worksheet intersection operator creates a reference that is common to two references (e.g., the expression F4:F6 E5:I5 returns the reference F5). The syntax of the corresponding VBA **Intersect** method is **Intersect**(*range1*, *range2*). Both *range1* and *range2* must be range objects.

Examples of Expressions to Refer to a Cell or Range

1. Using the **Range** keyword with an address

   Range("B1:D10")

2. Using the **Cells** keyword with row and column numbers

   Cells(15, 5)

   This expression refers to cell E15.

3. Using the **Range** keyword with a range name

   Range("addr1")

   The range name addr1 was assigned previously using **Insert→Name→ Define**. This method is useful if the user can possibly modify the spreadsheet so that the addresses of cells needed by the procedure are changed.

4. Using the **Cells** keyword with variables

   Cells(RowNum, ColNum)

5. Using the **Range** keyword with a variable

   Range(addr2)

   The variable addr2 was previously defined by means of a statement such as

   addr2 = **Selection.Address**

_. Using the **Range** keyword with ampersand

> TopRow = 2: BtmRow = 12

> **Range**("F" & TopRow & ":G" & BtmRow)

The **Range** argument evaluates to "F2:G12")

7. Using the **Range** keyword with two **Cells** expressions

> **Range(Cells**(1, 1), **Cells**(5, 5))

This expression refers to the range A1:E5. This method is useful when both row and column numbers of the reference must be "computed."

8. Using the **Range** keyword with **Cells**(index)

> **Range**("A5:A12")**.Cells(3)**

This expression refers to cell A7; it provides a way to select individual cells within a specified range.)

> **Range**("A1:J10")**.Cells**(13)

Accesses first across rows, then by columns; this example selects cell C2.

9. Using the **Range** keyword with **Offset**

> **Range**("A1")**.Offset**(3, 1)

This example selects cell B4.

> **Range**("A1:A12")**.Offset**(3, 1)

This example selects the range B4:B15.

10. Using the **Range** keyword with **Offset** and **Resize**

> **Range**("A1:A12")**.Offset**(3, 1)**.Resize**(1, 1)

Use the **Resize** keyword to select a single cell offset from a range. This example selects cell B4.

Getting Values from a Worksheet

To transfer values from worksheet cells to a procedure, use a reference to a worksheet range in an assignment statement like the following.

> *variablename* = **ActiveCell.Value**

> *variablename* = **Worksheets**("Sheet1")**.Range**("A9")**.Value**

The **Value** keyword can usually be omitted:

variablename = **Range**("A" & x)

variablename = **Cells**(StartRow+x,StartCol)

The corresponding **Formula** property is used to obtain the formula in a cell, rather than its value.

Sending Values to a Worksheet

To send values from a module sheet back to a worksheet, simply use an assignment statement like the ones shown in the following examples. You can send a label

Range("E1").**Value** = "Jan.-Mar."

a constant

Cells(1, 2).**Value** = 5

the value of a variable

Worksheets("Sheet1").**Range**("A1") = variable2

or even a worksheet formula

Cells(1, 3).**Formula** = "=sum(F1:F10)"

to a cell in a worksheet. Again, the **.Value** keyword can usually be omitted.

Interacting with the User

VBA provides two built-in dialog boxes for display of messages or for input, **MsgBox** and **InputBox**. These are often incorporated in **Sub** procedures; they should never be used in **Function** procedures.

MsgBox

The **MsgBox** dialog box allows you to display a message, such as "Please wait…" or "Access denied." The box can display one of four message icons, and there are many possibilities in the number and function of buttons that can be displayed.

The syntax of the **MsgBox** function is

MsgBox (*prompt_text, buttons, title_text, helpfile, context*)

where *prompt_text* is the message displayed within the box, *buttons* specifies the buttons to be displayed, and *title_text* is the title to be displayed in the Title Bar of the box. For information about *helpfile* and *context*, refer to *Microsoft Excel Visual Basic Reference*. The value of *buttons* determines the type of message icon and the number and type of response buttons; it also determines which button is the default button. The possible values are listed in Table 2-8. The values 0–5 specify the number and type of buttons, values 16–64 specify the type of message icon and values 0, 256, 512 specify which button is the default button. You add together one number from each group to form a value for *buttons*. For example, to specify a dialog box with a Warning Query icon, with Yes, No and Cancel buttons, and with the No button as default, the values 32 + 3 + 256 = 291.

Table 2-8. Values for the *buttons* Parameter of **MsgBox**

buttons Value	Equivalent Constant	Description
0	vbOKOnly	Display OK button only.
1	vbOKCancel	Display OK and Cancel buttons.
2	vbAbortRetryIgnore	Display Abort, Retry and Ignore buttons.
3	vbYesNoCancel	Display Yes, No and Cancel buttons.
4	vbYesNo	Display Yes and No buttons.
5	vbRetryCancel	Display Retry and Cancel buttons.
0		No icon.
16	vbCritical	Display Critical Message icon.
32	vbQuestion	Display Warning Query icon.
48	vbExclamation	Display Warning Message icon.
64	vbInformation	Display Information Message icon.
0	vbDefaultButton1	First button is default.
256	vbDefaultButton2	Second button is default.
512	vbDefaultButton3	Third button is default.

For example, the VBA expression,

MsgBox "You entered " & incr & "." & **Chr**(13) & **Chr**(13) & _
"That value is too large." & **Chr**(13) & **Chr**(13) & "Please try again.", 48

where the VBA variable incr has the value 50, produces the message box shown in Figure 2-14.

Figure 2-14. A **Msgbox** display.

The values of *buttons* are built-in constants—for example, the value 64 for *buttons* can be replaced by the variable name vbInformation. The same result, a dialog box with a Warning Query icon, with Yes, No and Cancel buttons and with the No button as default, can be obtained by using the expression

vbInformation + vbYesNoCancel + vbDefaultButton2

in the **MsgBox** function instead of the value 323.

MsgBox Return Values

MsgBox can return a value that indicates which button was pressed. This allows you to take different actions depending on whether the user pressed the Yes, No or Cancel buttons, for example. To get the return value of the message box, use an expression like

ButtonValue **= MsgBox** (*prompt_text, buttons, title_text, helpfile, context*)

(Note that the arguments of **MsgBox** must be enclosed in parentheses in order for it to return a value.)

The return values of the buttons are as follows: OK, 1; Cancel, 2; Abort, 3; Retry, 4; Ignore, 5; Yes, 6; No, 7.

InputBox

The **InputBox** allows you to pause a macro and request input from the user. There are both an **InputBox** function and an **InputBox** method.

The syntax of the **InputBox** function is

InputBox(*prompt_text, title_text, default, x_position, y_position, helpfile, context*)

where *prompt_text* and *title_text* are as in **MsgBox**. *Default* is the expression displayed in the input box, as a string. The horizontal distance of the left edge of the box from the left edge of the screen, and the vertical distance of the top edge from the top of the screen are specified by *x_position* and *y_position*, respectively. For information about *helpfile* and *context*, refer to *Microsoft Excel Visual Basic Reference*.

If the user presses the OK button or the RETURN key, the **InputBox** function returns as a value whatever is in the text box. If the Cancel button is pressed, the function returns a null string. The following example produces the input box shown in Figure 2-15.

ReturnValu = **InputBox**("Enter validation code number", _
"Validation of this copy of SOLVER.STATS")

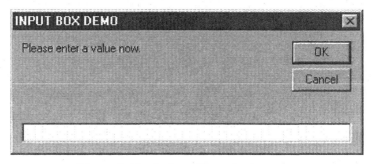

Figure 2-15. An **InputBox** display.

The syntax of the **InputBox** method is

Object.InputBox(*prompt_text, title_text, default, x_position, y_position, helpfile, context, type_num*)

The differences between the **InputBox** function and the **InputBox** method are the following: (i) *default* can be any data type and (ii) the additional argument *type_num* specifies the data type of the return value. The values of *type_num* and the corresponding data types are listed in Table 2-9. Values of *type_num* can be added together. For example, to specify an input dialog box that would accept number or string values as input, use the value $1 + 2 = 3$ for *type_num*.

Table 2-9. InputBox Data Type Values

type_num	Data Type
0	Formula
1	Number
2	String
4	Logical
8	Reference (as a Range object)
16	Error value
64	Array

The following example causes the **InputBox** method to return a **Range** object (so that you can use its **Address** property in addition to its **Value** property, for example):

```
Set known_Ys = Application.InputBox _
    ("Select the range of Y values", "STEP 1 OF 2", , , , , , 8)
```

Visual Basic Arrays

If you're familiar with other programming languages you are probably familiar with the concept of an array. An array is a collection of related variables denoted by a single name, such as Sample. You can then specify any element in the array by using an index number: Sample(1), Sample(7), etc.

Many scientists make extensive use of arrays in their calculations. Because some aspects of arrays in VBA can be confusing, this chapter provides detailed coverage of this important topic.

Dimensioning an Array

The **Dim** (short for Dimension) statement is used to declare the size of an array. Unless specified otherwise, VBA arrays begin with an index of 0. Thus the statement

Dim Sample(10)

establishes array storage for 11 elements, Sample(0) through Sample(10). However, you can specify that the arrays in your procedure begin with an array index of 1. Since worksheet ranges, worksheet functions and worksheet arrays use (or assume) a lower array index of 1, always specifying VBA arrays with lower array index of 1 can eliminate a lot of confusion.

There are two ways to specify the lower array index. You can specify the lower bound of an array in the **Dim** statement. For example,

Dim Sample (1 **To** 10)

sets the lower array index = 1 for the array Sample. It's considered good programming practice to put the **Dim** statements at the beginning of the procedure.

Alternatively, you can use the **Option Base 1** statement, which specifies that *all* arrays in the procedure begin with a lower index of 1. The **Option Base 1** statement is used at the module level: that is, it must appear in a module sheet before any procedures.

Use the Name of the Array Variable to Specify the Whole Array

You can refer to the complete array by using the array variable name in your code. The array name can be used with or without parentheses.

Multidimensional Arrays

Arrays can be multidimensional. Two-dimensional arrays are common; to create a 2-D array called Spectrum, with dimensions 500 rows × 2 columns, use the statement

Dim Spectrum (500,2)

Declaring the Variable Type of an Array

Since multidimensional arrays such as the one above can use up significant amounts of memory, it's a good idea to define the data type of the variable. The complete syntax of the **Dim** statement is

Dim VariableName(Lower **To** Upper) **As** Type

The optional Lower **To** can be omitted. Type can be **Integer**, **Single**, **Double**, **Variant**, etc. See the complete list of data types in "VBA Data Types" earlier in this chapter.) A **Variant** array can hold values of different data types, such as integer and string, in the same array.

Several variables can be dimensioned in a single **Dim** statement, but there must be a separate **As Type** for each variable. Thus

Dim J **As** Integer, K **As** Integer

is OK but **Dim** J, K **As Integer** declares only the variable J as integer.

Returning the Size of an Array

Use the **LBound** and **UBound** functions to obtain the size of an array during execution of your procedure. The **LBound** function returns the lower index of an array. For example, for the array Sample described previously, **LBound**(Sample) returns 1 and **UBound**(Sample) returns 10.

The complete syntax of **LBound** and **UBound** is **LBound**(arrayname, dimension). For the array Spectrum dimensioned thus:

Dim Spectrum (500,2)

the statement **UBound**(Spectrum,1) returns 500 and **UBound**(Spectrum,2) returns 2.

Dynamic Arrays

If you don't know what array size you will need to handle a particular problem, you can create a *dynamic array*. This will allow you to declare a variable as an array but set its size later. Dimension the array using the **Dim** command, using empty parentheses, and use the **ReDim** command later to specify the array size, as, for example, in Figure 2-16.

```
Dim MeanX(), MeanY()
:
'Get number of cells to use in calculation
Ncells = XValues.Count
ReDim MeanX(Ncells), MeanY(Ncells)
:
```

Figure 2-16. Re-dimensioning an array.

You can also use the **ReDim** command to change the number of dimensions of an array.

The **ReDim** command can appear more than once in a procedure. If you use the **ReDim** command to change the size of an array after it has been "populated" with values, the values will be erased.

Preserving Values in Dynamic Arrays

You can preserve the values in an existing array by using the **Preserve** keyword, e.g.,

```
Dim MeanX(), MeanY()
:
ReDim Preserve MeanX(Ncells / 2), MeanY(Ncells / 2)
```

But, there's a limitation. Only the upper bound of the last dimension of a multidimensional array can be changed. Thus, the following code is valid:

```
Dim MeanXandY(2, 1000)
:
ReDim Preserve MeanXandY (2,Ncells / 2)
```

but the following code will generate a run-time error:

```
Dim MeanXandY(1000, 2)
:
ReDim Preserve MeanXandY (Ncells / 2, 2)
```

If you use **Preserve**, you can't use the **ReDim** command to change the number of dimensions of an array.

Working with Arrays in Sub Procedures: Passing Values from Worksheet to VBA Module

There are two ways to get values from a worksheet into a VBA array. You can either set up a loop to read the value of each worksheet cell and store the value in the appropriate element of an array, or you can assign the VBA array to a worksheet range. The former method is straightforward; the latter method is described in the following section.

Depending on which of these two methods you use, there can be a definite difference with respect to execution speed that could become important if you are working with extremely large arrays. An appreciable time is required to read values from a range of worksheet cells and store them in an internal array, while calculation using values in an internal array is much faster. Thus, if you need to access array elements a number of times, it will probably be more time-efficient to store the values in an internal array.

A Range Specified in a Sub Procedure Can Be Used as an Array

If a variable in a VBA **Sub** procedure is set equal to a range of cells in a worksheet, that variable can be used as an array. No **Dim** statement is necessary. Thus the following expression creates a variable called TestArray that can be treated as an array:

TestArray = **Range**("A2:A10")

The worksheet array can be a range reference or a name that refers to a reference. Thus, if the name XRange had been assigned to the range "A2:A10," then the following expression would also create a worksheet array called TestArray:

TestArray = **Range**("XRange")

A one-row or one-column reference becomes a one-dimensional array; a rectangular range becomes a two-dimensional array of dimensions *array(rows, columns)*.

The lower index of these arrays is always 1. Although arrays created *within* VBA have a lower array index of zero unless specified otherwise (by means of the **Option Base 1** statement, for example), when you assign a variable name to a range of worksheet cells, an array is created with lower array index of 1.

Note that the values in the range of cells have not been transferred to an internal VBA array; the VBA variable simply "points" to the range on the worksheet. However, the values in the range can be accessed in the same way that elements in a true array are accessed; for example, XRange(3) returns the third element in the "array."

Some Worksheet Functions Used Within VBA
Create an Array Automatically

If you use a worksheet function within VBA that returns an array, the lower array index will be 1. Such worksheet functions include: LINEST, TRANSPOSE, MINVERSE and MMULT. That's why it's important to use **Option Base 1**; otherwise, you will have some arrays with lower array index of zero and others with lower array index of one.

An Array of Object Variables

There is an important difference between equating a range of cells in a worksheet to a simple variable in VBA, e.g.,

   ar = **Range**("A2:B9")

or equating a range of cells in a worksheet an object variable by using the **Set** command, e.g.,

   Set ar = **Range**("A2:B9")

Equating a variable in VBA to a worksheet range creates an array in VBA in which each array element contains the value stored in the cell. Using the **Set** command to equate an object variable in VBA to a worksheet range creates a Range object.

For an array of object variables, you must use a different approach to obtain the upper or lower bounds of the array indices, e.g.,

   ar.**Rows**.**Count**

or

   ar.**Columns**.**Count**.

Working with Arrays in Sub Procedures:
Passing Values from a VBA Module to a Worksheet

There are at least two ways to send values from a VBA array to a worksheet. You can set up a loop and write the value of each array element to a worksheet cell, or you can assign the value of the VBA array to the value of a worksheet range. The latter method can cause a problem when you use this method with a 1-D range, as described next.

A One-Dimensional Array
Assigned to a Worksheet Range
Can Cause Problems

Arrays can cause some confusion when you write the array back to a worksheet by assigning the value of the array to a worksheet range.

VBA considers a one-dimensional array to have the elements of the array in a row. This can cause problems when you select a range of cells in a column and assign an array to it, as in the following:

Range("E1:E10").**Value** = TestArray

The preceding statement causes the same value, the first element of the array, to be entered in all cells in the column. However, if you write the array to a row of cells instead of a column, e.g.,

Range("E1:N1").**Value** = TestArray

each cell of the range will receive the correct array value.

There are at least three ways to "work around" this problem caused by a "horizontal" array and a "vertical" destination range. One obvious way is to use a loop to write the elements of the array to individual worksheet cells in a column.

A second way is to specify both the row and the column dimensions of the array, so as to make it an array in a column, as illustrated in the **Sub** procedure shown in Figure 2-16.

```
Sub ArrayDemo1()
'Second method to "work around" the row-column problem:
'specify the row and column dimensions.

Dim TestArray(10, 1)
     statements to populate the array
'Then writes the array elements to cells E1:E10.
Range("E1:E10").Value = TestArray
End Sub
```

Figure 2-16. A "work around" for the row–column problem.

A third way is to use the TRANSPOSE worksheet function (Figure 2-17):

```
Sub ArrayDemo2()
'Another method to "work around" the row-column problem: use
Transpose.
'Note that Transpose creates a 1-base array.

Dim TestArray(10)
    statements to populate the array
Range("E1:E10").Value = Application.Transpose(TestArray)
End Sub
```

Figure 2-17. Another "work around" for the row–column problem.

Custom Functions

Chapter 1 provided an introduction to **Sub** procedures and **Function** procedures. By now it should be clear that a **Sub** procedure (a command macro) is a computer program that you "run"; it can perform actions such as formatting, opening or closing documents and so on. A **Function** procedure (a user-defined function) is a computer program that calculates a value and returns it to the cell in which it is typed. A **Function** procedure cannot change the worksheet environment (e.g., it can't make a cell Bold).

The following sections provide some examples of more advanced features of custom functions.

Specifying the Data Type of an Argument

You can specify the data type of an argument passed to a **Function** procedure by using the **As** keyword in the **Function** statement. For example, the **Function** procedure MolWt takes two arguments: formula (a string) and decimals (an integer). The statement

Function MolWt (formula **As String**, decimals **As Integer**)

declares the type of each variable. If an argument of an incorrect type is supplied to the function, a #VALUE! error message will be displayed.

Specifying the Data Type
Returned by a Function Procedure

You can also specify the data type of the return value. If none is specified, the **Variant** data type will be returned. In the example of the preceding section, MolWt returns a floating-point result. The **Variant** data type is satisfactory; however, if you wanted to specify double precision floating point, use an additional **As Type** expression in the statement, for example,

Function MolWt (formula **As String**, decimals **As Integer**) **As Double**

Returning an Error Value from a Function Procedure

If, during execution, a function procedure detects an incorrect value or an incipient error such as a potential divide-by-zero error, we need to return an error value. You could specify a text message as the return value of the function procedure, like this:

If (*error found*) **Then** FunctionName = "error message": **Exit Function**

but this is not the best way to handle an error. Use the **CVErr(*errorvalue*)** keyword to return one of Excel's worksheet error values that Excel can handle appropriately. For example, if a result cannot be calculated by the function, then a #N/A error message should be returned. This is accomplished by means of the following:

If (*error found*) **Then** FunctionName = **CVErr(xlErrNA): Exit Function**

The error values are listed in Appendix 1.

A Custom Function that Takes an Optional Argument

A custom function can have optional arguments. Use the **Optional** keyword in the list of arguments to declare an optional argument. The optional argument or arguments must be last in the list of arguments.

Within the procedure, you will need to determine the presence or absence of optional arguments by using the **IsMissing** keyword. As well, you will usually need to provide a default value if an argument is omitted.

Arrays in Function Procedures

You can create **Function** procedures that use arrays as arguments, or return an array of results.

A Range Passed to a Function Procedure
Can Be Used as an Array

If a range argument is passed in a function macro, the range can be treated as an array in the VBA procedure. No **Dim** statement is necessary. Thus the expression

Function MyLINEST(known_ys, known_xs)

passes the worksheet ranges known_ys and known_xs to the VBA procedure where they can be used as arrays. A one-row or one-column reference becomes a one-dimensional array; a rectangular range becomes a two-dimensional array of dimensions *array(rows, columns)*.

Passing an Indefinite Number of Arguments Using the ParamArray Keyword

Occasionally a **Function** procedure needs to accept an indefinite number of arguments. The SUM worksheet function is an example of such a function; its syntax is =SUM(number1,number2,...). To enable a **Function** procedure to accept an indefinite number of arguments, use the **ParamArray** keyword in the argument list of the function, as in the following expression

Function ArrayMaker(**ParamArray** rng())

Only one argument can follow the **ParamArray** keyword, and it must be the last one in the function's list of arguments. The argument declared by the **ParamArray** keyword is an array of **Variant** elements. Empty parentheses are required.

The lower bound of the array is zero, even if you have used the **Option Base 1** statement. Use **UBound(**rng**)** to find the upper array index.

Elements in the array of arguments passed using the **ParamArray** keyword can themselves be arrays. The following code illustrates how to access individual elements of each array in an array of elements passed using **ParamArray**.

```
Function ArrayMaker(ParamArray rng())

For J = 0 To UBound(rng)
    YSize = rng(J).Columns.Count
    For K = 1 To YSize
        statements
    Next K
Next J
```

Figure 2-18. Handling an array of array arguments passed by using **ParamArray**.

Returning an Array of Values as a Result

The most obvious way to enable a **Function** procedure to return an array of values is to assemble the values in an array and return the array. The procedure shown in Figure 2-19 illustrates a function that returns an array of three values. To use the function, the user must select a horizontal range of three cells, enter the function and press CONTROL+SHIFT+ENTER.

```
Function MyLINEST(known_ys, known_xs)
Dim Results(3)
    code to calculate slope, intercept and R-squared
Results(1) = MySlope
Results(2) = MyIntercept
Results(3) = MyRSq
MyLINEST = Results
End Function
```

Figure 2-19. A **Function** procedure that returns an array of results.

A second approach is to use the **Array** keyword. The **Array** function returns a variant that contains an array.

```
Function MyLINEST(known_ys, known_xs)
    code to calculate slope, intercept and R-squared
MyLINEST = Array(MySlope,My Intercept, MyRSq)
End Function
```

Figure 2-20. Using the **Array** keyword in a **Function** procedure.

The **Array** keyword can accommodate only a one-dimensional array. To use this approach to return a two-dimensional array of results, you must create an array of arrays, as illustrated in Figure 2-21. Both arrays must contain the same number of values.

```
Function MyLINEST2(known_ys, known_xs)
    code to calculate slope, intercept, R-squared,
        std dev of slope, std dev of intercept, std error of y values.
MyLINEST2 = Array(Array(MySlope, MyIntercept, MyRSq), _
Array(stdev_m, _ stdev_b, SE_y))
End Function
```

Figure 2-21. Using the **Array** keyword to return a 2-D array.

Creating Add-In Function Macros

Saving a custom function as an Add-In is by far the most convenient way to use it. Here are some of the advantages:

- An Add-In custom function is listed in the Paste Function list box without the workbook name preceding the name of the function, making it virtually indistinguishable from Excel's built-in functions.

- If the Add-In workbook is placed in the AddIns folder, the Add-In will be available every time you start Excel.

How to Create an Add-In Macro

To save a workbook as an Add-In, choose **Save As...** from the **File** menu. Choose Microsoft Excel Add-In from the Save File As Type drop-down list box, then press OK. In Excel for Windows, Add-In workbooks are automatically given the filename extension .xla.

When you save a workbook as an Add-In, the default location is the AddIns folder.

Command macros can also be saved as Add-Ins.

Testing and Debugging

When an error occurs during execution of a procedure, VBA will stop execution and display a run-time error message. There are a large number (over 50) of these run-time error messages. Some (but not all) of these error messages are self-explanatory. Here are some examples:

Subscript out of range   Attempted to access an element of an array outside its specified dimensions.

Property or method not found   Object does not have the specified property or method.

Argument not optional   A required argument was not provided.

The line of code in which the error occurred, or the first line of the procedure (containing the **Sub** or **Function** keyword) will be highlighted, usually in yellow (see Figure 2-22). After you have corrected the error in your VBA code, the line will still be highlighted. Press F5 to continue execution.

```
Function MySLOPE(known_ys, known_xs)
N = known_ys.Count

For z = 1 To N
Sx = Sx + known_xs(z)
Sy = Sy + known_ys(z)
Sxx = Sxx + known_xs(z) ^ 2
Syy = Syy + known_ys(z) ^ 2
Sxy = Sxy + known_xs(z) * known_ys(z)
Next z

Slope = (N * Sxy - Sx * Sy) / (N * Sxx - Sx * Sx)
MySLOPE = Slope
End Function
```

Figure 2-22. VBA code with a highlighted line.

Tracing Execution

When your program produces an error during execution, or executes but doesn't produce the correct answer, it is often helpful to execute the code one statement at a time and examine the values of selected variables during execution. If your procedure contains logical constructions (**If** or **Select Case**, for example), simply stepping through code will allow you to verify the logic.

Stepping Through Code

There are two ways to begin the process of stepping through the code of a **Sub** procedure:

- Select the name of the procedure in the Macro Name list box and press the Step Into button. This will display the code module containing the procedure; the first line of the procedure will be highlighted in yellow, as in Figure 2-22).

- Add a breakpoint as described in the following section, then run the **Sub** procedure in the usual way.

When the code window is displayed, with a line of code highlighted, you can step through the code by pressing F8 or by using the Step Into toolbutton 🔣. The Step Into toolbutton is on the Debug toolbar; choose **Toolbars** from the **View** menu and **Debug** from the submenu to display the Debug toolbar (Figure 2-23).

The highlighted line of code is the statement to be executed next.

Figure 2-23. The VBA Debug toolbar.

Adding a Breakpoint

A breakpoint allows you to halt execution at a specified line of code, rather than having to step through the code from the beginning. There are several ways to add a breakpoint:

- Opposite the line of code where you want to set the breakpoint, click in the gray bar on the left side of the VBA module sheet. The line of code will be highlighted (usually in red-brown) and a breakpoint indicator, a large dot of the same color, will be placed in the margin (see Figure 2-24).

- Place the cursor in the line of code where you want to set a breakpoint. Press the Toggle Breakpoint button 🖐 on the Debug toolbar.

- Insert a **Stop** statement in the VBA code.

- Enter a break expression in the Add Watch dialog box (see "Examining the Values of Variables" later in this chapter).

```
Function MySLOPE(known_ys, known_xs)
N = known_ys.Count

For z = 1 To N
Sx = Sx + known_xs(z)
Sy = Sy + known_ys(z)
Sxx = Sxx + known_xs(z) ^ 2
Syy = Syy + known_ys(z) ^ 2
Sxy = Sxy + known_xs(z) * known_ys(z)
Next z

Slope = (N * Sxy - Sx * Sy) / (N * Sxx - Sx * Sx)
MySLOPE = Slope
End Function
```

Figure 2-24. VBA code with a breakpoint.

When you run the macro, the code will execute until the breakpoint is reached, at which point execution will stop. You can now step through the code one statement at a time or examine the values of selected variables, as described in the following sections.

Since you can't "run" a **Function** procedure, the only way to step through a **Function** procedure is to add a breakpoint, then recalculate a formula containing the custom function.

To remove a breakpoint, click on the breakpoint indicator, or place the cursor on the highlighted line and press the Toggle Breakpoint button, or delete a **Stop** statement.

Examining the Values of Variables While in Break Mode

You can examine the values of selected variables while in Break Mode. You get to be in Break Mode by one of the following:

- Your procedure generated a run-time error and halted.

- Your procedure reached a line with a breakpoint or a **Stop** statement

To see the current value of a variable, highlight the variable by double-clicking on it, or simply place the cursor over the variable. The current value of the variable will be displayed in a yellow "InfoBox" next to the cursor, as illustrated in Figure 2-25.

```
Function MySLOPE(known_ys, known_xs)
N = known_ys.Count

For z = 1 To N
Sx = Sx + known_xs(z)
Sy = Sy + known_ys(z)
Sxx = Sxx + known_xs(z) ^ 2
Syy = Syy + known_ys(z) ^ 2
Syy = 8507.926157  + known_xs(z) * known_ys(z)
Next z

Slope = (N * Sxy - Sx * Sy) / (N * Sxx - Sx * Sx)
MySLOPE = Slope
End Function
```

Figure 2-25. Displaying the value of a variable while in break mode.

Examining the Values of Variables During Execution

You can also display the values of selected variables as the code is executed. There are several ways to select variables or expressions to be displayed:

- Highlight the variable or expression and then choose **Quick Watch...**

  from the Debug menu or press the Quick Watch button 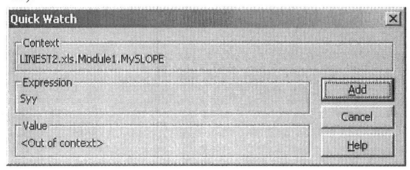 on the Debug toolbar, to display the Quick Watch dialog box (Figure 2-26).

- Highlight the variable or expression and then choose **Add Watch...** from the **Debug** menu to display the Add Watch dialog box (Figure 2-27).

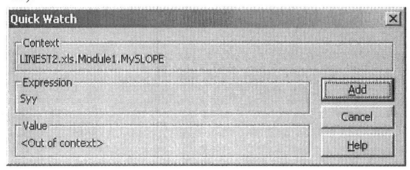

Figure 2-26. The VBA Quick Watch dialog box.

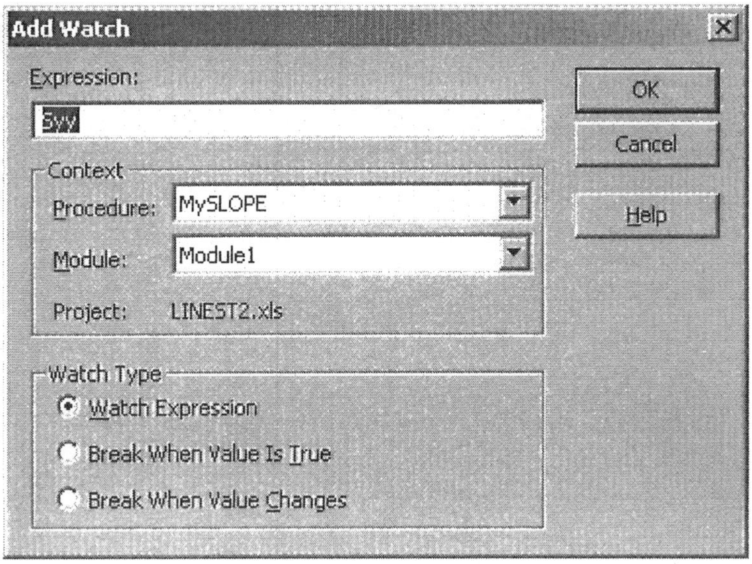

Figure 2-27. The VBA Add Watch dialog box.

To see the values of the selected variables or expressions, you must be in Step mode. The variables will be listed in the Watches pane (Figure 2-28), which is usually located below the Code window. The current values of the variables will be displayed as you step through the code.

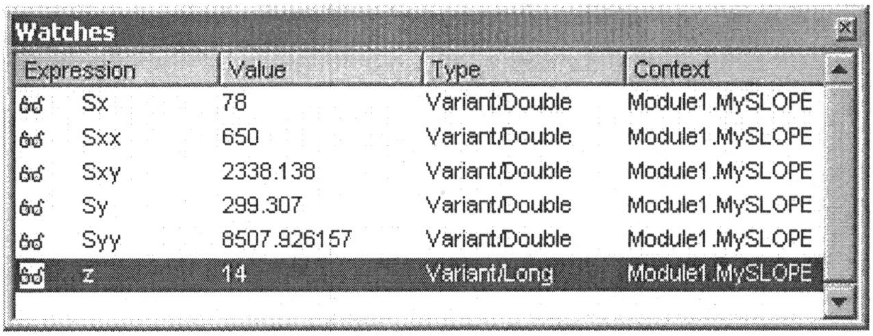

Figure 2-28. The VBA Watches pane.

To remove a variable or expression from the Watches window, select it in the Watches window, choose **Edit Watch** from the **Debug** menu and press the Delete button. Or you can simply select it in the Watches window and press the Delete key.

Watch expressions are not saved with your code.

Chapter 3

Worksheet Functions for Working with Matrices

Arrays, Matrices and Determinants

Spreadsheet calculations lend themselves almost automatically to the use of arrays of values. Arrays in Excel can be either one- or two-dimensional. For the solution of many types of problem, it is convenient to manipulate an entire rectangular array of values as a unit. Such an array is termed a *matrix*. (In Excel, the terms "range," "array" and "matrix" are virtually interchangeable.) An $m \times n$ matrix (m rows and n columns) of values is illustrated below:

$$\begin{bmatrix} a_{11} & a_{12} & \cdots & a_{1n} \\ a_{21} & a_{22} & \cdots & a_{2n} \\ \vdots & \vdots & \vdots & \vdots \\ a_{m1} & a_{m2} & \cdots & a_{mn} \end{bmatrix}$$

The values comprising the array are called *matrix elements*. Mathematical operations on matrices have their own special rules, to be discussed in the following sections.

Some Types of Matrices

A matrix which contains a single column of m rows or a single row of n columns is called a *vector*.

A *square matrix* has the same number of rows and columns. The set of elements a_{ij} for which $i = j$ ($a_{11}, a_{22},..., a_{nn}$) is called the *main diagonal* or *principal diagonal*.

If all the elements of a square matrix are zero except those on the main diagonal, the matrix is termed a *diagonal matrix*. A diagonal matrix whose diagonal elements are all 1 is a *unit matrix*.

An upper triangular matrix has values on the main diagonal and above, but the values of all elements below the main diagonal are zero; similarly, a lower triangular matrix has zero values for all elements above the main diagonal.

A *tridiagonal matrix* contains all zeros except on the main diagonal and the two adjacent diagonals.

A *symmetric* matrix is a square matrix in which $a_{ij} = a_{ji}$.

A *determinant* is a property of a square matrix; there is a procedure for the numerical evaluation of a determinant, so that an $N \times N$ matrix can be reduced to a single numerical value. The value of the determinant has properties that make it useful in certain tests and equations. (See, for example, "Cramer's Rule" in Chapter 9.)

An Introduction to Matrix Mathematics

Matrix algebra provides a powerful method for the manipulation of sets of numbers. Many mathematical operations, such as addition, subtraction, multiplication and division, have their counterparts in matrix algebra. Our discussion will be limited to the manipulations of square matrices. For purposes of illustration, two 3×3 matrices will be defined, namely

$$\mathbf{A} = \begin{bmatrix} a & b & c \\ d & e & f \\ g & h & i \end{bmatrix} = \begin{bmatrix} 2 & 3 & 4 \\ 3 & 2 & 1 \\ 4 & 3 & 7 \end{bmatrix}$$

and

$$\mathbf{B} = \begin{bmatrix} r & s & t \\ u & v & w \\ x & y & z \end{bmatrix} = \begin{bmatrix} 2 & 0 & 2 \\ 0 & 3 & 3 \\ 3 & 2 & 1 \end{bmatrix}$$

Addition or Subtraction. The following examples illustrate addition or subtraction.

Addition of a constant: $\mathbf{A} + q = \begin{bmatrix} a+q & b+q & c+q \\ d+q & e+q & f+q \\ g+q & h+q & i+q \end{bmatrix}$

Addition of two matrices (both must have the same dimensions, i.e., contain the same numbers of rows and columns):

$$\mathbf{A} + \mathbf{B} = \begin{bmatrix} a & b & c \\ d & e & f \\ g & h & i \end{bmatrix} + \begin{bmatrix} r & s & t \\ u & v & w \\ x & y & z \end{bmatrix} = \begin{bmatrix} a+r & b+s & c+t \\ d+u & e+v & f+w \\ g+x & h+y & i+z \end{bmatrix}$$

Multiplication or Division. Multiplication or division by a constant:

$$qA = \begin{bmatrix} qa & qb & qc \\ qd & qe & qf \\ qg & qh & qi \end{bmatrix}$$

Multiplication of two matrices can be either *scalar* or *matrix* multiplication. Scalar multiplication of two matrices consists of multiplying the elements of a matrix by a constant, as shown above, or multiplying corresponding elements of two matrices:

$$A \times B = \begin{bmatrix} a & b & c \\ d & e & f \\ g & h & i \end{bmatrix} \times \begin{bmatrix} r & s & t \\ u & v & w \\ x & y & z \end{bmatrix} = \begin{bmatrix} a \times r & b \times s & c \times t \\ d \times u & e \times v & f \times w \\ g \times x & h \times y & i \times z \end{bmatrix}$$

Thus it's clear that both matrices must have the same dimensions $m \times n$. Scalar multiplication is commutative, that is, $A \times B = B \times A$.

Matrix Multiplication. The matrix multiplication of two matrices is somewhat more complicated. The individual matrix elements of the matrix product C of two matrices A and B are

$$C_{ij} = \sum_{k=1}^{n} A_{ik} B_{kj}$$

where i is the row number and j is the column number. Thus, for example,

$$A \cdot B = \begin{bmatrix} a & b & c \\ d & e & f \\ g & h & i \end{bmatrix} \cdot \begin{bmatrix} r & s & t \\ u & v & w \\ x & y & z \end{bmatrix} = \begin{bmatrix} ar + bu + cx & as + bv + cy & at + bw + cz \\ dr + eu + fx & ds + ev + fy & dt + ew + fz \\ gr + hu + ix & gs + hv + iy & gt + hw + iz \end{bmatrix}$$

Matrix multiplication is not generally commutative, that is $A \cdot B \neq B \cdot A$.

Transposition. The transpose of matrix A, most commonly written as A^T, is the matrix obtained by exchanging the rows and columns of A; that is, the matrix element a_{ij} becomes the element a_{ji} in the transposed matrix. The transpose of a matrix of N rows and M columns is a matrix of M rows and N columns.

Matrix Inversion. The process of *matrix inversion* is analogous to obtaining the reciprocal of a number a. The matrix relationship that corresponds to the algebraic relationship $a \times (1/a) = 1$ is

$$A A^{-1} = I$$

where $\mathbf{A}^{-1}$ is the inverse matrix and $\mathbf{I}$ is the unit matrix. The process for manual calculation of the inverse of a matrix is complicated and need not be described here, since matrix inversion can be done conveniently using Excel's worksheet function MINVERSE.

Evaluation of the Determinant. A determinant is a mathematical value that can be calculated for a square matrix. Determinants are useful for the solution of systems of simultaneous equations, as will be discussed in chapter 9. The "pencil-and-paper" evaluation of the determinant of a matrix of N rows × N columns is tedious, but it can be done simply by using Excel's worksheet function MDETERM.

Excel's Built-in Matrix Functions

Performing matrix mathematics with Excel is very simple. Let's begin by assuming that the matrices **A** and **B** have been defined by selecting the 3R × 3C arrays of cells containing the values shown in Figure 3-1 and naming them by using **Define Name**. Remember, we're simply assigning a range name to a range of cells. We usually refer to it as a range or an array; the fact that we are calling it a matrix simply indicates what we intend to do with it.

	B	C	D
3	Matrix A		
4	2	3	4
5	3	2	-1
6	4	3	7

	F	G	H
3	Matrix B		
4	2	0	2
5	0	3	-3
6	-3	-2	1

Figure 3-1. Ranges of cells defined as A and B.
(folder 'Chapter 03 (Matrices) Examples, workbook 'Matrix Math', sheet 'Sheet1')

Addition or Subtraction. To add a constant (e.g., 3) to matrix **A**, simply select a range of cells the same size as the matrix, enter the formula =A+3, then press COMMAND+RETURN or CONTROL+SHIFT+RETURN (Macintosh) or CONTROL+SHIFT+ENTER (Windows). When you "array-enter" a formula by pressing e.g., CONTROL+SHIFT+ENTER, Excel puts braces around the formula, as shown below:

{=A+3}

Do not type the braces; if you do, the result will not be recognized by Excel as a formula.

	D	E	F
8	5	6	7
9	6	5	2
10	7	6	10

Figure 3-2. Result matrix {A + 3}.
(folder 'Chapter 03 (Matrices) Examples, workbook 'Matrix Math', sheet 'Sheet1')

Subtraction of a constant, multiplication or division by a constant, or addition of two matrices is performed in the same way by using standard Excel algebraic operators.

Scalar Multiplication. Scalar multiplication can be either multiplication of the elements of a matrix by a constant, e.g., a formula such as {=3*A}, or multiplication of corresponding elements of two matrices, e.g., {=A*B}. The result of the latter formula is shown in Figure 3-3.

	D	E	F
16	4	0	8
17	0	6	3
18	-12	-6	7

Figure 3-3. Result matrix {A × B}.
(folder 'Chapter 03 (Matrices) Examples, workbook 'Matrix Math', sheet 'Sheet1')

Matrix multiplication can be accomplished easily by the use of Excel's worksheet function MMULT(*matrix1, matrix2*). For the matrices **A** and **B** defined above, entering the formula =MMULT(A,B) yields the result shown in Figure 3-4 while the formula =MMULT(B,A) yields the result shown in Figure 3-5.

	D	E	F
24	-8	1	-1
25	9	8	-1
26	-13	-5	6

Figure 3-4. Result matrix **A·B**.
(folder 'Chapter 03 (Matrices) Examples, workbook 'Matrix Math', sheet 'Sheet1')

	D	E	F
28	12	12	22
29	-3	-3	-24
30	-8	-10	-3

Figure 3-5. Result matrix **B·A**.
(folder 'Chapter 03 (Matrices) Examples, workbook 'Matrix Math', sheet 'Sheet1')

Matrix multiplication of two matrices is possible only if the matrices are *conformable*, that is, if the number of columns of **A** is equal to the number of rows of **B**. The opposite condition, if the number of *rows* of **A** is equal to the number of *columns* of **B**, is not equivalent. The following examples, involving multiplication of a matrix and a vector, illustrate the possibilities:

MMULT (4×3 matrix, 3×1 vector) = 3×1 result vector

MMULT (4×3 matrix, 1×4 vector) = #VALUE!

MMULT (1×4 vector, 4×3 matrix) = 1×4 result vector

In other words, the two inner indices must be the same.

Transposition. The *transpose* of a matrix may be calculated by using the worksheet function TRANSPOSE(*array*) or obtained manually by using the Transpose option in the **Paste Special...** menu command.

The size of the array that can be transposed is limited only by the size of the Excel spreadsheet; the number of rows or columns cannot be greater than 256.

Matrix Inversion. The process for inverting a matrix "manually" (i.e., using pencil, paper and calculator) is complicated, but the operation can be carried out readily by using Excel's worksheet function MINVERSE(*array*). The inverse of the matrix **B** above is shown in Figure 3-6.

	D	E	F
36	-0.25	-0.33333333	-0.5
37	0.75	0.66666667	0.5
38	0.75	0.33333333	0.5

Figure 3-6. Result matrix $\mathbf{B}^{-1}$.
(folder 'Chapter 03 (Matrices) Examples, workbook 'Matrix Math', sheet 'Sheet1')

The size of the matrix must not exceed 52 rows by 52 columns.

Evaluation of the Determinant. The determinant of a matrix of N rows $\times$ N columns can be obtained by using the worksheet function MDETERM(*array*).

The function returns a single numerical value, not an array, and thus you do not have to use CONTROL+SHIFT+ENTER. The value of the determinant of **B**, represented by |**B**|, is 12.

Some Additional Matrix Functions

Some additional functions useful for working with arrays or matrices are provided on the CD that accompanies this book. The additional functions are as follows:

Identity Matrix. The function MIDENT(*size*) returns an identity matrix of a specified size. The *size* argument is optional. Use *size* when you want to use an identity matrix in a formula. Omit *size* when you want to fill a range of cells on a worksheet with an identity matrix; the size of the matrix is then determined by the size of the selection. If the selection is not a square matrix, the function returns the #REF! error value.

The maximum allowable size is 63 × 63 (larger gives #VALUE! error).

Examples:

The expression MIDENT(3) returns {1,0,0;0,1,0;0,0,1}.

The formula =MIDENT() entered in the range A1:E5 returns {1,0,0,0,0;0,1,0,0,0;0,0,1,0,0;0,0,0,1,0;0,0,0,0,1}.

The formula =MIDENT() entered in the range A1:E6 returns #REF! in the cells (the selection has five rows and six columns).

Finding the Position of a Value in an Array. The function MIndex(*lookup_value, array_, match_type*) returns a horizontal 2-element array containing the row and column numbers of a specified value in an array. The argument *lookup_value* is the value you use to find the value you want in *array_*. The argument *array_* is a contiguous range of cells containing possible lookup values. The argument *match_type* is a number (−1, 0, or 1) that specifies the value found in *array_*. If *match_type* is 0 or omitted, the function returns the position of the value that is exactly equal to *lookup_value*, or #N/A. If *match_type* is 1, the function returns the position of the largest value that is less than or equal to *lookup_value*. If *match_type* is −1, the function returns the position of the smallest value that is greater than or equal to *lookup_value*. Unlike Excel's INDEX worksheet function, if *match_type* is −1 or 1, the values do not have to be sorted in descending or ascending order, respectively.

The array must contain only numbers. If any cells contain text or error values, MIndex returns the #VALUE! error value. Empty cells are treated as zero.

Examples:

In the following example the range B13:D15, containing the values {13,0,–1;5,12,22;–5,0,1}, was assigned the name A.

The expression MIndex(MAX(A),A) returns the array of values {2,3}.

The expression MIndex(7,A) returns the array of values {#N/A,#N/A}.

The expression MIndex(15,A,1) returns the array of values {1,1}.

Scaling Arrays. The function MSCALE(*array, scale_factor_logical*) calculates and applies scale factors for a $N \times M$ matrix and returns a $N \times M$ scaled matrix. All values in a row are scaled by dividing by the largest element in that row. The function also creates a column vector of N elements, containing the scale factors.

If the optional argument *scale_factor_logical* = False or omitted, the function returns the scaled matrix; if *scale_factor_logical* = True, returns the scale factor vector.

Examples:

In the following examples the range A5:C7, assigned the name B, contains the values {3,20,1000;-0.1,3,100;5,10,-5}.

The formula =MSCALE(B) returns the array {0.003,0.02,1;-0.001,0.03,1;0.5,1,-0.5}.

The formula =MSCALE(B,TRUE) returns the array {0.001;0.01;0.1}.

Combining Separate Ranges into a Single Array. An array in Excel must be a contiguous range of cells. It sometimes happens that one would like to combine noncontiguous ranges into a single array. The function Arr(*range1*, *range2*...) combines individual 1-D or 2-D arrays into a 2-D array. All individual arrays must be vertical and must have the same number of rows. The VBA code for the function is shown in Figure 3-7.

This custom function makes use of the **ParamArray** keyword, which allows the function to accept an arbitrary number of ranges.

Some uses for this custom function include the following:

In the solution of a system of simultaneous equations by the Gaussian Elimination method (see Chapter 9), an augmented matrix of N rows $\times N + 1$ columns is created by combining the $N \times N$ matrix of coefficients with the N rows $\times 1$ column vector of constants. This can conveniently be done by using the custom function.

The LINEST worksheet function for multiple linear regression (see Chapter 13) requires that the argument *known_x's* be a contiguous selection of cells. The custom function can be used to convert a series of noncontiguous ranges into an array that can be used as the argument *known_x's* in LINEST.

```vba
Option Explicit
Option Base 1
Function Arr(ParamArray rng())
'Combines individual 1-D or 2-D arrays into a final 2-D array.
'In this version all individual arrays must be "vertical".
'All individual arrays must have same number of rows.
Dim Result()
Dim I As Integer, J As Integer, K As Integer
Dim TempX As Integer, TempY As Integer, XDim As Integer, YDim As Integer
Dim YStart As Integer, YSize As Integer

'First, get sizes of individual arrays, check to make sure all are same size.
For J = 0 To UBound(rng)
'Handles either range, name or array constant arguments
If IsObject(rng(J)) = True Then    'reference is to a range or a name
    TempX = rng(J).Rows.Count
    TempY = rng(J).Columns.Count
ElseIf IsArray(rng(J)) Then
    TempX = UBound(rng(J), 1)
    TempY = UBound(rng(J), 2)
End If
If J = 0 Then XDim = TempX
If XDim <> TempX Then Arr = CVErr(xlErrRef): Exit Function
YDim = YDim + TempY
Next J

'Now combine each individual array into final array.
'I index is used to select within array of arrays.
'K and J are column & row indices of individual arrays.
ReDim Result(XDim, YDim)
YStart = 0
For I = 0 To UBound(rng)
  YSize = rng(I).Columns.Count
  For K = 1 To YSize
  For J = 1 To XDim
    Result(J, YStart + K) = Application.Index(rng(I), J, K)
  Next J, K
  YStart = YStart + YSize
Next I
Arr = Result()
End Function
```

Figure 3-7. VBA function procedure to combine separate ranges into a single array. (folder 'Chapter 03 (Matrices) Examples, workbook 'ArrayMaker', module 'Module1')

Problems

Answers to the following problems are found in the folder "Ch. 03 (Matrices)" in the "Problems & Solutions" folder on the CD.

1. Find the inverse and the determinant of the following matrices:

(a)
$$\begin{bmatrix} 2 & 9 & 4 \\ 7 & 5 & 3 \\ 6 & 1 & 8 \end{bmatrix}$$

(b)
$$\begin{bmatrix} 2 & -1 & 0 \\ -1 & 2 & -1 \\ 0 & -1 & 2 \end{bmatrix}$$

(c)
$$\begin{bmatrix} 0.75 & 0.5 & 0.25 \\ 0.5 & 1 & 0.5 \\ 0.25 & 0.5 & 0.75 \end{bmatrix}$$

(d)
$$\begin{bmatrix} 2 & 1 & 1 \\ 1 & 1 & 1 \\ 1 & 2 & 1 \end{bmatrix}$$

2. Find the value of the determinant of each of the following.

(a)
$$\begin{bmatrix} 1 & 1 & 3 \\ 2 & 2 & 2 \\ 3 & 3 & 9 \end{bmatrix}$$

(b)
$$\begin{bmatrix} 2 & -1 & 1 \\ 1 & 3 & 2 \\ 3 & 2 & 3 \end{bmatrix}$$

(c) $\begin{bmatrix} 1 & 1 & 1 & -1 \\ 1 & -1 & -1 & 1 \\ 2 & 1 & -1 & 2 \\ 3 & 1 & 2 & -1 \end{bmatrix}$

Chapter 4

Number Series

Number series, such as

$$1, \frac{1}{2}, \frac{1}{3}, \frac{1}{4}, \ldots, \frac{1}{n}, \ldots$$

are important in many areas of mathematics, such as the evaluation of transcendental functions, integrals or differential equations. Often, the sum of a number series is used as an approximation to a function that can't be evaluated directly. The approximation becomes more and more accurate as more terms are added to the sum; for example, the value of e, the base of natural logarithms, can be evaluated by means of the sum of an infinite series:

$$e = 1 + \sum_{k=1}^{\infty} \frac{1}{k!} \tag{4-1}$$

If the sum of a series approaches a finite value as the number of terms approaches infinity, the series is said to be convergent. A series is divergent if the sum approaches infinity (or does not converge to a definite value) when the number of terms approaches infinity. Only convergent series will be discussed in this chapter.

An alternating series in one in which the sign of each successive term is the opposite of the preceding one. Such a series will always converge if the absolute value of the nth term approaches zero.

Instead of a series of constant terms, a series may consist of variables, as exemplified by the series

$$a_0 + a_1 x + a_2 x^2 + \cdots + a_n x^n + \cdots \tag{4-2}$$

A series of the form shown above, in which the terms are multiples of non-negative integral powers of x, is called a power series.

Functions such as e^x, $\sin x$, $\cos x$ and others can be expressed in terms of the sum of an infinite series. Of course, Excel already provides worksheet functions to evaluate e^x, $\sin x$ or $\cos x$, but the ability to use number series in Excel formulas increases the scope of calculations that you can perform.

Evaluating Series Formulas

The obvious way to evaluate a series formula is to evaluate individual terms in the series formula in separate rows of the spreadsheet, and then sum the terms. Figure 4-1 illustrates the evaluation of *e* by using equation 4-1, summing terms until the contribution from the next term in the series is less than 1E-15.

	A	B	C
1	k	1/k!	sum
2			1
3	1	1	2
4	2	0.5	2.5
5	3	0.166666667	2.66667
6	4	0.041666667	2.7083333
7	5	0.008333333	2.7166666667
8	6	0.001388889	2.71805555555556
9	7	0.000198413	2.71825396825397
10	8	2.48016E-05	2.71827876984127
11	9	2.75573E-06	2.71828152557319
18	16	4.77948E-14	2.71828182845904
19	17	2.81146E-15	2.71828182845905

Figure 4-1. Evaluation of the terms of a series row-by-row.
The spreadsheet calculates the value of *e* by using equation (4-1).
Note that some rows of calculation have been hidden.

A more compact way to evaluate the sum of a series is by summing terms in a single worksheet formula. For example, a value for *e* can be calculated from equation 4-1 by using the following worksheet formula

=1+1/FACT(1)+1/FACT(2)+1/FACT(3)+1/FACT(4)+1/FACT(5)

where we sum the first 5 terms of the series. The true value of *e* to 15 decimal places) is 2.718 281 828 459 045. The formula returns 2.717 (0.06% error). Unfortunately, most power series converge much more slowly than this, and many more terms are required. Hence this is not a practical way to evaluate a series in a single cell — apart from the fact that it requires a lot of typing, a worksheet formula is limited to 1024 characters. Fortunately there are other ways to evaluate the sum of a series in a single worksheet formula.

Using Array Constants to Create Series Formulas

An array constant is an array of values, separated by commas and enclosed in braces, used as an argument of a function. An example of an array constant, sometimes referred to as an array literal, is {40,21,300,10}.

You can use an array constant to make the evaluation of a series formula much more compact and accurate. For example, to evaluate equation 4-1, the formula

    =1+SUM(1/FACT({1,2,3,4,5,6,7,8,9,10}))

returns the value 2.718 281 801 146 38 (1 x 10^{-6} % error).

Using the ROW Worksheet Function to Create Series Formulas

The ROW worksheet function provides a convenient way to generate a series of integers. To illustrate the use of this function in a formula, enter the formula

    =ROW(1:100)

in a worksheet cell. Now highlight the formula in the formula bar or in the cell and press F9 (Windows) or COMMAND+= (Macintosh) to display the result of the formula. You will see the array of integers from 1 to 100, as shown below.

{1;2;3;4;5;6;7;8;9;10;11;12;13;14;15;16;17;18;19;20;21;22;23;24;25;26;27;28;29; 30;31;32;33;34;35;36;37;38;39;40;41;42;43;44;45;46;47;48;49;50;51;52;53;54;55 ;56;57;58;59;60;61;62;63;64;65;66;67;68;69;70;71;72;73;74;75;76;77;78;79;80;8 1;82;83;84;85;86;87;88;89;90;91;92;93;94;95;96;97;98;99;100}

Using this method you can evaluate series formulas conveniently. For example, the formula for *e* becomes

    {=1+SUM(1/FACT(ROW(1:100)))}

and returns a value for *e* of 2.718 281 828 459 05, identical to the value returned by Excel's built-in function.

This formula is an array formula, so after typing the formula in the cell, you must enter it by pressing CTRL+SHIFT+ENTER. Excel indicates that the formula is an array formula by enclosing it in braces. Don't type the braces as part of the formula; they are added automatically by Excel.

One problem associated with using the ROW function in a formula is that the row numbers will be adjusted if you insert or delete rows. For example, if you insert a row above the row in which the expression ROW(1:100) is entered, the expression will become ROW(2:101). You can avoid this problem by using the INDIRECT worksheet function, described in the next section.

The INDIRECT Worksheet Function

The INDIRECT worksheet function creates a reference specified by a text string. Thus, for example, the formula

    =INDIRECT("A1")

entered in a cell (other than cell A1, of course) creates a reference to cell A1 and returns the value contained in cell A1. Since the reference is text, it will not change to A2 if a row is inserted above. The INDIRECT function can be used to create powerful and versatile worksheet formulas. Some examples will serve to illustrate.

The formula

=INDIRECT(B1)

(notice the absence of quotation marks) returns the value in cell A27 if cell B1 contains the text value A27.

Since the argument of INDIRECT is a text string, the use of the concatenation operator (the "&" character) is common. For example, the formula

=INDIRECT("A" & B1)

returns the value in cell A27 if cell B1 contains the value 27.

Using the INDIRECT Worksheet Function with the ROW Worksheet Function to Create Series Formulas

The INDIRECT function can be used with the ROW function to create formulas to evaluate number series. The series formula for e that was shown previously becomes the formula

{=1+SUM(1/FACT(ROW(INDIRECT("1:20"))))}

if you wish to evaluate the first 20 terms, or

{=1+SUM(1/FACT(ROW(INDIRECT("1:"&B1))))}

where the value in cell B1 specifies the number of terms to be evaluated. For some, but not all, series you can evaluate 65536 (2^{16}) terms conveniently in this way.

Again, you must enter the array formula by pressing CTRL+SHIFT+ENTER.

The Taylor Series

A series known as the Taylor series is frequently used in the evaluation of functions by numerical methods. The Taylor series for the evaluation of a function F at the point $x + h$, given the value of the function and its derivatives at the point x, is

$$F(x + h) = F(x) + \sum_{k=1}^{\infty} \frac{F^k(x)h^k}{k!} + \xi \qquad (4\text{-}3)$$

where $F^k(x)$ is the kth derivative of the function at the point x, and ξ is the remainder or error term. As has been illustrated by examples we have seen earlier, the magnitude of ξ decreases as k (the number of terms) increases.

To obtain a result that closely approximates the true value of a function, we need to sum a number of terms. Clearly, we will not have available to us (without a lot of work) values of a large number of derivatives of the function F, up to the kth derivative. Fortunately, we will usually need only the first derivative, the first and second derivatives, or the first, second and third derivatives to obtain results of sufficient accuracy. We will use the Taylor series expansion of a function in several of the subsequent chapters.

The order of the approximation is determined by the highest-derivative term that is included in the approximation; thus the first-order Taylor series approximation is

$$F(x + h) \approx F(x) + hF'(x) \qquad (4\text{-}4)$$

the second-order approximation is

$$F(x + h) \approx F(x) + hF'(x) + \frac{h^2}{2}F''(x) \qquad (4\text{-}5)$$

and the third-order approximation is

$$F(x + h) \approx F(x) + hF'(x) + \frac{h^2}{2}F''(x) + \frac{h^3}{6}F'''(x) \qquad (4\text{-}6)$$

Obviously, the accuracy of the approximation increases as the number of terms is increased. It is also obvious that the accuracy of the approximation will increase as h is made smaller. Higher-order terms will become more important as h is increased, or if the function is nonlinear.

The Taylor Series: An Example

The following example will illustrate the use of the Taylor series to evaluate a function. Consider the polynomial $ax^3 + bx^2 + cx + d$, with $a = 1.25$, $b = 9$, $c = -5$ and $d = 11$. At $x = 1$, $F(x) = 16.25$. We wish to evaluate the function at $x = 1.6$. (Since we are dealing with a known function, we could just evaluate it at $x = 1.6$, but here we use a known function for purposes of illustration. In subsequent chapters Taylor series will be used to evaluate functions whose value is known at a certain point but whose form is unknown.)

From simple calculus, $F'(x) = 3ax^2 + 2bx + c = 3.75x^2 + 18x - 5$, $F''(x) = 6ax + 2b = 7.5x + 18$ and $F'''(x) = 6a = 7.5$. At $x = 1$, $F'(x) = 16.75$, $F''(x) = 25.5$ and $F'''(x) = 7.5$. Substituting these values, along with $h = 0.6$, into equations 4-4, 4-5 and 4-6 yields the results shown in Figure 4-2. As expected, the third-order approximation provides the highest accuracy.

	A	B	C	D	E
10	x	F(x) exact	F(x) calc		error
11	1	16.25			
12	1.6	31.16			
13	1.6		26.3	(1 term)	16%
14	1.6		30.89	(2 terms)	0.87%
15	1.6		31.16	(3 terms)	0.00%

Figure 4-2. Evaluation of Taylor series.

Problems

Answers to the following problems are found in the folder "Ch. 04 (Number Series)" in the "Problems & Solutions" folder on the CD.

1. Evaluate the following infinite series:

    (a) $1/2^n$ (b) $1/n^2$ (c) $1/n!$

2. Evaluate the following:

    $$S = 1/1! - 1/2! + 1/3! - 1/4! \ldots$$

3. Evaluate the following infinite series:

    $$\Sigma ax^n, \text{ where } a > 1, x < 1$$

4. Evaluate the following:
    $$S = 1/2^n + 1/3^n$$

5. Evaluate the following:
    $$S = 1/2^n - 1/3^n$$

6. Evaluate Wallis' series for π:

    $$\pi = 2 \prod \left[\frac{(2n)^2}{(2n-1)(2n+1)} \right]$$

    over the first 100 terms of the series.

7. Evaluate Wallis' series for π, summing over 65,536 terms. Use a worksheet formula that uses ROW and INDIRECT to create the series of integers.

8. A simple yet surprisingly efficient method to calculate the square root of a number is variously called Heron's method, Newton's method, or the divide-and-average method. To find the square root of the number a:

    1. Begin with an initial estimate x.
    2. Divide the number by the estimate (i.e., evaluate a/x), to get a new estimate
    3. Average the original estimate and the new estimate (i.e., $(x + a/x)/2$) to get a new estimate

   4. Return to step 2.

Use this method to calculate the square root of a number. The value of the initial estimate x must be greater than zero.

9. In the divide-and-average method, the better the initial estimate, the faster the convergence. Devise an Excel formula to provide an effective initial estimate.

10. The series

$$\pi = \sum_{k=1}^{\infty} \frac{16(-1^{k+1})}{(2k-1)5^{2k-1}} - \sum_{k=1}^{\infty} \frac{4(-1^{k+1})}{(2k-1)239^{2k-1}}$$

proposed by Machin in 1706, converges quickly. Determine the value of π to 15 digits by using this series

Chapter 5

Interpolation

Given a table of x, y data points, it is often necessary to determine the value of y at a value of x that lies between the tabulated values. This process of interpolation involves the approximation of an unknown function. It will be up to the user to choose a suitable function to approximate the unknown one. The degree to which the approximation will be "correct" depends on the function that is chosen for the interpolation. A large number of methods have been developed for interpolation; this chapter illustrates some of the most useful ones, either in the form of spreadsheet formulas or as custom functions. Although some interpolation formulas require uniformly spaced x values, all of the methods described in this chapter are applicable to non-uniformly spaced values.

Obtaining Values from a Table

Since interpolation usually involves the use of values obtained from a table, we begin by examining methods for looking up values in a table.

Using Excel's Lookup Functions to Obtain Values from a Table

Excel provides three worksheet functions for obtaining values from a table: VLOOKUP for vertical lookup in a table, HLOOKUP for horizontal lookup and LOOKUP. The first two functions are similar and have virtually identical syntax. The LOOKUP function is less versatile than the others but can sometimes be used in situations where the others fail.

The function VLOOKUP(*lookup_value, table_array, column_index_num, range_lookup*) looks for a match between *lookup_value* and values in the leftmost column of *table_array* and returns the value in a specified column in the row in which the match was found. The argument *column_index_num* specifies the column from which the value is to be obtained. The column number is relative; for example, a *column_index_num* of 7 returns a value from the seventh column of *table_array*.

The optional argument *range_lookup* (I would have called this argument *match_type_logical*) allows you to specify the type of match to be found. If *range_lookup* is TRUE or omitted, VLOOKUP finds the largest value that is less than or equal to *lookup_value*; the values in the first column of *table_array* must be in ascending order. If *range_lookup* is FALSE, VLOOKUP returns an exact match or, if one is not found, the #N/A! error value; in this case, the values in *table_array* can be in any order. You can use 0 and 1 to represent FALSE and TRUE, respectively.

Using VLOOKUP to Obtain Values from a Table

The spreadsheet in Figure 5-1 (see folder 'Chapter 05 Interpolation', workbook 'Interpolation I', sheet 'Freezing Point') lists the freezing point, boiling point and refractive index of aqueous solutions of ethylene glycol; the complete table, on the CD-ROM, contains data for concentrations up to 95% and extends to row 54.

	A	B	C	D
1	**Freezing and Boiling Points of Heat Transfer Fluid**			
2	Wt% Ethylene Glycol	Freezing Point, °F	Boiling Point, °F (at 1 atm)	Refractive Index (at 22°C)
3	0.0	32.0	212	1.3328
4	5.0	29.4	213	1.3378
5	10.0	26.2	214	1.3428
6	15.0	22.2	215	1.3478
7	20.0	17.9	216	1.3530
8	21.0	16.8	216	1.3540
9	22.0	15.9	216	1.3551
10	23.0	14.9	217	1.3561
11	24.0	13.7	217	1.3572
12	25.0	12.7	218	1.3582
13	26.0	11.4	218	1.3593
14	27.0	10.4	218	1.3603
15	28.0	9.2	219	1.3614
16	29.0	8.0	219	1.3624
17	30.0	6.7	220	1.3635
18	31.0	5.4	220	1.3646
19	32.0	4.2	220	1.3656
20	33.0	2.9	220	1.3667
21	34.0	1.4	220	1.3678
22	35.0	-0.2	221	1.3688

Figure 5-1. Portion of a data table.
(folder 'Chapter 05 Interpolation', workbook 'Interpolation I', sheet 'Freezing Point')

Using VLOOKUP to find the freezing point of a 33% solution is illustrated in Figure 5-2. The formula

=VLOOKUP(F3,$A$3:$D$54,2,0)

was entered in cell G3 and the lookup value, 33, in cell F3.

	F	G
	Wt% Ethylene	Freezing
2	Glycol	Point, °F
3	33.0	2.9

Figure 5-2. Using VLOOKUP to obtain a value from a table.
(folder 'Chapter 05 Interpolation', workbook 'Interpolation I', sheet 'Freezing Point')

The third argument, *column_index_num*, is 2 since we want to return freezing point values from relative column 2 of the database. If we wanted to return the refractive index of the solution we would use *column_index_num* = 4.

The fourth argument, *range_lookup*, is set to FALSE because in this case we want to find an exact match. The formula returns the value 2.9.

HLOOKUP(*lookup_value, table_array, row_index_num*, range_lookup) is similar to VLOOKUP, except that it "looks up" in the first row of the array and returns a value from a specified row in the same column.

Using the LOOKUP Function to Obtain Values from a Table

When you use VLOOKUP, you must always "look up" in the first column of the table, and retrieve associated information from columns to the right in the same row; you cannot use VLOOKUP to look up to the left. If it is necessary to look to the left in a table (maybe it's not convenient or possible to rearrange the data table so as to put the columns in the proper order to use VLOOKUP), you can sometimes accomplish this by using the LOOKUP function.

LOOKUP(*lookup_value,lookup_vector,result_vector*) has two syntax forms: vector and array. The vector form of LOOKUP looks in a one-row or one-column range (known as a vector) for a value and returns a value from the same position in another one-row or one-column range. The values in *lookup_vector* must be sorted in ascending order. If LOOKUP can't find *lookup_value*, it returns the largest value in *lookup_vector* that is less than or equal to *lookup_value*.

Creating a Custom Lookup Formula
to Obtain Values from a Table

A second way to "lookup" to the left in a table is to construct your own lookup formula using Excel's MATCH and INDEX worksheet functions. The MATCH and INDEX functions are almost mirror images of one another: MATCH looks up a value in an array and returns its numerical position, INDEX looks in an array and returns a value from a specified numerical position.

The following example illustrates how to use INDEX and MATCH to lookup to the left in a table. In the table of production figures for phosphoric acid shown in Figure 5-3 (see folder 'Chapter 05 Interpolation', workbook 'Interpolation I', sheet 'VLOOKUP to left'), it is desired to find the month with the largest production.

	A	B
4	Month	Production
5	Jan	76212
6	Feb	15379
7	Mar	62220
8	Apr	83119
9	May	33872
10	Jun	80881
11	Jul	54263
12	Aug	35427
13	Sep	50361
14	Oct	71600
15	Nov	133
16	Dec	22477

Figure 5-3. A table requiring "lookup" to the left.
(folder 'Chapter 05 Interpolation', workbook 'Interpolation I', sheet 'VLOOKUP to left')

Use Excel's MAX worksheet function to find the maximum value in the range of production figures. The expression

=MAX($B$5:$B$16)

returns the value 83119. Now we want to return the month value in the column to the left in the same row. We do this in two steps, as follows. First, use the MATCH function to find the position of the maximum value in the range.

The syntax of MATCH is similar to that of VLOOKUP: MATCH(*lookup_value,lookup_array*,match_type_num). If match_type_num = 0, MATCH returns the position of the first value that is equal to lookup_value. The expression

=MATCH(83119,$B$5:$B$16,0)

returns 4, the maximum value is the fourth value in the range. Second, use the INDEX function to return the value in the same position in the array of months:

=INDEX($A$5:$A$16,4)

The specific values 83119 and 4 can now be replaced by the formulas that produced them, to yield the following "megaformula."

=INDEX($A$5:$A$16,MATCH(MAX($B$5:$B$16),$B$5:$B$16,0))

This example could not be handled using LOOKUP, since LOOKUP requires that the lookup values (in this case in column B) be in ascending order.

Using Excel's Lookup Functions to Obtain Values from a Two-Way Table

A two-way table is a table with two ranges of independent variables, usually in the leftmost column (x values) and in the top row (y values) of the table; a two-dimensional array of z values forms the body of the table. Figure 5-4 shows an example of such a two-way table (see folder 'Chapter 05 Interpolation', workbook 'Interpolation I', sheet 'Viscosity'), containing the viscosity of solutions of ethylene glycol of various concentrations at temperatures from 0 to 250°F. The table can also be found on the CD; the data extends down to row 32.

The desired z value from a two way table is found at the intersection of the row and column where the x and y lookup values, respectively, are located. Unlike in the preceding example showing the application of VLOOKUP, where *column_index_num* was the value 2 (a value was always returned from column 2 of the array), we must calculate the value of *column_index_num* based on the y lookup value. There are several ways this can be done. A convenient formula is the following, where names have been used for references. Temp and Percent are the lookup values, P_Row is the range $B$3:$K$3 that contains the y independent variable and Table is the table $A$4:$K$32, containing the x independent variable in column 1. The following formula was entered in cell M2 of Figure 5-5.

=VLOOKUP(Temp,Table,MATCH(Percent,P_Row,1)+1,1)

The corresponding expression using references instead of names is

=VLOOKUP(M2, $A$4:$I$32,MATCH(N2, $B$3:$K$3,1)+1,1)

	A	B	C	D	E	F	G	H	I	J	K
1					Viscosity of Heat Transfer Fluid (cps)						
2					Volume Percent Ethylene Glycol						
3	Temp, °F	0%	10%	20%	30%	40%	50%	60%	70%	80%	90%
4	-30							89.67	128.79	185.22	
5	-20						40.38	60.46	89.93	131.32	284.48
6	-10						27.27	42.05	63.50	91.88	169.83
7	0					13.76	19.34	30.08	45.58	65.04	107.77
8	10				6.83	10.13	14.26	22.06	33.31	46.89	71.87
9	20			3.90	5.38	7.74	10.85	16.56	24.79	34.48	49.94
10	30		2.16	3.14	4.33	6.09	8.48	12.68	18.77	25.84	35.91
11	40	1.53	1.82	2.59	3.54	4.91	6.77	9.90	14.45	19.71	26.59
12	50	1.30	1.56	2.18	2.95	4.04	5.50	7.85	11.31	15.29	20.18
13	60	1.12	1.35	1.86	2.49	3.38	4.55	6.33	8.97	12.05	15.65
14	70	0.98	1.18	1.61	2.13	2.87	3.81	5.17	7.22	9.62	12.37
15	80	0.86	1.04	1.41	1.84	2.46	3.23	4.28	5.88	7.79	9.93
16	90	0.76	0.93	1.24	1.60	2.13	2.76	3.58	4.85	6.38	8.10
17	100	0.68	0.83	1.11	1.41	1.87	2.39	3.03	4.04	5.28	6.68
18	110	0.61	0.75	0.99	1.25	1.64	2.08	2.58	3.40	4.41	5.58
19	120	0.55	0.68	0.90	1.11	1.46	1.82	2.23	2.88	3.73	4.71
20	130	0.51	0.62	0.81	1.00	1.30	1.61	1.93	2.47	3.17	4.01
21	140	0.46	0.57	0.74	0.90	1.17	1.43	1.69	2.13	2.72	3.45
22	150	0.43	0.53	0.68	0.82	1.05	1.28	1.49	1.86	2.35	2.98
23	160	0.39	0.49	0.63	0.75	0.95	1.15	1.32	1.63	2.05	2.60
24	170	0.37	0.46	0.58	0.68	0.87	1.04	1.18	1.43	1.80	2.28
25	180	0.34	0.43	0.54	0.63	0.79	0.94	1.06	1.27	1.58	2.01
26	190	0.32	0.40	0.50	0.58	0.73	0.85	0.95	1.14	1.40	1.79

Figure 5-4. Portion of a two-way data table.
(folder 'Chapter 05 Interpolation', workbook 'Interpolation I', sheet 'Viscosity')

	M	N	O
4	Temp	Percent	Viscosity
5	120	60%	2.23

Figure 5-5. Using VLOOKUP and MATCH to obtain a value from a two-way table.
(folder 'Chapter 05 Interpolation', workbook 'Interpolation I', sheet 'Viscosity')

Interpolation

Often it's necessary to interpolate between values in a table. You can use simple linear interpolation, which uses a straight line relationship between two adjacent values. Linear interpolation can be adequate if the table values are close together, as in Figure 5-6. Most often, though, an interpolation formula that fits a curve through several data points is necessary; cubic interpolation, in which four data points are used for interpolation, is common. The following sections describe methods for performing linear interpolation or cubic interpolation.

Linear Interpolation in a Table
by Means of Worksheet Formulas

To find the value of y at a point x that is intermediate between the table values x_0, y_0 and x_1, y_1, use the equation for simple linear interpolation (equation 5-1).

$$y_x = y_0 + \frac{(x - x_0)}{(x_1 - x_0)}(y_1 - y_0)$$
(5-1)

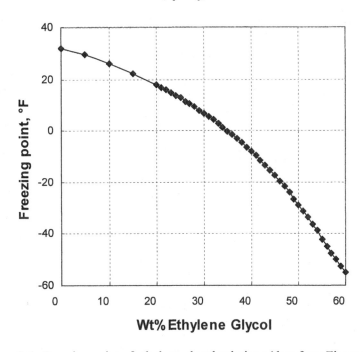

Figure 5-6. Freezing point of ethylene glycol solutions (data from Figure 5-1).
(folder 'Chapter 05 Interpolation', workbook 'Interpolation I', sheet 'Linear Interpolation')

In the following example, we'll assume that values of the independent variable x in the table are in ascending order, as in Figure 5-1, where the independent variable is wt% ethylene glycol. We want to find the freezing point for certain wt% values. Figure 5-2 shows the data (see folder 'Chapter 05 Interpolation', workbook 'Interpolation I', sheet 'Linear Interpolation'); it's clear that, since most of the points are close together, we can use linear interpolation without introducing too much error.

You can create a linear interpolation formula using Excel's MATCH and INDEX functions. If *match_type_num* = 1, MATCH returns the position of the largest array value that is less than or equal to *lookup_value*. The array must be in ascending order. Use this value in the INDEX function to return the values of x_0, y_0, x_1 and y_1, as shown in the following:

position	=MATCH(lookup_value,known_x´s,1)
x_0	=INDEX(known_x´s,position)
x_1	=INDEX(known_x´s,position+1)
y_0	=INDEX(known_y´s,position)
y_1	=INDEX(known_y´s,position+1)

The preceding formulas were applied to the data shown in Figure 5-1 to find the freezing point of a 33.3 wt% solution of ethylene glycol. The following named ranges were used in the calculations: known_x's ($A$3:$A$47), known_y's ($B$3:$B$47), lookup_value ($F$6), position ($G$6). The intermediate calculations and the final interpolated value are shown in Figure 5-7.

	F	G	H	I
3	*Stepwise calculations*			
4	*to develop formula*			
5	LookupValue	Value		Formula used in column G
6	33.3	18	(position)	=MATCH(LookupValue,XValues,1)
7		33	(x_0)	=INDEX(XValues,G6)
8		34	(x_1)	=INDEX(XValues,G6+1)
9		2.9	(y_0)	=INDEX(YValues,G6)
10		1.4	(y_1)	=INDEX(YValues,G6+1)
11	*result*	2.45		=G9+(F6-G7)*(G10-G9)/(G8-G7)

Figure 5-7. Linear interpolation: intermediate calculations.
(folder 'Chapter 05 Interpolation', workbook 'Interpolation I', sheet 'Linear Interpolation')

The formulas in cells G6:G11 can be combined into a single "megaformula" for linear interpolation, shown below and used in cell G15.

=INDEX(YValues,MATCH(LookupValue,XValues,1))+(F15-INDEX(XValues, MATCH(LookupValue,XValues,1)))*(INDEX(YValues,MATCH(LookupValue, XValues,1)+1)-INDEX(YValues,MATCH(LookupValue,XValues,1)))/ (INDEX(XValues,MATCH (LookupValue,XValues,1)+1)-INDEX(XValues, MATCH(LookupValue,XValues,1)))

	F	G
13	Megaformula version	
14	LookupValue	Value
15	33.3	2.45

Figure 5-8. Linear interpolation: final interpolated value.
(folder 'Chapter 05 Interpolation', workbook 'Interpolation I', sheet 'Linear Interpolation')

If you use the megaformula, the formulas in cells G6:G11 are no longer required.

Linear Interpolation in a Table by Using the TREND Worksheet Function

Excel provides the TREND worksheet function to perform linear interpolation in a table of data by means of a linear least-squares fit to all the data points in the table. But TREND can be used to perform linear interpolation between two adjacent data points.

The syntax of the TREND function is

TREND(***known_y's***, *known_x's*, *new_x's*, *const*)

where *known_y's* and *known_x's* are one-row or one-column ranges of known values. The argument *new_x's* is a range of cells containing *x* values for which you want the interpolated value. Use the argument *const* to specify whether the linear relationship $y = mx + b$ has an intercept value; if *const* is set to FALSE or zero, *b* is set equal to zero.

The TREND worksheet function provides a way to perform linear interpolation between two points without the necessity of creating a worksheet formula. Using the TREND function to perform the linear interpolation calculation that was illustrated in Figure 5-7 is shown in Figure 5-9. Cell G18 contains the formula

=TREND(B20:B21,A20:A21,F18,1)

	E	F	G	H
16	Other methods for linear interpolation:			
17	Using TREND worksheet function			
18		wt%	FP, °F	
19		33.3	2.45	

Figure 5-9. Using the TREND worksheet function for linear interpolation.
(folder 'Chapter 05 Interpolation', workbook 'Interpolation I', sheet 'Linear Interpolation')

Note that although TREND can be used to find the least-squares straight line through a whole set of data points, to perform linear interpolation you must select only two bracketing points, in this example in rows 20 and 21. It should be clear from Figure 5-6 that the least-squares straight line through all the data points will not provide the correct interpolated value.

You can also use TREND for polynomial (e.g., cubic) interpolation by regressing against the same variable raised to different powers (see "Cubic Interpolation in a Table by Using the TREND Worksheet Function" later in this chapter.)

Linear Interpolation in a Table by Means of a Custom Function

The linear interpolation formula can also be easily coded as a custom function, as shown in Figure 5-10.

```
Function InterpL(lookup_value, known_x´s, known_y´s)

Dim pointer As Integer
Dim X0 As Double, Y0 As Double, X1 As Double, Y1 As Double

pointer = Application.Match(lookup_value, known_x´s, 1)
X0 = known_x´s(pointer)
Y0 = known_y´s(pointer)
X1 = known_x´s(pointer + 1)
Y1 = known_y´s(pointer + 1)
InterpL = Y0 + (lookup_value - X0) * (Y1 - Y0) / (X1 - X0)
End Function
```

Figure 5-10. **Function** procedure for linear interpolation.
(folder 'Chapter 05 Interpolation', workbook 'Interpolation I', module 'LinearInterpolation')

The syntax of the function is

InterpL(*lookup_value,known_x´s,known_y´s*).

The argument *lookup_value* is the value of the independent variable for which you want the interpolated *y* value; *known_x's* and *known_y's* are the arrays of independent and dependent variables, respectively, that comprise the table. The table must be sorted in ascending order of *known_x's*. Figure 5-11 illustrates the use of the custom function to interpolate values in the table shown in Figure 5-1; cell G24 contains the formula

=InterpL(F22,$A$3:$A$54,$B$3:$B$54)

	E	F	G	H
21	Other methods for linear interpolation:			
22	Using a custom function for interpolation			
23		wt%	FP, °F	
24		33.3	2.45	

Figure 5-11. Using the InterpL function for linear interpolation.
(folder 'Chapter 05 Interpolation', workbook 'Interpolation I', sheet 'Linear Interpolation')

The custom function can be applied to tables in either vertical or horizontal format.

Cubic Interpolation

Often, values in a table change in such a way that linear interpolation is not suitable. Cubic interpolation uses the values of four adjacent table entries (e.g., at x_0, x_1, x_2 and x_3) to obtain the coefficients of the cubic equation $y = a + bx + cx^2 + dx^3$ to use as an interpolating function between x_1 and x_2. For example, to find the freezing point for a 33.3 wt% solution of ethylene glycol using cubic interpolation requires the four table values in Figure 5-12 whose *x* values are highlighted.

A convenient way to perform cubic interpolation is by means of the Lagrange fourth-order polynomial

$$y_x = \frac{(x-x_2)(x-x_3)(x-x_4)}{(x_1-x_2)(x_1-x_3)(x_1-x_4)}y_1 + \frac{(x-x_1)(x-x_3)(x-x_4)}{(x_2-x_1)(x_2-x_3)(x_2-x_4)}y_2$$
$$+ \frac{(x-x_1)(x-x_2)(x-x_4)}{(x_3-x_1)(x_3-x_2)(x_3-x_4)}y_3 + \frac{(x-x_1)(x-x_2)(x-x_3)}{(x_4-x_1)(x_4-x_2)(x_4-x_3)}y_4 \quad (5-2)$$

	A	B	C	D
1	**Freezing and Boiling Points of Heat Transfer Fluid**			
2	Wt% Ethylene Glycol	Freezing Point, °F	Boiling Point, °F (at 1 atm)	Refractive Index (at 22°C)
16	29.0	8.0	219	1.3624
17	30.0	6.7	220	1.3635
18	31.0	5.4	220	1.3646
19	32.0	4.2	220	1.3656
20	33.0	2.9	220	1.3667
21	34.0	1.4	220	1.3678
22	35.0	-0.2	221	1.3688
23	36.0	-1.5	221	1.3699
24	37.0	-3.0	221	1.3709
25	38.0	-4.5	221	1.3720
26	39.0	-6.4	221	1.3730

Figure 5-12. Four bracketing x values required
to perform cubic interpolation at $x = 33.3\%$.
(folder 'Chapter 05 Interpolation', workbook 'Interpolation I', sheet Cubic Interpolation')

The Lagrange fourth-order polynomial is cumbersome to use in a worksheet function, but convenient to use in the form of a custom function. A compact and elegant implementation of cubic interpolation in the form of an Excel 4.0 Macro Language custom function was provided by Orvis[*]. A slightly modified version, in VBA, is provided here (Figure 5-13). The syntax of the custom function is InterpC(*lookup_value, known_x's, known_y's*). The argument *lookup_value* is the value of the independent variable for which you want the interpolated y value; *known_x's* and *known_y's* are the arrays of independent and dependent variables, respectively, that comprise the table. The table must be sorted in ascending order of *known_x's*.

---

[*] William J. Orvis, *Excel 4 for Scientists and Engineers*, Sybex Inc., Alameda, CA, 1993.

```
Function InterpC(lookup_value, known_x's, known_y's)
'  Performs cubic interpolation, using an array of known_x's, known_y's.
'  The known_x's must be in ascending order.
'  Based on XLM code from Excel for Chemists", page 239,
'  which was based on W. J. Orvis' code.

Dim row As Integer
Dim i As Integer, j As Integer
Dim Q As Double, Y As Double

row = Application.Match(lookup_value, known_x's, 1)
  If row < 2 Then row = 2
  If row > known_x's.Count - 2 Then row = known_x's.Count - 2

For i = row - 1 To row + 2
  Q = 1
For j = row - 1 To row + 2
  If i <> j Then Q = Q * (lookup_value - known_x's(j)) / (known_x's(i) - _
known_x's(j))
Next j
  Y = Y + Q * known_y's(i)
Next i
InterpC = Y
End Function
```

Figure 5-13. Cubic interpolation function procedure.
(folder 'Chapter 05 Interpolation', workbook 'Interpolation I', module 'CubicInterpolation')

Figure 5-14 illustrates the use of the custom function to interpolate values in the table shown in Figure 5-12; cell H22 contains the formula

=InterpC(G22,$A$3:$A$47,$B$3:$B$47)

	F	G	H	I
20	Using a custom function for cubic interpolation			
21		wt%	FP, °F	
22		33.3	2.47	

Figure 5-14. Using the InterpC function procedure for cubic interpolation.
(folder 'Chapter 05 Interpolation', workbook 'Interpolation I', sheet 'Linear Interpolation')

Cubic Interpolation in a Table by Using the TREND Worksheet Function

In the TREND function, the array *known_x's* can include one or more sets of independent variables. For example, suppose column A contains x values. You can enter x^2 values in column B and x^3 in column C and then regress columns A through C against the y values in column D to obtain a cubic interpolation function. But instead of actually entering values of the square and the cube of the *x* values, you can use an array constant in an array formula, thus

    {=TREND(C19:C22,A19:A22^{1,2,3},F9^{1,2,3},1)}

This example of using the TREND function is found in folder 'Chapter 05 Interpolation', workbook 'Interpolation I', sheet Cubic Interpolation').

Linear Interpolation in a Two-Way Table by Means of Worksheet Formulas

To perform linear interpolation in a two-way table (a table with two ranges of independent variables, *x* and *y* and a two-dimensional array of *z* values forming the body of the table), we can use the same linear interpolation formula that was employed earlier. Consider the example shown in Figure 5-15; we want to find the viscosity value in the table for *x* = 76°F, *y* = 56.3 wt% ethylene glycol. The shaded cells are the values that bracket the desired *x* and *y* values.

	A	B	C	D	E	F	G	H	I
1				Viscosity of Heat Transfer Fluid (cps)					
2				Volume Percent Ethylene Glycol					
3	Temp, °F	20%	30%	40%	50%	60%	70%	80%	90%
4	0			13.76	19.34	30.08	45.58	65.04	107.77
5	10		6.83	10.13	14.26	22.06	33.31	46.89	71.87
6	20	3.90	5.38	7.74	10.85	16.56	24.79	34.48	49.94
7	30	3.14	4.33	6.09	8.48	12.68	18.77	25.84	35.91
8	40	2.59	3.54	4.91	6.77	9.90	14.45	19.71	26.59
9	50	2.18	2.95	4.04	5.50	7.85	11.31	15.29	20.18
10	60	1.86	2.49	3.38	4.55	6.33	8.97	12.05	15.65
11	70	1.61	2.13	2.87	3.81	5.17	7.22	9.62	12.37
12	80	1.41	1.84	2.46	3.23	4.28	5.88	7.79	9.93
13	90	1.24	1.60	2.13	2.76	3.58	4.85	6.38	8.10
14	100	1.11	1.41	1.87	2.39	3.03	4.04	5.28	6.68

Figure 5-15. Linear interpolation in a two-way table.
The shaded cells are the ones used in the interpolation.
(folder 'Chapter 05 Interpolation', workbook 'Interpolation II', module ' Linear Interpolation 2-Way')

We must perform three linear interpolations. First, as shown in Figure 5-16, for the two bracketing values of *x* we calculate the value of *z* at *y* = 56.3. The formula used in cell B32 is

    =InterpL(0.563,$E$3:$F$3,E11:F11)

	A	B	C	D	E	F
31	Temp, °F	z(interp)				
32	70	4.67	(value of z at x=70°F, y = 56.3%)			
33	80	3.89	(value of z at x=80°F, y = 56.3%)			

Figure 5-16. First steps in linear interpolation in a two-way table.
(folder 'Chapter 05 Interpolation', workbook 'Interpolation II', module ' Linear Interpolation 2-Way')

Then, in this one-way table (A32:B33), we use these two interpolated values of z to interpolate at $x = 76°F$, as illustrated in Figure 5-17. The formula in cell B36 is

=InterpL(A36,A32:A33,B32:B33)

	A	B
35	Temp, °F	z(interp)
36	76	4.20

Figure 5-17. Final step in linear interpolation in a two-way table.
(folder 'Chapter 05 Interpolation', workbook 'Interpolation II', module ' Linear Interpolation 2-Way')

The resulting interpolated value suffers from the usual errors expected from linear interpolation (and in this example may be in error by as much as 3%). A more accurate value can be obtained by performing cubic interpolation, using four bracketing values to obtain the coefficients of the interpolating cubic. There are at least two ways to obtain these coefficients: by using LINEST (the multiple linear regression worksheet function, described in detail in Chapter 13), or by using the cubic interpolation function. The latter will be described here, in the following sections.

Cubic Interpolation in a Two-Way Table by Means of Worksheet Formulas

To perform cubic interpolation between data points in a two-way table, we use a procedure similar to the one for linear interpolation. Figure 5-18 shows the table of viscosities that was used earlier. In this example we want to obtain the viscosity of a 63% solution at 55°F. The shaded cells are the values that bracket the desired x and y values.

	A	B	C	D	E	F	G	H	I
1	**Viscosity of Heat Transfer Fluid (cps)**								
2		Volume Percent Ethylene Glycol							
3	Temp, °F	20%	30%	40%	50%	60%	70%	80%	90%
4	0			13.76	19.34	30.08	45.58	65.04	107.77
5	10		6.83	10.13	14.26	22.06	33.31	46.89	71.87
6	20	3.90	5.38	7.74	10.85	16.56	24.79	34.48	49.94
7	30	3.14	4.33	6.09	8.48	12.68	18.77	25.84	35.91
8	40	2.59	3.54	4.91	6.77	9.90	14.45	19.71	26.59
9	50	2.18	2.95	4.04	5.50	7.85	11.31	15.29	20.18
10	60	1.86	2.49	3.38	4.55	6.33	8.97	12.05	15.65
11	70	1.61	2.13	2.87	3.81	5.17	7.22	9.62	12.37
12	80	1.41	1.84	2.46	3.23	4.28	5.88	7.79	9.93
13	90	1.24	1.60	2.13	2.76	3.58	4.85	6.38	8.10
14	100	1.11	1.41	1.87	2.39	3.03	4.04	5.28	6.68
15	110	0.99	1.25	1.64	2.08	2.58	3.40	4.41	5.58

Figure 5-18. Cubic interpolation in a two-way table.
The shaded cells are the ones used in the interpolation.
(folder 'Chapter 05 Interpolation', workbook 'Interpolation II', module ' Cubic Interpolation 2-Way')

We'll use the InterpC function to perform the interpolation. Figure 5-19 shows the z values, interpolated at $y = 63\%$ using the four bracketing y values, for the four bracketing x values. The formula in cell M8 is

=InterpC(63%,$E$3:$H$3,E8:H8)

	L	M
7	x	z at y=63%
8	40	11.15
9	50	8.80
10	60	7.05
11	70	5.73

Figure 5-19. First steps in cubic interpolation in a two-way table.
(folder 'Chapter 05 Interpolation', workbook 'Interpolation II', module ' Cubic Interpolation 2-Way')

Then, in this one-way table, we use the formula

=InterpC(L15,$L$8:$L$11,$M$8:$M$11)

in cell M15 to obtain the final interpolated result, as shown in Figure 5-20.

	L	M
14	x	z(interp)
15	55	7.86

Figure 5-20. Final step in cubic interpolation in a two-way table.
(folder 'Chapter 05 Interpolation', workbook 'Interpolation II', module ' Cubic Interpolation 2-Way')

Cubic Interpolation in a Two-Way Table by Means of a Custom Function

The cubic interpolation macro was adapted to perform cubic interpolation in a two-way table. The calculation steps were similar to those described in the preceding section. The cubic interpolation function shown in Figure 5-13 was converted into a subroutine CI; the main program is similar to the Lagrange fourth-order interpolation program of Figure 5-12.

The VBA code is shown in Figure 5-21. The syntax of the function is

InterpC2(*x_lookup,y_lookup,known_x´s,known_y´s,known_z´s*)

The arguments *x_lookup* and *y_lookup* are the lookup values. The arguments *known_x´s* and *known_y´s* are the one-dimensional ranges of the *x* and *y* independent variables (in Figure 5-20, the column of temperature values and the row of volume percent values). The argument *known_z´s* is the table of dependent variables (the two-dimensional body of the table).

```
Option Explicit
Option Base 1
'++++++++++++++++++++++++++++++++++++++++++++++++++++++++++++++++++++
Function InterpC2(x_lookup, y_lookup, known_x´s, known_y´s, _ known_z´s)

' known_x´s are in a column, known_y´s are in a row, or vice versa.
' In this version, known_x´s and known_y´s must be in ascending order.
' In first call to Sub, XX is array of four known_y´s
'    and YY is array of corresponding Z values, pointer is y_lookup.
' This call is made 4 times in a loop,
'    obtaining 4 interpolated Z values, ZZ
' In second call to Sub, XX is array of four known_x´s
' and YY is the array of interpolated Z values, pointer is x_lookup.

Dim M As Integer, N As Integer
Dim R As Integer, C As Integer
Dim XX(4) As Double, YY(4) As Double, ZZ(4) As Double, ZInterp(4) As _
Double

R = Application.Match(x_lookup, known_x´s, 1)
C = Application.Match(y_lookup, known_y´s, 1)
If R < 2 Then R = 2
If R > known_x´s.Count - 2 Then R = known_x´s.Count - 2
```

```
If C < 2 Then C = 2
If C > known_y´s.Count - 2 Then C = known_y´s.Count - 2

For N = 1 To 4
' Create array of four known_y´s, four known_z´s, four known_x´s
' Check values to see whether ascending or descending,
'and transfer input data to arrays in ascending order always.
XX(N) = known_x´s(R + N - 2)
If known_y´s(C + 2) > known_y´s(C - 1) Then
   For M = 1 To 4
      YY(M) = known_y´s(C + M - 2)
      If known_z´s(R + N - 2, C + M - 2) = "" Then InterpC2 = _
 CVErr(xlErrNA): Exit Function
      ZZ(M) = known_z´s(R + N - 2, C + M - 2)
   Next M
Else
   For M = 1 To 4
      YY(M) = known_y´s(C - M + 3)
      If known_z´s(R + N - 2, C - M + 3) = "" Then InterpC2 = _
 CVErr(xlErrNA): Exit Function
      ZZ(M) = known_z´s(R + N - 2, C - M + 3)
   Next M
End If
ZInterp(N) = CI(y_lookup, YY, ZZ)
'This is array of interpolated Z values at y_lookup
Next N

InterpC2 = CI(x_lookup, XX, ZInterp)
End Function
'+++++++++++++++++++++++++++++++++++++++++++++++++++++++++++++++++++
Private Function CI(lookup_value, known_x´s, known_y´s)
'   Performs cubic interpolation, using an array of known_x´s, known_y´s (four
values of each)
'   This is a modified version of the function InterpC.

Dim i As Integer, j As Integer
Dim Q As Double, Y As Double

For i = 1 To 4
   Q = 1
For j = 1 To 4
   If i <> j Then Q = Q * (lookup_value - known_x´s(j)) / (known_x´s(i) - _
      known_x´s(j))
Next j
   Y = Y + Q * known_y´s(i)
Next i
CI = Y
End Function
```

Figure 5-21. Cubic interpolation function procedure for use with a two-way table.
(folder 'Chapter 05 Interpolation', workbook 'Interpolation II', module 'Cubic2Way')

The function InterpC2 was used to obtain the viscosity of a 74.5% weight percent solution of ethylene glycol at 195°F, as illustrated in Figure 5-22. The formula in cell M7 was

=InterpC2(K7,L7,$A$4:$A$29,$B$3:$I$3,$B$4:$I$29)

This custom function provides a convenient way to perform interpolation in a two-way table.

	K	L	M
5	Using CubicInterp2Way function		
6	Temp	Percent	Viscosity
7	195	74.5%	1.18

Figure 5-22. Result returned by the cubic interpolation function.
(folder 'Chapter 05 Interpolation', workbook 'Interpolation II', sheet 'Cubic Interp 2-Way by Custom Fn')

Problems

Data for, and answers, to the following problems are found in the folder "Ch. 05 (Interpolation)" in the "Problems & Solutions" folder on the CD.

1. Using the table "Freezing and Boiling Points of Heat Transfer Fluid" shown in Figure 5-1 (also found on the CD-ROM), obtain the freezing point of 30.5% and 34.5% solutions of ethylene glycol.

3. Using the table "Freezing and Boiling Points of Heat Transfer Fluid," find the wt% ethylene glycol that has a freezing point of 0°F.

3. Using the following table (also found on the CD-ROM)

Table 5-27. Data Table for Two-Way Interpolation

	y = 0.0	0.4	0.8	1.2	1.6	2.0
x = 0.0	1.00000	0.92106	0.69671	0.36236	-0.02920	-0.41615
0.5	2.43916	2.30901	1.93911	1.38787	0.74230	0.10433
1.0	5.00564	4.79106	4.18120	3.27235	2.20798	1.15615
1.5	8.95215	8.59837	7.59289	6.09444	4.33960	2.60542
2.0	14.10791	13.52462	11.86685	9.39633	6.50309	3.64392
2.5	19.47338	18.51170	15.77851	11.70530	6.93516	2.22118

obtain an interpolated value for z at the following values of x and y by cubic interpolation: $x = 1\ 1/3$, $y = 1\ 2/3$; $x = 1.55$, $y = 1.425$.

4. Using the table "Viscosity of Heat Transfer Fluid" shown in Figure 5.4 (also found on the CD-ROM), obtain the viscosity of a 30.5% solution of ethylene glycol at 95°C, and the viscosity of a 74.5% solution of ethylene glycol at 195°C.

5. Using the following table (also found on the CD-ROM), obtain a value for the refractive index of benzene at the following pressure and wavelength values: 1 atm, 5000 Å; 1 atm, 6600 Å; 500 atm, 5000 Å; 900 atm, 5000 Å; 1 atm, 4600 Å.

Table 5-28. Refractive Index of Benzene at Various Wavelengths as a Function of Pressure

		Wavelength						
		4678 Å	4800 Å	4922 Å	5016 Å	5086 Å	5876 Å	6438 Å
Pressure, atm	1	1.50690	1.50477	1.50284	1.50151	1.50050	1.49221	1.48822
	246	1.51946	1.51724	1.51532	1.51391	1.51286	1.50438	1.50025
	485	1.52986	1.52762	1.52557	1.52421	1.52316	1.51445	1.51029
	757	1.53992	1.53761	1.53555	1.53415	1.53305	1.52418	1.51991
	1108	1.55102	1.54867	1.54657	1.53614	1.54401	1.53489	1.53052

6.　Using the following table (also found on the CD-ROM)

Table 5-29. Data Table for Interpolation

x	y
0.0	1.0000
0.5	2.2373
1.0	3.7560
1.5	4.7875
2.0	3.6439
2.5	-2.4690
3.0	-17.0501
3.5	-42.6275
4.0	-77.0077
4.5	-106.9697
5.0	-100.2178
5.5	0.7658

obtain an interpolated value for y at the following values of x by cubic interpolation: 1.81, 3.11, 5.2, 5.4.

Chapter 6
Differentiation

The analysis of scientific or engineering data often requires the calculation of the first (or higher) derivative of a function or of a curve defined by a table of data points. These derivative values may be needed to solve problems involving the slope of a curve, the velocity or acceleration of an object, or for other calculations.

Students in calculus courses learn mathematical expressions for the derivatives of many types of functions. But there are many other functions for which it is difficult to obtain an expression for the derivative, or indeed the function may not be differentiable. Fortunately, the derivative can always be obtained by numerical methods, which can be implemented easily on a spreadsheet. This chapter provides methods for calculation of derivatives of worksheet formulas or of tabular data.

First and Second Derivatives of Data in a Table

The simplest method to obtain the first derivative of a function represented by a table of x, y data points is to calculate Δx and Δy, the differences between adjacent data points, and use $\Delta y / \Delta x$ as an approximation to dy/dx. The first derivative or slope of the curve at a given data point x_i, y_i can be calculated using either of the following forward, backward, or central difference formulas, respectively (equations 6-1, 6-2, and 6-3).

$$\frac{dy}{dx} \approx \frac{\Delta y}{\Delta x} = \frac{y_{i+1} - y_i}{x_{i+1} - x_i} \qquad \text{(forward difference)} \qquad (6\text{-}1)$$

$$\frac{dy}{dx} \approx \frac{y_i - y_{i-1}}{x_i - x_{i-1}} \qquad \text{(backward difference)} \qquad (6\text{-}2)$$

$$\frac{dy}{dx} \approx \frac{y_{i+1} - y_{i-1}}{x_{i+1} - x_{i-1}} \qquad \text{(central difference)} \qquad (6\text{-}3)$$

The second derivative, d^2y/dx^2, of a data set can be calculated in a similar manner, namely by calculating $\Delta(\Delta y/\Delta x)/\Delta x$.

Calculation of the first or second derivative of a data set tends to emphasize the "noise" in the data set; that is, small errors in the measurements become relatively much more important. The central difference formula tends to reduce noise resulting from experimental error.

Points on a curve of x, y values for which the first derivative is a maximum, a minimum, or zero are often of particular importance and are termed *critical points*, that is, points where the curvature (the second derivative) changes sign are termed *inflection points*. For example, in the analysis of data from an acid-base titration, the inflection point is used to determine the equivalence point.

Calculating First and Second Derivatives

A pH titration (measured volumes of a base solution are added to a solution of an acid and the pH measured after each addition) is shown in Figure 6-1, and a portion of the spreadsheet containing the titration data in Figure 6-2. The end-point of the titration corresponds to the point on the curve with maximum slope, and this point can be estimated visually in Figure 6-1. The first and second derivatives of the data are commonly used to determine the inflection point of the curve mathematically.

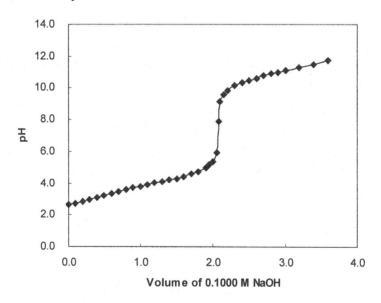

Figure 6-1. Chart of titration data.
(folder 'Chapter 06 Examples', workbook 'Derivs of Titration Data', worksheet 'Derivs')

	A	B	C	D	E	F
2	V/mL	pH	ΔV	ΔpH	V(avge)	ΔpH/ΔV
22	1.90	4.981	0.100	0.229	1.850	2.29
23	1.95	5.157	0.050	0.176	1.925	3.52
24	2.00	5.389	0.050	0.232	1.975	4.64
25	2.05	5.928	0.050	0.539	2.025	10.78
26	2.08	7.900	0.030	1.972	2.065	65.73
27	2.10	9.115	0.020	1.215	2.090	60.75
28	2.15	9.604	0.050	0.489	2.125	9.78
29	2.20	9.856	0.050	0.252	2.175	5.04
30	2.30	10.125	0.100	0.269	2.250	2.69

Figure 6-2. First derivative of titration data, near the endpoint.
(folder 'Chapter 06 Examples', workbook 'Derivs of Titration Data', worksheet 'Derivs')

Columns A through F of the spreadsheet shown in Figure 6-2 are used to calculate the first derivative, $\Delta pH/\Delta V$. Since the derivative has been calculated over the finite volume $\Delta V = V_{i+1} - V_i$, the most suitable volume to use when plotting the $\Delta pH/\Delta V$ values, as shown in column E of Figure 6-2, is

$$V_{average} = \frac{V_{i+1} + V_i}{2} \qquad (6\text{-}4)$$

The maximum in $\Delta pH/\Delta V$ indicates the location of the inflection point of the titration (Figure 6-3).

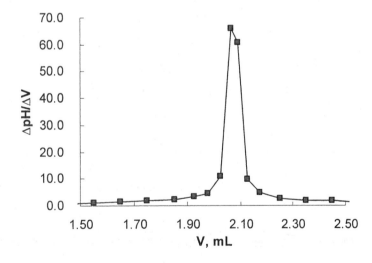

Figure 6-3. First derivative of titration data, near the endpoint.
(folder 'Chapter 06 Examples', workbook 'Derivs of Titration Data', worksheet 'Derivs')

The maximum in the first derivative curve must still be estimated visually. The second derivative, $\Delta(\Delta pH/\Delta V)/\Delta V$, calculated by means of columns E through J of the spreadsheet (shown in Figure 6-4) can be used to locate the inflection point more precisely. The second derivative, shown in Figure 6-5, passes through zero at the inflection point. Linear interpolation can be used to calculate the point at which the second derivative is zero.

	E	F	G	H	I	J
2	V(avge)	ΔpH/ΔV	ΔV	Δ(ΔpH)	V(avge)	Δ(ΔpH)/ΔV
22	1.850	2.29	0.100	0.57	1.800	5.7
23	1.925	3.52	0.075	1.23	1.888	16.4
24	1.975	4.64	0.050	1.12	1.950	22.4
25	2.025	10.78	0.050	6.14	2.000	122.8
26	2.065	65.73	0.040	54.95	2.045	1373.8
27	2.090	60.75	0.025	-4.98	2.078	-199.3
28	2.125	9.78	0.035	-50.97	2.108	-1456.3
29	2.175	5.04	0.050	-4.74	2.150	-94.8
30	2.250	2.69	0.075	-2.35	2.213	-31.3

Figure 6-4. Second derivative of titration data, near the endpoint.
(folder 'Chapter 06 Examples', workbook 'Derivs of Titration Data', worksheet 'Derivs')

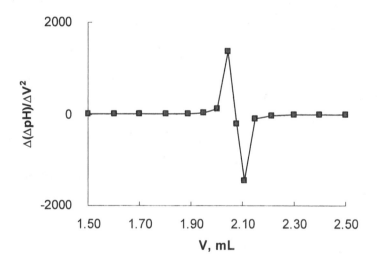

Figure 6-5. Second derivative of titration data, near the endpoint.
(folder 'Chapter 06 Examples', workbook 'Derivs of Titration Data', worksheet 'Derivs')

There are other equations for numerical differentiation that use three or more points instead of two points to calculate the derivative. Since these equations usually require equal intervals between points, they are of less generality. Again, their main advantage is that they minimize the effect of "noise." Table 6-1 lists equations for the first, second and third derivatives, for data from a table at equally spaced interval h.

These difference formulas can be derived from Taylor series. Recall from Chapter 4 that the first-order approximation is

$$F(x + h) \approx F(x) + hF'(x) \tag{6-5}$$

or, in the notation used in Table 6-1

$$y_{i+1} = y_i + hy'_i \tag{6-6}$$

which, upon rearranging, becomes

$$y'_i = \frac{y_{i+1} - y_i}{h} \tag{6-7}$$

admittedly, an obvious result.

The second derivative can be written as

$$y''_i = \frac{y'_{i+1} - y'_i}{h} \tag{6-8}$$

When each of the y' terms is expanded according to the preceding expression for y', the expression for the second derivative becomes

$$y''_i = \frac{(y_{i+2} - y_{i+1})/h - (y_{i+1} - y_i)/h}{h} \tag{6-9}$$

or

$$y''_i = \frac{y_{i+2} - 2y_{i+1} + y_i}{h^2} \tag{6-10}$$

The same result can be obtained from the second-order Taylor series expansion

$$F(x + h) \approx F(x) + hF'(x) + \frac{h^2}{2!}F''(x) \tag{6-11}$$

which is written in Table 6-1 as

$$y_{i+1} = y_i + hy'_i + \frac{h^2}{2!}y''_i \tag{6-12}$$

by substituting the backward-difference formula for F from Table 6-1. Expressions for higher derivatives or for derivatives using more terms can be obtained in a similar fashion.

Table 6-1. Some Formulas for Computing Derivatives
(For tables with equally spaced entries)

First derivative, using two points:

Forward difference $$y'_i = \frac{y_{i+1} - y_i}{h}$$

Central difference $$y'_i = \frac{y_{i+1} - y_{i-1}}{2h}$$

Backward difference $$y'_i = \frac{y_i - y_{i-1}}{h}$$

First derivative, using three points:

Forward difference $$y'_i = \frac{-y_{i+2} + 4y_{i+1} - 3y_i}{2h}$$

First derivative, using four points:

Central difference $$y'_i = \frac{-y_{i+2} + 8y_{i+1} - 8y_{i-1} + y_{i-2}}{12h}$$

Second derivative, using three points:

Forward difference $$y''_i = \frac{y_{i+2} - 2y_{i+1} + y_i}{h^2}$$

Central difference $$y''_i = \frac{y_{i+1} - 2y_i + y_{i-1}}{h^2}$$

Backward difference $$y''_i = \frac{y_i - 2y_{i-1} + y_{i-2}}{h^2}$$

Second derivative, using four points:

Forward difference $$y''_i = \frac{2y_i - 5y_{i+1} + 4y_{i+2} - y_{i+3}}{h^2}$$

Second derivative, using five points:

Central difference $$y''_i = \frac{-y_{i+2} + 16y_{i+1} - 30y_i + 16y_{i-1} - y_{i-2}}{12h^2}$$

Third derivative, using four points

Forward difference $$y'''_i = \frac{y_{i+3} - 3y_{i+2} + 3y_{i+1} - y_i}{h^3}$$

Using LINEST as a Fitting Function

Instead of calculating a derivative at an x value corresponding to a table entry, it may be necessary to obtain the derivative at an intermediate x value. This problem is related to the process of interpolation, and indeed some of the techniques from the preceding chapter can be applied here (see "Cubic Interpolation" in Chapter 5). For example, we can obtain a piecewise fitting function that applies to a localized region of the data set, and use the parameters of the fitting function to calculate the derivative. In this section and the following one, we will use a cubic equation

$$F(x) = ax^3 + bx^2 + cx + d \qquad (6\text{-}13)$$

as the fitting function, using four data points to obtain the four coefficients of the cubic. (The fitted curve will pass exactly through all four points and R^2 will be exactly 1.) Once we have obtained the coefficients, the derivatives are calculated from them; the first derivative is

$$F'(x) = 3ax^2 + 2bx + c \qquad (6\text{-}14)$$

and the second derivative is

$$F''(x) = 6ax + 2b \qquad (6\text{-}15)$$

We can use the LINEST worksheet function (the multiple linear regression worksheet function, described in detail in Chapter 13) to obtain the coefficients a, b, c and d, then use the coefficients a, b, and c in equation 6-14 or 6-15 to calculate the first or second derivatives.

The LINEST method will be illustrated using a table of absorbance data taken at 5-nm increments, part of which is shown in Figures 6-6 and 6-7; the complete range of x values is in \$A\$5:\$A\$85 and the y values in \$B\$5:\$B\$85. We wish to obtain the first derivative of this data set at 2-nm increments over the range 390–415 nm.

	A	B
3	Original Data	
4	Wavelength	Absorbance
23	390	0.552
24	395	0.582
25	400	0.598
26	405	0.600
27	410	0.586
28	415	0.559
29	420	0.521

Figure 6-6. Data used to calculate first and second derivatives.
(folder 'Chapter 06 Examples', workbook 'Derivs Using LINEST', sheet 'Using megaformula')

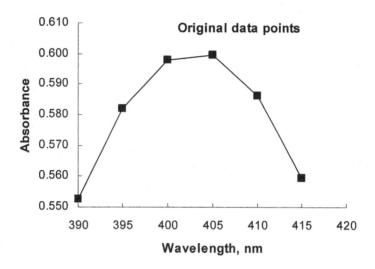

Figure 6-7. Chart of some data used to calculate first and second derivatives.
(folder 'Chapter 06 Examples', workbook 'Derivs Using LINEST', sheet 'Using megaformula')

The steps required in the calculation of the first or second derivative at a specified value of x are as follows:

(i)   Use the MATCH function to find the position of the lookup value x in the table of x values. The lookup value is in cell D5 in Figure 6-8.

=MATCH(D5, $A$5:$A$85,1)

(ii) Use the OFFSET function to select the four bracketing x values:

=OFFSET($A$5:$A$85,D5-2,0,4,1)

(iii) Use a similar formula to obtain the four bracketing y values:

=OFFSET($B$5:$B$85,D5-2,0,4,1)

(iv) Use these two arrays in the LINEST formula, raising the range of x values to an array of powers; the LINEST formula must be entered in a horizontal range of three cells, and you must press CONTROL+SHIFT+ENTER:

=LINEST(OFFSET(known_ys,MATCH(D6,known_xs,1)-2,0,4,1),
OFFSET(known_xs,MATCH(D6,known_xs,1)-2,0,4,1)^{1,2,3},1,0)

(v)   Use the INDEX function to obtain each of the regression coefficients a, b and c from the LINEST array. (To simplify the formula, the cells containing the preceding LINEST formula have been given the name LINEST_array.) The following equation returns the coefficient a:

=INDEX(LINEST_array,1)

(vi) Use the coefficients a, b, and c to calculate the first or second derivative:

If these formulas are combined into one "megaformula", the result (entered in cell E5 in Figure 6-8) is

```
=3*INDEX(LINEST(OFFSET(known_ys,MATCH(D5,x_values,1)-2,0,4,1),
OFFSET(x_values,MATCH(D5,x_values,1)-2,0,4,1)^{1,2,3},1,0),1)*x^2
+2*INDEX(LINEST(OFFSET(known_ys,MATCH(D5,x_values,1)-2,0,4,1),
OFFSET(x_values,MATCH(D5,x_values,1)-2,0,4,1)^{1,2,3},1,0),2)*x
+INDEX(LINEST(OFFSET(known_ys,MATCH(D5,x_values,1)-2,0,4,1),
OFFSET(x_values,MATCH(D5,x_values,1)-2,0,4,1)^{1,2,3},1,0),3)
```

which is rather confusing. A better approach is to use named formulas. The following table lists the named formulas and ranges used to calculate the first derivative shown in Figure 6-7.

x_values	=Sheet2!$A$5:$A$85
y_values	=Sheet2!$B$5:$B$85
lookup_value	=Sheet2!$D$5:$D$17
pointer	=MATCH(INDIRECT(ROW()&":"&ROW()) lookup_value ,x_values,1)
known_xs	=OFFSET(x_values,pointer-2,0,4,1)
known_ys	=OFFSET(y_values,pointer-2,0,4,1)
LIN_array	=LINEST(Sheet2!known_ys,Sheet2!known_xs^{1,2,3},1,0)
aa	=INDEX(LINEST_array,1)
bb	=INDEX(LINEST_array,2)
cc	=INDEX(LINEST_array,3)

Using these named formulas, the formula for the first derivative becomes

```
=3*aa*x^2+2*bb*x+cc
```

Note the formula used for pointer. It incorporates an "implicit intersection" expression. Since both lookup_value and x_values are arrays, the formula

```
=MATCH(lookup_value ,x_values,1)
```

returns an array of values instead of a single value. The formula using the expression INDIRECT(ROW()&":"&ROW()) lookup_value returns a single value, the value in the array lookup_value that is in the same row as the formula.

	D	E	F	G
4	x	y	F'(x)	F"(x) x 10
5	390	0.552	0.00710	-4.53E-03
6	392		0.00616	-4.87E-03
7	394		0.00516	-5.20E-03
8	396		0.00405	-5.46E-03
9	398		0.00294	-5.65E-03
10	400	0.598	0.00176	-5.84E-03
11	402		0.00059	-5.85E-03
12	404		-0.00058	-5.87E-03
13	406		-0.00179	-5.80E-03
14	408		-0.00293	-5.65E-03
15	410	0.586	-0.00408	-5.49E-03
16	412		-0.00515	-5.18E-03
17	414		-0.00615	-4.88E-03

Figure 6-8. First derivative calculated using LINEST function.
The *y* values indicate the known experimental points.
(folder 'Chapter 06 Examples', workbook 'Derivs Using LINEST', sheet 'Using named formulas')

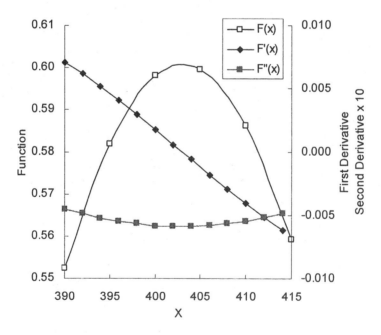

Figure 6-9. Chart of values of first and second derivative
calculated using LINEST.
(folder 'Chapter 06 Examples', workbook 'Derivs Using LINEST', sheet 'Using named formulas')

Part of the table of calculated first derivative values is shown in Figure 6-8, and the values are charted in Figure 6-9. The formula used in cell F5, for example, is

=3*aa*x^2+2*bb*x+cc

One could use the x value where $F'(x) = 0$ to locate the maximum in the spectrum.

Depending on the data table being differentiated, the errors in the values returned by this method may be as great as several percent.

Derivatives of a Worksheet Formula

Instead of calculating the first or second derivative of a curve represented by data points, we may wish to find the derivative of a function (a worksheet formula). In the following, two different methods are illustrated to calculate the first or second derivative of a worksheet formula by using a user-defined function. The calculation of the first derivative of the function $y = 3x^3 + 5x^2 - 5x + 11$ is used as the example for each method

Derivatives of a Worksheet Formula
Calculated by Using a VBA Function Procedure

The first example is a **Function** procedure that returns the first derivative of a specific worksheet formula. The expression for the derivative is "hard-coded" in the VBA procedure. The user must be able to provide the expression for the derivative and must modify the VBA code to apply it to a different formula. The function's only argument is the value of x, the independent variable for which the derivative is to be calculated. The main advantage of this approach is that the returned value of the derivative is exact. This approach will execute the fastest and would be suitable if the same formula is to be used many times in a worksheet.

```
Function Deriv1(x)
'User codes the expression for the derivative here.
Deriv1 = 9 * x ^ 2 + 10 * x - 5
End Function
```

Figure 6-10. Function procedure to demonstrate calculation of a first derivative. (folder 'Chapter 06 Examples', workbook 'Derivs by VBA (Part 1)', module 'Module1')

First Derivative of a Worksheet Formula Calculated by Using the Finite-Difference Method

The second example is a **Function** procedure that uses the finite-difference method. The first derivative of a formula in a worksheet cell can be obtained with a high degree of accuracy by evaluating the formula at x and at $x + \Delta x$. Since Excel carries 15 significant figures, Δx can be made very small. Under these conditions $\Delta y/\Delta x$ approximates dy/dx very well.

The user must "hard-code" the worksheet formula in VBA, in a suitable form; the derivative is calculated by numerical differentiation. Again, the function's only argument is the value of x, the independent variable. This approach would be useful if the user is unable to provide an expression for the derivative.

```
Function Deriv2(x)
OldY = fn(x)
xx = (1.00000001) * x
NewY = fn(xx)
Deriv2 = (NewY - OldY) / (xx - x)
End Function

Function fn(x)
'User codes the expression for the function here.
fn = 3 * x ^ 3 + 5 * x ^ 2 - 5 * x + 11
End Function
```

Figure 6-11. Function procedure to demonstrate calculation of first derivative.
(folder 'Chapter 06 Examples', workbook 'Derivs by VBA (Part 1)', module 'Module1')

The Newton Quotient

In the previous section, the finite-difference method was shown to provide an excellent estimate of the first derivative of a function expressed as a worksheet formula. The multiplier used in the preceding user-defined function was 1.00000001. What is the optimum value of this multiplier, so that the Newton quotient $\Delta y/\Delta x$ gives the best approximation to dy/dx?

There are two sources of error in this finite-difference method of computing dy/dx: the *approximation error*, inherent in using a finite value of Δx, and the *roundoff error*, due to the limited precision of the numbers stored in the computer. We want to find the value of Δx that strikes the best balance between these two errors. If Δx is made too large, then the approximation error is large, since $dy/dx \rightarrow \Delta y/\Delta x$ only when $\Delta x \rightarrow 0$. If Δx is made too small, then the roundoff error is large, since we are obtaining Δy by subtracting two large and nearly equal numbers, $F(x)$ and $F(x + \Delta x)$.

Excel carries 15 digits in its calculations, and it turns out that multiplying x by a factor of 1.00000001 (a change in the 8th place) produces the minimum error, before round-off error begins to have an effect. Figure 6-12 illustrates this, using a quadratic equation as an example; other functions give similar results. The values in Figure 6-12 show that we can expect accuracy up to approximately the tenth digit.

	A	B	C	D	E	F	G	H
1				$y = 3x^2 - 11x + 30$				
2	x	y	Δx	$x+\Delta x$	$y+\Delta y$	$\Delta y/\Delta x$	exact	% error
3	7.5	116.25	1.0E-05	7.5001	116.253	34.0002	34	6.6E-04
4	7.5	116.25	1.0E-06	7.50001	116.2503	34.00002	34	6.6E-05
5	7.5	116.25	1.0E-07	7.500001	116.25003	34.000002	34	6.7E-06
6	7.5	116.25	1.0E-08	7.5000001	116.250003	34.0000003	34	8.4E-07
7	7.5	116.25	1.0E-09	7.50000001	116.2500003	34.000001	34	4.2E-06
8	7.5	116.25	1.0E-10	7.500000001	116.25000003	34.00002	34	4.9E-05
9	7.5	116.25	1.0E-11	7.5000000001	116.250000003	34.0001	34	4.2E-04

Figure 6-12. Newton quotient $\Delta y/\Delta x$ as a function of the magnitude of Δx (folder 'Chapter 06 Examples', workbook 'Derivs by VBA (Part 1)', sheet 'Newton Quotient')

Derivative of a Worksheet Formula Calculated by Using the Finite-Difference Method

The spreadsheet shown in Figure 6-13 (see folder 'Chapter 06 Examples', workbook 'Derivs by Sub Procedure') illustrates the calculation of the first derivative of a function $y = x^3 - 3x^2 - 130x + 150$ by evaluating the function at x and at $x + \Delta x$. Here a value of Δx of 1×10^{-8} was used. For comparison, the first derivative was calculated from the exact expression from differential calculus: $F'(x) = 3x^2 - 6x - 130$.

The Excel formulas in cells B11, C11, D11, E11, F11, G11 and H11 (columns C–F are hidden) are

B11 = t*x^3+u*x^2+v*x + w $F(x)$

C11 =A11*(1+delta) $x + \Delta x$

D11 = t*C11^3+u*C11^2+v*C11 + w $F(x + \Delta x)$

E11 =A11*delta Δx

F11 =D11-B11 Δy

G11 =F11/E11 $\Delta y/\Delta x$

H11 =3*t*A11^2+2*u*A11+v dy/dx from calculus

	A	B	G	H
1		**Numerical Differentiation**		
2		$F(x) = tx^3 + ux^2 + vx + w$		
3		t	1	
4		u	-3	delta
5		v	-130	1.00E-08
6		w	150	
7			Δy/Δx	
8	x	y	By worksheet formula	From calculus
9	-10	150	230.0000006	230
10	-9	348	167.000005	167
11	-8	486	110.000002	110
12	-7	570	59.000001	59
13	-6	606	14.000002	14
14	-5	600	-24.9999994	-25
15	-4	558	-57.999998	-58
16	-3	486	-84.9999992	-85
17	-2	390	-105.999999	-106
18	-1	276	-120.9999994	-121
19	0	150	#DIV/0!	-130

Figure 6-13. First derivative calculated on a worksheet by using Δx.
(folder 'Chapter 06 Examples', workbook 'Derivs by Sub Procedure', sheet 'Deriv')

The value in cell G21 illustrates that, using this technique, an *x* value of zero will have to be handled differently, since multiplying zero by 1.00000001 does not produce a change in *x*. This problem will be dealt with in a subsequent section.

First Derivative of a Worksheet Formula Calculated by Using a VBA Sub Procedure Using the Finite-Difference Method

The approach used in the preceding section can be performed by using a VBA **Sub** procedure. The VBA code is shown in Figure 6-14. By means of an input box the user identifies the range of cells containing the formulas for which the derivative is to be calculated, with a second input box, the corresponding cells containing the independent variable *x*, and with a third input box, the range of cells to receive the first derivative.

```
Option Explicit
Option Base 1
'+++++++++++++++++++++++++++++++++++++++++++++
Sub Derivs()
Dim z As Integer, N As Integer
Dim Old_Ys() As Double, New_Ys() As Double, Old_Xs() As Double,
Dim Derivs() As Double, increment As Double
Dim known_Xs As Object, known_Ys As Object, cel As Object

increment = 0.00000001

'Use the Set keyword to create an object variable
Set known_Ys = Application.InputBox _
("Select the range of Y values", "STEP 1 OF 3", , , , , , 8)
N = known_Ys.Count
ReDim Old_Ys(N), New_Ys(N), Old_Xs(N), Derivs(N)
z = 1
For Each cel In known_Ys
  Old_Ys(z) = cel.Value
  z = z + 1
Next cel

Set known_Xs = Application.InputBox _
("Select the range of X values", "STEP 2 OF 3", , , , , , 8)
z = 1
For Each cel In known_Xs
  Old_Xs(z) = cel.Value
  cel.Value = Old_Xs(z) * (1 + increment)
  z = z + 1
Next cel
z = 1
For Each cel In known_Ys
  New_Ys(z) = cel.Value
  z = z + 1
Next cel
z = 1
For Each cel In known_Xs
  cel.Value = Old_Xs(z)
  z = z + 1
Next cel

Application.InputBox("Select the destination for derivatives", _
"STEP 3 OF 3", , , , , , 8).Select
For z = 1 To N
  Derivs(z) = (New_Ys(z) - Old_Ys(z)) / (increment * Old_Xs(z))
  ActiveCell.Offset(z - 1, 0).Value = Derivs(z)
Next

End Sub
```

Figure 6-14. Sub procedure to calculate first derivative.
(folder 'Chapter 06 Examples', workbook 'Derivs by Sub Procedure', module 'Derivs')

	A	B	G	H	I
1			**Numerical Differentiation**		
2			F(x) = tx^3 + ux^2 + vx + w		
3		t	1		
4		u	-3	delta	
5		v	-130	1.00E-08	
6		w	150		
7				Δy/Δx	
8	x	y	By worksheet formula	From calculus	By macro
9	-10	150	230.0000006	230	230.000001
10	-9	348	167.000005	167	167.000005
11	-8	486	110.000002	110	110.000002
12	-7	570	59.000001	59	59.0000013
13	-6	606	14.000002	14	14.0000016
14	-5	600	-24.9999994	-25	-24.9999994
15	-4	558	-57.999998	-58	-57.999998
16	-3	486	-84.9999992	-85	-84.9999992
17	-2	390	-105.999999	-106	-105.999999
18	-1	276	-120.9999994	-121	-121
19	0	150	#DIV/0!	-130	
20	1	18	-132.999998	-133	-133

Figure 6-15. Calculating the first derivative of a formula.
(folder 'Chapter 06 Examples', workbook 'Derivs by Sub Procedure', sheet 'Deriv')

The **Sub** procedure saves the values of x and y from the worksheet (OldX and OldY), then writes the incremented value of x (NewX) to the worksheet cell. This causes the worksheet to recalculate and display the corresponding value of $y + \Delta y$ (NewY). The derivative is calculated and written to the destination cell. Finally, the original value of x is restored. Figure 6-15 illustrates the spreadsheet of Figure 6-13 after the **Sub** procedure has been run. The errors produced by this method are much smaller than those produced by the function based on LINEST.

The code in Figure 6-14 can easily be modified to calculate the partial derivatives of a function with respect to one or several parameters of the function (e.g., dy/da, dy/db, etc.) for a cubic equation. Similar code is used in the SolvStat macro (see Chapter 14, "The Solver Statistics Add-In") and a similar approach is used in the Solver itself (see "How the Solver Works" in Chapter 14).

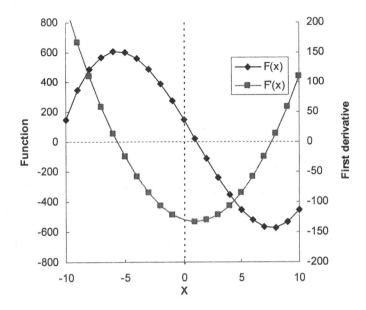

Figure 6-16. A chart of a function and its first derivative.
(folder 'Chapter 06 Examples', workbook 'Derivs by Sub Procedure', sheet 'Deriv')

The advantage of using a **Sub** procedure is that the derivative can be obtained easily, even for the most complicated worksheet formulas. All of the difficult calculations are done when the spreadsheet updates after the new value of x is entered in, for example, cell A9. The disadvantage of a **Sub** procedure is that if changes are made to precedent cells in the worksheet, the **Sub** procedure must be run in order to update the calculations.

First Derivative of a Worksheet Formula Calculated by Using a VBA Function Procedure Using the Finite-Difference Method

Unlike the **Sub** procedure described in the preceding section, a **Function** procedure automatically recalculates each time changes are made to precedent cells. A **Function** procedure to calculate the first derivative of a formula in a cell would be very useful. However, a function procedure can't use the approach of the preceding section (i.e., changing the value of the cell containing the x value), since a function procedure can't change the contents of other cells. A different approach will have to be found.

The following VBA code illustrates a simple **Function** procedure to calculate the first derivative dy/dx of a formula in cell, using the same approach that was used in the preceding section: the procedure calculates OldX, OldY,

NewX and NewY in order to calculate $\Delta x/\Delta y$. But in this function procedure, both the worksheet formula and the independent variable are passed to the function as arguments. The procedure is shown simply to illustrate the method; a number of modifications, to be described later, will be necessary in order to produce a "bulletproof" procedure.

The basic principle used in this **Function** procedure is the following:

(i)   The two arguments of the function are references to the independent variable x and the cell containing the formula to be differentiated, $F(x)$.

(ii) Use the **Value** property to obtain the values of the arguments; these are OldX and OldY.

(iii) Use the **Formula** property of the cell to get the worksheet formula to be differentiated as the text variable FormulaText.

(iv) Use the SUBSTITUTE worksheet function to replace references to the x variable in FormulaText by the incremented x value, NewX.

(v)   Use the **Evaluate** method to get the new value of the formula. This is NewY.

Since other procedures in this chapter and in subsequent chapters will use the same method for modifying and evaluating a formula, it will be worthwhile to examine the VBA code shown in Figure 6-17. The syntax of the function is FirstDerivDemo(**expression,variable**). The nine lines of code in this procedure perform the following actions:

(1)   Get FormulaString, the worksheet formula (as text) by using the **Formula** property of *expression*.

(2)   Get OldY, the value of the worksheet formula, by using the **Value** property of *expression*.

(3)   Get XRef, the reference to the independent variable x, by using the **Address** property of *variable*. The address will be an A1-style absolute reference

(4)   Get OldX, the value of the independent variable x, by using the **Value** property of *variable*.

(5)   Calculate NewX, the incremented value of the independent variable, by multiplying OldX by 1.000000001.

(6)   Convert all references in FormulaString to absolute by using the **ConvertFormula** method.

(7)   Replace all instances of XRef in FormulaString by the value of the new variable NewX. This is done by using the SUBSTITUTE worksheet function. For example, the formula string

```
=3*$B$3^3+5*$B$3^2-5*$B$3+11
```

when cell $B$3 contains the value 2, is converted to

```
=3*2.00000002^3+5*2.00000002^2-5*x+11.
```

(8)   Calculate NewY, the new value of the function, by applying the **Evaluate** method to the new formula string.

(9)   Calculate and return the first derivative.

```
Option Explicit
Function FirstDerivDemo(expression, variable) As Double
'Custom function to return the first derivative of a formula in a cell.

Dim OldX As Double, OldY As Double, NewX As Double, NewY As Double
Dim FormulaString As String, XAddress As String

FormulaString = expression.Formula
OldY = expression.Value
XAddress = variable.Address   'Default is absolute reference
OldX = variable.Value
NewX = OldX * 1.00000001
FormulaString = Application.ConvertFormula(FormulaString, xlA1, xlA1, _
xlAbsolute)            'Convert all references in formula to absolute
FormulaString = Application.Substitute(FormulaString, XAddress, NewX)
NewY = Evaluate(FormulaString)
FirstDerivDemo = (NewY - OldY) / (NewX - OldX)
End Function
```

Figure 6-17. Function procedure to demonstrate calculation of first derivative.
(folder 'Chapter 06 Examples', workbook 'Derivs by VBA (Part 2)', module 'Demo')

Examples of the first derivative of some worksheet formulas calculated by the custom function are shown in Figure 6-18. The formula in cell D3 is

= FirstDerivDemo (C3,B3)

The formulas labeled "exact" in column E are the appropriate formulas from differential calculus for the first derivative of the respective functions.   For example, the formula in cell E3 is

=9*B3^2+10*B3-5

	A	B	C	D	E	F
1	Demo to Illustrate Use of Simple First Derivative Function					
2	Function	x	F(x)	F'(x)	exact	% error
3	$y=3x^3+5x^2-5x+11$	2	45	51.0000003	51	-5.2E-07
4	$y = \sin x$	1	0.84147	0.5403023	0.5403023	-5.8E-08
5	$y=e^{-x}$	-1	0.36788	0.3678794	0.3678794	2.5E-07
6	$y = a^x$ (e.g., $a = 3.5$)	2.4	19.4734	24.3955256	24.3955252	-1.5E-06

Figure 6-18. Using a simple **Function** procedure to calculate some first derivatives.
(folder 'Chapter 06 Examples', workbook 'Derivs by VBA (Part 2)', sheet 'Demo Function')

Improving the VBA Function Procedure

The simple procedure shown in Figure 6-17 requires some modification.

First, the simple procedure replaces all instances of XRef, the reference to the independent variable x, in FormulaString with a number value. For example, a cell reference such as A2 will be replaced with a number value such as 0.05. But there are cases where the substring A2 should not be replaced. Our procedure needs to handle the following possibilities, all of which contain the substring A2 within FormulaString:

(i)   the reference XRef and references in FormulaString may be relative, absolute or mixed,

(ii) FormulaString contains a name such as BETA2,

(iii) FormulaString contains a reference such as AA2, or

(iv) FormulaString contains a reference such as A25.

By using the **Address** property to obtain an absolute reference (e.g., $A$2) and using the **ConvertFormula** method to convert all references in FormulaString to absolute, we have already eliminated problems arising from cases (i), (ii), and (iii). Only case (iv) poses a problem: the substring $A$2 in $A$25 will be substituted by 0.05, yielding 0.055. And so, as is often the case with computer programming, a project that initially appeared to be simple requires some additional programming.

We could write a formula parser that would break FormulaString into its component parts and inspect each one. Not impossible, but that would require extensive programming. A much simpler solution turns out to be the following: by means of a loop, we replace each instance of, for example, A2 individually, and, instead of replacing the reference with a number (e.g., 0.05), we replace the reference with the number concatenated with the space character (e.g., 0.05 0). We then evaluate the resulting string after each substitution. The reference $A$25 yields the string 0.05 5. When evaluated, this gives rise to an error, and an **On Error GoTo** statement is used so that the faulty substitution is not incorporated into the FormulaString to be evaluated. Inspection of the code in the latter half of the procedure in Figure 6-21 should make the process clear.

A second problem with the simple procedure of Figure 6-17 is that when x = 0, NewX = OldX, NewY = OldY and the procedure returns a #VALUE! error. The error produced by a zero value for the independent variable x is handled by adding an additional optional argument *scale_factor*. The syntax of the function is dydx(*expression, reference,* **Optional** *scale_factor*). If x is zero, a value for *scale_factor* must be entered by the user. *Scale_factor* is used to calculate the Δx for numerical differentiation. *Scale_factor* should be the same order of magnitude as typical x values used in the formula.

The **Function** procedure is shown in Figure 6-19.

```
Option Explicit
Function dydx(expression, variable, Optional scale_factor) As Double
'Custom function to return the first derivative of a formula in a cell.
'expression is F(x), variable is x.
'scale_factor is used to handle case where x = 0.
'Workbook can be set to either R1C1- or A1-style.

Dim OldX As Double, NewX As Double, OldY As Double, NewY As Double
Dim delta As Double
Dim NRepl As Integer, J As Integer
Dim FormulaString As String, XRef As String, dummy as String
Dim T As String, temp As String

delta = 0.00000001

'Get formula and value of cell formula (y).
FormulaString = expression.Formula     'Returns A1-style formula; default is
absolute.
OldY = expression.Value
'Get reference and value of argument (x).
OldX = variable.Value
XRef = variable.Address     'Default is A1-style absolute reference.

'Handle the case where x = 0.
'Use optional scale_factor to provide magnitude of x.
'If not provided, returns #DIV0!
If OldX <> 0 Then
  NewX = OldX * (1 + delta)
Else
  If IsMissing(scale_factor) Or scale_factor = 0 Then _
  dydx = CVErr(xlErrDiv0): Exit Function
  NewX = scale_factor * delta
End If

'Convert all references to absolute
'so that only text that is a reference will be replaced.
T = Application.ConvertFormula(FormulaString, xlA1, xlA1, xlAbsolute)

'Do substitution of all instances of x reference with value.
'Substitute reference, e.g., $A$2,
'with a number value, e.g., 0.2, followed by a space
'so that $A$25 becomes 0.2 5, which results in an error.
'Must replace from last to first.
NRepl = (Len(T) - Len(Application.Substitute(T, XRef, ""))) / Len(XRef)
For J = NRepl To 1 Step -1
    temp = Application.Substitute(T, XRef, NewX & " ", J)
    If IsError(Evaluate(temp)) Then GoTo pt1
    T = temp
pt1: Next J
NewY = Evaluate(T)
dydx = (NewY - OldY) / (NewX - OldX)
End Function
```

Figure 6-19. Improved **Function** procedure to calculate first derivative.
(folder 'Chapter 06 Examples', workbook 'Derivs by VBA (Part 2)', module 'FirstDeriv')

	A	B	C	D	E	F
1	Demo to Illustrate Use of Advanced First Derivative Function					
2	Reference in formula or in argument can be absolute, relative, mixed or a name.					
3	Function	x	F(x)	F'(x)	exact	% error
4	y=3x³+5x²-5x+11	2	45	51.00000027	51	-5.2E-07
5	y = sin x	1	0.84147	0.54030231	0.5403023	-5.8E-08
6	y=e⁻ˣ	-1	0.36788	0.36787944	0.3678794	2.5E-07
7	y = aˣ (e.g., a = 3.5)	2.4	19.4734	24.39552511	24.395525	3.8E-07
8	y=3x³+5x²-5x+11	0	11	#VALUE!	-5	#VALUE!
9	y=3x³+5x²-5x+11	0	11	-4.99999988	-5	2.4E-06

Figure 6-20. Using the improved function procedure to calculate some first derivatives. The optional argument *scale_factor* is used in row 9 to eliminate the #VALUE! error seen in row 8. (folder 'Chapter 06 Examples', workbook 'Derivs by VBA (Part 2)', sheet Better Function')

The examples in Table 6-20 illustrate the values of the first derivative calculated by using the function dydx, compared with the "exact" values.

The worksheet formulas in column C and the corresponding functions in column D are:

C4 =3*B4^3+5*B4^2-5*B4+11   D4 =dydx($C$4,$B$4)

C5 =SIN($B5)   D5 =dydx(C5,B5)

C6 =EXP($B$6)   D6 =dydx(C6,B6)

C7 =a^B7   D7 =dydx(C7,B7)

C8 =3*B8^3+5*B8^2-5*B8+11   D8 =dydx(C8,B8)

C9 =3*B9^3+5*B9^2-5*B9+11   D9 =dydx(C9,B9,1)

Rows 4–6 illustrate that relative, absolute or mixed references can be used in the worksheet formula or in the arguments of the custom function. Row 9 illustrates the use of the optional argument *scale_factor* when the x value is zero.

Second Derivative of a Worksheet Formula

The VBA code for the **Function** procedure shown in Figure 6-21 requires only slight modification to provide a function that returns the second derivative of a function as a cell formula. The syntax of the d2xdy2 function is identical to that of the function dydx.

The code is shown in Figure 6-21. The function calculates the central derivative uing three points (see the formula in Table 6-1). Note that the multiplier used to calculate Δx is 1E-4 instead of 1E-8.

```
Option Explicit
Function d2ydx2(expression, variable, Optional scale_factor) As Double
'Custom function to return the second derivative of a formula in a cell.
'expression is F(x), variable is x.
'Uses central difference formula.
'scale_factor is used to handle case where x = 0.
'Workbook can be set to either R1C1- or A1-style.

Dim OldX As Double, OldY As Double
Dim NewX1 As Double, NewX2 As Double
Dim NewY1 As Double, NewY2 As Double
Dim XRef As String
Dim delta As Double
Dim FormulaString As String, T As String
Dim temp As String
Dim NRepl As Integer, J As Integer

delta = 0.0001

'Get formula and value of cell formula (y).
FormulaString = expression.Formula     'Returns A1-style formula
OldY = expression.Value
'Get reference and value of argument (x).
OldX = variable.Value
XRef = variable.Address     'Default is A1-style absolute reference

'Handle the case where x = 0.
'Use optional scale_factor to provide magnitude of x.
'If not provided, returns #DIV0!
If OldX <> 0 Then
  NewX1 = OldX * (1 + delta)
  NewX2 = OldX * (1 - delta)
Else
  If IsMissing(scale_factor) Or scale_factor = 0 Then _
  d2ydx2 = CVErr(xlErrDiv0): Exit Function
  NewX1 = scale_factor * delta
  NewX2 = -scale_factor * delta
End If

'Convert all references to absolute
'so that only text that is a reference will be replaced.
FormulaString = Application.ConvertFormula(FormulaString, xlA1, xlA1, _
xlAbsolute)

T = FormulaString
NRepl = (Len(T) - Len(Application.Substitute(T, XRef, ""))) / Len(XRef)
'Do substitution of all instances of x reference with incremented x value
For J = NRepl To 1 Step -1
  temp = Application.Substitute(T, XRef, NewX1 & " ", J)
  If IsError(Evaluate(temp)) Then GoTo pt1
  T = temp
pt1: Next J
'Evaluate the expression.
NewY1 = Evaluate(T)
```

```
T = FormulaString
'Now do substitution of all instances of x reference with decremented x value
For J = NRepl To 1 Step -1
    temp = Application.Substitute(T, XRef, NewX2 & " ", J)
    If IsError(Evaluate(temp)) Then GoTo pt2
    T = temp
pt2: Next J
NewY2 = Evaluate(T)
d2ydx2 = (NewY1 + NewY2 - 2 * OldY) / Abs((NewX1 - OldX) * (NewX2 - OldX))
End Function
```

Figure 6-21. Function procedure to calculate second derivative.
(folder 'Chapter 06 Examples', workbook 'Derivs by VBA (Part 2)', module 'SecondDeriv')

Figure 6-22 illustrates the use of the dydx and d2ydx2 custom functions. The formula in cell B4 is

=aa*A4^3+bb*A4^2+cc*A4+dd

(aa, bb, cc, dd are named ranges. The formula in cell C4 is

=dydx(B4,A4,1)

	A	B	C	D	E	F	G	H
1			**First and Second Derivative Functions**					
2			$y = 2x^3 - 20x^2 + 11x + 30$					
3	x	F(x)	F'(x)	exact	% error	F''(x)	exact	% error
4	-5	-775	361.0000021	361	5.8E-07	-100.0000002	-100	-2.0E-07
5	-4	-462	267.0000003	267	1.0E-07	-88.0000002	-88	-2.0E-07
6	-3	-237	185.0000020	185	1.1E-06	-75.9999997	-76	-4.5E-07
7	-2	-88	114.9999996	115	3.9E-07	-64.0000003	-64	-5.0E-07
8	-1	-3	57.0000001	57	1.6E-07	-52.0000000	-52	-7.5E-08
9	0	30	10.9999998	11	1.4E-06	-40.0000001	-40	-2.8E-07
10	1	23	-22.9999999	-23	-3.9E-07	-28.0000002	-28	-6.6E-07
11	2	-12	-45.0000001	-45	-2.0E-07	-15.9999999	-16	-6.1E-07
12	3	-63	-55.0000004	-55	-7.0E-07	-4.0000003	-4	-8.3E-06
13	4	-118	-52.9999997	-53	-5.0E-07	7.9999998	8	2.8E-06
14	5	-165	-38.9999993	-39	-1.7E-06	19.9999999	20	2.5E-07

Figure 6-22. Using **Function** procedures to calculate
first and second derivatives of a function.
(folder 'Chapter 06 Examples', workbook 'Derivs by VBA (Part 2)', sheet 'First and Second Derivs')

Note the use of the optional argument *scale_factor* that prevents an error in cells C9 and F9 when the value of the independent variable in cell A9 is zero.

Concerning the Choice of Δx
for the Finite-Difference Method

In preceding sections, the $x + \Delta x$ used for the calculation of the derivatives was calculated by multiplying x by 1.00000001. Thus Δx is a "scaled" increment. An alternative approach would have been to use a constant Δx of, e.g., 0.00000001. Either approach has its advantages and disadvantages.

The constant-increment method eliminates the need to handle the case of $x = 0$ separately. However, the method fails when x is very large, e.g., 10^8. The scaled-increment method handles a wide range of x values, but fails in some special cases, such as for sin x when $x = 1000$.

You should be aware of these limitations when using the dydx and d2ydx2 custom functions.

Problems

Answers to the following problems are found in the folder "Ch. 06 (Differentiation)" in the "Problems & Solutions" folder on the CD.

1. Using the data file "Titration Curve", obtain the first and second derivative. The "endpoint" of a titration is considered to be the volume at the "inflexion point": that is, where the curve $y = F(x)$ has maximum slope, or where the first derivative reaches a maximum, or where the second derivative passes through zero; the last is the easiest to determine graphically or mathematically.

2. Using the data file "Student Potentiometric Data", obtain the first and second derivative.

3. Using Excel's SIN function, create a table of $\sin\theta$, in one degree increments of θ (remember that Excel's trigonometric functions require angles in radians). Now calculate $d\sin\theta$, using one of the formulas in Table 6-1. Compare your answer with the exact: $d\sin\theta = \cos\theta$. Experiment with different formulas from Table 6-1 to compare the errors.

4. Determine the first and second derivatives of the function $y = 2x^3 - 20x^2 + 11x + 30$ over the range $x = -5$ to $x = 10$.

5. Determine the first derivative of the function $y = x^2 - 1 \times 10^{-6} x + 1 \times 10^{-15}$ over the range $x = 0$ to $x = 2 \times 10^{-6}$.

6. Determine the first derivative of the following functions over suitable ranges of x:

(a) $$y = \frac{4}{1 + x^2}$$

(b) $$y = e^{-x^2}$$

(c) $$y = \sqrt{1 - \frac{\sin^2 x}{2}}$$

(d)
$$y = \frac{x}{(1+x)\sqrt{x}}$$

(e)
$$y = \frac{\exp[(x-\mu)^2 / 2\sigma^2]}{\sigma\sqrt{2\pi}}$$

7. Show that the slope of the logistic equation

$$y = \frac{1}{1 + e^{-ax}}$$

at its midpoint (the Hall slope) is equal to $a/4$.

8. The van der Waals equation is an equation of state that applies to real gases. For 1 mole of a gas, the van der Waals equation is

$$\left(P + \frac{a}{V^2}\right)(V - b) = RT$$

where R is the gas constant (0.0821 L atm K^{-1} mol^{-1}) and T is the Kelvin temperature. The constants a and b are constants particular to a given gas, and correct for the attractive forces between gas molecules, and for the volume occupied by the gas molecules, respectively. For methane (CH_4), the constants are $a = 2.253$ L^2 atm and $b = 4.278 \times 10^{-2}$ L. Using the rearranged form of the van der Waals equation

$$P = \frac{RT}{V - b} - \frac{a}{V^2}$$

calculate the pressure of 1 mole of methane as a function of container volume at 0°C (273 K) at suitable volumes from 22.4 L to 0.05 L. Use one of the custom functions described in this chapter to calculate the first and second derivatives of the P-V relationship. Compare with the exact expressions

$$\frac{dP}{dV} = -\frac{RT}{(V - b)^2} + \frac{2a}{V^3}$$

$$\frac{d^2P}{dV^2} = \frac{2RT}{(V - b)^3} - \frac{6a}{V^4}$$

Chapter 7

Integration

The solution of scientific and engineering problems sometimes requires integration of an expression. *Symbolic integration* involves the use of the methods of calculus to yield a closed-form analytical expression: the *indefinite integral*, or mathematical function $F(x)$ whose derivative dy/dx is given. We will not attempt to find the indefinite integral — Excel is not equipped to do symbolic algebra — but instead find the area under the curve bounded by a function $F(x)$ and the x-axis. This area is the *definite integral*.

It may be difficult or even impossible to obtain an expression for the integral of a particular function. But by using numerical methods we can always obtain a value for the definite integral. The result of *numeric integration* is the area under the curve, between specified limits, from $x = a$ to $x = b$. The calculation will involve a curve described either by a table of experimental x, y values or by a function $y = F(x)$.

This chapter provides methods for calculating the area under a curve that is described by a table of x, y values on a worksheet or by a worksheet formula. Some methods require evenly spaced x values, while for others the x values can be irregularly spaced.

Area under a Curve

By "area under a curve" we mean the area bounded by a curve and the x-axis (the line $y = 0$), between specified limits. The area can be positive if the curve lies above the x-axis or negative if it is below.

Calculation of the area under a curve is sometimes referred to as *quadrature*, since it involves subdividing the area under the curve into a number of "panels" whose areas can be calculated. The sum of the areas of the panels will be an approximation to the area under the curve. The three most common approaches are the rectangle method, in which the panels are rectangles, the trapezoid method, in which the panels are trapezoids and Simpson's method, which approximates the curvature of the function. These methods require that we have a table of values of the function; the three methods are illustrated in Figure 7-1. Only Simpson's method requires panels of equal width.

The simplest approach is to approximate the area of the panel by a rectangle whose height is equal to the value of one of the two data points, illustrated in Figure 7-1. If we have a table of n data points, we will have $n-1$ panels.

As the x increment (the interval between the data points) decreases, this rather crude approach becomes a better approximation to the area. The area under the curve bounded by the limits $x_{initial}$ and x_{final} is the sum of the n individual rectangles, as given by equation 7-1.

$$\text{area A} = \sum_{i=1}^{n-1} y_i (x_{i+1} - x_i) \tag{7-1}$$

A better approximation is to use the average of the two y values as the height of the rectangle. This is equivalent to approximating the area by a trapezoid rather than a rectangle. The area under the curve is given by equation 7-2.

$$A = \sum_{i=1}^{n-1} \frac{y_i + y_{i+1}}{2} (x_{i+1} - x_i) \tag{7-2}$$

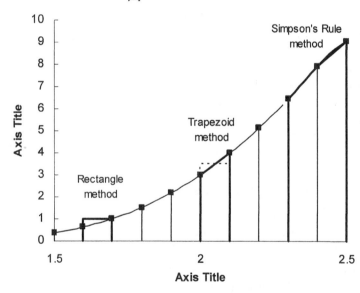

Figure 7-1. Graphical illustration of methods of calculating the area under a curve.

Simpson's 1/3 rule approximates the curvature of the function by means of a quadratic interpolating polynomial. The 1/3 rule, calculated by means of equation 7-3, requires two intervals of equal width h; thus each element of area is evaluated by using three data points.

$$A = \frac{h}{3} \sum_{i=1,3,5...}^{n-2} (y_i + 4y_{i+1} + y_{i+2}) \qquad (7\text{-}3)$$

The 1/3 rule requires an even number of panels; thus the number of data points n must be an odd number. If n is even, the area of the first or last panel can be calculated using the trapezoid formula. The end panel to be so calculated should be the one in which the function is more linear.

Simpson's 3/8 rule (equation 7-4) approximates the area by a cubic interpolating polynomial, evaluates the area of three panels of equal width, and requires four data points for each element of area.

$$A = \frac{3h}{8} \sum_{i=1}^{n} (y_i + 3y_{i+1} + 3y_{i+2} + y_{i+3}) \qquad (7\text{-}4)$$

The 3/8 rule is often used when evaluating the area under a curve described by an odd number of panels: the first or last three panels are evaluated using the 3/8 rule, and the remainder by the 1/3 rule.

Calculating the Area under a Curve Defined by a Table of Data Points

In the fields of toxicology and pharmacology, the area under the curve of a plot of plasma concentration of a drug *versus* elapsed time after administration of the drug has a number of important uses. The area can used to calculate the total body clearance and the apparent volume of distribution.

In a study, a drug was administered intravenously to a patient. Blood samples were taken at intervals of time, plasma was separated from each blood sample, and the plasma samples were analyzed for drug concentration. The data are shown in Figure 7-2. The dashed line indicate extrapolation of the data.

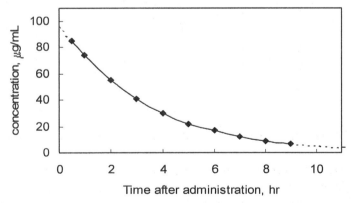

Figure 7-2. Plot of drug concentration versus time.
(folder 'Chapter 07 Examples', workbook 'Area under Curve', worksheet 'Curve1 by worksheet')

	A	B	C
1	Time, hr	Conc, µg/mL	area
2	0	95	
3	0.5	85	45
4	1	74	39.75
5	2	55	64.5
6	3	41	48
7	4	30	35.5
8	5	22	26
9	6	17	19.5
10	7	12	14.5
11	8	9.1	10.55
12	9	6.7	7.9
13	11	4.0	10.7
14	20	0	18
15		Sum =	340

Figure 7-3. Calculating the area under a curve.
(folder 'Chapter 07 Examples', workbook 'Area under Curve', worksheet 'Curve1 by worksheet')

The formula in cell C3, used to calculate the area increment by the trapezoidal approximation, is

=(B2+B3)/2*(A3-A2)

The area increments were summed to obtain the area under the curve.

Calculating the Area under a Curve Defined by a Table of Data Points by Means of a VBA Function Procedure

A simple VBA custom function to find the area under a curve defined by a table of x, y data points, using the trapezoidal approximation, is shown in Figure 7-4. The syntax of the function is CurvArea(*x_values, y_values*).

```
Function CurvArea(x_values, y_values)
'Simple trapezoidal area integration

N1 = y_values.Count
For J = 2 To N1
area = area + (x_values(J) - x_values(J - 1)) * (y_values(J) + y_values(J - 1)) / 2
Next J
CurvArea = area
End Function
```

Figure 7-4. Simple VBA function CurvArea to calculate the area under a curve.
(folder 'Chapter 07 Examples', workbook 'Area under Curve', module 'CurvArea')

Calculating the Area under a Curve Defined by a Formula

Instead of determining the area under a curve defined by a table of data points, you may need to determine the area under a curve defined by a formula. For example, you may need to determine the area under the curve defined by equation 7-6

$$y = \frac{x^3}{e^x - 1} \tag{7-6}$$

which is shown in Figure 7-5. It is clear from the figure that summing areas of panels from $x = 0$ to $x = 15$ will provide an accurate determination of the area. In the calculation of the area, you are not limited by a table of values, as in the previous section, but instead you can create your own table by calculating values of the function for a range of suitable x values. Nor are you limited to using Panels of equal width. You can increase the accuracy obtained from the simple trapezoidal function by choosing panels of smaller width in regions where the curvature is greater. A chart of the function will show where the x increments should be made smaller; this should be evident from Figure 7-5.

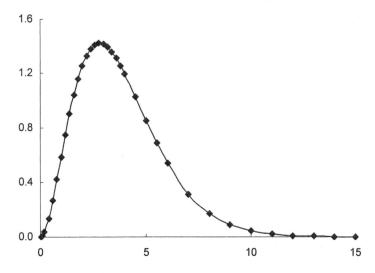

Figure 7-5. Graph of the function $y = x^3/(e^x - 1)$.
(folder 'Chapter 07 Examples', workbook 'Area under Curve', worksheet 'Curve2 by worksheet')

Part of the data table is shown in Figure 7-6, along with the area under the curve calculated by the trapezoidal approximation. The result returned by the custom function

=curvarea($B$4:$B$39,$A$4:$A$39)

is 6.514. The exact value for the area under the curve is $\pi^4/15 = 6.494$; the error in the value returned by the custom function is 0.3%.

	A	B	C
1	**Integration of Area Under a Curve**		
2		$y = x^3/(e^x - 1)$	
3	x	y	area
4	0	0	
5	0.05	0.002438	0.000061
6	0.1	0.009508	0.000299
7	0.2	0.036133	0.002282
8	0.4	0.130128	0.016626
9	0.6	0.262736	0.039286
10	0.8	0.417775	0.068051
11	1	0.581977	0.099975
12	1.2	0.744790	0.132677
38	14	0.002282	0.003624
39	15	0.001032	0.001657
40		Sum =	6.514127

Figure 7-6. Portion of data table for calculation of area under a curve.
Note that rows 13–37 have been hidden.
(folder 'Chapter 07 Examples', workbook 'Area under Curve', worksheet 'Curve2 by worksheet')

Area between Two Curves

The area between two curves can be determined by using any of the calculation methods described previously. The area is determined by the absolute value of the difference between the two curves, as in equation 7-7.

$$A = \int_a^b |f(x) - g(x)| dx \qquad (7\text{-}7)$$

There are several possibilities for the "area between two curves": the area can either be bounded by the curves *f(x)* and *g(x)* between specified limits (for example, the vertical lines $x = a_1$ and $x = b_1$ in Figure 7-7) or by the two curves *f(x)* and *g(x)* between two points where they cross (the points $x = a_2$ and $x = b_2$ in Figure 7-7).

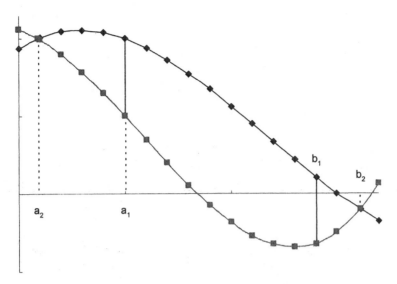

Figure 7-7. Areas bounded by two curves (between a_1 and a_2 or between b_1 and b_2).
(folder 'Chapter 07 Examples', workbook 'Area between two curves', worksheet 'Sheet1')

For the first case (area bounded by two curves between specified limits) the calculation is straightforward. In the second case, it is necessary to find the two values of x where the curves intersect. This can be done "manually," by inspecting the table of values for $f(x)$ and $g(x)$, or by methods described later in this book (see "Finding Values Other Than Zeroes of a Function" in Chapter 8).

Integrating a Function

Instead of finding the area under a curve defined by a set of data points, you may wish to integrate a function $F(x)$. You could simply create a table of function values and use one of the methods described in earlier sections to calculate the area. But a more convenient solution would be to create a custom function that uses the **Formula** property of the cell to get the worksheet formula to be integrated, in the same way that was used in the preceding chapter, and uses the formula to find the area under the curve. This approach will be described in subsequent sections.

Integrating a Function
Defined by a Worksheet Formula
by Means of a VBA Function Procedure

In this section, the trapezoidal and Simpson's rule methods are implemented as VBA custom functions, using an approach similar to that used in the differentiation functions of the previous chapter. The **Formula** property of the cell is used to get the worksheet formula to be differentiated into the VBA code as text. Then the SUBSTITUTE worksheet function is used to replace the variable of interest by an incremented value, and the **Evaluate** method used to get the new value of the formula. These values are used to calculate the area of each panel, and the areas of the panels are summed to obtain the area under the curve.

This function procedure can be used to integrate an expression $F(x)$ defined by a worksheet formula, between specified lower and upper limits a and b respectively. A table of function values is not required.

$$A = \int_a^b F(x)dx \qquad\qquad (7\text{-}8)$$

The syntax of the function is Integrate(***expression, variable, from_lower, to_upper***). The argument *expression* is the integrand, the expression to be integrated. The argument *variable* is the variable of integration, and the arguments *from_lower* and *to_upper* are the lower and upper limits of integration, respectively. The VBA code is shown in Figure 7-8. Function procedures for both trapezoidal (IntegrateT) and Simpson's rule (IntegrateS) methods are shown.

The range of x values over which the integration is to be performed (*to_upper* - *from_lower*) is divided into N panels. The user can adjust the accuracy of the integration by changing the value of N in the procedure, with a concomitant increase in calculation time.

```
Option Explicit
Function IntegrateT(expression, variable, from_lower, to_upper)
'Simple trapezoidal area integration

Dim FormulaString As String, T As String, Xref As String
Dim H As Double, area As Double, X As Double
Dim N As Integer, K As Integer, J As Integer
Dim NRepl As Integer
Dim temp As String
Dim F1 As Double, F2 As Double

FormulaString = expression.Formula
T = Application.ConvertFormula(FormulaString, xlA1, xlA1, xlAbsolute)
XRef = variable.Address

N = 1000
H = (to_upper - from_lower) / N
area = 0
X = from_lower
NRepl = (Len(T) - Len(Application.Substitute(T, XRef, ""))) / Len(XRef)

For K = 1 To N
```

```
For J = NRepl To 1 Step -1
   temp = Application.Substitute(T, XRef, X & " ", J)
   If IsError(Evaluate(temp)) Then GoTo pt1
   T = temp
pt1: Next J
F1 = Evaluate(T)
T = Application.ConvertFormula(FormulaString, xlA1, xlA1, xlAbsolute)
For J = NRepl To 1 Step -1
   temp = Application.Substitute(T, XRef, X + H & " ", J)
   If IsError(Evaluate(temp)) Then GoTo pt2
   T = temp
pt2: Next J
F2 = Evaluate(T)

area = area + H * (F1 + F2) / 2
X = X + H
Next K
IntegrateT = area
End Function
```

Figure 7-8. VBA **Function** procedure to integrate a worksheet formula
by the trapezoidal approximation method.
(folder 'Chapter 07 Examples,' workbook 'Integration,' module 'SimpleIntegration')

```
Function IntegrateS(expression, variable, from_lower, to_upper)
'Simpson's 1/3 rule area integration

Dim FormulaString As String, T As String, Xref As String
Dim H As Double, area As Double, X As Double
Dim N As Integer, K As Integer, J As Integer
Dim NRepl As Integer
Dim temp As String
Dim Y0 As Double, Y1 As Double, Y2 As Double

FormulaString = expression.Formula
XRef = variable.Address

N = 1000
H = (to_upper - from_lower) / N / 2

For K = 0 To N - 1
X = 2 * K * H
T = Application.ConvertFormula(FormulaString, xlA1, xlA1, xlAbsolute)
NRepl = (Len(T) - Len(Application.Substitute(T, XRef, ""))) / Len(XRef)
For J = NRepl To 1 Step -1
   temp = Application.Substitute(T, XRef, from_lower + X & " ", J)
   If IsError(Evaluate(temp)) Then GoTo pt1
   T = temp
pt1: Next J
Y0 = Evaluate(T)
```

```
T = Application.ConvertFormula(FormulaString, xlA1, xlA1, xlAbsolute)
For J = NRepl To 1 Step -1
   temp = Application.Substitute(T, XRef, from_lower + X + H & " ", J)
   If IsError(Evaluate(temp)) Then GoTo pt2
   T = temp
pt2: Next J
Y1 = Evaluate(T)
T = Application.ConvertFormula(FormulaString, xlA1, xlA1, xlAbsolute)
For J = NRepl To 1 Step -1
   temp = Application.Substitute(T, XRef, from_lower + X + 2 * H & " ", J)
   If IsError(Evaluate(temp)) Then GoTo pt3
   T = temp
pt3: Next J
Y2 = Evaluate(T)
area = area + H * (Y0 + 4 * Y1 + Y2) / 3
Next K
IntegrateS = area
End Function
```

Figure 7-9. VBA function procedure to integrate a worksheet formula
by Simpson's method.
(folder 'Chapter 07 Examples', workbook 'Integration', module 'SimpleIntegration')

Some results returned by the IntegrateT and IntegrateS functions are shown in Figures 7-10 and 7-11, respectively. In general, results are more accurate when using the Simpson's method function.

	A	B	C	D	E	F	G	H
1	Integration function using simple trapezoidal approx.							
2	Function	x	F(x)	from	to	Area	exact	% error
3	x^3	1	1	0	1	0.2500003	0.25	1.0E-04
4	$4\sqrt{(1-x^2)}$	1	0	0	1	3.14156	3.14159	1.2E-03
5	triangle*	1	2	0	2	4.00000000	4	0.0E+00
6	Gaussian**	95	0.035	20	180	1.00000000	1	3.1E-12
7								
8	* slope = 2, intercept = 4							
9	** $\mu = 100, \sigma = 10$							

Figure 7-10. Some results returned by the IntegrateT custom function.
(folder 'Chapter 07 Examples', workbook 'Integration', sheet 'Trapezoidal Integration Fn')

	A	B	C	D	E	F	G	H
1	**Integration function using Simpson's method**							
2	Function	x	F(x)	from	to	Area	exact	% error
3	x^3	1	1	0	1	0.2500000	0.25	4.4E-14
4	$4\sqrt{(1-x^2)}$	1	0	0	1	3.141588	3.141593	1.6E-04
5	triangle*	1	2	0	2	4.0000000	4	2.2E-14
6	Gaussian**	95	0.035	20	180	1.0000000	1	1.3E-13
7								
8	* slope = 2, intercept = 4							
9	** μ = 100, σ = 10							

Figure 7-11. Some results returned by the IntegrateS custom function.
(folder 'Chapter 07 Examples', workbook 'Integration', sheet Simpson Integration Fn')

Because some functions may require a large number of iterations, there may be a noticeable delay in calculation.

Gaussian Quadrature

The preceding methods for numerical integration employ evenly spaced values of x at which the function is evaluated. Other formulas have been developed whereby the function is evaluated at specially selected values of x. These *Gaussian quadrature* formulas are significantly more efficient, in terms of the accuracy of the evaluation.

Gaussian quadrature formulas involve the evaluation of the function at a set of x_i values (nodes), with the use of a corresponding set of weights w_i, in the following formula

$$A = \int_{-1}^{1} F(x)dx = \sum_{i=1}^{N} w_i F(x_i) \tag{7-9}$$

The nodes and weights can be derived from certain kinds of polynomials. The Legendre polynomials will be used here to determine the values of x_i and w_i. The Legendre polynomials are a set of polynomials of degree N. Increasing N provides an increase in accuracy of evaluation but requires a concomitant increase in computation time. Values of Legendre polynomials for N up to 100 have been published.

The integration need not be limited solely to the interval -1 to 1. By employing a change of variable

$$z = \frac{2x - (a+b)}{(b-a)} \tag{7-10}$$

the integral expression is

$$A = \int\limits_{a}^{b} F(x)dx = \frac{b-a}{2} \int\limits_{-1}^{1} F\left(\frac{(b-a)z + (b+a)}{2} \right) dz \qquad (7\text{-}11)$$

and equation 7-9 becomes

$$A = \int\limits_{a}^{b} F(x)dx = \frac{b-a}{2} \sum_{i=1}^{N} w_i F\left(\frac{(b-a)z_i + (b+a)}{2} \right) \qquad (7\text{-}12)$$

which permits integration over any range.

The code shown in Figure 7-12 performs Gaussian quadrature using equation 7-12 and a tenth-order Legendre polynomial. Some results returned by the function are shown in Figure 7-13.

```
Option Explicit
'++++++++++++++++++++++++++++++++++++++++++++++++++++++++++++++++++
Function Integrate(expression, variable, from_lower, to_upper, Optional _
    tolerance)

Dim FormulaString As String, XAddress As String
Dim result As Double

FormulaString = expression.Formula
XAddress = variable.Address    'Default is absolute
FormulaString = Application.ConvertFormula(FormulaString, xlA1, xlA1, _
    xlAbsolute)
Call GaussLeGendre10(FormulaString, XAddress, from_lower, to_upper, _
    tolerance, result)
Integrate = result
End Function
'++++++++++++++++++++++++++++++++++++++++++++++++++++++++++++++++++
Sub GaussLeGendre10(expression, XRef, from_lower, to_upper, tolerance,
    result)
'Uses ten-point Gauss-Legendre quadrature formula.
'Adapted from Shoup, p.203

Dim XJ As Variant, AJ As Variant
Dim TotalArea As Double, OldArea As Double, area As Double

Dim T As String, temp As String
Dim I As Integer, J As Integer, K As Integer, JJ As Integer
Dim N As Integer, NRepl As Integer
Dim A As Double, B As Double, C As Double, D As Double, F As Double
Dim H As Double

XJ = Array(-0.973906528517172, -0.865063366688984, -0.679409568299024, -
    0.433395394129247, -0.148874338981631, 0.973906528517172,
```

```
   0.865063366688984, 0.679409568299024, 0.433395394129247,
   0.148874338981631)
AJ = Array(0.066671344308688, 0.149451349915058, 0.219086362515982,
   0.269266719309996, 0.295524224714753, 0.066671344308688,
   0.149451349915058, 0.219086362515982, 0.269266719309996,
   0.295524224714753)

If IsMissing(tolerance) Then tolerance = 0.0000000001
OldArea = 0
N = 1
For K = 1 To 10 'increments divided by 1,2,4,8,16,32,64,128,256,512
area = 0
H = (to_upper - from_lower) / N

For I = 1 To N
A = from_lower + (I - 1) * H
B = A + H
C = (B + A) / 2
D = (B - A) / 2

For J = 1 To 10
T = expression
NRepl = (Len(T) - Len(Application.Substitute(T, XRef, ""))) / Len(XRef)
For JJ = NRepl To 1 Step -1
   temp = Application.Substitute(T, XRef, C + D * XJ(J) & " ", JJ)
   If IsError( Evaluate(temp)) Then GoTo pt1
   T = temp
pt1: Next JJ
F = Evaluate(T)
  area = area + AJ(J) * F
Next J
Next I
area = area * D
If Abs((area - OldArea) / area) < tolerance Then GoTo AllDone
OldArea = area
N = 2 * N
Next K
AllDone:
result = area
End Sub
```

Figure 7-12. Integrate custom function.
(folder 'Chapter 07 Examples', workbook 'Integration', module 'LegendreIntegration')

	A	B	C	D	E	F	G	H
1	Custom Function to Integrate Area Under a Curve							
2	=Integrate(formula_in_cell,variable,from_lower,to_upper,tolerance)							
3	Function	x	F(x)	from	to	area	exact value	% error
4	4√(1-x²)dx	1	0	-1	1	3.1415928	3.1415927	4.0E-06
5	x³dx	1	1	0	1	0.2500000002	0.25	7.9E-08
6	(mx+b)dx	2	0	0	2	4.000000003	4	7.6E-08
7	sin(x)dx	0	0	0	3.14	2.000000001	2	7.4E-08
8	(x e⁻ˣ)dx	1	0.37	0	1000	1.000000001	1	9.5E-08
9	(1/x) dx	1	1	1	2	0.69314718	0.69314718	7.7E-08

Figure 7-13. Some results returned by the Integrate custom function.
(folder 'Chapter 07 Examples', workbook 'Integration', sheet 'GaussLegendre Integration Fn')

Early versions of this program returned inaccurate results when the range $b - a$ was large. The function Integrate illustrates one approach to overcoming this problem. First, the integral is evaluated over the total range $b - a$. Then the interval is divided into two halves and each "panel" is integrated separately. The sum of the two panels is compared to the previous value. If the difference is larger than a tolerance value, the interval is divided into quarters, the areas summed and so on. The process is continued for 10 cycles of iteration (512 panels) or until the area difference is less than a specified tolerance.

Because some functions may require a large number of iterations, there may be a noticeable delay in calculation. Increasing the value of *tolerance* should speed up calculation, but only at the expense of accuracy.

Integration with an Upper or Lower Limit of Infinity

Integrals such as

$$A = \int_{a}^{\infty} F(x)dx \tag{7-13}$$

can be evaluated by summing the areas of a number of panels covering the range from $x = a$ to $x = a$ suitably large value. It is to be expected that as $x \to \infty$ the area of panel$(x) \to$ zero. Thus the integral can be evaluated by summing the integrals of a series of panels of increasing width (e.g., from 0–1, 1–10, 10–100, etc), ending the summation when the area of the last panel is suitably small. Manual adjustment of the panel widths is easily done by inspection of the results. Figure 7-14 shows a typical result.

	A	B	C	D	E	F	G	H
32			Integrating to upper limit of infinity					
33	Function	x	F(x)	from	to	integrated value	Σ	% error
34	y = 1/((1+x)*sqrt(x)	1	0.5	0	0.01	0.1989708	0.1989708	93.67
35		1	0.5	0.01	0.1	0.4132174	0.6121882	80.51
36		1	0.5	0.1	1	0.9582416	1.5704298	50.01
37		1	0.5	1	10	0.9582416	2.5286714	19.51
38		1	0.5	10	100	0.4132174	2.9418888	6.36
39		1	0.5	100	1000	0.1361128	3.0780016	2.02
40		1	0.5	1E+03	1E+04	0.0432252	3.1212268	0.65
41		1	0.5	1E+04	1E+05	0.0136748	3.1349016	0.21
42		1	0.5	1E+05	1E+06	0.0043245	3.1392261	0.08
43		1	0.5	1E+06	1E+08	0.0018000	3.1410261	0.02
44		1	0.5	1E+08	1E+10	0.0001800	3.1412061	0.01
45		1	0.5	1E+10	1E+14	0.0000198	3.1412259	0.01
46		1	0.5	1E+14	1E+18	0.0000002	3.1412261	0.01
47						exact value:	3.1415927	

Figure 7-14. Integrating from a lower limit to an upper limit of infinity.
Results returned by the Integrate custom function.
(folder 'Chapter 07 Examples', workbook 'Integration', sheet 'Integrating to infinity by sum')

Distance Traveled Along a Curved Path

The length of a plane curve can be estimated by dividing the curve into segments, as in Figure 7-15, and approximating the length of the curve segment by the straight line AB. The length of AB = $\sqrt{(\Delta x)^2 + (\Delta y)^2}$. The distance along the curve is found by summing the lengths of the segments.

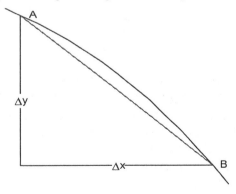

Figure 7-15. Approximating the distance along a curve AB
by the length of the straight line segment AB.
(folder 'Chapter 07 Examples', workbook 'Curve Distance', sheet 'Curve Distance (Circle)')

	A	B	C
1	Distance Travelled Along a Curve		
2	1/4 circle with r = 1		
3	(distance should be $\pi/2$)		
4	x	y	d
5	0.000	1.000	
6	0.050	0.999	0.050
7	0.075	0.997	0.025
8	0.100	0.995	0.025
9	0.125	0.992	0.025
51	0.980	0.199	0.024
52	0.985	0.173	0.027
53	0.990	0.141	0.032
54	0.9925	0.122	0.019
55	0.9950	0.100	0.023
56	0.9975	0.071	0.029
57	0.999	0.045	0.026
58	1.000	0.000	0.045
59		Sum x 2 =	3.14145
60		% error =	4.6E-03

Figure 7-16. Approximating the circumference of a circle of radius 1.
Note that the rows between 9 and 51 are hidden.
(folder 'Chapter 07 Examples', workbook 'Curve Distance', sheet 'Curve Distance (Circle)')

The procedure is illustrated by estimating the length of one quarter of a circle of radius $r = 1$. The equation of the circle is $x^2 + y^2 = 1$, or $y = \sqrt{1 - x^2}$. As shown in Figure 7-16, the value of y and the distance d between successive points was calculated from $x = 0$ to $x = 1$, using an x increment of 0.025. Near the end of the range of x values, where y changes more rapidly, the x increment was decreased. The formula in cell C6 is

=SQRT((A8-A5)^2+(B8-B5)^2)

The sum of the distances × 2, in cell C59 is a reasonable estimate of π.

Problems

Answers to the following problems are found in the folder "Ch. 07 (Integration)" in the "Problems & Solutions" folder on the CD.

1. Find the area under the curve of the function $\int\limits_{0}^{\infty}\dfrac{x^2}{e^x-1}dx$ by Simpson's method.

2. Integrate the following expressions, using one of the custom functions for integration.

   (a) $\int\limits_{0}^{1}x^n\,dx$

   (b) $\int\limits_{0}^{1}e^{-x^2}\,dx$

   (c) $\int\limits_{0}^{\pi}\sin x\,dx$

   (d) $\int\limits_{0}^{1}\dfrac{\ln x}{1+x}dx$

   (e) $\int\limits_{0}^{1}\dfrac{\ln x}{1-x^2}dx$

   (f) $\int\limits_{0}^{1}(\ln x)^3\,dx$

   (g) $\int\limits_{0}^{1}\dfrac{(x^3-x^2)}{\ln x}dx$

3. Evaluate the elliptic integral

$$\int\limits_{0}^{\pi/2}\sqrt{1-(1/2)\sin^2 x}\,dx$$

4. An ellipse is a plane figure described by the locus of a point $P(x, y)$ that moves such that the sum of its distances from two fixed points (foci) is a constant. If the ellipse has foci located at A $(-c, 0)$ and B $(c, 0)$ and the distance ACB is $2a$, then by setting $b = \sqrt{a^2 - c^2}$, the equation of the ellipse is simplified to

$$\frac{x^2}{a^2} + \frac{y^2}{b^2} = 1$$

(a and b are termed the semiaxes of the ellipse).

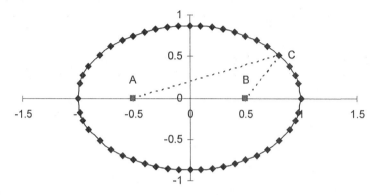

Figure 7-17. Approximating the circumference of an ellipse.

For the ellipse shown in Figure 7-17, with foci at $x = -0.5$, $y = 0$ and $x = 0.5$, $y = 0$ and $a = 1$, determine the circumference of the ellipse.

5. Determine the area of the ellipse of problem 7-4.

6. Find the area between the curve $y = 2x - x^2$ and the line $y = -3$.

7. Find the area between the curve $y = 2x - x^2$ and the line $y = 2.5x - 2.3$.

8. Find the area enclosed between the two curves shown in Figure 7-7: $y_1 = x^3 - 20x^2 - 100x + 2000$ and $y_2 = 2x^3 - 5x^2 - 300x + 1000$. The curves intersect in the region between $x = -5$ and $x = 15$.

9. The area between the curve $y = x^2$ and the horizontal line $y = 4$ is divided into two equal areas by the horizontal line $y = c$. Find c.

10. The area between the curve $y = x^2 + 3$ and the line $y = 12$ is divided into two equal areas by the line $y = c$. Find c.

11. Integrate the following expression.

$$\int_0^\infty \frac{x^3}{e^x - 1} dx$$

12. Integrate the following expressions, using the custom function for integration.

(a) $$\int_0^\infty e^{-x} dx$$

(b) $$\int_0^\infty x e^{-x} dx$$

(c) $$\int_0^\infty e^{-x^2} dx$$

(d) $$\int_0^\infty e^{-ax^2} dx$$

(e) $$\int_0^\infty \frac{e^{-x^2}}{\sqrt{x}} dx$$

Chapter 8

Roots of Equations

Many problems in science and engineering can be expressed in the form of an equation in a single unknown, i.e., $y = F(x)$. A value of x that makes $y = 0$ is called a root of the function; often the solution to a scientific problem is a root of a function. If the function to be solved is a quadratic equation, there is a familiar formula to find the two roots of the expression. But for almost all other functions, similar formulas aren't available; the roots must be obtained by successive approximations, beginning with an initial estimate and then refining it. This chapter presents a number of methods for obtaining the roots or zeroes of a function.

A Graphical Method

As a preliminary step in finding the roots of a complicated or unfamiliar function, it is helpful to make a chart of the function, in order to get preliminary estimates of the roots, and indeed to find out how many roots there are. A cubic equation such as the one shown in equation 8-1 and Figure 8-1,

$$y = x^3 + 0.13x^2 - 0.0005x - 0.0009 \qquad (8\text{-}1)$$

always has three roots, either three real roots as in Figure 8-1, or one real and two imaginary roots. Figure 8-27 later in this chapter shows an example of the latter case.

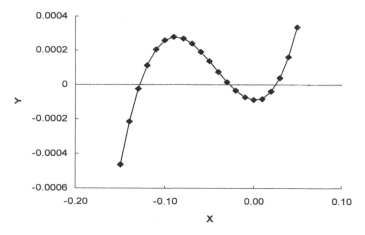

Figure 8-1. A regular polynomial with three real roots.

But the number of roots of other functions, such as

$$y = -1.04 \ln x - 1.26 \cos x + 0.0307\,e^x \qquad (8-2)$$

may not be obvious. A chart of the function is useful to show the number and approximate value of the roots of the function. The chart in Figure 8-2 shows that the function shown in equation 8-2 has two real roots.

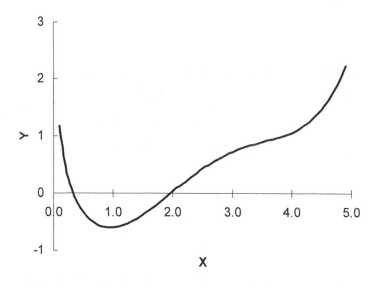

Figure 8-2. A function with two real roots.

	A	B
1	X	Y
15	1.4	-0.4396
16	1.5	-0.37322
17	1.6	-0.29995
18	1.7	-0.22146
19	1.8	-0.1393
20	1.9	-0.05493
21	2.0	0.030316
22	2.1	0.115193
23	2.2	0.198584
24	2.3	0.27949
25	2.4	0.35704

Figure 8-3. Portion of data table of x and y values
showing the pair of values that bracket a root of the function shown in Figure 8-2.
(folder 'Chapter 08 Examples', workbook 'Roots of Equations', worksheet 'Graphical Method')

Once a chart has been created, it is very easy to expand the scales of the axes to examine the crossing region at higher and higher magnification. Figure 8-3 shows part of the data table used to create Figure 8-2; the formula in column B is the function shown in equation 8-1. The two values that bracket one of the roots of the function are highlighted.

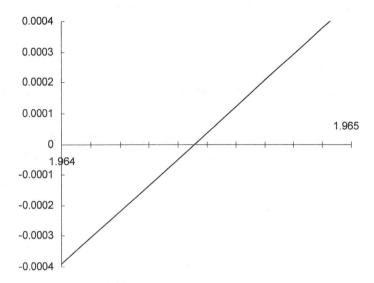

Figure 8-4. Expanded chart of a function, for graphical estimation of a root.
(folder 'Chapter 08 Examples', workbook 'Roots of Equations', worksheet 'Graphical Method')

The expanded portion of the chart, shown in Figure 8-4, was created by selecting the four cells A20:B21, creating a chart and changing the x- and y-axis scales. From the figure, one can estimate that the root that lies between $x = 1.9$ and $x = 2.0$ has the value 1.96446. This is probably adequate for most purposes. Remember to choose the Smoothed Lines option in the ChartWizard.

The Interval-Halving or Bisection Method

This method and the one that follows make use of the fact that, as can be seen for example in Figure 8-3, a real root of a function lies between two adjacent x values for which y exhibits a change in sign. In order to obtain a root of a function by this method, you need to create a table of x values and the corresponding y values of the function, and identify two adjacent y values, one positive and the other negative. These and the corresponding x values will be the starting values for a binary search.

Once you have obtained the two starting x values, x_1 and x_2, the midpoint of the interval between them, x_3, is an approximation to the root. Now choose the pair of x values with opposite signs, either x_1 and x_3 or x_2 and x_3 and bisect the interval between them to get a further improvement. Repeat the process until a desired level of accuracy is attained. Figure 8-5 illustrates the application of this method, using equation 8-2. Only a portion of the table is shown; 34 rows were required to reach convergence at the 1E-10 level, at which point $x = 1.96445854473859$.

	A	B	C	D
1	Interval-Halving Method			
2	X1	Y	X2	Y
3	5	2.525054	1	-0.59733
4	3	0.72146	1	-0.59733
5	2	0.030316	1	-0.59733
6	1.5	-0.37322	2	0.030316
7	1.75	-0.18074	2	0.030316
8	1.875	-0.07615	2	0.030316
9	1.9375	-0.02299	2	0.030316
10	1.96875	0.003661	1.9375	-0.02299
11	1.953125	-0.00967	1.96875	0.003661
12	1.9609375	-0.003	1.96875	0.003661
13	1.96484375	0.000329	1.9609375	-0.003
14	1.962890625	-0.00134	1.96484375	0.000329
15	1.963867188	-0.0005	1.96484375	0.000329
16	1.964355469	-8.8E-05	1.96484375	0.000329
17	1.964599609	0.00012	1.964355469	-8.8E-05

Figure 8-5. Using the binary search method to find a real root of a function.
(folder 'Chapter 08 Examples', workbook 'Roots of Equations', worksheet 'Binary Search Method')

To construct the worksheet of Figure 8-5, the initial values x_1 and x_2 were entered in cells A3 and C3, respectively, and the formula for the function in cells B3 and D3. Next, the formulas that perform the binary search were entered in row 4; the formula in cell A4 calculates the midpoint value between the x values in the previous row

=(C3+A3)/2

and the formula in cell C4 selects the y value that has the opposite sign to the value in the previous row.

=IF(SIGN(B4)<>SIGN(B3),A3,C3).

Cells B4 and D4 contain the formula for the function. Finally, the formulas in A4:D4 were filled down into subsequent rows. Each row constitutes an iteration cycle; convergence was observed visually.

Although unsophisticated, this method will always find a root.

The Interval Method with Linear Interpolation (the *Regula Falsi* Method)

The interval-halving method can be made much more efficient in the following way. Instead of simply bisecting the difference between the two estimates of the root, you can obtain a better estimate of the root by using linear interpolation, as illustrated in Figure 8-6.

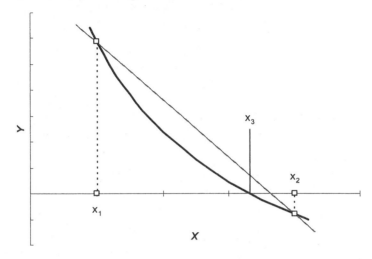

Figure 8-6. The binary search method with linear interpolation
(the *Regula Falsi* method)

The equation for linear interpolation is either

$$x_3 = x_1 + y_1 \frac{x_2 - x_1}{y_2 - y_1} \qquad (8\text{-}3)$$

or

$$x_3 = x_1 - y_2 \frac{x_2 - x_1}{y_2 - y_1} \qquad (8\text{-}4)$$

Again, two starting values of x must be obtained, for which the y values have opposite signs.

When applied to the same function as in the preceding example, this method converges efficiently to a root, as illustrated in Figure 8-7.

Again, cells A3 and C3 contain the initial values for x_1 and x_2, respectively, and cells B3 and D3 contain the formula for the function. Cell A4 contains the linear interpolation formula:

=C3-D3*(C3-A3)/(D3-B3)

and cell C4 contains the same formula as used in the previous example to select the *y* value that has the opposite sign to the value in the previous row:

	A	B	C	D
1	Interval Method with Linear Interpolation			
2	X1	Y1	X2	Y2
3	5	2.525054	1	-0.59733
4	1.765222575	-0.1682	5	2.525054
5	1.967236444	0.00237	1.765222575	-0.1682
6	1.964429524	-2.5E-05	1.967236444	0.00237
7	1.964458545	-1.6E-10	1.967236444	0.00237
8	1.964458545	-1.2E-15	1.967236444	0.00237
9	1.964458545	0	1.964458545	-1.2E-15

Figure 8-7. Using the *Regula Falsi* method to find a real root of a function.
(folder 'Chapter 08 Examples', workbook 'Roots of Equations', worksheet 'Regula Falsi Method')

In general this method converges more efficiently to the root than does the binary search method, although unfavorable situations can occur, as illustrated in Figure 8-8. In this example, one end of the interval is "stuck," and even after 19 cycles of iteration, convergence has only reached the 1E-03 level.

	A	B	C	D
1	Slow convergence			
2	X1	Y1	X2	Y2
3	0.01000	3.560449	1	-0.59733
4	0.85777	-0.59226	0.01	3.560449
5	0.73686	-0.55142	0.01	3.560449
6	0.63939	-0.48778	0.01	3.560449
7	0.56355	-0.41478	0.01	3.560449
8	0.50579	-0.34243	0.01	3.560449
9	0.46229	-0.27658	0.01	3.560449
10	0.42969	-0.2198	0.01	3.560449
11	0.40529	-0.1726	0.01	3.560449
12	0.38701	-0.13433	0.01	3.560449
13	0.37330	-0.10385	0.01	3.560449
14	0.36301	-0.07989	0.01	3.560449
15	0.35526	-0.06123	0.01	3.560449
16	0.34942	-0.04679	0.01	3.560449
17	0.34502	-0.03568	0.01	3.560449
18	0.34170	-0.02717	0.01	3.560449
19	0.33919	-0.02066	0.01	3.560449
20	0.33729	-0.0157	0.01	3.560449
21	0.33585	-0.01192	0.01	3.560449
22	0.33476	-0.00904	0.01	3.560449

Figure 8-8. A case with slow convergence of the *Regula Falsi* method.
(folder 'Chapter 08 Examples', workbook 'Roots of Equations', worksheet 'Regula Falsi (2)')

The *Regula Falsi* Method
with Correction for Slow Convergence

The preceding example shows that an unlucky choice of starting values can lead to slow convergence. By examination of the example in Figure 8-7, it can be seen that the ideal situation for rapid convergence occurs when, in almost every cycle, there is a change in the value of both x_1 and x_2, y_1 and y_2 or in the sign of y_1 or y_2. Any one of these can be used to test for slow convergence.

The slow-convergence situation in Figure 8-8 was remedied by changing the interpolation calculation so that if the value of x_2 does not change from one cycle to the next, the value of y_2 used in the interpolation is halved. The performance of the modified formula is illustrated in Figure 8-9. The only change is the formula in cell D4

```
=IF(C4=C3,D3/2,-1.04*LN(C4)-1.26*COS(C4)+0.0307*EXP(C4))
```

This formula divides the value of y_2 by 2 if there has been no change in x_2 in the preceding two iteration cycles (this has occurred in rows 5, 6 and 7, for example). Otherwise the function is calculated by means of the usual formula.

A nested IF could be used to handle the case where either x_1 or x_2 is "stuck."

	A	B	C	D
1	Modified formula improves convergence			
2	X1	Y1	X2	Y2
3	0.01000	3.560449	1	-0.59733
4	0.85777	-0.59226	0.01	3.560449
5	0.73686	-0.55142	0.01	1.780224
6	0.56496	-0.41636	0.01	0.890112
7	0.38810	-0.13669	0.01	0.445056
8	0.29926	0.092106	0.3881	-0.13669
9	0.33503	-0.00974	0.29926	0.092106
10	0.33161	-0.00062	0.29926	0.046053
11	0.33117	0.000538	0.33161	-6E-04
12	0.33137	-2.5E-07	0.33117	5E-04
13	0.33137	-9.9E-11	0.33117	3E-04
14	0.33137	9.93E-11	0.33137	-1E-10
15	0.33137	-1.9E-16	0.33137	1E-10

Figure 8-9. Modifying the *Regula Falsi* method to handle slow convergence. (folder 'Chapter 08 Examples', workbook 'Roots of Equations', worksheet 'Regula Falsi (3)')

The Newton-Raphson Method

The preceding methods require manual selection of a pair of starting values with opposite signs. The Newton-Raphson method (sometimes referred to simply as Newton's method) requires only a single function value as the starting value, and is therefore *self-starting*. The Newton-Raphson method is a classic exercise from freshman calculus—it uses the first derivative of the function (the slope of the curve) at the initial estimate, x_1, and extrapolates this tangent line to the x axis to obtain an improved value, x_2. The process is repeated to obtain further approximations to the root, as illustrated in Figure 8-10, until the desired convergence level is reached.

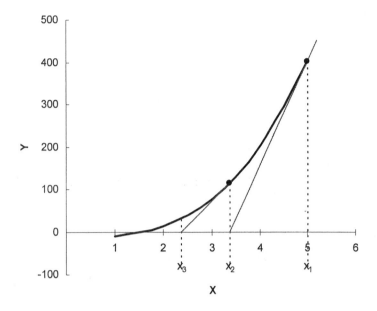

Figure 8-10. The Newton-Raphson method for obtaining a root of a function.

The slope of the curve at x_1 is the first derivative of the function, dy/dx. The improved estimate can be calculated by rearranging the expression for the slope, $m = (y_2 - y_1)/(x_2 - x_1)$, and setting $y_2 = 0$. This results in the equation

$$x_2 = (mx_1 - y_1)/m \tag{8-5}$$

or the equivalent

$$x_2 = x_1 - (y_1/m) \tag{8-6}$$

sometimes written as

$$x_2 = x_1 - y_1/y_1' \tag{8-6a}$$

In pencil-and-paper calculations the slope would be obtained by calculating the first derivative using calculus, but in spreadsheet calculations you can use numerical differentiation (see Chapter 6, "Differentiation"). Increase x by a small amount Δx, which increases the y value by a small amount Δy. If you make Δx small enough, $\Delta y / \Delta x$ will be a good approximation to the first derivative dy/dx. In the following example, $x + \Delta x$ was obtained by multiplying x by 1.00000001. (See "The Newton Quotient" in Chapter 6.)

The calculations of the Newton-Raphson method are illustrated in Figure 8-11. The function for which a root is sought is the regular polynomial

$$y = 3x^3 + 2.5x^2 - 5x - 11 \tag{8-7}$$

	A	B	C	D	E	F	G	H
1				Newton-Raphson Method				
2				delta =	1.00E-08			
3		X1	Y1	X2	Y2	m	new X1	
4		5	401.5	5.00000005	401.50001	245	3.36122451	
5								
6		3.36122451	114.36208	3.36122454	114.36209	113.48659	2.35351003	
7		2.35351003	30.188317	2.35351005	30.188318	56.618636	1.82032311	
8		1.82032311	6.277663	1.82032313	6.2776637	33.923802	1.63527123	
9		1.63527123	0.6276192	1.63527125	0.6276196	27.243364	1.61223373	
10		1.61223373	0.0091011	1.61223374	0.0091015	26.454847	1.61188970	
11		1.61188970	2.013E-06	1.61188972	2.439E-06	26.443144	1.61188963	
12		1.61188963	1.066E-13	1.61188964	4.262E-07	26.443142	1.61188963	

Figure 8-11. Calculation of a root of a function by the Newton–Raphson method.
The formulas in row 6 were filled down until convergence was observed.
(folder 'Chapter 08 Examples', workbook 'Roots of Equations', worksheet 'Newton-Raphson Method')

The starting value, in this case 5, was entered in cell B4. The formulas in cells C4, D4, E4, F4 and G4 are, respectively,

C4: =3*B4^3+2.5*B4^2-5*B4-11   (the function y)

D4: =B4+0.0000001*B4   (increment x by a small amount Δx)

E4: =3*D4^3+2.5*D4^2-5*D4-11   (this is $y + \Delta y$)

F4: =(E4-C4)/(D4-B4)   ($m = \Delta x/\Delta y$)

G4: =(F4*B4-C4)/F4   ($x_{new} = (m \times x_{old} - y_{old})/m$)

Then the formula =G4 was entered in cell B6, so as to use the improved x value as the starting value in the next row (row 5 was left empty for purposes of illustration only). The formulas in C4:G4 were copied and pasted into the corresponding cells in row 6. Finally, the formulas in cells B6:G6 were Filled Down into succeeding rows until convergence was observed in column G or a sufficiently small value of y was obtained in column C.

Using Goal Seek...

Excel provides a built-in way to find a real root of a function. The **Goal Seek...** command in the **Tools** menu can be used to perform what is sometimes called "backsolving"; that is, it varies x in order to make y reach a specified value. Thus you can use **Goal Seek...** to find a value of x that makes the value of the function y become zero, or at least very close to zero. The computer code that performs the Goal Seek function probably involves the Newton-Raphson method.[*]

As an example to illustrate the use of **Goal Seek...**, we'll return to the cubic equation 8-1, $y = x^3 + 0.13x^2 - 0.0005x - 0.0009$. Figure 8-12 shows a part of the data table that was used to produce the chart shown in Figure 8-1.

	A	B
3	X	Y
4	-0.15	-4.65E-04
5	-0.14	-2.16E-04
6	-0.13	-2.50E-05
7	-0.12	1.14E-04
8	-0.11	2.07E-04
9	-0.10	2.60E-04

Figure 8-12. Part of a data table.
(folder 'Chapter 08 Examples', workbook 'Roots of Equations', worksheet 'Using Goal Seek')

It can be seen that one of the roots of this function must lie between $x = -0.13$ and $x = -0.12$, since there is a change in sign of the function somewhere in this interval. To use **Goal Seek...**, enter a trial value of x in a cell and the function in another cell, as illustrated in Figure 8-13. The cell containing the value of x is referred to as the *changing cell*, the cell containing the function as the *target cell* or the *objective*.

	A	B
26	Changing cell	Target cell
27	-0.2	-2.79E-03

Figure 8-13. Target Cell and Changing Cell for **Goal Seek**.
(folder 'Chapter 08 Examples', workbook 'Roots of Equations', worksheet 'Using Goal Seek')

Now choose **Goal Seek...** from the **Tools** menu to display the Goal Seek dialog box (Figure 8-14). (Although not necessary, it's convenient to select the target cell before beginning.)

---

[*] According to Microsoft, "Goal Seek uses an iterative process in which the source cell is incremented or decremented at varying rates until the target value is reached."

Enter a reference to the target cell in the Set Cell box (the cell reference will appear there if you selected that cell before choosing **Goal Seek...**). Enter 0 in the To Value box and a reference to the changing cell in the By Changing Cell box, and press OK.

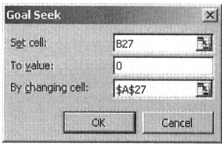

Figure 8-14. The Goal Seek dialog box.

After a few iteration cycles the Goal Seek Status dialog box (Figure 8-15) will be displayed. When you press OK the final values of the changing cell and target cell will be displayed in the worksheet cells, as shown in Figure 8-16.

Figure 8-15. The Goal Seek Status dialog box.

	A	B
	Changing cell	Target cell
26		
27	-0.1284371	-1.86E-18

Figure 8-16. Obtaining a root of a function by using Goal Seek.
(folder 'Chapter 08 Examples', workbook 'Roots of Equations', worksheet 'Using Goal Seek')

For scientific and engineering problems, it's critical that you set the convergence limit (the stopping parameter) of Goal Seek to suit your problem. Choose **Options...** from the **Tools** menu and choose the Calculation tab (see

Figure 8-17). The Maximum Change parameter sets the convergence limit; when the value of the target cell becomes less than this value, iteration ceases. The default value for Maximum Change is 0.001, which is suitable for this problem, but will not be suitable for many other problems. For a problem where the magnitude of the result (the changing cell value) is a very small number, you can set Maximum Change to a value such as 1E-15. Alternatively, you can set it to zero, which will usually result in Goal Seek completing 100 iteration cycles before quitting.

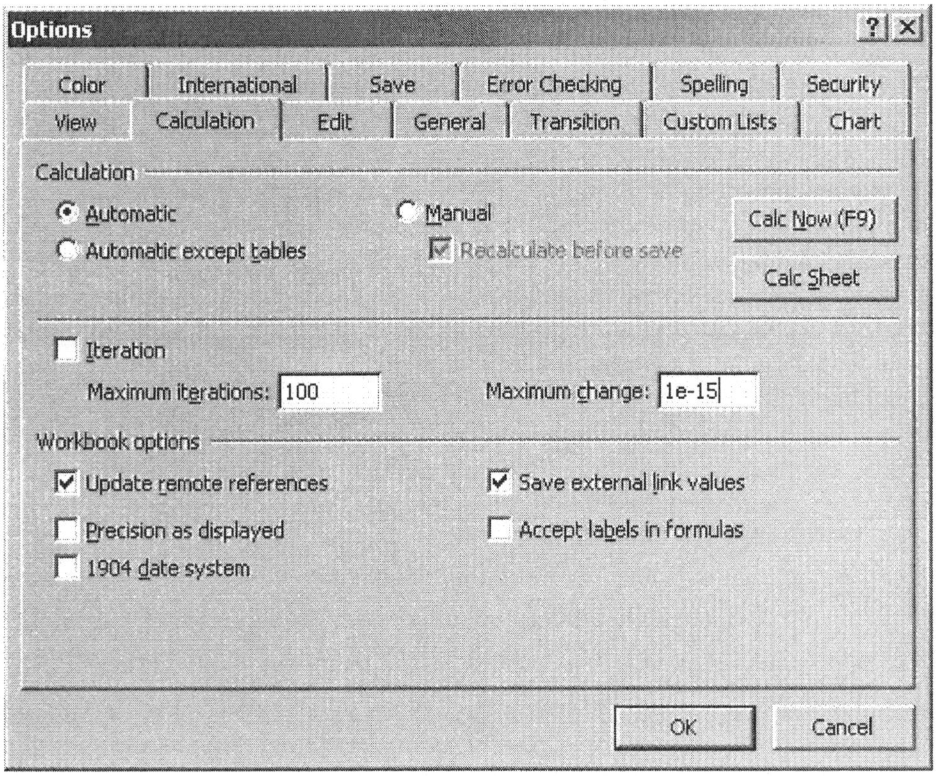

Figure 8-17. The Calculation Options dialog box.

Since **Goal Seek...** almost certainly uses something like the Newton-Raphson method to find a root, it should be clear from Figure 8-1 that the trial value that you use will determine the root that is found. The cubic equation that we used in our example, shown in Figure 8-1, has three real roots. It is clear that if 0.01 is used as initial estimate, the largest of the three roots will be calculated, while using –0.2 as an initial estimate will result in the smallest of the three roots. Thus, to obtain a particular root, some guidance must be provided by the user.

Figure 8-18 illustrates the three roots of the function obtained by using different initial estimates.

Starting Value	Root Found
0.01	0.025701
-0.20	-0.128437
-0.01	-0.027264

Figure 8-18. Different starting values lead to different roots.
(folder 'Chapter 08 Examples', workbook 'Roots of Equations', worksheet 'Using Goal Seek')

The Secant Method

The secant method is similar to the Newton-Raphson method, except that it is not necessary to calculate the slope of the curve. Instead, the slope is approximated by using two values of x, as illustrated in Figure 8-19. Although this may be a poor approximation to the tangent to the curve, it becomes more and more accurate as the iterations approach the root. This method is not self-starting, since values of the function at two adjacent x values must be provided to begin the calculation. The calculations are illustrated in Figure 8-20, applied to the function shown in equation 8-1.

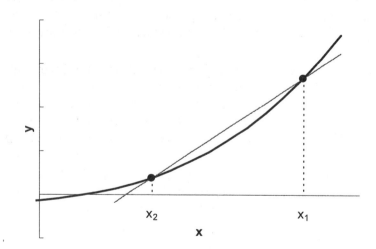

Figure 8-19. The secant method for obtaining a root of a function.

	A	B	C	D	E	F
1	Secant Method					
2	X1	Y1	X2	Y2	m	new X2
3	5	2.5251	4.9	2.2349	2.90168	4.129796266
4	4.9	2.2349	4.1297963	1.1268	1.43875	3.346645771
5	4.1297963	1.1268	3.3466458	0.8494	0.35412	0.947915289
6	3.3466458	0.8494	0.9479153	-0.6002	0.60434	1.941087368
7	0.9479153	-0.6002	1.9410874	-0.0199	0.58426	1.975206929
8	1.9410874	-0.0199	1.9752069	0.0092	0.85302	1.964457031
9	1.9752069	0.0092	1.964457	0.0000	0.85314	1.964458545
10	1.9644570	0.0000	1.9644585	0.0000	0.85314	1.964458545
11	1.9644585	0.0000	1.9644585	0.0000	0.85313	1.964458545

Figure 8-20. Using the secant method to obtain a root of a function.
(folder 'Chapter 08 Examples', workbook 'Roots of Equations', worksheet 'Secant Method')

The formulas in row 3 are identical to those in Figure 8-10, except that cell C3 contains a value rather than a formula.

The Newton-Raphson Method
Using Circular Reference and Iteration

The Newton-Raphson method discussed in a previous section requires the user to fill down formulas until convergence is observed visually. One can create a Newton-Raphson calculation that runs automatically by using an intentional circular reference.

A circular reference is created when a formula refers to itself, either directly or indirectly. If a circular reference occurs, Excel issues a "Cannot resolve circular references" message and displays a zero value in the cell. Usually, circular references occur because the user entered an incorrect cell reference in an equation. But occasionally a problem can be solved by intentionally creating a circular reference.

The calculation is illustrated in Figure 8-21. A single change was made to the worksheet in Figure 8-11. After entering the formulas in row 4, the initial value 5 in cell B4 was replaced by the formula =G4. In this way the improved estimate of x was entered as the start value of the process.

	A	B	C	D	E	F	G	H
1		Newton-Raphson Method with Circular Reference						
2				delta =	1E-08			
3		X1	Y1	X2	Y2	m	new X1	
4		5	401.5	5.00000005	401.5	245.0000	3.36122451	
5								

Figure 8-21. Calculation of a root of a function by the Newton–Raphson method (before creating intentional circular reference).
(folder 'Chapter 08 Examples', workbook 'Roots of Equations', worksheet 'Newton-Raphson circular')

When you press ENTER after typing the formula in cell G4, the "Cannot resolve circular references" message is displayed, and Excel displays a zero in the cell to indicate a circular reference, as shown in Figure 8-22.

	A	B	C	D	E	F	G	H
1		Newton-Raphson Method with Circular Reference						
2				delta =	1E-08			
3		X1	Y1	X2	Y2	m	new X1	
4		0	401.5	5.00000005	401.5	245.0000	3.36122451	
5								

Figure 8-22. Creating an intentional circular reference.
(folder 'Chapter 08 Examples', workbook 'Roots of Equations', worksheet 'Newton-Raphson circular')

To force Excel to evaluate the circular reference, using the results of the previous calculation cycle as start values for the next cycle, choose **Options...** from the **Tools** menu and choose the Calculation tab. Check the Iteration box and enter 0 in the Maximum Change box. (The default settings are Maximum Iterations = 100 and Maximum Change = 0.001.) When you press the OK button the circular reference will be evaluated. The results of the calculations are shown in Figure 8-23.

	A	B	C	D	E	F	G	H
1		Newton-Raphson Method with Circular Reference						
2				delta =	1E-08			
3		X1	Y1	X2	Y2	m	new X1	
4		1.61188963	0	1.61188964	4.3E-07	26.4431	1.61188963	
5								

Figure 8-23. Finding a root by the Newton-Raphson method and circular reference.
(folder 'Chapter 08 Examples', workbook 'Roots of Equations', worksheet 'Newton-Raphson circular')

A Newton-Raphson Custom Function

The Newton-Raphson method can also be used in the form of a custom function. The VBA code is shown in Figure 8-24.

```vba
Option Explicit
Function NewtRaph(expression, variable, Optional initial_value)
'Finds a root of a function by Newton-Raphson method.
'Expression must be a reference to a cell containing a formula.
'Variable must be a cell reference (cannot be a name).
'Initial_value can be a number, reference or omitted.
'Reference style can be either A1-style or R1C1-style.

Dim FormulaString As String, XRef As String
Dim delta_x As Double, tolerance As Double
Dim X1 As Double, X2 As Double, X3 As Double
Dim Y1 As Double, Y2 As Double
Dim m As Double
Dim I As Integer, J As Integer, NRepl As Integer
Dim temp As String, T As String, dummy As String

'Get F(x) and x.
FormulaString = expression.Formula
If Left(FormulaString, 1) <> "=" _
    Then NewtRaph = CVErr(xlErrNA): Exit Function
XRef = variable.Address

'Convert all references to absolute
'so that only text that is a reference will be replaced.
FormulaString = Application.ConvertFormula(FormulaString, xlA1, xlA1, _
xlAbsolute)

'Handle initial values that cause problems
If IsMissing(initial_value) Then initial_value = variable
If initial_value = "" Then initial_value = variable

'Set delta_x for numerical differentiation, stopping tolerance
delta_x = 0.00000001
tolerance = 0.0000000001

'Perform the Newton-Raphson procedure
X1 = initial_value
For I = 1 To 100    '100 iterations maximum
T = FormulaString       'Start with original formula each time thru loop
'Do substitution of all instances of x reference with value.
'Substitute reference, e.g., $A$2,
'with a number value, e.g., 0.2, followed by a space
'so that $A$25 becomes 0.2 5, which results in an error.
NRepl = (Len(T) - Len(Application.Substitute(T, XRef, ""))) / Len(XRef)
For J = NRepl To 1 Step -1
  temp = Application.Substitute(T, XRef, X1 & " ", J)
```

```
    If IsError(Evaluate(temp)) Then GoTo pt1
    T = temp
pt1: Next J
Y1 = Evaluate(T)

T = FormulaString      'Begin with original formula again.
If X1 = 0 Then X1 = delta_x
X2 = X1 + X1 * delta_x
For J = NRepl To 1 Step -1
    temp = Application.Substitute(T, XRef, X2 & " ", J)
    If IsError(Evaluate(temp)) Then GoTo pt2
    T = temp
pt2: Next J
Y2 = Evaluate(T)
m = (Y2 - Y1) / (X1 * delta_x)
X3 = X1 - Y1 / m
'Exit here if a root is found
If Abs(X3 - X1) < tolerance Then NewtRaph = X3: Exit Function
X1 = X3
Next I
'Exit here with error value if no root found
NewtRaph = CVErr(xlErrNA)
End Function
```

Figure 8-24. VBA code for the Newton-Raphson custom function.
(folder 'Chapter 08 Examples', workbook 'Newton-Raphson Function', module 'Module1')

The syntax of the custom function is

NewtRaph(*expression*,*variable*,*initial_value*)

Expression is a reference to a cell that contains the formula of the function, *Variable* is the cell reference of the argument to be varied (the x value of $F(x)$ or Goal Seek's changing cell) and *initial_value* is an optional argument that can be used to determine which root will be found.

To illustrate the use of the custom function, we will use it to find a root of the cubic equation $y = -2x^3 + 16x^2 + 60x - 300$. A chart of the function is shown in Figure 8-25. A portion of the data table to generate the chart is shown in columns A and B of Figure 8-26. The formula in cell B7 is

=aa*A7^3+bb*A7^2+cc*A7+dd

where aa, bb, cc and dd are the coefficients of the cubic.

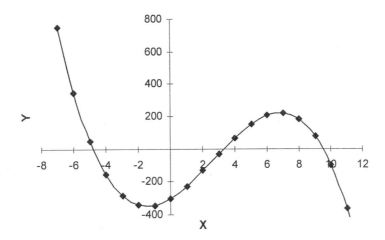

Figure 8-25. Root of a function returned by the Newton-Raphson custom function.
(folder 'Chapter 08 Examples', workbook 'Newton-Raphson Function', sheet 'Newton-Raphson')

To use the custom function, enter the function in cell C7 by typing it following the syntax above, or choose **Insert→Function...**, choose the User Defined category and choose the function from the list box. For the *expression* argument, enter a reference to a cell containing the worksheet function (e.g., cell B7 in Figure 8-26). For the variable argument, enter A7, the cell reference of the independent variable in the formula *expression*. If you do not enter a value for the optional *initial_value* argument, the value of the independent variable will be used as the starting value. When you press ENTER, a root of the function is returned, as shown in Figure 8-26.

	A	B	C	D
4	x	y	root	trial value
5	-7	750	-4.79212051203765	-100
6	-6	348	3.29634999529599	0
7	-5	50	9.49577051674166	100
8	-4	-156	-4.79212051203764	

Figure 8-26. Root of a function returned by the Newton-Raphson custom function.
(folder 'Chapter 08 Examples', workbook 'Newton-Raphson Function', sheet 'Newton-Raphson')

The root that is returned depends on the initial or trial value used by the Newton-Raphson procedure. In this example, if a relatively large negative value is used (e.g., −7), the root near −5 will be obtained. (See Figure 8-10 if this is not clear.) Some caution must be exercised in choosing a trial value to direct the procedure towards a particular root, as illustrated by the results for the same polynomial shown in Figure 8-27.

	A	B	C
4	x	y	root
17			3.29634999529599
18			-4.79212051203765
19			9.49577051674166

Figure 8-27. The root that is returned can be very sensitive to the choice of trial value. (folder 'Chapter 08 Examples', workbook 'Newton-Raphson Function', sheet 'Newton-Raphson')

If no root is found after 100 cycles of iteration, the function returns the #N/A error value.

The advantage of this custom function compared to **Goal Seek...** is, of course, that if the coefficients aa, bb, cc, or dd are changed, the value of the root is automatically updated.

Bairstow's Method
to Find All Roots of a Regular Polynomial

A regular polynomial is one that contains only integer powers of x. The Bairstow (or Bairstow-Lin) method finds all roots, both real and imaginary, of a regular polynomial with real coefficients. The method involves the successive extraction of quadratic factors from the original polynomial of degree N and subsequent reduced polynomials of degree $N–2$, $N–4$ and so on. The quadratic formula is then used to obtain pairs of roots, either real or complex, from the quadratic factors. If the degree of the polynomial is odd, then the remainder, after extracting quadratic factors, will be a linear factor, yielding the final root directly.

The calculation proceeds as follows. For the polynomial

$$y = a_n x^n + a_{n-1} x^{n-1} + \ldots + a_1 x + a_0 \tag{8-8}$$

performing *synthetic division* by a trial quadratic

$$x^2 + px + q \tag{8-9}$$

yields a quotient and a remainder.

$$y = (x^2 + px + q)(b_n x^{n-2} + b_{n-1} x^{n-3} + \ldots + b_2) + (Rx + S) \tag{8-10}$$

If $(x^2 + px + q)$ is an exact divisor, then the remainder $(Rx + S)$ will be zero. Our task therefore is to find the values of p and q that make $(Rx + S)$ equal to zero. This will make $(x^2 + rx + s)$ a quadratic factor of the polynomial.

Examination of the process of synthetic division reveals that there is a correspondence between the coefficients of the two preceding forms of the polynomial:

$$b_n = a_n \tag{8-11}$$

$$b_{n-1} = a_{n-1} - p b_n \tag{8-12}$$

$$b_{n-2} = a_{n-2} - p b_{n-1} - q b_n \tag{8-13}$$

$$\vdots$$

$$b_{n-k} = a_{n-k} - p b_{n-k+1} - q b_{n-k+2} \ (k = 2, 3, \ldots, n-1) \tag{8-14}$$

$$R = a_1 - p b_2 - q b_3 \tag{8-15}$$

$$S = a_0 - q b_2 \tag{8-16}$$

If the polynomial has been normalized so that $a_n = 1$, then the equations are simplified somewhat.

The trial quadratic will be a factor of the polynomial if the remainder is zero, that is, $R = S = 0$. Since R and S are functions of p and q:

$$R = R(p, q) \tag{8-17}$$

$$S = S(p, q) \tag{8-18}$$

we need to find the values of p and q that make R and S equal to zero. We will do this by means of a two-dimensional analog of the Newton-Raphson method. If p^* and q^* are the desired solution, then the solution can be expressed as a Taylor series

$$R(p^*, q^*) = R(p, q) + \frac{\partial b_1}{\partial p} \Delta p + \frac{\partial b_1}{\delta q} \Delta q + \cdots \tag{8-19}$$

and

$$S(p^*, q^*) = S(p, q) + \frac{\partial b_0}{\partial p} \Delta p + \frac{\partial b_0}{\partial q} \Delta q + \cdots \tag{8-20}$$

where

$$\Delta p = p^* - p \tag{8-218}$$

and

$$\Delta q = q^* - q \tag{8-22}$$

ignoring terms other that the first, since as we approach the correct answer the higher terms become negligible. The preceding result in two equations in two unknowns, which can be solved to obtain

$$\Delta p = \frac{S \dfrac{\partial R}{\partial q} - R \dfrac{\partial S}{\partial q}}{\dfrac{\partial R}{\partial p}\dfrac{\partial S}{\partial q} - \dfrac{\partial S}{\partial p}\dfrac{\partial R}{\partial q}} \qquad (8\text{-}23)$$

$$\Delta q = \frac{R \dfrac{\partial S}{\partial q} - S \dfrac{\partial R}{\partial q}}{\dfrac{\partial R}{\partial p}\dfrac{\partial S}{\partial q} - \dfrac{\partial S}{\partial p}\dfrac{\partial R}{\partial q}} \qquad (8\text{-}24)$$

To find the partial derivatives $\delta R/\delta p$, etc, we could follow the usual procedure of making a small change in p to find the corresponding change in b. Instead, we will calculate the partial derivatives using analytical expressions. Differentiating the expressions 8-11 to 8-14 with respect to p yields the following:

$$c_n = \frac{\partial b_n}{\partial p} \qquad (8\text{-}25)$$

$$c_{n-1} = \frac{\partial b_{n-1}}{\partial p} = -b_n - p\frac{\partial b_n}{\partial p} \qquad (8\text{-}26)$$

$$c_{n-2} = \frac{\partial b_{n-2}}{\partial p} = -b_{n-1} - p\frac{\partial b_{n-1}}{\partial p} - q\frac{\partial b_n}{\partial p} \qquad (8\text{-}27)$$

$$c_{n-k} = \frac{\partial b_{n-k}}{\partial p} = -b_{n-k+1} - p\frac{\partial b_{n-k+1}}{\partial p} - q\frac{\partial b_{n-k+2}}{\partial p} \qquad (8\text{-}28)$$

$$c_0 = \frac{\partial b_0}{\partial p} = -q\frac{\partial b_2}{\partial p} \qquad (8\text{-}29)$$

Equations 8-25 to 8-29 can be written in the form

$$c_n = 0 \tag{8-30}$$

$$c_{n-1} = b_n - pc_n \tag{8-31}$$

$$c_{n-2} = b_{n-1} - pc_{n-1} - qc_n \tag{8-32}$$

$$\vdots$$

$$c_{n-k} = b_{n-k} - pc_{n-k+1} - qc_{n-k+2} \tag{8-33}$$

$$c_0 = -qc_2 \tag{8-34}$$

The simultaneous equations to be solved are

$$c_2 \Delta p + c_3 \Delta q = -b_1 \tag{8-35}$$

$$c_1 \Delta p + c_2 \Delta q = -b_0 \tag{8-36}$$

Using Cramer's rule, we obtain

$$\Delta p = \frac{\begin{vmatrix} -b_1 & c_3 \\ -b_0 & c_2 \end{vmatrix}}{\begin{vmatrix} c_2 & c_3 \\ c_1 & c_2 \end{vmatrix}} \tag{8-37}$$

$$\Delta q = \frac{\begin{vmatrix} c_2 & -b_1 \\ c_1 & -b_0 \end{vmatrix}}{\begin{vmatrix} c_2 & c_3 \\ c_1 & c_2 \end{vmatrix}} \tag{8-38}$$

The procedure for calculating the roots therefore is as follows: with initial estimates of p and q (zero or one can be used), calculate the values of b_j and c_j. Use these values to calculate Δp and Δq, and correct the initial values. Continue until convergence is reached. Obtain the two roots by use of the quadratic formula. Use the result of synthetic division of the polynomial as the new polynomial, and repeat the process. Continue until the polynomial is of order one or zero.

The VBA code is shown in Figure 8-28. The portion of the code that performs the Bairstow calculation is based on code found in Shoup, T. E., *Numerical Methods for the Personal Computer*, Prentice-Hall, 1983.

This procedure contains code, not found in other procedures in this book, that allows the macro to accept a polynomial equation as a reference to a cell that contains a formula or as a reference to a cell that contains a formula as text. The procedure also handles an implicit reference.

```
Option Explicit
'+++++++++++++++++++++++++++++++++++++++++++++++++++++++++++++
Function Bairstow(equation, reference)
'Obtains the coefficients of a regular polynomial (maximum order = 6).
'Polynomial is a cell formula.
'Polynomial can contain cell references or names.
'Poynomial can be text.
'Reference can be a cell reference or a name.

Dim A() As Double, Root() As Double
Dim J As Integer, N As Integer
Dim p1 As Integer, p2 As Integer, p3 As Integer
Dim expnumber As Integer, ParenFlag As Integer
Dim R As Integer, C As Integer
Dim FormulaText As String, RefText As String, NameText As String
Dim char As String, term As String
ReDim A(6)

' GET equation EITHER AS CELL FORMULA OR AS TEXT.
If Application.IsText(equation) Then
  FormulaText = equation
'If in quotes, remove them.
  If Asc(Left(FormulaText, 1)) = 34 Then _
  FormulaText = Mid(FormulaText, 2, Len(FormulaText) - 1)
Else
  FormulaText = equation.Formula
End If
If Left(FormulaText, 1) = "=" Then FormulaText = Mid(FormulaText, 2, 1024)
FormulaText = Application.ConvertFormula(FormulaText, xlA1, xlA1, _
xlAbsolute)
FormulaText = Application.Substitute(FormulaText, " ", "") 'remove all spaces

'GET THE NAME CORRESPONDING TO reference
NameText = ""
On Error Resume Next  'Handles case where no name has been assigned
NameText = reference.Name.Name
On Error GoTo 0
NameText = Mid(NameText, InStr(1, NameText, "!") + 1)

'HANDLE CASE WHERE reference IS A RANGE
'by finding cell in same row or column as cell containing function.
If reference.Rows.Count > 1 Then
  R = equation.Row
  Set reference = Intersect(reference, Range(R & ":" & R))
ElseIf reference.Columns.Count > 1 Then
  C = equation.Column
  Set reference = Intersect(reference, Range(C & ":" & C))
```

```
End If
RefText = reference.Address

'PARSE THE FORMULA INTO TERMS
'pointers: p1, beginning; p2, end of string.
FormulaText = FormulaText & " " 'add extra character for parsing
p1 = 1
ParenFlag = 0   'Keep track of left and right parentheses
For J = 1 To Len(FormulaText)
 char = Mid(FormulaText, J, 1)
  If char = "(" Then ParenFlag = ParenFlag + 1
  If char = ")" Then ParenFlag = ParenFlag - 1
  If ((char = "+" Or char = "-") And ParenFlag = 0) Or J = Len(FormulaText) _
Then
    term = Mid(FormulaText, p1, J - p1)
    term = Application.Substitute(term, NameText, RefText)
    p2 = J: p1 = p2

'GET THE EXPONENT AND COEFFICIENT FOR EACH TERM
'p3: location of reference in term.
If InStr(1, term, RefText & "^") Then   'function returns zero if not found
'These are the x^2 and higher terms
  p3 = InStr(1, term, RefText & "^")
  expnumber = Mid(term, p3 + Len(RefText) + 1, 1)
  term = Left(term, p3 - 1) 'term is now the coefficient part
ElseIf InStr(1, term, RefText) Then
'This is the x term
  p3 = InStr(1, term, RefText)
  expnumber = 1
  term = Left(term, p3 - 1) 'term is now the coefficient part
Else
'This is the constant term
  expnumber = 0
End If

If term = "" Then term = "=1"   'If missing, Evaluate will require a string.
If term = "+" Or term = "-" Then term = term & "1"
If Right(term, 1) = "*" Then term = Left(term, Len(term) - 1)
A(expnumber) = Evaluate(term)
End If
Next J

'RESIZE THE ARRAY
For J = 6 To 0 Step -1
If A(J) <> 0 Then N = J: Exit For
Next
ReDim Preserve A(N)
ReDim Root(1 To N, 1)

'REDUCE POLYNOMIAL SO THAT FIRST COEFF = 1
For J = 0 To N: A(J) = A(J) / A(N): Next

'SCALE THE POLYNOMIAL, IF NECESSARY
'<code to be added later>
```

```
Call EvaluateByBairstowMethod(N, A, Root)
Bairstow = Root()

End Function
'++++++++++++++++++++++++++++++++++++++++++++++++++++++++++++
Sub EvaluateByBairstowMethod(N, A, Root)
'Code adapted from Shoup, "Numerical Methods for the Personal Computer".

Dim B() As Double, C() As Double
Dim M As Integer, I As Integer, J As Integer, IT As Integer
Dim P As Double, Q  As Double, delP  As Double, delQ  As Double
Dim denom As Double, S1 As Double
Dim tolerance As Double

ReDim B(N + 2), C(N + 2)
tolerance = 0.000000000000001
M = N

While M > 0
If M = 1 Then Root(M, 0) = -A(0): Call Sort(Root, N): Exit Sub
P = 0: Q = 0: delP = 1: delQ = 1
For I = 0 To N: B(I) = 0: C(I) = 0: Next
For IT = 1 To 20
If Abs(delP) < tolerance And Abs(delQ) < tolerance Then Exit For
  For J = 0 To M
    B(M - J) = A(M - J) + P * B(M - J + 1) + Q * B(M - J + 2)
    C(M - J) = B(M - J) + P * C(M - J + 1) + Q * C(M - J + 2)
  Next J
    denom = C(2) ^ 2 - C(1) * C(3)
    delP = (-B(1) * C(2) + B(0) * C(3)) / denom
    delQ = (-C(2) * B(0) + C(1) * B(1)) / denom
    P = P + delP
    Q = Q + delQ
Next IT

S1 = P ^ 2 + 4 * Q
If S1 < 0 Then
  'Handle imaginary roots
  Root(M, 0) = P / 2: Root(M, 1) = Sqr(-S1) / 2
  Root(M - 1, 0) = P / 2: Root(M - 1, 1) = -Sqr(-S1) / 2
Else
  'Handle real roots
  Root(M, 0) = (P + Sqr(S1)) / 2
  Root(M - 1, 0) = (P - Sqr(S1)) / 2
End If
For I = M To 0 Step -1: A(I) = B(I + 2): Next
M = M - 2
Wend
End Sub
'++++++++++++++++++++++++++++++++++++++++++++++++++++++++++++
Sub Sort(Root, N)
'SORT ROOTS IN ASCENDING ORDER
Dim I As Integer, J As Integer
```

```
Dim temp0 As Double, temp1 As Double

For I = 1 To N
 For J = I To N
  If Root(I, 0) > Root(J, 0) Then
    temp0 = Root(I, 0): temp1 = Root(I, 1)
    Root(I, 0) = Root(J, 0): Root(I, 1) = Root(J, 1)
    Root(J, 0) = temp0: Root(J, 1) = temp1
  End If
 Next J
Next I
End Sub
```

Figure 8-28. VBA code for the Bairstow custom function.
(folder 'Chapter 08 Examples', workbook 'Bairstow', module 'BairstowFn')

The syntax of the Bairstow function is

Bairstow(*equation,reference*)

Equation is a reference to a cell that contains the formula of the function, *reference* is the cell reference of the argument to be varied (the *x* value of *F(x)*).

The Bairstow function is an array function. To return the roots of a polynomial of order N, you must select a range of cells 2 columns by N rows, enter the function and then press CONTROL+SHIFT+ENTER.

Figure 8-29 shows a chart of the polynomial

$$y = x^3 - 0.0031x^2 + 2.3 \times 10^{-8}x + 5 \times 10^{-9}$$

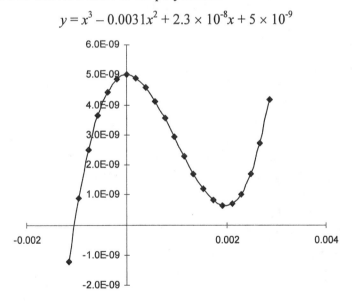

Figure 8-29. A regular polynomial with one real root and two imaginary roots.
(folder 'Chapter 08 Examples', workbook 'Bairstow', sheet 'Example')

The function has one real root and a pair of imaginary roots. Figure 8-30 shows a portion of the spreadsheet in which the Bairstow custom function is used to obtain the roots of the function.

	A	B
25		Roots:
26	Real part	Imaginary part
27	-0.001090	0
28	0.002095	-0.000447311
29	0.002095	0.000447311

Figure 8-30. Calculation of all roots (real and imaginary) of a regular polynomial by the Bairstow custom function.
(folder 'Chapter 08 Examples', workbook 'Bairstow', sheet 'Example 2')

The formula

=A2^3-0.0031*A2^2+0.000000023*A2+0.000000005

was entered in cell B2 and the Bairstow custom function

{=Bairstow(B2,A2)}

in cells A27:B29. The real part of the root is in the left cell and the imaginary part in the right cell. Note that, since the custom function handles only polynomials with real coefficients, the complex roots (if any) occur in conjugate pairs.

Finding Values Other than Zeroes of a Function

Many of the preceding methods can be modified so as to find the x of a function for a y value other than zero. In this way you can find, for example, the point of intersection of two curves (the x value where the y value of one function equals the y value of another function). Some examples follow.

Using Goal Seek...
to Find the Point of Intersection of Two Lines

It is a simple matter to use **Goal Seek...** to find the intersection of two lines, as illustrated in Figure 8-31

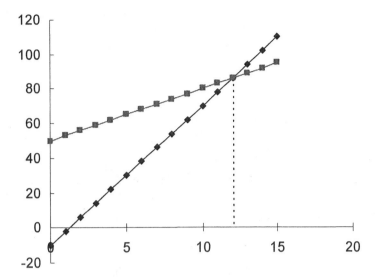

Figure 8-31. Finding the intersection of two lines in a chart.
(folder 'Chapter 08 Examples', workbook 'Intersecting Lines', sheet 'Two Straight Lines')

In the spreadsheet cells shown in Figure 8-32, the formula in cell B24 is

=slope1*A24+int1

and the formula in cell C24 is

=slope2*A24+int2

Both formulas use A24 as input. The formula in cell D24 (the target cell) is

=B24-C24

Now use **Goal Seek**… to vary A24 to make the target cell, D24, equal to zero. The result is shown in Figure 8-32.

	A	B	C	D
22	Table for intersection			
23	x	y1	y2	y1-y2
24	12	86	86	0

Figure 8-32. Using Goal Seek to find the intersection of two lines.
(folder 'Chapter 08 Examples', workbook 'Intersecting Lines', sheet 'Two Straight Lines')

This approach is very simple, but it has one major drawback—you must run **Goal Seek...** each time you want to find the point of intersection. A much more satisfactory approach is to use the Newton-Raphson technique to find the intersection point, as illustrated in the following section.

The "drop line" in Figure 8-31 was added to the chart to emphasize the intersection point. The line was added to the chart in the following way: cell A25 contains the formula =A24 and cell B25 contains the value 0. The highlighted cells A24:B25 were copied and pasted in the chart to create a new series, as follows: **Copy** A24:B25, activate the chart, choose **Paste Special** from the **Edit** menu, check the boxes for Add Cells As New Series and X Values In First Column, press OK. Figure 8-33 shows the portion of the worksheet where the drop line is specified.

	A	B	C	D
22	Table for intersection & for drop line			
23	x	y1	y2	y1-y2
24	12	86	86	0
25	12	0		

Figure 8-33. Adding a "drop line" from the intersection of two lines.
(folder 'Chapter 08 Examples', workbook 'Intersecting Lines', sheet 'Two Straight Lines')

Using the Newton-Raphson Method
to Find the Point of Intersection of Two Curves

The Newton-Raphson method can be modified to find the x value that makes a function have a specified value, instead of the zero value that was used in a previous section. Equation 8-5 becomes

$$x_2 = (mx_1 - y_1 + y_2)/m \qquad (8-38)$$

You can set up the calculation in the same way that was used for the Newton-Raphson method with intentional circular reference. In the following example we will find the intersection of a straight line and a curve (Figure 8-34).

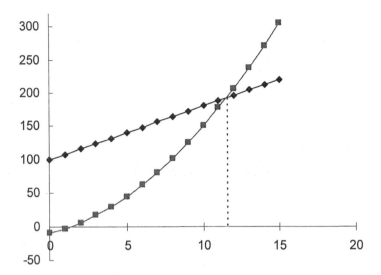

Figure 8-34. Finding the intersection of two lines in a chart.
(folder 'Chapter 08 Examples', workbook 'Intersecting Lines', sheet 'Using Circular Reference')

A portion of the data table that generated the two lines is shown in Figure 8-35.

	A	B	C
4	x	y1	y2
5	0	100	-10
6	1	108	-3
7	2	116	6
8	3	124	17
9	4	132	30
10	5	140	45

Figure 8-35. Portion of the data table for Figure 8-32.
(folder 'Chapter 08 Examples', workbook 'Intersecting Lines', sheet 'Using Circular Reference')

The formula in cell B5 is

=slope*A5+int

and in cell C5

=aa*A5^2+bb*A5+cc

Using the same method as in the preceding section, y_1 is the function for which the slope is calculated, and y_2 is the value used as the "constant." Of course, both y_1 and y_2 change as the value of x changes.

	A	B	C	D	E	F	G
36	Using modified Newton-Raphson approach to find intersection						
37	x	y1	y2	x+Δx	y1+Δy	slope	new x
38	11.536	192.285	192.285	11.536	192.285	29.07130865	11.536
39	11.536	0					

Figure 8-36. Using the Newton-Raphson method to find the intersection of two lines. (folder 'Chapter 08 Examples', workbook 'Intersecting Lines', sheet 'Using Circular Reference')

Figure 8-36 shows the cells where the Newton-Raphson calculation is performed, using an intentional circular reference (refer to the section "The Newton-Raphson Method Using Circular Reference and Iteration" earlier in this chapter if the method of calculation is not apparent). The formula in cell G38 is

=(C38+F38*A38-B38)/F38

The advantage of using the Newton-Raphson method with circular references, compared to using **Goal Seek...**, is that calculation of the x, y coordinates of the intersection occurs automatically, "in the background." If you change one or more of the parameters (for example, if you change the slope of the straight line), the new intersection point and new drop line will be calculated and displayed on the chart.

Using the Newton-Raphson Method to Find Multiple Intersections of a Straight Line and a Curve

The preceding technique can be easily extended to find multiple intersections of two curves. The following figure illustrates how to find the two intersections of a horizontal straight line with a parabola, but many other types of curve can be handled.

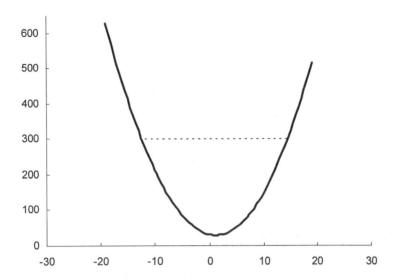

Figure 8-37. Two intersections of a straight line and a curve, calculated by using the
Newton-Raphson method with intentional circular references.
(folder 'Chapter 08 Examples', workbook 'Intersecting Lines', sheet 'Using Circular Reference (2)')

It is merely necessary to use two identical Newton-Raphson formulas and
provide two different start values that will result in convergence to the two
different "roots." Figure 8-38 illustrates the set-up of the table. Cells C66 and
C67 contain the formula

=$I$5

(pointing to the cell that contains a constant). Guided by Figure 8-37, initial x
values of 10 and −10 were chosen. Figure 8-38 shows the cell values before the
intentional circular references have been created.

	A	B	C	D	E	F	G
64	Table set-up before establishing circular references						
65	x	y1	y2	x+Δx	y1+Δy	slope	new x
66	10.000	150.0	300.0	10.00	150	27.00	15.5556
67	-10.000	210.0	300.0	-10.00	210	-33.00	-12.727

Figure 8-38. Calculating two intersections of a line and a curve
by the Newton–Raphson method (before creating intentional circular references).
(folder 'Chapter 08 Examples', workbook 'Intersecting Lines', sheet 'Using Circular Reference (2)')

Once the formulas have been entered, replace the initial x values in cells A66
and A67 by the formulas =G66 and =G67, respectively, to create the two circular
references. The "Cannot resolve circular references" message will be displayed

and the two cells will display zero values. Now choose **Options...** from the **Tools** menu and choose the Calculation tab. Check the Iteration box and press OK. Figure 8-39 shows the final values in the table, after circular reference iteration is complete.

	A	B	C	D	E	F	G
64	Table after establishing circular references						
65	x	y1	y2	x+Δx	y1+Δy	slope	new x
66	14.454	300.0	300.0	14.45	300	40.36	14.4536
67	-12.454	300.0	300.0	-12.45	300	-40.36	-12.454

Figure 8-39. Calculating two intersections of a line and a curve by the Newton–Raphson method (after creating intentional circular references). (folder 'Chapter 08 Examples', workbook 'Intersecting Lines', sheet 'Using Circular Reference (2)')

A Goal Seek Custom Function

The Newton-Raphson custom function described in a previous section was modified to create a custom function that performs goal seeking. This custom function can be used in the same way as Excel's built-in **Goal Seek** tool — to find the value of x (the changing cell) that makes the function y (the target cell) have a specified value. The VBA code is shown in Figure 8-40.

```
Option Explicit
Function GoalSeek(target_cell, changing_cell, objective_value, Optional _
initial_value) As Double
'Finds value of X to make Y have a desired value
'This is a modified version of NewtRaph

Dim tolerance As Double, incr As Double
Dim XRef As String, FormulaString As String
Dim I As Integer
Dim X1 As Double, Y1 As Double, X2 As Double, Y2 As Double
Dim m As Double

If IsMissing(initial_value) Then initial_value = changing_cell
If initial_value = "" Then initial_value = changing_cell

tolerance = 0.0000000001
incr = 0.00000001

XRef = changing_cell.Address
FormulaString = target_cell.Formula
FormulaString = Application.ConvertFormula(FormulaString, xlA1, xlA1, _
xlAbsolute)
```

```
X1 = initial_value
For I = 1 To 100
Y1 = Evaluate(Application.Substitute(FormulaString, XRef, X1))
If X1 = 0 Then X1 = incr
X2 = X1 + X1 * incr
Y2 = Evaluate(Application.Substitute(FormulaString, XRef, X2))
m = (Y2 - Y1) / (X2 - X1)
X2 = (m * X1 - Y1 + objective_value) / m
'Exit here if a root is found
If Abs((X2 - X1) / X2) < tolerance Then GoalSeek = X2: Exit Function
X1 = X2
Next I
'Exit here with error value if no root found
GoalSeek = CVErr(xlErrNA): Exit Function
End Function
End Sub
```

Figure 8-40. VBA code for the GoalSeek custom function.
(folder 'Chapter 08 Examples', workbook 'GoalSeek Fn', module 'Module1')

This custom function can be used in the same way as Excel's built-in **Goal Seek...** tool to find the value of x (the changing cell) that makes the function y (the target cell) have a specified value.

The syntax of the function is

GoalSeek(***target_cell, changing_cell, objective_value,*** *initial_value*)

The argument *target_cell* is a reference to a cell containing a formula $F(x)$. The argument *changing_cell* is a cell reference corresponding to x, the independent variable. (The formula in *target_cell* must depend on *changing_cell*.) These two arguments correspond exactly to the **Goal Seek** tool's inputs Set Cell and By Changing Cell. The argument *objective_value* (**Goal Seek**'s To Value input) is the value you want *target_cell* to attain. The optional argument *initial_value* is used, in cases where more that one value of x can result in the function $F(x)$ having the desired value, to control the value of x that is returned.

Note that when using the **Goal Seek** tool, To Value can only be a fixed value, not a cell reference, whereas when using the GoalSeek custom function, the argument can be a cell reference. Thus, when *objective_value* is changed, the GoalSeek return value updates automatically.

As an illustration, we will use the GoalSeek custom function to find the value of x that makes the function $y = x^2 + 6x - 10$ have a specified value, namely $y = 210$. In the spreadsheet shown in Figure 8-41 the table in \$A\$5:\$B20 provides the x, y values of the function that are plotted in Figure 8-42. The adjustable parameters of the function are in \$E\$5:\$E\$7. The adjustable value of the intersection point H is in cell E10. Cell D14 contains the formula

=goalseek(B5,A5,E10)

Note that the GoalSeek function does not modify the value of the changing cell (in this example cell A5) nor does it result in a change in the cell containing the function (in this example cell B5). These values are merely copied and used as inputs for the VBA code. The final value of the changing cell is returned by the GoalSeek function (in this example in cell D14). As a check, the target cell formula was entered in cell E14 so as to calculate $F(x)$ using the value of x returned by GoalSeek.

Some functions have more than one value of x that can satisfy the relationship $F(x) = objective\_value$; in these cases the user must use the optional argument *initial_value* to control the value of x that is returned.

	A	B	C	D	E
1	\multicolumn{5}{c}{**Intersecting Lines in a Chart**}
2	\multicolumn{5}{c}{(Using GoalSeek custom function to find the intersection of curve y and horizontal H)}
3	\multicolumn{5}{c}{y = aa·x² + bb·x + cc}
4	x	y		\multicolumn{2}{c}{Parameters of y}
5	0	-10		aa	1
6	1	-3		bb	6
7	2	6		cc	-10
8	3	17			
9	4	30		\multicolumn{2}{c}{Value of H}
10	5	45			210
11	6	62			
12	7	81		\multicolumn{2}{c}{Using GoalSeek Fn}
13	8	102		x	y
14	9	125		12.1327	210
15	10	150			
16	11	177			
17	12	206			
18	13	237			
19	14	270			
20	15	305			

Figure 8-41. Using the GoalSeek custom function to find the value of x
that makes the function $y = x^2 + 6x - 10$ have a specified value (here, $y = 210$).
(folder 'Chapter 08 Examples', workbook 'GoalSeek Fn', sheet 'Intersection of line with h (2)')

If you change the values of aa, bb, cc, or H, the function value will update to find the new intersection value. In contrast, if you use the **Goal Seek...** tool, you must repeat the action of goal-seeking each time you change any of the parameters.

A limitation of the GoalSeek custom function is that *target_cell* must contain the complete expression dependent on *changing_cell*. Only the instances of *changing_cell* that appear in the formula in *target_cell* will be used in the Newton-Raphson calculation.

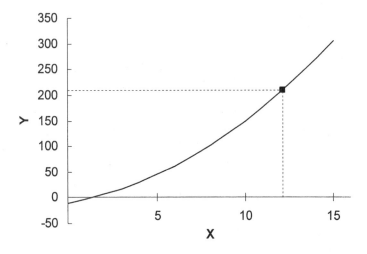

Figure 8-42. The value of x that makes the function $y = x^2 + 6x - 10$ have the value 210. (folder 'Chapter 08 Examples', workbook 'GoalSeek Fn', sheet 'Intersection of line with h (2)')

The CD contains an example of the use of the GoalSeek function to find approximately 180 intersection points of lines with a curve in a chart (see folder 'Chapter 08 Examples', workbook 'Diatomic Molecule', sheet 'Vibrational Energy Levels'). The resulting chart is shown in Figure 8-43. The chart contains two data series. The first data series shows the continuous function of energy as a function of distance r. The second data series shows the approximately 90 horizontal vibrational energy levels.

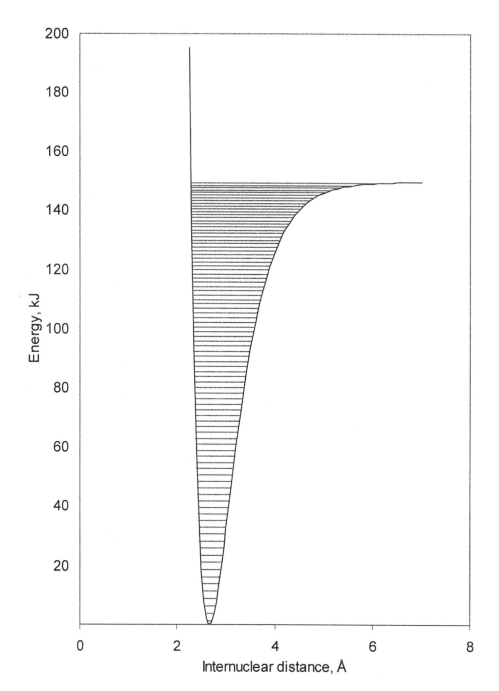

Figure 8-43. Using the GoalSeek custom function
to find multiple intersections of lines in a chart.
(folder 'Chapter 08 Examples', workbook 'Diatomic Molecule', sheet 'Sheet1')

Problems

Answers to the following problems are found in the folder "Ch. 08 (Roots of Equations)" in the "Problems & Solutions" folder on the CD.

1. A circuit consisting of a source, a resistor and a load, has a current i that oscillates as a function of time t according to the following:

$$i = 2.5\sin(\frac{\pi}{4})e^{-2.5t} + 2.5\sin(2.5t - \frac{\pi}{4})$$

Find the first time after $t = 0$ when the current reaches zero.)

2. In pipe flow problems the relationship

$$aD^3 + bD + c = 0$$

is encountered. Solve for D, if $a = 700$, $b = -2.9$, $c = -300$.

3. When the sparingly soluble salt $BaCO_3$ is dissolved in water, the following simultaneous equilibria apply:

$BaCO_3 \leftrightharpoons Ba^{2+} + CO_3^{2-}$ $K_{sp} = [Ba^{2+}][CO_3^{2-}] = 5.1 \times 10^{-9}$

$CO_3^{2-} + H_2O \leftrightharpoons HCO_3^- + OH^-$ $K_b = [OH^-][HCO_3^-]/[CO_3^{2-}] = 2.1 \times 10^{-4}$

Employing mass- and charge-balance equations, the following relationship can be obtained for a saturated solution of $BaCO_3$ in water:

$$[Ba^{2+}]^2 - \sqrt{K_b K_{sp}}\,[Ba^{2+}]^{1/2} - K_{sp} = 0$$

Find the concentration of free Ba^{2+} in the saturated solution.

4. A solution of 0.10 M nitric acid (HNO_3) is saturated with silver acetate (AgAc), a sparingly soluble salt. The system of mass- and charge-balance equations describing the system is

$[NO_3^-] = 0.10$ (mass balance)

$[Ag^+] = S$ (mass balance)

$[Ac^-] + [HAc] = S$ (mass balance)

$[Ag^+] + [H^+] = [Ac^-] + [NO_3^-]$ (charge balance)

$[Ag^+][Ac^-] = 4.0 \times 10^{-3}$ K_{sp}

$[H^+][Ac^-]/[HAc] = 1.8 \times 10^{-5}$ K_a

where S is the mol/L of silver acetate that dissolve. Using the preceding relationships, the following expression is obtained for the solubility S of silver acetate:

$$K_a\left(\frac{S^2}{K_{sp}}-1\right)+S=\frac{K_{sp}}{S}+0.10$$

Find the solubility S.

5. Find the two sets of coordinates of the intersection of the straight line $y = mx + b$, where $m = 5$ and $b = 50$, with the parabola $y = ax^2 + bx + c$, where $a = 1.1$, $b = -2.3$ and $c = -30.5$. Make a chart of the two series to show the intersections.

6. Find the two sets of coordinates of the intersection of the straight line with $y = h$ and the circle of radius r (the equation of a circle is $x^2 + y^2 = r$; thus $y = \sqrt{1-x^2}$). For example, use $r = 1$ and $h =$ some value between 0 and 1. The intersections will be at x, $y = h$ and $-x$, $y = h$. Make a chart to show the circle (values of x from -1 to 1 and calculated values of y, also same values of x and $-y$).

7. Having solved problem #8, and having created the chart, use the values of the intersections to create a chart series that shows the circumscribed rectangle (four sets of coordinates: x, $y = h$; $-x$, $y = h$; x, $y = -h$; $-x$, $y = -h$). Use any suitable method to find the coordinates of the circumscribed square.

8. For the chemical reaction

$$2A \rightleftharpoons B + 2C$$

the equilibrium constant expression is

$$K = \frac{[B][C]^2}{[A]^2}$$

For this reaction, the value of the equilibrium constant K at a certain temperature is 0.288 mol L^{-1}.

A reaction mixture is prepared in which the initial concentrations are $[A] = 1$, $[B] = 0$, $[C] = 0$ mol L^{-1}. From mass balance and stoichiometry, the concentrations at equilibrium are $[A] = 1 - 2x$, $[B] = x$, $[C] = 2x$ mol L^{-1}, from which the expression for K is $\dfrac{4x^3}{1-4x-4x^2}$. Find the value of x that makes the expression have a value of 0.288, and calculate the concentrations of A, B and C at equilibrium.

9. For the gas-phase chemical reaction

$$A + B \rightleftharpoons C + 2D$$

the equilibrium constant expression for reaction is

$$K = \frac{[C][D]^2}{[A][B]} = 15.9 \text{ atm at } 400°C.$$

A reaction mixture is prepared in which the initial concentrations are [A] = 1 atm, [B] = 2 atm, [C] = 0, [D] = 0. From mass balance and stoichiometry, the concentrations at equilibrium are [A] = 1 − x, [B] = 2 − x, [C] = x, [D] = 2x, from which the expression for K is $\dfrac{4x^3}{x^2 - 3x + 2}$. Find the value of x that makes the expression have a value of 15.9, and calculate the partial pressures of A, B, C and D at equilibrium.

10. The Reynolds number is a dimensionless quantity used in calculations of fluid flow in pipes. The Reynolds number is defined as

$$N_{Re} = \frac{D_i V \rho}{\mu}$$

where D_i is the inside diameter of the pipe, V is the average velocity of the fluid in the pipe, ρ is the fluid density and μ is the absolute viscosity of the fluid. For flow in pipes, a Reynolds number of less than 2000 indicates that the flow is laminar, while a value of greater than 10,000 indicates that the flow is turbulent. For a pipe diameter of 5 cm, and fluid of density 1 g/cm^3 and viscosity of 1 centipoise, find the minimum velocity that results in turbulent flow.

11. Find the value of the (1,1) element of the following matrix that gives a determinant value of zero.

$$\begin{bmatrix} 0.75 & 0.5 & 0.25 \\ 0.5 & 1 & 0.5 \\ 0.25 & 0.5 & 0.75 \end{bmatrix}$$

Which elements in the matrix cannot be changed in order to give a determinant of zero?

12. Use the Bairstow custom function to find all of the roots of the polynomial

$$x^5 - 10x^4 + 30x^3 - 20x^2 - 31x + 30$$

13. Use the Bairstow custom function to find all of the roots of the polynomial

$$16200000x^4 - 64800000x^3 + 97199996x^2 - 64800000x + 16200000$$

Chapter 9

Systems of Simultaneous Equations

Sometimes a scientific or engineering problem can be represented by a set of n linear equations in n unknowns, for example

$$x + 2y = 15$$
$$3x + 8y = 57$$

or, in the general case

$$a_{11}x_1 + a_{12}x_2 + a_{13}x_3 + \cdots + a_{1n}x_n = c_1$$

$$a_{21}x_1 + a_{22}x_2 + a_{23}x_3 + \cdots + a_{2n}x_n = c_2$$

$$\vdots$$

$$a_{n1}x1 + a_{n2}x_2 + a_{n3}x_3 + \cdots + a_{nn}x_n = c_n$$

where x_1, x_2, x_3,..., x_n are the experimental unknowns, c is the experimentally measured quantity, and the a_{ij} are known coefficients. The equations must be linearly independent; in other words, no equation is simply a multiple of another equation, or the sum of other equations.

A familiar example is the spectrophotometric determination of the concentrations of a mixture of n components by absorbance measurements at n different wavelengths. The coefficients a_{ij} are the ε, the molar absorptivities of the components at different wavelengths (for simplicity, the cell path length, usually 1.00 cm, has been omitted from these equations). For example, for a mixture of three species P, Q and R, where absorbance measurements are made at λ_1, λ_2 and λ_3, the equations are

$$\varepsilon_{\lambda_1}^P [P] + \varepsilon_{\lambda_1}^Q [Q] + \varepsilon_{\lambda_1}^R [R] = A_{\lambda 1}$$

$$\varepsilon_{\lambda_2}^P [P] + \varepsilon_{\lambda_2}^Q [Q] + \varepsilon_{\lambda_2}^R [R] = A_{\lambda 2}$$

$$\varepsilon_{\lambda_3}^P [P] + \varepsilon_{\lambda_3}^Q [Q] + \varepsilon_{\lambda_3}^R [R] = A_{\lambda 3}$$

This chapter describes direct methods (involving the use of matrices) and indirect (iterative) methods for the solution of such systems. The chapter begins by describing methods for the solution of systems of linear equations, and concludes by describing a method for handling nonlinear systems of equations.

Cramer's Rule

According to Cramer's rule, a system of simultaneous linear equations has a unique solution if the determinant D of the coefficients is nonzero. To obtain the solution, each unknown is expressed as a quotient of two determinants: the denominator is D and the numerator is obtained from D by replacing the column in the determinant corresponding to the desired unknown with the column of constants.

Thus, for example, for the set of equations

$$2x + y - z = 0$$
$$x - y + z = 6$$
$$x + 2y + z = 3$$

the determinant is

$$D = \begin{vmatrix} 2 & 1 & -1 \\ 1 & -1 & 1 \\ 1 & 2 & 1 \end{vmatrix}$$

The coefficients and constants lend themselves readily to spreadsheet solution, as illustrated in Figure 9-1. Using the formula =MDETERM(A2:C4), the value of the determinant is found to be –9, indicating that the system is soluble.

	A	B	C	D
1	Coefficients			Constants
2	2	1	-1	0
3	1	-1	1	6
4	1	2	1	3

Figure 9-1. Spreadsheet data for three equations in three unknowns.
(folder 'Chapter 09 Simultaneous Equations', workbook 'Simult Eqns I', sheet 'Cramer's Rule')

	A	B	C
8	0	1	-1
9	6	-1	1
10	3	2	1

Figure 9-2. The determinant for obtaining x.
(folder 'Chapter 09 Simultaneous Equations', workbook 'Simult Eqns I', sheet 'Cramer's Rule')

The x values that comprise the solution of the set of equations can be calculated in the following manner: x_k is given by a quotient in which the denominator is D and the numerator is obtained from D by replacing the kth column of coefficients by the constants c_1, c_2, ... The unknowns are obtained readily by copying the coefficients and constants to appropriate columns in another location in the sheet. For example, to obtain x, the determinant is shown in Figure 9-2, and $x = 2$ is obtained from the formula

=MDETERM(A8:C10)/MDETERM(A2:C4)

$y = -1$ and $z = 3$ are obtained from appropriate forms of the same formula.

Cramer's method is very inefficient and should be used only for systems of only a few equations.

Solving Simultaneous Equations by Matrix Inversion

Simultaneous equations can be represented in matrix notation by

$$\mathbf{AX} = \mathbf{C} \tag{9-1}$$

where $\mathbf{A}$ is the matrix of coefficients, $\mathbf{B}$ the matrix of unknowns, and $\mathbf{C}$ the matrix of constants. Multiplying both sides of equation 9-1 by $\mathbf{A}^{-1}$ yields

$$\mathbf{X} = \mathbf{A}^{-1}\mathbf{C} \tag{9-2}$$

In other words, the solution matrix is obtained by multiplying the matrix of constants by the inverse matrix of the coefficients. To return the solution values shown in Figure 9-3, the array formula

{=MMULT(MINVERSE(A2:C4),D2:D4)}

was entered in cells E2:E4.

	A	B	C	D	E
1	Coefficients			Constants	Solution
2	2	1	-1	0	2
3	1	-1	1	6	-1
4	1	2	1	3	3

Figure 9-3. Solving a set of simultaneous equations by means of matrix methods.
(folder 'Chapter 09 Simultaneous Equations', workbook 'Simult Eqns I', sheet 'Matrix Inversion')

Solving Simultaneous Equations by Gaussian Elimination

A system of linear equations such as

$$x + 2y = 15$$
$$3x + 8y = 57$$

can be solved by successive substitution and elimination of variables. For example, you can multiply the first equation by 3, so that the coefficient of x is the same as in the second equation, and then subtract it from the second equation, thus

$$3x + 8y = 57$$
$$\underline{-3x + 6y = 45}$$
$$2y = 12$$

to produce a single equation in one unknown from which $y = 6$. Using the value of y, you can now calculate x.

To extend this procedure to a system of n equations in n unknowns requires that one work in a systematic fashion. The solution process is equivalent to converting the n x n matrix above into a triangular matrix, such as the upper triangular matrix

$$a_{11}x_1 + a_{12}x_2 + a_{13}x_3 + \cdots + a_{1n}x_n = b_1$$
$$a_{22}x_2 + a_{23}x_3 + \cdots + a_{2n}x_n = b_2$$
$$a_{33}x_3 + \cdots + a_{3n}x_n = b_3$$
$$\vdots$$
$$a_{nn}x_n = b_n$$

which corresponds to a system of equations in which one of the equations contains only one unknown, and successive equations contain only one additional unknown. A similar solution process can be carried out using a lower triangular matrix.

There are several methods for the solution of systems of equations that involve a triangular matrix. The Gaussian elimination process reduces a system of linear equations to an upper triangular matrix. In the example at the beginning of this chapter, we used the first equation to eliminate x_1 from the other equation. To eliminate x_1 in a system of n equations:

$$a_{11}x_1 + a_{12}x_2 + a_{13}x_3 + \cdots + a_{1n}x_n = b_1$$
$$a_{21}x_1 + a_{22}x_2 + a_{23}x_3 + \cdots + a_{2n}x_n = b_2$$
$$a_{31}x_1 + a_{32}x_2 + a_{33}x_3 + \cdots + a_{3n}x_n = b_3$$
$$\text{etc.}$$

we multiply equation 1 by the factors a_{21}/a_{11}, a_{31}/a_{11}, ..., a_{n1}/a_{11} and subtract from equations 2, 3, ..., n. This eliminates x_1 from equations 2...n. Equation 1 is termed the pivot equation, and the coefficient of x_1 the *pivot*.

We then use equation 2 as the pivot equation, the coefficient of x_2 as the pivot, and eliminate x_2 from equations 3, ..., n.

If the pivot equation is normalized by dividing it by the coefficient of x_j, the coefficient of x_j is 1 and the calculations are simplified somewhat.

It will be instructive to show the progress of the calculations with a simple example, such as the following:

$$5x_1 + x_2 + x_3 + x_4 = 685$$
$$2x_1 - x_2 - x_3 + x_4 = 165$$
$$3x_1 - x_2 + 2x_3 - 2x_4 = 256$$
$$5x_1 - 4x_2 + 3x_3 - 2x_4 = 361$$

The Gaussian elimination method operates on an $n \times n$ matrix of coefficients, augmented by the vector of constants. In our example this matrix will be a 4×5 matrix, as shown:

$$\begin{bmatrix} 5 & 1 & 1 & 1 & 685 \\ 2 & -1 & -1 & 1 & 165 \\ 3 & -1 & 2 & -2 & 256 \\ 5 & -4 & 3 & -2 & 361 \end{bmatrix}$$

First, row 1 is normalized:

$$\begin{bmatrix} 1 & 0.2 & 0.2 & 0.2 & 137 \\ 2 & -1 & -1 & 1 & 165 \\ 3 & -1 & 2 & -2 & 256 \\ 5 & -4 & 3 & -2 & 361 \end{bmatrix}$$

The x_1 terms are eliminated from column 1 of rows 2, 3 and 4 by subtracting:

$$\begin{bmatrix} 1 & 0.2 & 0.2 & 0.2 & 137 \\ 0 & -1.4 & -1.4 & 0.6 & -109 \\ 0 & -1.6 & 1.4 & -2.6 & -155 \\ 0 & -5 & 2 & -3 & -324 \end{bmatrix}$$

Row 2 is normalized:

$$\begin{bmatrix} 1 & 0.2 & 0.2 & 0.2 & 137 \\ 0 & 1 & 1 & -0.4286 & 77.857 \\ 0 & -1.6 & 1.4 & -2.6 & -155 \\ 0 & -5 & 2 & -3 & -324 \end{bmatrix}$$

The x_2 terms are eliminated from column 2 of rows 3 and 4:

$$\begin{bmatrix} 1 & 0.2 & 0.2 & 0.2 & 137 \\ 0 & 1 & 1 & -0.4286 & 77.857 \\ 0 & 0 & 3 & -3.2857 & -30.429 \\ 0 & 0 & 7 & -5.1429 & 65.286 \end{bmatrix}$$

Row 3 is normalized and the x_3 terms are eliminated from column 3 of row 4:

$$\begin{bmatrix} 1 & 0.2 & 0.2 & 0.2 & 137 \\ 0 & 1 & 1 & -0.4286 & 77.857 \\ 0 & 0 & 1 & -1.0952 & -10.143 \\ 0 & 0 & 0 & 2.5238 & 136.29 \end{bmatrix}$$

Row 4 is normalized:

$$\begin{bmatrix} 1 & 0.2 & 0.2 & 0.2 & 137 \\ 0 & 1 & 1 & -0.4286 & 77.857 \\ 0 & 0 & 1 & -1.0952 & -10.143 \\ 0 & 0 & 0 & 1 & 54 \end{bmatrix}$$

As you can see, the coefficients matrix is now an upper triangular matrix, with the diagonal elements equal to one. The results are obtained by successive substitution, beginning with the last row. The last row corresponds to $x_4 = 154$, the third row corresponds to $x_3 - 0.272727x_4 = 107$, from which $x_3 = 149$, and so on. The results, x_1, x_2, x_3 and x_4 are 106, 52, 49, 54, respectively. You can see the steps in Gaussian elimination calculation by using the demo program provided on the CD (folder 'Chapter 09 Simultaneous Equations', workbook 'Simult Lin Eqns', sheet 'Gaussian Elimination Demo').

The Gaussian elimination method can also be performed by using the VBA custom function GaussElim. The VBA code is shown in Figure 9-4.

The syntax of the function is GaussElim(***coeff_matrix,const_vector***). The function returns the results vector; since the function is an array function, you must select an appropriately sized range of cells and press CTRL+SHIFT+ENTER (Windows) or COMMAND+RETURN or CTRL+SHIFT+RETURN (Macintosh).

```
Option Base 1
Option Explicit
Function GaussElim(coeff_matrix, const_vector)

Dim AugMatrix() As Double, ResultVector() As Double
Dim NormFactor As Double
Dim temp As Double, term As Double, ElimFactor As Double
Dim I As Integer, J As Integer, K As Integer
Dim C As Integer, R As Integer
Dim N As Integer

N = coeff_matrix.Rows.Count
ReDim AugMatrix(N, N + 1), ResultVector(N)

'Create augmented matrix with dimensions N x (N+1)
For I = 1 To N
For J = 1 To N
  AugMatrix(I, J) = coeff_matrix(I, J)
Next J, I
For J = 1 To N
  AugMatrix(J, N + 1) = const_vector(J)
Next

For K = 1 To N
'Normalize each row, from column K to right.
'If normalization factor zero, swap rows
NormFactor = AugMatrix(K, K)
If NormFactor = 0 Then
  For J = 1 To N + 1
    temp = AugMatrix(K, J)
    AugMatrix(K, J) = AugMatrix(K + 1, J)
    AugMatrix(K + 1, J) = temp
  Next J
NormFactor = AugMatrix(K, K)
End If
For C = K To N + 1
  AugMatrix(K, C) = AugMatrix(K, C) / NormFactor
Next C

'Eliminate
For R = K + 1 To N
  ElimFactor = AugMatrix(R, K)
  For C = K To N + 1
    AugMatrix(R, C) = AugMatrix(R, C) - AugMatrix(K, C) * ElimFactor
  Next C
Next R

Next K

'Calculate and return the coefficients.
'Selected range can be either horizontal or vertical.
For K = N To 1 Step -1
```

```
ResultVector(K) = AugMatrix(K, N + 1)
term = 0
For C = N To K + 1 Step -1
  term = term + AugMatrix(K, C) * ResultVector(C)
Next C
ResultVector(K) = AugMatrix(K, N + 1) - term
Next K
If Range(Application.Caller.Address).Rows.Count > 1 Then
  GaussElim = Application.Transpose(ResultVector)
Else
  GaussElim = ResultVector
End If
End Function
```

Figure 9-4. VBA code for the Gaussian Elimination custom function.
(folder 'Chapter 09 Simultaneous Equations', workbook 'Simult Eqns II', module 'GaussianElimFunction')

The calculation proceeds essentially as described in the example. First, the elements of the working matrix AugMatrix are populated by reading in the values from the *coeff_matrix* and *const_vector* arguments. Then, in a loop, each row is normalized by dividing by the appropriate diagonal element, and Gaussian elimination is performed on the following rows. When all rows have been done, the results are calculated, beginning with the last row of the upper diagonal matrix.

The custom function GaussElim contains some features not discussed in the worked-out example. As you can see from the example, the diagonal elements of the coefficients matrix are the pivots and are used to normalize the matrix. If the process of elimination results in a zero diagonal element, subsequent normalization using that pivot value will result in a divide-by-zero error. Thus it is necessary to check that the pivot value is not zero before normalizing. If the pivot is zero, one can swap this row with one below it before normalizing and proceeding with the elimination step. However, if we have reached the last row of the matrix, we swap the last and first rows, but in this case we must swap rows in the original matrix and start over from the beginning.

The Gauss-Jordan Method

The Gauss-Jordan method utilizes the same augmented matrix [A|C] as was used in the Gaussian elimination method. In the Gaussian elimination method, only matrix elements below the pivot row were eliminated; in the Gauss-Jordan method, elements both above and below the pivot row are eliminated, resulting in a unit coefficient matrix:

$$\begin{bmatrix} 1 & 0 & 0 & 0 & 116 \\ 0 & 1 & 0 & 0 & 72 \\ 0 & 0 & 1 & 0 & 149 \\ 0 & 0 & 0 & 1 & 154 \end{bmatrix}$$

The advantage of this method is that the calculation of the vector of results is simplified.

The VBA custom function GaussJordan1, shown in Figure 9-5 incorporates partial pivoting. Two versions are provided on the CD that accompanies this book: the first version, GaussJordan1, has the syntax GaussJordan1(*coeff_matrix, const_vector, value_index*). The *value_index* argument specifies the element of the results vector to be returned. The second version, GaussJordan2, has the syntax GaussJordan2(*coeff_matrix, const_vector*), and returns the vector of results. You must select an appropriately sized range of cells and press CTRL+SHIFT+ENTER (Windows) or COMMAND+RETURN or CTRL+SHIFT+RETURN (Macintosh).

```
Option Base 1
Option Explicit
'Solving systems of linear equations by the Gauss-Jordan elimination method
'++++++++++++++++++++++++++++++++++++++++++++++++++++++++++++++
Function GaussJordan1(coeff_matrix, const_vector, value_index)
' This version returns a single element of the solution vector,
' specified by value_index.

Dim X() As Double, AugMatrix() As Double, PivotRow() As Integer
Dim PivotLogical() As Boolean
Dim I As Integer, J As Integer
Dim R As Integer, C As Integer, P As Integer
Dim N As Integer
Dim TempMax As Double, factor As Double

N = coeff_matrix.Rows.Count
ReDim X(N), AugMatrix(N, N + 1), PivotRow(N), PivotLogical(N)

'Create augmented matrix (A|B) with dimensions N x (N+1)
For I = 1 To N
For J = 1 To N
   AugMatrix(I, J) = coeff_matrix(I, J)
Next J, I
For J = 1 To N
  AugMatrix(J, N + 1) = const_vector(J)
Next J

'Initialize pivot elements for each row
For J = 1 To N: PivotLogical(J) = False: Next
```

```
'Do the elimination by columns.
For C = 1 To N

'Find maximum value in column
TempMax = 0
For R = 1 To N
If Abs(AugMatrix(R, C)) <= TempMax Then GoTo LoopEnd
If PivotLogical(R) = True Then GoTo LoopEnd
PivotRow(C) = R
TempMax = Abs(AugMatrix(R, C))
LoopEnd: Next R

'Test the coefficient matrix for singularity.
If TempMax < 1E-100 Then
GaussJordan1 = CVErr(xlErrDiv0)
Exit Function
End If

'Matrix element(P,C) is pivot element.
P = PivotRow(C)
PivotLogical(P) = True
For J = 1 To N
   If J <> P Then
      factor = AugMatrix(J, C) / AugMatrix(P, C)
      For R = C + 1 To N + 1
      AugMatrix(J, R) = AugMatrix(J, R) - factor * AugMatrix(P, R)
      Next R
   End If
Next J
Next C

'Calculate the solution vector and return the specified element.
For C = 1 To N
   P = PivotRow(C)
   X(C) = AugMatrix(P, N + 1) / AugMatrix(P, C)
Next C
GaussJordan1 = X(value_index)
End Function
```

Figure 9-5. VBA code for the Gauss-Jordan custom function.
(folder 'Chapter 09 Simultaneous Equations', workbook 'Simult Eqns II', module 'GaussJordanFunction')

Figures 9-6 and 9-7 illustrate the use of the GaussElim and GaussJordan functions to solve systems of simultaneous equations, in this case the spectrophotometric determination of the concentrations of a mixture of n components by absorbance measurements at n different wavelengths, as described in the beginning of this chapter. The absorbance of a six-component mixture was measured at six wavelengths; in Figure 9-3 the sample absorbances are in column H and the known molar absorptivities of the six components are in B5:G10.

	A	B	C	D	E	F	G	H
3		molar absorptivities of species 1-6						
4	Wavelength, nm	ε_1	ε_2	ε_3	ε_4	ε_5	ε_6	absorbance
5	400	192	19.1	51.8	1.59	3.2	0.11	0.3548
6	450	17.5	190	53.5	6.3	6.6	0.0	0.4805
7	500	3.5	55.9	157	29.5	12.7	0.19	0.5185
8	550	2.5	7.9	15.9	223	27.9	0.79	0.5075
9	600	0.83	1.4	3.1	38.2	218	1.3	0.2598
10	650	0.19	0.16	0.15	15.9	105	0.80	0.1167

Figure 9-6. Data table for use with the GaussElim or GaussJordan functions.
(folder 'Chapter 09 Simultaneous Equations', workbook 'Simult Eqns II', sheet 'Elimination Fns')

Figure 9-7 shows the results returned by the GaussElim and GaussJordan2 functions. The results vector is the vector of concentrations of the six components in the mixture. The percentage error figures in columns L and N are the errors between the known concentrations and the concentrations returned by the functions.

As the number of simultaneous equations becomes larger, the errors can increase drastically. In this system of equations, the values of the first through fifth variables can be obtained with good precision, since each has a maximum where the other species do not absorb strongly. The concentration of the sixth species is subject to significant error. And if the absorbance measurements are changed randomly by just ± 1 in the last figure (Figure 9-8), the errors increase significantly.

	J	K	L	M	N
3	Results				
4	Concs used	GaussElim	% error	GaussJordan	% error
5	0.001043	0.001043	0.02	0.001043	0.02
6	0.001711	0.001711	0.02	0.001711	0.02
7	0.002239	0.002239	0.03	0.002239	0.03
8	0.001935	0.001935	0.02	0.001935	0.02
9	0.000789	0.000788	0.05	0.000788	0.05
10	0.002825	0.002925	9.6	0.002925	9.6

Figure 9-7. Results from the GaussElim or GaussJordan functions.
(folder 'Chapter 09 Simultaneous Equations', workbook 'Simult Eqns II', sheet 'Elimination Fns')

	J	K	L	M	N
3	Results				
4	Concs used	GaussElim	% error	GaussJordan	% error
5	0.001043	0.001044	0.06	0.001044	0.06
6	0.001711	0.001711	0.03	0.001711	0.03
7	0.002239	0.002239	0.03	0.002239	0.03
8	0.001935	0.001936	0.09	0.001936	0.09
9	0.000789	0.000792	0.25	0.000792	0.25
10	0.002825	0.002364	44	0.002364	44

Figure 9-8. Results from the GaussElim or GaussJordan functions
when small changes are made in the coefficients (compare Figure 9-7),
(folder 'Chapter 09 Simultaneous Equations', workbook 'Simult Eqns II', sheet 'Elimination Fns')

Solving Linear Systems by Iteration

The equations shown at the beginning of this chapter for a system of n equations in n unknowns can be rearranged so as to give a set of equations for the n variables

$$x_1 = (c_1 - a_{12}x_2 - a_{13}x_3 \ldots - a_{1n}x_n)/a_{11}$$

$$x_2 = (c_2 - a_{23}x_3 \ldots - a_{2n}x_n - a_{21}x_1)/a_{22}$$

and so on.

The variables can be evaluated by means of an iterative procedure: with initial guesses of the $x_1 \ldots x_n$ values, new values of the variables are calculated, using the above equations. These values are used in successive cycles of iteration until the value of each of the variables has converged, based on a specified tolerance.

Compared to the direct methods that have been described, iterative methods are particularly efficient for the solution of *sparse matrices*. Sparse matrices are ones in which most of the elements are zero. Physical systems in which the equations involve only a few of the variables are described by sparse matrices.

The following sections describe two iterative methods: the Jacobi method and the Gauss-Seidel method.

The Jacobi Method
Implemented on a Worksheet

In the Jacobi method, new values for all the n variables are calculated in each iteration cycle, and these values replace the previous values only when the iteration cycle is complete. The Jacobi method is sometimes called the *method of simultaneous replacement.* Improvement in one of the variables does not have an effect until the next cycle of iteration. For this reason it does not converge as rapidly as the Gauss-Seidel method, to be described in the following section.

To illustrate, consider a system of order 3,

$$a_{11}x_1 + a_{12}x_2 + a_{13}x_3 = c_1$$
$$a_{21}x_1 + a_{22}x_2 + a_{23}x_3 = c_2$$
$$a_{31}x_1 + a_{32}x_2 + a_{33}x_3 = c_3$$

These equations can be rearranged to give

$$x_1 = \frac{c_1 - a_{12}x_2 - a_{13}x_3}{a_{11}}$$

$$x_2 = \frac{c_2 - a_{21}x_1 - a_{23}x_3}{a_{22}}$$

$$x_3 = \frac{c_3 - a_{31}x_1 - a_{32}x_2}{a_{33}}$$

Begin with initial estimates for x_1, x_2 and x_3; in the following example, initial estimates of zero were used. Then solve for each unknown value; thus

$$x_1 = \frac{c_1 - 0 - 0}{a_{11}}$$

$$x_2 = \frac{c_2 - 0 - 0}{a_{22}}$$

$$x_3 = \frac{c_3 - 0 - 0}{a_{33}}$$

In the second iteration,

$$x_1 = \frac{c_1 - a_{12}x_2 - a_{13}x_3}{a_{11}}$$

and so on.

The Jacobi method is shown implemented on a spreadsheet. Figure 9-9 shows the table of coefficients and constants.

	B	C	D	E
3	coefficients matrix			constants
4	3	1	-1	181.05
5	1	2	-1	108.35
6	1	1	5	142.55

Figure 9-9. Data table for use with the Jacobi method.
(folder 'Chapter 09 Simultaneous Equations', workbook 'Simult Eqns II', sheet 'Jacobi Method')

Figure 9-10 illustrates the portion of the spreadsheet where the Jacobi method is implemented. Row 9 contains suitable initial values.

	B	C	D	E
8	x1	x2	x3	% error (x1)
9	0	0	0	
10	60	54	29	735.0
11	51.8	38.3	5.6	120.5
12	49.5	31.1	10.5	353.3
13	53.5	34.7	12.4	49.0
14	52.9	33.6	10.9	8.0
15	52.8	33.2	11.2	23.6
16	53.03	33.39	11.33	3.3
17	52.99	33.32	11.22	0.5
18	52.98	33.29	11.25	1.6
19	53.002	33.306	11.255	0.2
20	53.000	33.301	11.248	0.04
21	52.999	33.299	11.250	0.1
22	53.0001	33.3004	11.2503	0.015
23	53.0000	33.3001	11.2499	2.38E-03
24	52.9999	33.3000	11.2500	6.98E-03
25	53.000010	33.300027	11.250023	9.68E-04
26	52.999998	33.300007	11.249993	1.59E-04
27	52.999995	33.299997	11.249999	4.65E-04
28	53.0000006	33.3000018	11.2500015	6.45E-05
29	52.9999999	33.3000004	11.2499995	1.06E-05
30	52.9999997	33.2999998	11.2499999	3.10E-05
31	53.00000004	33.30000012	11.25000010	4.30E-06
32	53	33.3	11	7.05E-07

Figure 9-10. Satisfactory convergence is reached with the Jacobi method after 23 iteration cycles.
(folder 'Chapter 09 Simultaneous Equations', workbook 'Simult Eqns II', sheet 'Jacobi Method')

Cells B10, C10 and D10 contain, respectively, the formulas

=($E$4-$C$4*C9-$D$4*D9)/$B$4

=($E$5-$B$5*B9-$D$5*D9)/$C$5

=($E$6-$B$6*B9-$C$6*C9)/$D$6

When these formulas are filled down into successive rows, as shown in Figure 9-10, the values of the variables x_1, x_2 and x_3 converge. Convergence to a suitable level is observed visually. In this particular example, twenty-three iteration cycles were required to get below the 10^{-6} percent error level (here, the percentage error in the variable x_1 is shown).

The Gauss-Seidel Method Implemented on a Worksheet

In the Gauss-Seidel method, an improved value of one of the variables is used in the iteration cycle as soon as it has been calculated. The Gauss-Seidel method is sometimes called the *method of successive replacement*.

To illustrate, consider the same system of order 3 that was used previously to illustrate the Jacobi method. Again, begin with initial estimates of zero for x_1, x_2 and x_3. Now solve for each unknown value in turn, using the latest values of the variables as they are calculated; thus

$$x_1 = \frac{c_1 - 0 - 0}{a_{11}}$$

$$x_2 = \frac{c_2 - a_{21}x_1 - 0}{a_{22}}$$

$$x_3 = \frac{c_3 - a_{31}x_1 - a_{32}x_2}{a_{33}}$$

In the second iteration,

$$x_1 = \frac{c_1 - a_{12}x_2 - a_{13}x_3}{a_{11}}$$

and so on.

Using the same constants and coefficients that were used in the preceding example (Figure 9-10), the spreadsheet formulas in Figure 9-11 can be modified to implement the Gauss-Seidel method, in which the value of a variable is used as soon as it is calculated. The formulas in cells B14, C14 and D14 are, respectively,

=($E$8-$C$8*C13-$D$8*D13)/$B$8

=($E$9-$B$9*B14-$D$9*D13)/$C$9

=($E$10-$B$10*B14-$C$10*C14)/$D$10

and, as can be seen in Figure 9-11, the formulas converge more rapidly to the specified level of precision.

	A	B	C	D	E
12	iteration	x1	x2	x3	% error (X1
13		0	0	0	
14	1st	60	24	12	735.0
15	2nd	56.2	31.9	10.9	323.0
16	3rd	53.4	32.9	11.3	35.3
17	4th	53.1	33.2	11.2	11.9
18	5th	53.0	33.3	11.2	1.6
19	6th	53.0	33.3	11.2	0.5
20	7th	53.00	33.30	11.25	0.1
21	8th	53.00	33.30	11.25	0.0
22	9th	53.00	33.30	11.25	0.0
23	10th	53.000	33.300	11.250	0.0
24	11th	53.000	33.300	11.250	0.00
25	12th	53.000	33.300	11.250	0.0
26	13th	53.0000	33.3000	11.2500	0.000
27	14th	53.0000	33.3000	11.2500	1.03E-06
28	15th	53.0000	33.3000	11.2500	1.93E-07
29	16th	53.000000	33.300000	11.250000	4.08E-08
30	17th	53.000000	33.300000	11.250000	7.79E-09

Figure 9-11. Satisfactory convergence is reached with the Gauss-Seidel method after 15 iteration cycles.
(folder 'Chapter 09 Simultaneous Equations', workbook 'Simult Eqns II', sheet 'Gauss-Seidel 1')

You may wish to experiment with changing the values of the coefficients. In particular, see the effect of making the diagonal elements large, or off-diagonal elements large.

The Gauss-Seidel Method
Implemented on a Worksheet
Using Circular References

The worksheet in the preceding section can be easily modified to use intentional circular references, as follows. After entering the starting values in row 13 and the formulas in row 14 as before (Figure 9-11), change the cell references in the formulas in cells B14 and C14 from references to row 13 to references to row 14.   The formulas in cells B14, C14 and D14 are now, respectively,

=($E$8-$C$8*C14-$D$8*D14)/$B$8

=($E$9-$B$9*B14-$D$9*D14)/$C$9

=($E$10-$B$10*B14-$C$10*C14)/$D$10

This produces the "Cannot resolve circular references" error message.   Then choose **Tools→Options…**, choose the Calculation tab, check the Iteration box and change the Maximum Change parameter to a suitable small value, such as 1E-10 or even zero.   When you press OK, the final values of the variables are returned, as shown in Figure 9-12.   Cell A14 contains the formula =A14+1, and shows that, in this example, one hundred cycles of iteration (the default value in **Tools→Options→Calculation**) were performed.

	A	B	C	D	E
12	iteration	x1	x2	x3	% error (X1)
13					
14	100	53.000000	33.300000	11.250000	0.00E+00

Figure 9-12. The Gauss-Seidel method using intentional circular references.
(folder 'Chapter 09 Simultaneous Equations', workbook 'Simult Eqns II', sheet 'Gauss-Seidel 2')

A Custom Function Procedure for the Gauss-Seidel Method

The Gauss-Jacobi and the Gauss-Seidel methods can easily be implemented as a custom function.   Since the Gauss-Seidel method is more efficient, only the Gauss-Seidel custom function is presented here.   The VBA code is shown in Figure 9-13.

If any of the diagonal elements of the coefficients matrix are zero, a divide-by-zero error will be produced.   Thus it is necessary either to ensure that the coefficients matrix does not contain any zero diagonal terms before beginning the solution, or to incorporate code to swap rows if a zero diagonal element is encountered.   The GaussSeidel2 procedure (not shown) includes swapping if a diagonal element = 0.

```
Option Base 1
Option Explicit
'+++++++++++++++++++++++++++++++++++++++++++++++++++++++++++
Function GaussSeidel(coeff_matrix, const_vector, Optional init_values)
' Solving systems of linear equations by the GaussSeidel method.
' Coefficients matrix cannot have zero diagonal element.

Dim ResultVector() As Double
Dim I As Integer, J As Integer, K As Integer
Dim N As Integer, NIterations As Integer
Dim R As Integer, C As Integer
Dim ConvergeFlag As Boolean
Dim result As Double, sum As Double

N = coeff_matrix.Rows.Count
If coeff_matrix.Columns.Count <> N Or const_vector.Rows.Count _
<> N Then GaussSeidel = CVErr(xlErrRef): Exit Function
ReDim ResultVector(N)

' Following shows code for either fixed or adjustable iteration parameters.
' MaxChange and MaxIterations are set in the Tools/Options/Calculation menu.
tolerance = 0.00000001
NIterations = 100

' User can specify optional initial values for the calculation.
' This may be helpful for large arrays.
If Not (IsMissing(init_values)) Then
' Test if init_values is a Range.
  If Not (IsError(init_values.Address)) Then
    If init_values.Rows.Count = 1 Then
      K = init_values.Columns.Count
    Else
      K = init_values.Rows.Count
    End If
  Else
' init_values must be an expression.
    K = UBound(init_values)
  End If
  For I = 1 To K
    ResultVector(I) = init_values(I)
  Next I
End If

' Begin the iteration process.
For J = 1 To NIterations
' Flag will be set to false if any of the result values has not yet converged.
ConvergeFlag = True
' Do each row in the matrix.
For R = 1 To N
  sum = 0
'  Sum each term in the row, but skip term on the diagonal.
  For C = 1 To N
    sum = sum + coeff_matrix(R, C) * ResultVector(C)
```

```
Next C
sum = sum - coeff_matrix(R, R) * ResultVector(R)
' Calculate the current result value
result = (const_vector(R) - sum) / coeff_matrix(R, R)
' If result exceeds previous value by more than tolerance,set flag to false.
If Abs(ResultVector(R) - result) > tolerance Then ConvergeFlag = False
' Save the current value.
ResultVector(R) = result
Next R
' When all terms are done in this loop, exit if all have converged.
If ConvergeFlag = True Then GaussSeidel = _
Application.Transpose(ResultVector): Exit Function
Next J
' Did not converge, so send back an error value.
GaussSeidel = CVErr(xlErrNA)
End Function
```

Figure 9-13. VBA code for the Gauss-Seidel method.
(folder 'Chapter 09 Simultaneous Equations', workbook 'Simult Eqns II', module 'GaussSeidelFunction')

Solving Nonlinear Systems by Iteration

Systems of nonlinear equations, as exemplified by

$$w^3 + 2x^2 + 3y - 4z = -2.580$$
$$wx - xy + yx = -3.919$$
$$w^2 + 2wx + x^2 = 1.000$$
$$w + x + y - z = -3.663$$

or

$$2 \sin x + 3 \cos y = 0.4119$$
$$2 e^x + 3 \ln y = 3.427$$

can only be solved by iterative methods. Newton's iteration method is the most commonly used method for solving systems of nonlinear equations.

Newton's Iteration Method

In a manner similar to that in Chapter 6, we can express each of the n simultaneous equations:

$$F_1(x_1, x_2, \ldots, x_n) = c_1$$
$$F_2(x_1, x_2, \ldots, x_n) = c_2$$

$$F_n(x_1, x_2, \ldots, x_n) = c_n$$

as a Taylor series expansion, e.g.,

$$c_1 = F_1(x_1 + \Delta x_1, \cdots, x_n + \Delta x_n)$$

$$= F_1(x_1, x_2, \cdots, x_n) + \Delta x_1 \frac{\partial F_1}{\partial x_1} + \cdots + \Delta x_n \frac{\partial F_1}{\partial x_n} + \text{higher-order terms}$$

where the Δx_i values are the corrections to the initial estimates of the x_i values, for example, $x_1 = x_1 + \Delta x_1$.

As before, we can obtain a good approximation to the $\dfrac{\partial F_i}{\partial x_j}$ terms by

calculating $\Delta F_i / \Delta x_j$ (see Chapter 6, "Differentiation").

The problem has thus been reduced to a linear system

$$\begin{bmatrix} \dfrac{\partial F_1}{\partial x_1} & \dfrac{\partial F_1}{\partial x_2} & \cdots & \dfrac{\partial F_1}{\partial x_n} \\ \vdots & & & \\ \dfrac{\partial F_n}{\partial x_1} & \cdots & \cdots & \dfrac{\partial F_n}{\partial x_n} \end{bmatrix} \cdot \begin{bmatrix} \Delta x_1 \\ \vdots \\ \Delta x_n \end{bmatrix} = \begin{bmatrix} c_1 \\ \vdots \\ c_n \end{bmatrix}$$

that can be solved by methods that have already been described in this chapter.

The solution process is as follows: with initial estimates of the x_i values, we obtain the $\dfrac{\partial F_i}{\partial x_j}$ values by numerical differentiation. We set up the matrix of partial derivatives augmented by the vector of constants and solve for the Δx_j variables. We then use these to calculate improved estimates of the x_i values, calculate new values of the $\dfrac{\partial F_i}{\partial x_j}$ terms and solve for the Δx_j variables. We repeat the process until the magnitude of the Δx_j variables is smaller than a specified tolerance.

The VBA code for the SimultEqNL function is shown in Figure 9-14. The syntax of the function is SimultEqNL(**equations,variables,constants**).

The arguments have the same meaning as for the preceding GaussElim, GaussJordan, or GaussSeidel functions. The function returns the results vector; since the function is an array function, you must select an appropriately sized range of cells and press CTRL+SHIFT+ENTER (Windows) or COMMAND+RETURN or CTRL+SHIFT+RETURN (Macintosh).

```
Option Explicit
Option Base 1
'+++++++++++++++++++++++++++++++++++++++++++++++++++++++++++++++++
Function SimultEqNL(equations, variables, constants)
'Newton iteration method to find roots of nonlinear simultaneous equations

Dim I As Integer, J As Integer, K As Integer, N As Integer
Dim NIterations As Integer
Dim R As Integer, C As Integer
Dim VarAddr() As String, FormulaString() As String
Dim con() As Double, A() As Double, B() As Double
Dim V() As Double
Dim Y1 As Double, Y2 As Double
Dim tolerance As Double, incr As Double

N = equations.Rows.Count
K = variables.Rows.Count
If K = 1 Then K = variables.Columns.Count
If K <> N Then SimultEqNL = CVErr(xlErrRef): Exit Function
ReDim VarAddr(N), FormulaString(N), V(N), con(N)
ReDim A(N, N + 1), B(N, N + 1)

tolerance = 0.000000000001  'Convergence criterion.
incr = 0.0000000001   'Increment for numerical differentiation.
NIterations = 50

For I = 1 To N
VarAddr(I) = variables(I).Address
Next

'Initial values
For I = 1 To N
con(I) = constants(I).Value
V(I) = variables(I).Value: If V(I) = 0 Then V(I) = 1
Next

For J = 1 To NIterations
'Create N x N matrix of partial derivatives.
For R = 1 To N
 For C = 1 To N
'  FormulaString is formula in which all but one variable in each equation
'  is replaced by current values.
   FormulaString(R) = Application.ConvertFormula(equations(R).Formula, _
xlA1, xlA1, xlAbsolute)
     For I = 1 To N
     If I <> C Then FormulaString(R) = Application.Substitute( _
FormulaString(R), VarAddr(I), V(I))
     Next I
'Calculate partial derivative (central differences).
   Y2 = Evaluate(Application.Substitute(FormulaString(R), VarAddr(C), _
     V(C) * (1 + incr)))
   Y1 = Evaluate(Application.Substitute(FormulaString(R), VarAddr(C), _
```

```
      V(C) * (1 - incr)))
   A(R, C) = (Y2 - Y1) / (2 * incr * V(C))
  Next C
Next R

'Augment matrix of derivatives with vector of constants.
For R = 1 To N
  FormulaString(R) = Application.ConvertFormula(equations(R).Formula, _
     xlA1, xlA1, xlAbsolute)
  For C = 1 To N
   FormulaString(R) = Application.Substitute(FormulaString(R), VarAddr(C), _
     V(C))
  Next C
 A(R, N + 1) = con(R) - Evaluate(FormulaString(R))
Next R

For I = 1 To N
If Abs((A(I, N + 1)) / V(I)) > tolerance Then GoTo Refine
Next I
SimultEqNL = Application.Transpose(V)
Exit Function

Refine: Call GaussJordan3(N, A, B)
'Update V values
For I = 1 To N
V(I) = V(I) + A(I, N + 1)
Next I
Next J

' Exit here if no convergence after 50 cycles of iteration
SimultEqNL = CVErr(xlErrNA)
End Function
'++++++++++++++++++++++++++++++++++++++++++++++++++++++++++++++++
Sub GaussJordan3(N, AugMatrix, TempMatrix)
Dim I As Integer, J As Integer, K As Integer, L As Integer, P As Integer
Dim pivot As Double, temp As Double

For K = 1 To N
' Locate largest matrix element, use as pivot.
pivot = AugMatrix(K, K): P = K
For L = K + 1 To N
If Abs(AugMatrix(L, K)) < Abs(pivot) Then GoTo EndOfLoop
pivot = AugMatrix(L, K)
P = L
EndOfLoop: Next L

' Swap rows
For J = 1 To N + 1
temp = AugMatrix(K, J)
AugMatrix(K, J) = AugMatrix(P, J)
AugMatrix(P, J) = temp
Next J
```

```
' Normalize pivot row
For J = 1 To N + 1
TempMatrix(K, J) = AugMatrix(K, J) / pivot
Next J
' Do the Gauss elimination.
For I = 1 To N
If I = K Then GoTo EndOfLoop2
For J = 1 To N + 1
TempMatrix(I, J) = AugMatrix(I, J) - AugMatrix(I, K) * TempMatrix(K, J)
Next J
EndOfLoop2: Next I

For I = 1 To N
For J = 1 To N + 1
AugMatrix(I, J) = TempMatrix(I, J)
Next J
Next I

Next K
End Sub
```

Figure 9-14. VBA code for the SimultEqnNL function procedure.
(folder 'Chapter 09 Simultaneous Equations', workbook 'NonLinNewton', module 'NewtonIterationIFunction')

As an example of the use of the SimultEqNL function, consider the following set of four equations:

$$w^3 + 2w^2 + 3w + 4 = 12.828$$
$$wx + xy + yz = -3.919$$
$$w^2 + 2wx + x^2 = 1$$
$$w + x + y - z = -3.663$$

The corresponding Excel formulas were entered in E11:E14 of Figure 9-15, as follows:

```
=A11^3+2*A11^2+3*A11+4
```

```
=A11*B11+B11*C11+C11*D11
```

```
=A11^2+2*A11*B11+B11^2
```

```
=A11+B11+C11-D11
```

The constants were entered in cells F11:F14 and trial values of the unknowns in cells A11:D11.

	A	B	C	D	E	F	G
9		Variables					
10	w	x	y	z	Equations	Constants	Results
11	1	1	1	-1	10.000	12.828	1.250
12					1.000	-3.919	-0.250
13					4.000	1.000	-3.330
14					4.000	-3.663	1.333

Figure 9-15. A custom function for the Newton method for nonlinear equations.
(folder 'Chapter 09 Simultaneous Equations', workbook 'NonLinNewton', sheet 'Figure 9-16')

The custom function was entered in cells G11:G14 as an array formula:

{=SimultEqNL(E11:E14,A11:D11,F11:F14)}

and returned the values of the variables w, x, y and z shown in Figure 9-15. You can confirm for yourself that this set of results satisfies the set of equations by entering the results in the four variables cells and see that the values in the "Equations" cells agree with the values in the "Constants" cells.

The custom function can be entered in the "Variables" cells so that the "Results" appear there. This creates a circular reference, so you must check the iteration box in **Tools→Options→Calculation**.

Again, be aware that attempting to solve large systems of equations, or even small sets of ill-conditioned equations, can lead to erroneous results.

Problems

Answers to the following problems are found in the folder "Ch. 09 (Simultaneous Equations)" in the "Problems & Solutions" folder on the CD.

1. Solve the following system of four simultaneous equations:

$$3x_1 + 1.1x_2 - 2x_3 - 1.8x_4 = 11$$
$$3.2x_1 + 2.1x_2 + 3.2x_3 + 2.2x_4 = 0$$
$$3.4x_1 + 2.3x_2 + 4.1x_3 + 3.2x_4 = 6$$
$$1.6x_1 + 1.1x_2 - 3.2x_3 + 2.4x_4 = -5$$

2. Current flow in a circuit is described by Kirchhoff's laws. A particular circuit network yielded the following three simultaneous linear equations:

$$I_1 + I_2 - I_3 = 0$$
$$2I_1 + 5I_3 = 7$$
$$2I_1 - 4I_2 = 2$$

Find the currents I_1, I_2 and I_3 in the circuit network.

3. Solve the following system of four simultaneous equations:

$$2.829x_1 - 2.253x_2 + 6.777x_3 + 3.970x_4 = 6.235$$
$$1.212x_1 + 1.995x_2 + 2.265x_3 + 8.008x_4 = 7.319$$
$$4.553x_1 + 5.681x_2 + 8.850x_3 + 1.302x_4 = 5.730$$
$$5.808x_1 - 5.030x_2 + 0.098x_3 + 7.832x_4 = 9.574$$

4. The UV-visible spectra of aqueous solutions of $CoCl_2$, $NiCl_2$ and $CuCl_2$ are shown in Figure 9-16.

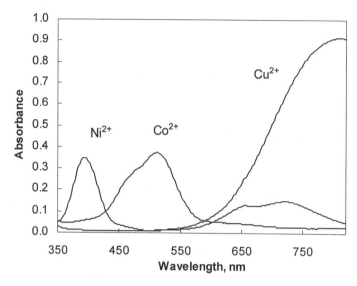

Figure 9-16. UV-visible spectra of cobalt, nickel and copper solutions.

Three wavelengths were chosen at which the absorbance of the three species, Co^{2+}, Ni^{2+} and Cu^{2+}, differed significantly. The molar absorptivities of the three species at the three wavelengths are shown in Table 9-1.

Table 9- 1. Molar Absorptivity ε, $M^{-1}cm^{-1}$

λ/nm	Co^{2+}	Ni^{2+}	Cu^{2+}
394	0.995	6.868	0.188
510	6.450	0.215	0.198
808	0.469	1.179	15.052

A mixture of the three metal ions gave the following absorbance readings at the three wavelengths: 394 nm, 0.845; 510 nm, 0.388; 808 nm, 1.696, when measured using a cell with a 1.00-cm path length. Calculate the concentration of the three metal ions in the mixture, using Beer's Law: $A = \varepsilon bc$ (A = absorbance, ε = molar absorptivity, b = cell path length in cm, c = concentration in mol/L).

5. The following sets of simultaneous equations may or may not be solvable by the Gaussian Elimination method. For each case, explain why. If solvable, solve.

(a)
$$x + y + 3z = 5$$
$$2x + 2y + 2z = 14$$
$$3x + 3y + 9z = 15$$

(b)
$$\begin{bmatrix} 2 & -1 & 1 \\ 1 & 3 & 2 \\ 3 & 2 & 3 \end{bmatrix} \begin{bmatrix} 4 \\ 12 \\ 16 \end{bmatrix}$$

(c)
$$2x - y + z = 0$$
$$x + 3y + 2z = 0$$
$$3x + 2y + 3z = 0$$

(d)
$$x_1 + x_2 + x_3 - x_4 = 2$$
$$x_1 - x_2 - x_3 + x_4 = 0$$
$$2x_1 + x_2 - x_3 + 2x_4 = 9$$
$$3x_1 + x_2 + 2x_3 - x_4 = 7$$

6. Solve the following system of six simultaneous equations:

$$\begin{bmatrix} 2.97 & 0.75 & 1.23 & 2.08 & 1.26 & 0 \\ 2.34 & 2.38 & 1.23 & 1.23 & 1.94 & 2.07 \\ 1.23 & 0.52 & 0 & 3.66 & 0.18 & 0.51 \\ 1.84 & 1.89 & 2.64 & 2.65 & 0.51 & 0.38 \\ 1.48 & 0.40 & 2.88 & 1.46 & 0 & 2.65 \\ 2.94 & 1.55 & 1.71 & 1.06 & 2.46 & 2.97 \end{bmatrix} = \begin{bmatrix} 7.93 \\ 9.79 \\ 26.19 \\ 5.10 \\ 8.43 \\ -15.74 \end{bmatrix}$$

7. Solve the following system of nonlinear equations:
$$x^2 + y^2 = 1$$
$$x^2 - y^2 = 0$$

8. Solve the following system of nonlinear equations:

$$xyz = 2$$
$$x^2 + y^2 + 4z^2 = 9$$
$$2x^2 + y^3 + 6z = 4$$

Chapter 10

Numerical Integration of Ordinary Differential Equations Part I: Initial Conditions

A differential equation is an equation that involves one or more derivatives. Many physical problems, when formulated mathematically, lead to differential equations. For example, the equation ($k > 0$)

$$\frac{dy}{dt} = -ky \tag{10-1}$$

describing the decrease in y as a function of time, occurs in the fields of reaction kinetics, radiochemistry or electrical engineering (where y represents concentration of a chemical species, or atoms of a radioactive element, or electrical charge, respectively) as well as in many other fields. Of course, a differential equation can be more complicated that the one shown in equation 10-1; another example from electrical engineering is shown in equation 10-2,

$$L\frac{di}{dt} + Ri = E \tag{10-2}$$

where R is the resistance in a circuit, L is the inductance, E is the applied potential, i is the current and t is time.

If a differential equation contains derivatives of a single independent variable, it is termed an ordinary differential equation (ODE), while an equation containing derivatives of more than one independent variable is called a partial differential equation (PDE). Partial differential equations are discussed in a subsequent chapter.

The general form of an ordinary differential equation is

$$\frac{dy}{dx} = F(x, y) \tag{10-3}$$

217

and although writing the differential equation, such as the above, may be simple, solving the problem is not. By "solving," we mean that we want to be able to calculate the value of y for any value of x. Some differential equations, such as 10-1, are solvable by symbolic integration (the integrated equation is $\ln y = -kt +$ const), but many others may not be amenable to solution by the "pencil-and-paper" approach. Numerical methods, however, can always be employed to find the value of the function at various values of t. Although we haven't found an expression for the function $F(x, y)$, but simply obtained a table of y values as a function of x, the process is often referred to as "integration."

You may remember from your freshman calculus class that when an expression is integrated, an arbitrary constant of integration is always part of the solution. For example, when equation 10-1 is integrated, the result is $\ln y = -kt + \ln y_0$, or $y_t = y_0 e^{-kt}$. A similar situation pertains when numerical methods are employed: to solve the problem, one or more values of the dependent variable and/or its derivative must be known at specific values of the independent variable. If these are given at the zero value of the independent variable, the problem is said to be an initial-value problem; if they are given at some other values of the independent variable, the problem is a boundary-value problem. This chapter deals with initial-value problems, while the following chapter deals with boundary-value problems.

Solving a Single
First-Order Differential Equation

This section describes methods for solving first-order differential equations with initial conditions (the *order* of a differential equation is determined by the order of the highest derivative in the equation). Two methods will be described: Euler's method and the Runge–Kutta method. Euler's method is simple in concept, but not of sufficient accuracy to be useful; it is included here because it illustrates the basic method of calculation and can be modified to yield methods of higher accuracy. The Runge-Kutta method, of which there are several variants, is the usual method of choice. A third method, the predictor-corrector method, will be described later in this chapter.

Euler's Method

Let us use in our first calculation an example of equation 10-1: the first-order kinetic process $A \rightarrow B$ with initial concentration $C_0 = 0.2000$ mol/L and rate constant $k = 5 \times 10^{-3}$ s^{-1}. We'll simulate the change in concentration of the species A vs. time over the interval from $t = 0$ to $t = 600$ seconds, in increments of 20 seconds.

The differential equation for the change in concentration of the species A as a function of time is

$$d[A]/dt = -k[A] \qquad (10\text{-}4)$$

Expressing this in terms of finite differences, the change in concentration $\Delta[A]$ that occurs during the time interval from $t = 0$ to $t = \Delta t$ is

$$\Delta[A] = -k[A]_t\, \Delta t \qquad (10\text{-}5)$$

Thus, if the concentration of A at $t = 0$ is 0.2000 M, then the concentration at $t = (0 + \Delta t)$ is $[A] = 0.2000 - (5 \times 10^{-3})(0.2000)(20) = 0.1800$ M. The calculation, known as *Euler's method*, is illustrated in Figure 10-1. The formula in cell B7 is

=B6-k*B6*DX.

The concentrations at subsequent time intervals are calculated in the same way. In general, the formula is

$$y_{n+1} = y_n + hF(x_n, y_n) \qquad (10\text{-}6)$$

where $h = x_{n+1} - x_n$.

	A	B	C	D
1	Simulation of first order kinetics by Euler's Method			
2	rate constant =	5.0E-03		(k)
3	time increment =	20		(DX)
4				
5	t	C_t (Euler)	C_t (exact)	
6	0	0.2000	0.2000	
7	20	0.1800	0.1810	
8	40	0.1620	0.1637	
9	60	0.1458	0.1482	
10	80	0.1312	0.1341	
11	100	0.1181	0.1213	
12	120	0.1063	0.1098	
13	140	0.0957	0.0993	

Figure 10-1. Simulation of first-order kinetics by Euler's method.
(folder 'Chapter 10 Examples', workbook 'ODE Examples', worksheet 'Euler')

The advantage of Euler's method is that it can be easily expanded to handle systems of any complexity. It is not particularly useful, however, since the error introduced by the approximation $d[A]/dt = \Delta[A]/\Delta t$ is compounded with each additional calculation. Compare the Euler's method result in column B of Figure

10-1 with the analytical expression for the concentration, $[A]_t = [A]_0 e^{-kt}$, in column C. At the end of approximately one half-life (seven cycles of calculation in this example), the error has already increased to 3.6%. Accuracy can be increased by decreasing the size of Δt, but only at the expense of increased computation. A much more efficient way of increasing the accuracy is by means of a series expansion. The Runge–Kutta methods, which are described next, comprise the most commonly used approach.

The Fourth-Order Runge–Kutta Method

The Runge–Kutta methods for numerical solution of the differential equation $dy/dx = F(x, y)$ involve, in effect, the evaluation of the differential function at intermediate points between x_n and x_{n+1}. The value of y_{n+1} is obtained by appropriate summation of the intermediate terms in a single equation. The most widely used Runge–Kutta formula involves terms evaluated at x_n, $x_{n+\Delta x/2}$ and $x_{n+\Delta x}$. The *fourth-order Runge–Kutta* equations for $dy/dx = F(x, y)$ are

$$y_{n+1} = y_n + \frac{T_1 + 2T_2 + 2T_3 + T_4}{6} \Delta x \qquad (10\text{-}7)$$

where
$$T_1 = F(x_n, y_n) \qquad (10\text{-}8)$$

$$T_2 = F(x_n + \frac{\Delta x}{2}, y_n + \frac{T_1}{2}) \qquad (10\text{-}9)$$

$$T_3 = F(x_n + \frac{\Delta x}{2}, y_n + \frac{T_2}{2}) \qquad (10\text{-}10)$$

$$T_4 = F(x_n + \Delta x, y_n + T_3) \qquad (10\text{-}11)$$

If more than one variable appears in the expression, then each is corrected by using its own set of T_1 to T_4 terms.

Fourth-Order Runge-Kutta Method Implemented on a Worksheet

The spreadsheet in Figure 10-2 illustrates the use of the RK method to simulate the first-order kinetic process A → B, again using initial concentration $[A]_0 = 0.2000$ and rate constant $k = 5 \times 10^{-3}$. The differential equation is, again, equation 10-4. This equation is of the simple form $dy/dx = F(y)$, and thus only the y_i terms of T_1 to T_4 need to be evaluated. The RK terms (note that T_1 is the Euler method term) are shown in equations 10-12 through 10-15.

$$T_1 = -k[A]_t \, \Delta x \tag{10-12}$$

$$T_2 = -k([A]_t + T_1/2) \, \Delta x \tag{10-13}$$

$$T_3 = -k([A]_t + T_2/2) \, \Delta x \tag{10-14}$$

$$T_4 = -k([A]_t + T_3) \, \Delta x \tag{10-15}$$

	A	B	C	D	E	F	G
1			Runge-Kutta simulation of first order kinetics				
2			rate constant=		5.0E-03	(k)	
3			time increment=		20	(DX)	
4							
5	t	TA1	TA2	TA3	TA4	RK	exact
6	0					0.2000	0.2000
7	20	-0.0200	-0.0190	-0.0191	-0.0181	0.1810	0.1810
8	40	-0.0181	-0.0172	-0.0172	-0.0164	0.1637	0.1637
9	60	-0.0164	-0.0156	-0.0156	-0.0148	0.1482	0.1482
10	80	-0.0148	-0.0141	-0.0141	-0.0134	0.1341	0.1341
11	100	-0.0134	-0.0127	-0.0128	-0.0121	0.1213	0.1213
12	120	-0.0121	-0.0115	-0.0116	-0.0110	0.1098	0.1098
13	140	-0.0110	-0.0104	-0.0105	-0.0099	0.0993	0.0993

Figure 10-2. Simulation of first-order kinetics by the Runge–Kutta method. (folder 'Chapter 10 Examples', workbook 'ODE Examples', worksheet 'RK1')

The RK equations in cells B7, C7, D7, E7 and F7, respectively, are (only part of the spreadsheet is shown; the formulas extend down to row 74):

=-k*F6*DX

=-k*(F6+TA1/2)*DX

=-k*(F6+TA2/2)*DX

=-k*(F6+TA3)*DX

=F6+(TA1+2*TA2+2*TA3+TA4)/6.

If you use the names TA1, ..., TA4 you can use **AutoFill** to generate the column labels TA1, ..., TA4. These names are accepted by Excel, whereas T1 is not a valid name. As well, the nomenclature is expandable to systems requiring more than one set of Runge–Kutta terms (e.g., TB1, ..., TB4, etc.).

Compare the RK result in column F of Figure 10-2 with the analytical expression for the concentration, $[A]_t = [A]_o e^{-kt}$, in column G. After one half-life (row 13) the RK calculation differs from the analytical expression by only

0.00006%. (Compare this with the 3.6% error in the Euler method calculation at the same point.) Even after 10 half-lives (not shown), the RK error is only 0.0006%.

In essence, the fourth-order Runge–Kutta method performs four calculation steps for every time interval. The percent error after one half-life ($t = 140$) is only 6×10^{-5}%. In contrast, in the solution by Euler's method, decreasing the time increment to 5 seconds to perform four times as many calculation steps still only reduces the error to 0.9% after 1 half-life.

If the spreadsheet is constructed as shown in Figure 10-2, you can't use a formula in which a name is assigned to the values of the calculated concentration in column F (the range $F$7:$F$74). This is because the formula in B7, for example, will use the concentration in F7; this is called an implicit intersection. An alternative arrangement that permits using a name for the concentration $[A]_t$ is shown in Figure 10-3. Each row contains the concentration at the beginning and at the end of the time interval. The name C_t can now be assigned to the array of values in column B; the former formulas (now in cells $C$7:$G$74) contain C_t in place of F6 and cell B7 contains the formula =G6.

	A	B	C	D	E	F	G	H
1	Runge-Kutta simulation of first order kinetics							
2			rate constant=		5.0E-03	(k)		
3			time increment=		20	(DX)		
4								
5	t	C_t	TA1	TA2	TA3	TA4	RK	exact
6	0	0.2000	-0.0200	-0.0190	-0.0191	-0.0181	0.1810	0.1810
7	20	0.1810	-0.0181	-0.0172	-0.0172	-0.0164	0.1637	0.1637
8	40	0.1637	-0.0164	-0.0156	-0.0156	-0.0148	0.1482	0.1482
9	60	0.1482	-0.0148	-0.0141	-0.0141	-0.0134	0.1341	0.1341
10	80	0.1341	-0.0134	-0.0127	-0.0128	-0.0121	0.1213	0.1213
11	100	0.1213	-0.0121	-0.0115	-0.0116	-0.0110	0.1098	0.1098
12	120	0.1098	-0.0110	-0.0104	-0.0105	-0.0099	0.0993	0.0993
13	140	0.0993	-0.0099	-0.0094	-0.0095	-0.0090	0.0899	0.0899
14	160	0.0899	-0.0090	-0.0085	-0.0086	-0.0081	0.0813	0.0813

Figure 10-3. Alternative spreadsheet layout for the Runge–Kutta method. (folder 'Chapter 10 Examples', workbook 'ODE Examples', worksheet 'RK2')

The RK equations in cells C6, D6, E6, F6 and G6, respectively, are

=-k*C_t*DX

=-k*(C_t+TA1/2)*DX

=-k*(C_t+TA2/2)*DX

=-k*(C_t+TA3)*DX

=C_t+(TA1+2*TA2+2*TA3+TA4)/6

and cell B7 contains the formula =G6.

Fourth-Order Runge-Kutta Method Applied to a Differential Equation Involving Both x and y

In the preceding examples, the differential equation involved only the dependent variable y. In the general case, the differential equation can be a function of both x and y. The following example illustrates the use of the Runge-Kutta method for $dy/dx = F(x, y)$.

A function is described by the differential equation

$$dy/dx = 2x^2 + 2y \qquad (10\text{-}16)$$

and the function has the value $y = 0.5$ at $x = 0$. We want to find the value of the function over the range $x = 0$ to $x = 1$. Figure 10-4 illustrates the use of the RK method to model the function. The formulas for the T_1–T_4 terms, in cells B11 to E11 are, respectively,

=2*A10^2+2*F10

=2*(A10+deltax/2)^2+2*(F10+B11*deltax/2)

=2*(A10+deltax/2)^2+2*(F10+C11*deltax/2)

	A	B	C	D	E	F	G	H
7			Formula for TA2: F(x+Δx/2, y+T1*Δx/2)					
8			Formula for Y: y + (T1+2*T2+2*T3+T4)*Δx/6					
9	X	TA1	TA2	TA3	TA4	Y	Y(exact)	% error
10	0.0					0.5000	0.5000	
11	0.1	1.000	1.105	1.116	1.243	0.6114	0.6114	1.8E-06
12	0.2	1.243	1.392	1.407	1.584	0.7518	0.7518	4.0E-06
13	0.3	1.584	1.787	1.807	2.045	0.9321	0.9321	6.6E-06
14	0.4	2.044	2.314	2.341	2.652	1.1655	1.1655	9.3E-06
15	0.5	2.651	3.001	3.036	3.438	1.4683	1.4683	1.2E-05
16	0.6	3.437	3.885	3.930	4.443	1.8601	1.8601	1.5E-05
17	0.7	4.440	5.009	5.066	5.713	2.3652	2.3652	1.7E-05
18	0.8	5.710	6.426	6.498	7.310	3.0130	3.0130	2.0E-05
19	0.9	7.306	8.202	8.291	9.304	3.8396	3.8396	2.2E-05
20	1.0	9.299	10.414	10.526	11.784	4.8889	4.8891	2.4E-05

Figure 10-4. The fourth-order Runge–Kutta method applied to $y' = 2x^2+2y$. (folder 'Chapter 10 Examples', workbook 'ODE Examples', worksheet 'Both x and y (Formulas)')

```
=2*(A10+deltax)^2+2*(F10+D11*deltax)
```

and the formula for y_{n+1}, in cell F11, is

```
=F10+(B11+2*C11+2*D11+E11)*deltax/6
```

Figure 10-4 shows the agreement between the RK values and the exact values (the unknown function is $y = e^{2x} - x^2 - x - 0.5$). The errors are small and increase only slowly with increasing x.

Fourth-Order Runge-Kutta Custom Function for a Single Differential Equation with the Derivative Expression Coded in the Procedure

The Runge-Kutta formulas can be implemented in the form of a VBA custom function. The VBA code is shown in Figure 10-5.

This first version can handle a single first-order ordinary differential equation; the expression for the derivative must be "hard-wired" in the VBA code. The syntax of the function is Runge(*x_variable, y_variable, interval*). The function returns the value of y (the dependent variable) at $x + \Delta x$, based on the values of x (the independent variable), y and a differential equation. The arguments *x_variable* and *y_variable* are references to cells containing the values of x and y in the derivative expression coded in the subroutine. The argument *interval* is a value or cell reference or formula that specifies the interval of x over which the Runge-Kutta integration is to be calculated.

```
Option Explicit
Function Runge(x_variable, y_variable, interval)
'Runge-Kutta method to solve a single first-order ODE.
'Expression for derivative must be coded in subroutine.
Dim T1 As Double, T2 As Double, T3 As Double, T4 As Double
' Calculate the RK terms
T1 = interval * deriv(x_variable, y_variable)
T2 = interval * deriv(x_variable + interval / 2, y_variable + T1 / 2)
T3 = interval * deriv(x_variable + interval / 2, y_variable + T2 / 2)
T4 = interval * deriv(x_variable + interval, y_variable + T3)
Runge = y_variable + (T1 + 2 * T2 + 2 * T3 + T4) / 6
End Function
'++++++++++++++++++++++++++++++++++++++++++++++++++++++++++++++++++
Function deriv(X, Y)
'Code the derivative here.
deriv = 2 * X ^ 2 + 2 * Y
End Function
```

Figure 10-5. Simple custom function for Runge-Kutta calculation.
(folder 'Chapter 10 Examples', workbook 'ODE Examples', module 'SimpleRungeKutta')

Figure 10-6 illustrates the use of the custom function. The formula in cell C9 is

=Runge(A8,C8,A9-A8)

	A	B	C	D
7	X	Y(exact)	Y(Runge)	% error
8	0.0	0.50000	0.50000	
9	0.1	0.61140	0.61140	1.8E-06
10	0.2	0.75182	0.75182	4.0E-06
11	0.3	0.93212	0.93211	6.6E-06
12	0.4	1.16554	1.16553	9.3E-06
13	0.5	1.46828	1.46826	1.2E-05
14	0.6	1.86012	1.86009	1.5E-05
15	0.7	2.36520	2.36516	1.7E-05
16	0.8	3.01303	3.01297	2.0E-05
17	0.9	3.83965	3.83956	2.2E-05
18	1.0	4.88906	4.88894	2.4E-05

Figure 10-6. The fourth-order Runge–Kutta method applied to $y' = 2x^2+2y$
by using a user-defined function.
(folder 'Chapter 10 Examples', workbook 'ODE Examples', worksheet 'Both x and y (Simple RK function)')

In following sections, procedures will be provided to handle systems of simultaneous differential equations. In addition, the VBA code will be modified so that the expression for the derivative is passed to the function as an argument.

Fourth-Order Runge-Kutta Custom Function for a Single Differential Equation with the Derivative Expression Passed as an Argument

The custom function Runge described in the preceding section simplifies the solution of an ordinary differential equation, but the VBA code must be modified for each case. The custom function to be described next permits the user to enter the expression for the derivative as an Excel formula in a worksheet cell and pass the expression to the custom function as an argument. This custom function uses the method employed in previous chapters: the **Formula** property is used to obtain the formula of (in this case) the derivative, the SUBSTITUTE function to replace a cell reference in the formula with a value, and the **Evaluate** method to calculate the value of the function. The VBA code is shown in Figure 10-7. The syntax of the function is Runge1(*x_variable, y_variable, deriv_formula, interval*). The arguments *x_variable* (the independent variable), *y_variable* (the dependent variable) and *interval* are as described in the previous section; the argument *deriv_formula* is a reference to a cell containing the derivative in the form of worksheet formula.

A more advanced version that handles multiple differential equations will be presented later.

```vba
Option Explicit
Function Runge1(x_variable, y_variable, deriv_formula, interval)
'Runge-Kutta method to solve ordinary differential equations.
'Solves problems involving a single first-order differential equation.
'Derivative expression passed as an argument.

Dim FormulaText As String
Dim XAddress As String, YAddress As String
Dim X As Double, Y As Double
Dim H As Double, result As Double

'GET THE FORMULA AND REFERENCE ARGUMENTS
FormulaText = deriv_formula.Formula
'Make all references absolute
FormulaText = Application.ConvertFormula(FormulaText, xlA1, xlA1, _
xlAbsolute)
XAddress = x_variable.Address     'absolute is default
X = x_variable.Value
YAddress = y_variable.Address     'absolute is default
Y = y_variable.Value
Runge1 = RK1(XAddress, YAddress, X, Y, interval, FormulaText)
End Function
'+++++++++++++++++++++++++++++++++++++++++++++++++++++++++++
Private Function RK1(XAddress, YAddress, X, Y, H, FormulaText)
' Calculate the RK terms
Dim T1 As Double, T2 As Double, T3 As Double, T4 As Double
Dim result As Double

Call eval(XAddress, YAddress, X, Y, FormulaText, result)
T1 = result * H
Call eval(XAddress, YAddress, X + H / 2, Y + T1 / 2, FormulaText, result)
T2 = result * H
Call eval(XAddress, YAddress, X + H / 2, Y + T2 / 2, FormulaText, result)
T3 = result * H
Call eval(XAddress, YAddress, X + H, Y + T3, FormulaText, result)
T4 = result * H
RK1 = Y + (T1 + 2 * T2 + 2 * T3 + T4) / 6
End Function
'+++++++++++++++++++++++++++++++++++++++++++++++++++++++++++
Sub eval(XRef, YRef, XValue, YValue, FormulaText, result)
'Evaluates the derivative formula.  Replaces each instance of, e.g., $A$2 in
formula with number value, e.g., 0.20, then evaluates.
'Must do this replacement from end of formula to beginning.
'Modified 03/08/06 to handle possible un-intended replacement of e.g., $A$2 in
$A$22.
'Method: replace $A$2 with value & " "
'so that $A$22 becomes "0.20 2" and this formula evaluates to an error.
```

```
Dim T As String, temp As String
Dim NRepl As Integer, J As Integer
Dim dummy As Double

T = FormulaText
'First, do substitution of all instances of x address with value
NRepl = (Len(T) - Len(Application.Substitute(T, XRef, ""))) / Len(XRef)
For J = NRepl To 1 Step -1
   temp = Application.Substitute(T, XRef, XValue & " ", J)
   On Error GoTo ErrorHandler1
   dummy = Evaluate(temp)
   T = temp
pt1: Next J
'Then do substitution of all instances of y address with value
NRepl = (Len(T) - Len(Application.Substitute(T, YRef, ""))) / Len(YRef)
For J = NRepl To 1 Step -1
   temp = Application.Substitute(T, YRef, YValue & " ", J)
   On Error GoTo ErrorHandler2
   dummy = Evaluate(temp)
   T = temp
pt2: Next J
result = Evaluate(T)
Exit Sub

'ERROR HANDLER ROUTINES.
ErrorHandler1:
'Trappable error number 13 (Type mismatch) is expected.
If Err.Number = 13 Then
   On Error GoTo 0      'Disable the error handler.
   Resume pt1      'and continue execution.
Else
   End      'Some other error, so quit completely
End If
ErrorHandler2:
If Err.Number = 13 Then
   On Error GoTo 0
   Resume pt2
Else
   End
End If
End Sub
```

Figure 10-7. Custom function for Runge-Kutta calculation.
(folder 'Chapter 10 Examples', workbook 'ODE Examples', module 'RungeKutta1')

In Figure 10-8, the custom function is applied to the same first-order reaction kinetics problem that was calculated on a worksheet in the preceding sections. The formulas in cells C6 and D7 are, respectively,

=-k*D6

and =Runge1(A6,D6,C6,A7-A6)

	A	B	C	D	E
1	First-Order Reaction (A->B) Using RK Custom Function				
2			rate constant =	5.00E-03	(k)
3			C(initial) =	0.2000	(C)
4			dC/dt = -kC		
5	t	C_t(exact)	dy/dx	C_t(Runge1)	% Error
6	0	0.200000	-1.00E-03	0.200000	
7	20	0.180967	-9.05E-04	0.180968	9.06E-06
8	40	0.163746	-8.19E-04	0.163746	1.81E-05
9	60	0.148164	-7.41E-04	0.148164	2.72E-05
10	80	0.134064	-6.70E-04	0.134064	3.62E-05
11	100	0.121306	-6.07E-04	0.121306	4.53E-05
12	120	0.109762	-5.49E-04	0.109762	5.44E-05
13	140	0.099317	-4.97E-04	0.099317	6.34E-05
14	160	0.089866	-4.49E-04	0.089866	7.25E-05
15	180	0.081314	-4.07E-04	0.081314	8.15E-05
16	200	0.073576	-3.68E-04	0.073576	9.06E-05
17	220	0.066574	-3.33E-04	0.066574	9.96E-05
18	240	0.060239	-3.01E-04	0.060239	1.09E-04
19	260	0.054506	-2.73E-04	0.054506	1.18E-04
20	280	0.049319	-2.47E-04	0.049319	1.27E-04
21	300	0.044626	-2.23E-04	0.044626	1.36E-04

Figure 10-8. Simulation of first-order kinetics by using a Runge-Kutta custom function.
(folder 'Chapter 10 Examples', workbook 'ODE Examples', worksheet 'First Order')

If you compare Figure 10-8 with Figure 10-3, you can see that the spreadsheet calculations are simplified considerably.

Systems of First-Order Differential Equations

Sometimes a system is described by several differential equations. For example, the coupled reaction scheme

$$A \underset{k_2}{\overset{k_1}{\rightleftharpoons}} B \underset{k_4}{\overset{k_3}{\rightleftharpoons}} C$$

results in the simultaneous equations

$$\frac{d[A]_t}{dt} = -k_1[A]_t + k_2[B]_t \tag{10-17}$$

$$\frac{d[B]_t}{dt} = k_1[A]_t - k_2[B]_t - k_3[B]_t + k_4[C]_t \tag{10-18}$$

$$\frac{d[C]_t}{dt} = k_3[B]_t - k_4[C]_t \qquad (10\text{-}19)$$

The Runge-Kutta formulas can be used to solve systems of simultaneous differential equations, such as equations 10-17, 10-18 and 10-19. For a system with independent variable x, N dependent variables y_i and N differential equations

$$dy_i/dx = F_i(x, y_1, y_2, ..., y_N) \qquad (10\text{-}20)$$

the relationships are

$$T_{1i} = F_i(x, y_1, y_2, ..., y_N)\,\Delta x \qquad (10\text{-}21)$$

$$T_{2i} = F_i(x + \Delta x/2, y_1 + T_{11}/2, y_2 + T_{12}/2, ..., y_N + T_{1N}/2)\,\Delta x \qquad (10\text{-}22)$$

etc., and

$$\Delta y_i = (T_{1i} + 2T_{2i} + 2T_{3i} + T_{4i})/6 \qquad (10\text{-}23)$$

Systems of simultaneous differential equations, such as equations 10-17, 10-18 and 10-19, can be solved by using worksheet formulas, but it is much more convenient to use a custom worksheet formula, described in the following section.

Fourth-Order Runge-Kutta Custom Function for Systems of Differential Equations

The simple Runge-Kutta custom function of Figure 10-4 was expanded so as to handle multiple differential equations, by using equations 10-21 through 10-23. The VBA code is shown in Figure 10-9.

The syntax of the custom function is

Runge3(*x_variable, y_variables, deriv_formulas, interval*, index).

The argument *x_variable* is a reference to the cell containing the independent variable, the argument *y_variables* is a reference to the range containing the values of the N dependent variables, and the argument *deriv_formulas* is a reference to the range containing the formulas of the N derivatives, in the same order as *y_variables*. For *y_variables* and *deriv_formulas*, the user can enter a range of cells or make a nonadjacent selection. The argument increment is the Δx used in the calculation. The optional argument index specifies the dependent variable to return; if omitted, the function returns the complete array of dependent variables. In this case the user must select a range of cells in a row, enter the formula and then press CONTROL+SHIFT+ENTER. Since the function always calculates the complete array, this can save calculation time if several dependent variables are being returned.

```
Option Explicit
Option Base 1
'++++++++++++++++++++++++++++++++++++++++++++++++++++++++++++++
Function Runge3(x_variable, y_variables, deriv_formulas, interval, Optional _
index)
'Runge-Kutta method to solve ordinary differential equations.
'Solves problems involving simultaneous first-order differential equations.

'x_variable is a reference to the independent variable x.
'y_variables is a reference to the dependent variables y(1) ... y(N).
'deriv_formulas is a reference to the derivatives dy(i)/dx, in same order.
'interval is a reference to delta x
'index specifies the y(i) to be returned.  If omitted, returns the array.

Dim FormulaText() As String, XAddr As String, YAddr() As String
Dim J As Integer, N As Integer

N = y_variables.Columns.Count
If N = 1 Then N = y_variables.Rows.Count
ReDim FormulaText(N), YAddr(N)

'GET THE X REFERENCE, Y REFERENCE AND DERIVATIVE FORMULA
XAddr = x_variable.Address
For J = 1 To N
   YAddr(J) = y_variables(J).Address
   FormulaText(J) = Application.ConvertFormula(deriv_formulas(J).Formula, _
xlA1, xlA1, xlAbsolute)
Next J

If IsMissing(index) Then
   Runge3 = RK3(N, FormulaText, XAddr, YAddr, x_variable, y_variables,
interval)
Else
   Runge3 = RK3(N, FormulaText, XAddr, YAddr, x_variable, y_variables, _
interval)  (index)
End If
End Function
'++++++++++++++++++++++++++++++++++++++++++++++++++++++++++++++
Private Function RK3(N, FormulaText, XAddr, YAddr, x_variable, y_variables, _
H)
Dim X As Double, Y() As Double, term() As Double
Dim J As Integer, K As Integer
ReDim term(4, N), Y(N)

K = 1: X = x_variable.Value
   For J = 1 To N: Y(J) = y_variables(J).Value: Next J
   Call eval3(N, FormulaText, XAddr, YAddr, X, Y, H, K, term)
K = 2: X = x_variable.Value + H / 2
   For J = 1 To N: Y(J) = y_variables(J).Value + term(1, J) / 2: Next J
   Call eval3(N, FormulaText, XAddr, YAddr, X, Y, H, K, term)
```

```
K = 3: X = x_variable.Value + H / 2
   For J = 1 To N: Y(J) = y_variables(J).Value + term(2, J) / 2: Next J
   Call eval3(N, FormulaText, XAddr, YAddr, X, Y, H, K, term)
K = 4: X = x_variable.Value + H
   For J = 1 To N: Y(J) = y_variables(J).Value + term(3, J): Next J
   Call eval3(N, FormulaText, XAddr, YAddr, X, Y, H, K, term)

For J = 1 To N
 Y(J) = y_variables(J).Value+(term(1, J)+2*term(2, J)+2*term(3, J)+term(4, J)) / 6
Next J
RK3 = Y
End Function
'+++++++++++++++++++++++++++++++++++++++++++++++++++++++++++++++++
Sub eval3(N, FormulaText, XAddr, YAddr, X, Y, H, K, term)
Dim I As Integer, J As Integer
Dim T As String

For J = 1 To N
   T = FormulaText(J)
   Call SubstituteInString(T, XAddr, X)
   For I = 1 To N
      Call SubstituteInString(T, YAddr(I), Y(I))
   Next I
   term(K, J) = H * Evaluate(T)
Next J
End Sub
'+++++++++++++++++++++++++++++++++++++++++++++++++++++++++++++++++
Sub SubstituteInString(T, Ref, Value)
'Replaces each instance of e.g., $A$2 in formula with number value, e.g., 0.20,
then evaluates.
'Must do this replacement from end of formula to beginning.
'Modified 03/08/06 to handle possible un-intended replacement of e.g., $A$2 in
$A$22.
'Method: replace $A$2 with value & " "
'so that $A$22 becomes "0.20 2" and this formula evaluates to an error.

Dim temp As String
Dim NReplacements As Integer, J As Integer
Dim dummy As Double

'Substitute all instances of address with value
NReplacements = (Len(T) - Len(Application.Substitute(T, Ref, ""))) / Len(Ref)
For J = NReplacements To 1 Step -1
   temp = Application.Substitute(T, Ref, Value & " ", J)
   On Error GoTo ErrorHandler
   dummy = Evaluate(temp)
   T = temp
pt1: Next J
Exit Sub

ErrorHandler:
'Trappable error number 13 (Type mismatch) is expected.
```

```
If Err.Number = 13 Then
    On Error GoTo 0     'Disable the error handler.
    Resume pt1     'and continue execution.
Else
    End     'Some other error, so quit completely
End If
End Sub
```

Figure 10-9. Fourth-order Runge-Kutta custom function
for systems of differential equations.
(folder 'Chapter 10 Examples', workbook 'ODE Examples', module 'RungeKutta3')

Figures 10-10, 10-11 and 10-12 illustrate the use of Runge3 to simulate some complex chemical reaction schemes. Figure 10-10 shows concentration vs. time for the consecutive first-order reaction scheme

$$A \rightarrow B \rightarrow C$$

for which the differential equations are

$$\frac{d[A]_t}{dt} = -k_1[A]_t \tag{10-24}$$

$$\frac{d[B]_t}{dt} = k_1[A]_t - k_2[B]_t \tag{10-25}$$

$$\frac{d[C]_t}{dt} = k_3[B]_t \tag{10-26}$$

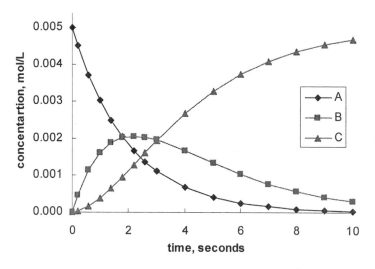

Figure 10-10. Runge-Kutta simulation of consecutive first order reactions.
(folder 'Chapter 10 Examples', workbook 'ODE Examples', worksheet 'A->B->C')

The parameters used in the simulation were $[A]_0 = 5.00 \times 10^{-3}$ mol L^{-1}, $k_1 = 0.5$ s^{-1} and $k_2 = 0.4$ s^{-1}.

Part of the spreadsheet is shown in Figure 10-11. The formulas for the derivatives, in cells G10, H10 and I10, are

=-k_1*J10

=k_1*J10-k_2*K10

=k_2*K10

and the formulas in cells J11, K11 and L11 are

=Runge3(A10,J10:L10,G10:I10,A11-A10,1)

=Runge3(A10,J10:L10,G10:I10,A11-A10,2)

=Runge3(A10,J10:L10,G10:I10,A11-A10,3)

	A	G	H	I	J	K	L
8	time		Using Runge-Kutta custom function				
9	(sec)	d[A]/dt	d[B]/dt	d[C]/dt	[A]ₜ	[B]ₜ	[C]ₜ
10	0.0	-2.50E-03	2.50E-03	0.00E+00	5.00E-03	0.00E+00	0.00E+00
11	0.2	-0.00226	0.00208	1.83E-04	4.52E-03	4.57E-04	1.88E-05
12	0.6	-1.85E-03	1.39E-03	4.58E-04	3.70E-03	1.15E-03	1.51E-04
13	1.0	-1.52E-03	8.78E-04	6.38E-04	3.03E-03	1.59E-03	3.73E-04
14	1.4	-1.24E-03	4.95E-04	7.46E-04	2.48E-03	1.87E-03	6.52E-04
15	1.8	-1.02E-03	2.15E-04	8.02E-04	2.03E-03	2.00E-03	9.63E-04
16	2.2	-8.32E-04	1.31E-05	8.19E-04	1.66E-03	2.05E-03	1.29E-03
17	2.6	-6.81E-04	-1.28E-04	8.09E-04	1.36E-03	2.02E-03	1.61E-03
18	3.0	-5.58E-04	-2.23E-04	7.81E-04	1.12E-03	1.95E-03	1.93E-03
19	4.0	-3.38E-04	-3.27E-04	6.65E-04	6.77E-04	1.66E-03	2.66E-03
20	5.0	-2.05E-04	-3.27E-04	5.32E-04	4.11E-04	1.33E-03	3.26E-03
21	6.0	-1.25E-04	-2.84E-04	4.09E-04	2.49E-04	1.02E-03	3.73E-03
22	7.0	-7.56E-05	-2.30E-04	3.06E-04	1.51E-04	7.65E-04	4.08E-03
23	8.0	-4.59E-05	-1.78E-04	2.24E-04	9.18E-05	5.61E-04	4.35E-03
24	9.0	-2.78E-05	-1.34E-04	1.62E-04	5.57E-05	4.05E-04	4.54E-03
25	10.0	-1.69E-05	-9.89E-05	1.16E-04	3.38E-05	2.89E-04	4.68E-03

Figure 10-11. Spreadsheet for the Runge-Kutta simulation
of consecutive first-order reactions.
(folder 'Chapter 10 Examples', workbook 'ODE Examples', worksheet 'A->B->C')

The arguments of the function can be entered in other ways. Two of these are illustrated in rows 12 and 13 of the spreadsheet. If the derivatives are located in non-adjacent cells, the deriv_formulas argument can be entered as a non-adjacent selection, as illustrated by the formula in cell J12:

=Runge3(A11,(J11,K11,L11),G11:I11,A12-A11,1)

The cell references must be enclosed in parentheses and separated by commas. The function can also be entered as an array formula, as in cells J13:L13

{=Runge3(A12,J12:L12,G12:I12,A13-A12)}

In this simulation, the largest errors are about 0.05%.

Figure 10-12 shows a second example, concentration vs. time for a second-order autocatalytic reaction scheme. An autocatalytic reaction is one in which a *product* acts as a catalyst for the reaction. The reaction has two pathways: an uncatalyzed path (A→B) and an autocatalytic path (A + B → 2B). The rate law (the differential equation) is

$$-d[A]_t/dt = d[B]_t/dt = k_0[A]_t + k_1[A]_t[B]_t \qquad (10\text{-}27)$$

The parameters used in the calculation were: $k_0 = 1.00 \times 10^{-4}$ s^{-1}, $k_1 = 0.50$ M^{-1} s^{-1}, $C = 0.0200$ M. The spreadsheet can be examined on the CD-ROM.

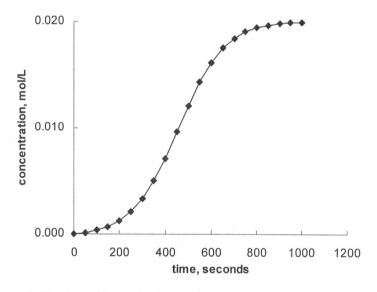

Figure 10-12. Runge-Kutta simulation of second-order autocatalytic reaction. (folder 'Chapter 10 Examples', workbook 'ODE Examples', worksheet 'Autocatalytic')

Predictor-Corrector Methods

The methods in the preceding sections are one-step methods. They need only the value of the preceding point to calculate the value of the new point. Thus they are self-starting methods. Predictor-corrector methods, on the other hand, use the values of two or more previous points to calculate the value of the new point. They are not self-starting; two or more known initial values are needed. Often a Runge-Kutta calculation is used to provide the needed values.

Predictor-corrector methods use two formulas, the predictor equation and the corrector equation. There are many forms of predictor and corrector equations, but all operate according to the same principle: calculate an approximate value of the function using a predictor equation, then use a corrector equation to correct the value.

A Simple Predictor-Corrector Method

To illustrate the method we will modify the simple Euler method, equation 10-6, as follows. The predictor equation is

$$y_{n+1} = y_{n-1} + 2hF(x_n, y_n) \tag{10-28}$$

which requires values at x_{n-1} and x_n to calculate y_{n+1}. Once we have an approximate value for y_{n+1}, we use the corrector equation

$$y_{n+1} = y_n + h\left(\frac{F'(x_n, y_n) + F'(x_{n+1}, y_{n+1})}{2}\right) \tag{10-29}$$

to get an improved value of y_{n+1}. The corrector equation is used iteratively: the value of y_{n+1} is used to obtain an improved value of y_{n+1} and the process is continued until a specified level of convergence is obtained. Two starting values are required, and generally only a single value at x_0 is provided as part of the statement of the problem; the fourth-order Runge-Kutta method can be used to obtain the other starting value.

The worksheet shown in Figure 10-13 illustrates the application of this simple predictor-corrector formula. Again we use as an example the simulation of the first-order kinetic process $A \rightarrow B$ with initial concentration $C_0 = 0.2000$ mol/L and rate constant $k = 5 \times 10^{-3}$ s^{-1}. Again, we use a time increment of 20 seconds.

	A	B	C	D	E	F
1			**Simulating First-Order Reaction** **Using Two-point Predictor-Corrector Method**			
2			(Values in bold are initial values)			
3	t	Pred	Corr1	Corr2	Corr3	Corr4
4	0	**0.2000**	*Difference between successive values (row 11)*			
5	20	**0.1810**	*-3E-05*	*2E-06*	*-8E-08*	*4E-09*
6	40	0.16381	0.16373	0.16373	0.16373	0.16373
7	60	0.14821	0.14821	0.14821	0.14821	0.14821
8	80	0.13417	0.13409	0.13409	0.13409	0.13409
9	100	0.12137	0.12139	0.12139	0.12139	0.12139
10	120	0.10989	0.10981	0.10981	0.10981	0.10981
11	140	0.09940	0.09943	0.09942	0.09942	0.09942
12	160	0.09001	0.08992	0.08993	0.08993	0.08993
13	180	0.08139	0.08144	0.08144	0.08144	0.08144
14	200	0.07373	0.07364	0.07364	0.07364	0.07364

Figure 10-13. Decreasing error in the Euler method
by a simple predictor-corrector method.
(folder 'Chapter 10 Examples', workbook 'ODE Examples', worksheet 'Predictor-Corrector Method')

The predictor formula was entered in column B. The first two values, shown in bold, are the starting values; the predictor formula, in cell B6, corresponds exactly to equation 10-28 and is

=B4+2*DX*-k*B5

The corrector formula, in cell C6, corresponds exactly to equation 10-29 and is

=$B5+DX*(-k*$B5-k*B6)/2

The preceding formula is used iteratively. The formula (note the use of relative and mixed references) was Filled Right to perform the iterations. The formulas in row 5 were added to display the difference between a corrected value and the preceding one (for example, the formula in cell C5 is

=B11-C11

and shows how the corrector formula converges).

A Simple Predictor-Corrector Method
Utilizing an Intentional Circular Reference

An intentional circular reference can be used in the corrector formula to eliminate the need to **Fill Right** the corrector formula in order to perform the iterations. The corrector formula in cell C6 is changed from the formula shown above to

=$B5+DX*(-k*$B5-k*C6)/2

which creates a circular reference, since cell C6 refers to itself. A circular reference is usually an error; Excel displays the "Cannot resolve circular references" error message and puts a zero in the cell. In this case, however, the circular reference is intentional. We can make Excel recalculate the value in each cell, using the result of the previous iteration. To "turn on" iteration, choose **Tools → Options → Calculation** and check the Iteration box. Unless you change the default settings for iteration, Microsoft Excel stops calculating after 100 iterations or after the circular reference value changes by less than 0.001 between iterations, whichever comes first. Enter 1E-9 in the Maximum Change box. When you press OK the iterative circular reference calculation will begin. You can **Fill Down** the formula into the remaining cells in column C. The calculations in columns D–F are no longer needed and can be deleted. The spreadsheet is shown in Figure 10-14.

The value displayed in cell C6 is identical to the value that would be obtained by extending the corrector formula to, in this case, the tenth iteration (these calculations can be seen in columns G–L in the spreadsheet of Figure 10-13).

The errors obtained by using the modified Euler method are significantly less than with the simple Euler method, but greater than with the fourth-order Runge-Kutta method.

	A	B	C	D	E	F
1		**Simulating First-Order Reaction**				
		Using Two-point Predictor-Corrector Method				
2		(A single corrector formula employing a **circular reference**)				
3	t	Pred	Corr			
4	0	**0.2000**				
5	20	**0.1810**				
6	40	0.16381	0.16373			
7	60	0.14821	0.14821			
8	80	0.13417	0.13409			
9	100	0.12137	0.12139			
10	120	0.10989	0.10981			
11	140	0.09940	0.09942			
12	160	0.09001	0.08993			
13	180	0.08139	0.08144			
14	200	0.07373	0.07364			

Figure 10-14. A simple predictor-corrector method utilizing a circular reference.
(folder 'Chapter 10 Examples', workbook 'ODE Examples', worksheet 'Predictor-Corrector Method (2)')

Higher-Order Differential Equations

Differential equations of higher order can also be solved using the methods described in this chapter, since a differential equation of order n can be converted into a set of n first-order differential equations. For example, consider the following second-order differential equation (equation 10-30) that describes the damped vibration of a mass m connected to a rigid support by a linear spring with coefficient k_s and a vibration damper with coefficient k_d, illustrated in Figure 10-15.

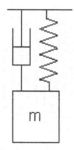

Figure 10-15. A damped vibration system.

$$m\frac{d^2x}{dt^2} + k_d\frac{dx}{dt} + k_s x = 0 \qquad (10\text{-}30)$$

Equation 10-30 can be rearranged to

$$\frac{d^2x}{dt^2} = \frac{k_d}{m}\frac{dx}{dt} - \frac{k_s}{m}x \qquad (10\text{-}30a)$$

The values of the mass, spring coefficient and damper coefficient are shown in Figure 10-16. We want to calculate the position x of the mass at time intervals from $t = 0$, when the mass has been given an initial displacement of 10 cm from its rest position.

	G	H	I
3	mass, kg	coefficient of spring, N/cm	coefficient of damper, N/cm
4	5	5	0.33
5	(m)	(ks)	(kd)

Figure 10-16. Parameters used in the damped vibration calculation in Figure 10-17. (folder 'Chapter 10 Examples', workbook 'ODE Examples', worksheet '2nd Order ODE')

We define x as the displacement of the mass from its rest position at any time t, and $x' = dx/dt$. Then, since $d^2 x / dt^2 = d / dt (dx / dt)$, equation 10-30 can be written as the two equations

$$\frac{dx}{dt} = x' \tag{10-31}$$

$$\frac{dx'}{dt} = -\frac{k_d}{m} x' - \frac{k_s}{m} x \tag{10-32}$$

You can now use the methods described previously for systems of first-order differential equations to solve the problem.

Figure 10-17 shows part of a spreadsheet describing the displacement x of the damped system as a function of time. The formula for the second derivative, in cell E6, is

=(-kd*C6-ks*B6)/(m*0.01)

(The mass m is multiplied by 0.01 to convert it from kg to N s^2 cm^{-1}, in order to obtain the displacement in cm.) The custom function Runge3 is used in columns B and C to calculate x (in column B) and x' (in column C); the array formula entered in cells B7 and C7 is

{=Runge3(A6,B6:C6,D6:E6,A7-A6)}

The value of x' is in both columns C and D, since the same value is both the x value (in column C) and the derivative (in column D); the formula in cell D6 is =C6.

	A	B	C	D	E
5	t	x	x'	x' = dx/dt	x" = dx'/dt
6	0.000	5	0	0.000	-500
7	0.025	4.853	-11.404	-11.404	-410
8	0.050	4.450	-20.419	-20.419	-310
9	0.075	3.853	-26.893	-26.893	-208
10	0.100	3.126	-30.841	-30.841	-109
11	0.125	2.331	-32.421	-32.421	-19
12	0.150	1.523	-31.903	-31.903	58
13	0.175	0.750	-29.634	-29.634	121
14	0.200	0.052	-26.013	-26.013	166
15	0.225	-0.542	-21.451	-21.451	196
16	0.250	-1.016	-16.353	-16.353	209
17	0.275	-1.359	-11.094	-11.094	209
18	0.300	-1.572	-5.998	-5.998	197

Figure 10-17. Portion of the spreadsheet for damped vibration calculation. The initial values for the calculation are in bold.
(folder 'Chapter 10 Examples', workbook 'ODE Examples', worksheet '2nd Order ODE')

The displacement as a function of time, from 0 to 1 second, is shown in Figure 10-18.

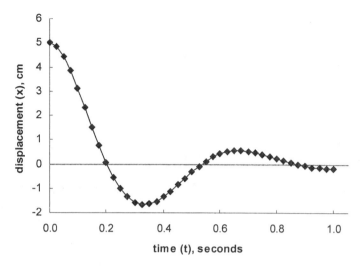

Figure 10-18. Damped vibration.
(folder 'Chapter 10 Examples', workbook 'ODE Examples', worksheet '2nd Order ODE')

Problems

Answers to the following problems are found in the folder "Ch. 10 (ODE)" in the "Problems & Solutions" folder on the CD.

1. A function is described by the differential equation $dy/dt = 1 - t\sqrt[3]{y}$. Calculate y for $t = 0$ to $t = 5$, in increments of 0.1.

2. A function is described by the differential equation
$$\frac{dy}{dx} = \frac{1 - 2x^2 /(1 + x^2)}{1 + x^2}$$
Calculate y for $x = 0$ to $x = 6$.

3. A function is described by the differential equation
$$\frac{dy}{dx} = -10\left(y - \arctan(x) + \frac{1}{1 + x^2} \right)$$
Calculate y for $x = 0$ to $x = 2.5$. Adjust the magnitude of Δx for different parts of the calculation, as appropriate.

4. **Trajectory I.** Consider the motion of a projectile that is fired from a cannon. The initial velocity of the projectile is v_0 and the angle of elevation of the cannon is θ degrees. If air resistance is neglected, the velocity component of the projectile in the x direction (x') is $v_0 \cos \theta$ and the component in the y direction is $v_0 \sin \theta - gt$. Use Euler's method to calculate the trajectory of the projectile. For the calculation, assume that the projectile is a shell from a 122-mm field howitzer, for which the muzzle velocity is 560 m/s. (Getting started: create five columns, as follows: t, x', y', x, y. Calculate x and y, the coordinates of distance traveled, from, e.g., $x_{t+1} = x_t + x_t'\Delta t$.) Verify that the maximum range attainable with a given muzzle velocity occurs when $\theta = 45°$.

5. **Trajectory II.** Without air resistance, the projectile should strike the earth with the same y' that it had when it left the muzzle of the cannon. Because of accumulated errors when using the Euler method, you will find that this is not true. Repeat the calculation of problem number 1 using RK4.

6. **Trajectory III.** To produce a more accurate estimate of a trajectory, air drag should be taken into account. For speeds of objects such as baseballs or cannonballs, air drag can be taken to be proportional to the square of the

velocity, $f = Dv^2$. The proportionality constant $D = 0.5\rho CA$, where ρ is the density of air, A is the cross-sectional area of the projectile and C, the drag coefficient, is a dimensionless quantity that depends on the shape of the projectile. The forces acting on a projectile in flight are illustrated in the following figure.

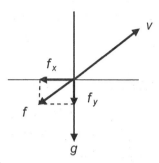

Combining the above equation for the air drag and the relationship between force and acceleration, $f = ma$, we get, for the "deceleration" in the x-direction, $x'' = -Dv_x^2/m$; $y'' = -Dv_y^2/m - g$.

Calculate the trajectory of a baseball hit at angle $\theta = 30°$ with initial velocity 50 m/s. The parameters of the baseball are: mass 145 g, circumference 23 cm (from *Rules of Baseball,* Major League Baseball Enterprises, 1998). For air resistance, use $\rho = 1.2$ kg/m^2 and the drag coefficient $C = 0.5$.

(Getting started: create eight columns, as follows: t, x'', y'', x', y', v, x, y. At $t = 0$, x' and y' are calculated as in the previous problem, but for subsequent t values, they are calculated by the Euler method, using the previous values of x'' and y''. Calculate x and y, the coordinates of distance traveled, using, e.g., $x_{t+1} = x_t + x_t'\Delta t + \frac{1}{2}x_t''(\Delta t)^2$.)

7. **Pendulum Motion I**. The motion of a simple pendulum, consisting of a mass M at the end of a rod of length L, is described by the following first-order differential equation:

$$\frac{d\omega}{d\theta} = \frac{-g}{L}\frac{\sin\theta}{\omega}$$

where ω = angular velocity (rad/s)
        θ = angle of displacement from equilibrium position
        $g = 9.81$ m/s^2
        $L = 1.0$ m

Calculate the angular velocity of the pendulum beginning with the initial conditions $\theta = 10°$, $\omega = 0.3$.

8. **Pendulum Motion II.** The motion of a simple pendulum as a function of time is described by the following second-order differential equation:

$$\frac{d^2\theta}{dt^2} + \frac{g}{L}\theta = 0$$

where the terms in the equation are as defined in the preceding problem. Generate a table of angle of displacement as a function of time from $t = 0$ to $t = 2$ seconds, with $\theta = 10°$ and $d\theta/dt = 0$ at $t = 0$.

9. **Liquid Flow.** A cylindrical tank of diameter D is filled with water to a height h. Water is allowed to flow out of the tank through a hole of diameter d in the bottom of the tank. The differential equation describing the height of water in the tank as a function of time is

$$\frac{dh}{dt} = -\frac{d^2}{D^2}\sqrt{2gh}$$

where g is the acceleration due to gravity. Produce a plot of height of water in the tank as a function of time for $D = 10$ ft, $d = 6$ in and $h_0 = 30$ ft. Compare your results with the analytical solution $h = \left(\sqrt{h_0} - kt/2\right)^2$, where $k = (d^2/D^2)\sqrt{2g}$.

10. **Chemical Kinetics I.** Calculate concentrations as a function of time for the second-order reaction

$$A + B \xrightarrow{k} C$$

for which $-d[A]/dt = -d[B]/dt = d[C]/dt = k[A][B]$. Use $[A]_0 = 0.02000$, $[B]_0 = 0.02000$, $k = 0.050$ s^{-1}. Calculate concentrations over the time range from 0 to 500 seconds.

11. **Chemical Kinetics II.** Use the Runge custom function to calculate [A], [B] and [C] for the coupled reaction scheme

$$A \underset{k_2}{\overset{k_1}{\rightleftharpoons}} B \underset{k_4}{\overset{k_3}{\rightleftharpoons}} C$$

using $[A]_0 = 0.1$, $[B]_0 = 0$, $[C]_0 = 0$ mol L^{-1}, $k_1 = 1$ s^{-1}, $k_2 = 1$ s^{-1}, $k_3 = 0.1$ s^{-1} and $k_4 = 0.01$ s^{-1}, over the range 0–100 s.

12. **Chemical Kinetics III.** Repeat #8, using $[A]_0 = 0$, $[B]_0 = 0.1$, $[C]_0 = 0$ mol L^{-1}.

13. **Chemical Kinetics IV**. Repeat #8, using $[A]_0 = 0$, $[B]_0 = 0$, $[C]_0 = 0.1$ mol L^{-1}.

Chapter 11

Numerical Integration of Ordinary Differential Equations Part II: Boundary Conditions

In the preceding chapter, we saw that a differential equation of order n could be converted into a set of n first-order differential equations. For example, if the problem to be solved is a second-order differential equation, it is converted into two first-order differential equations; two "known" values of the function or its derivative will be needed in order to solve the problem. In the second-order differential equation example illustrated in Figure 10-16, the value of the function and its first derivative were both known at $x = 0$. The problem was then solved using the standard methods described in Chapter 10.

If information about a second-order differential equation is known at two or more different values of the independent variable, then the problem is known as a *boundary-value problem* (BVP). The points where the function is known are usually (but not always) the limits of the domain of interest — hence the term boundary-value problem. Problems of this type must be solved by different methods than those we applied to initial-value problems.

Two approaches are commonly used to solve boundary-value problems: the "shooting" method and the finite-difference method. This chapter shows how to apply these methods to differential equations of order two; fortunately, most important physical systems are described by differential equations of order no higher than two.

The Shooting Method

The shooting method is a trial-and-error method. To solve a problem where the values of y are known at x_0 and x_n, the boundaries of the interval of interest, we set up the problem as though it were an initial-value problem, with two "knowns" given at the same boundary — for example, at x_0. (See Figure 10-17 for an example of an initial-value problem of this type: the two knowns, shown in bold, are the value of y at x_0 and a trial value of y' at x_0.) Using the trial value of

y', we calculate y for a suitable range of x values from x_0 to x_n, and compare the calculated value of y at x_n with the known value. If the calculated value does not agree with the known value, we repeat the calculations with a different trial value of y', until we calculate a value of y at the other boundary, x_n, that agrees with the boundary value, hence the name "shooting method."

An Example: Deflection of a Simply Supported Beam

A simply supported beam (a beam supported at the ends) is bent downwards by the applied load, consisting of the weight of the beam itself plus any other loads.

Figure 11-1. Diagram of a simply supported beam.

The simply supported steel beam shown in Figure 11-1 supports a uniformly distributed load of 2000 lb/ft. The length L of the span is 30 feet. The deflection (downward bending displacement) y of the beam as a function of distance x along the span of the beam is given by the second-order differential equation 11-1, known as the general equation of the elastic curve of a deflected beam.

$$\frac{d^2y}{dx^2} = \frac{M}{EI} \tag{11-1}$$

M, the bending moment at distance x, is given by equation 11-2

$$M = (wLx/2) - (wx^2/2) \tag{11-2}$$

where L is the length of the beam and w is the weight of the beam per unit length. E is the modulus of elasticity of the beam material; for carbon steel, $E = 2.9 \times 10^7$ psi, and I is the moment of inertia of the cross section of the beam, given by equation 11-3.

$$I = bh^3/12 \tag{11-3}$$

where b is the width and h the height of the beam cross section. In this example, for a beam 6 in wide × 16 in deep, $I = 2048$ in^4.

Equation 11-1 can be transformed into the two equations

$$\frac{dy}{dx} = z \tag{11-4}$$

ans
$$\frac{dz}{dx} = \frac{M}{EI} \tag{11-5}$$

where z is the slope of the beam.

We want to calculate the amount of deflection of the beam at the center of the span. Since the deflection is known to be zero at either end of the beam ($y = 0$ at $x = 0$ and $y = 0$ at $x = 30$), this is a boundary value problem. We will solve it by using the shooting method. We set up the problem as though it were an initial-value problem, with two "knowns" given at the same boundary, $x = 0$ in this example. The two known values are the value of y at $x = 0$ and a trial value of z at $x = 0$.

The spreadsheet used to solve the problem is shown in Figure 11-2. To ensure consistency in units, all dimensions have been converted to inches. The values of y along the beam were calculated at increments of 2 inches (rows 13–182 are hidden). For simplicity, the values of deflection y and slope z in rows 6 through 185 were calculated by using Euler's method; the formulas in cells B6 and C6 are, respectively,

=B5+C5*(A6-A5)

=C5+E5*(A6-A5)

	A	B	C	D	E
1	Beam Deflection Calculated by Using the Shooting Method				
2	(Calculations Performed by Using Euler Method)				
3	(all quantities must be in inches)				
4	Distance x (in)	Deflection y (in)	Slope z=dy/dx	Bending moment M	dz/dx=M/EI
5	0	**0.0000**	**0.00000**	0	0
6	2	0.0000	0.00000	59667	1.00E-06
7	4	0.0000	0.00000	118667	2.00E-06
8	6	0.0000	0.00001	177000	2.98E-06
9	8	0.0000	0.00001	234667	3.95E-06
10	10	0.0000	0.00002	291667	4.91E-06
11	12	0.0001	0.00003	348000	5.86E-06
12	14	0.0001	0.00004	403667	6.80E-06
183	356	1.8984	0.01090	118667	2.00E-06
184	358	1.9202	0.01091	59667	1.00E-06
185	360	**1.9420**	0.01091	0	0

Figure 11-2. Simulation of beam deflection by the shooting method. The boundary values of the deflection and the initial trial value of the slope are in bold. Note that the rows between 12 and 183 have been hidden.
(folder 'Chapter 11 Examples', workbook 'ODE-BVP', worksheet 'Beam deflection (Euler)')

	G	H	I
5	Trial	z	y
6	1	0	1.9420198
7	2	-0.1	-34.05798
8	3	-0.0053945	0

Figure 11-3. Calculating the boundary condition by linear interpolation.
(folder 'Chapter 11 Examples', workbook 'ODE-BVP', worksheet 'Beam deflection (Euler)')

With a trial value of $z = 0$, the value of y calculated at $x = 360$ is not zero, but 1.9420. We will now proceed to vary z in order to make $y = 0$. One method that can be used to find the correct value of z is to calculate two values of y at the upper boundary ($x = 360$), using two trial values of z at the lower boundary ($x = 0$), and then calculate an improved value of z by using linear interpolation to find the value that makes $y = 0$. Here, the trial values of z (the slope of the beam) that were used were zero and -0.1. These values of z were entered in cell C5; the resulting values of y that were obtained at $x = 360$ (in cell B185) are shown in Figure 11-3.

	A	B	C	D	E
1	Beam Deflection Calculated by Using the Shooting Method				
2	(Calculations Performed by Using Euler Method)				
3	(all quantities must be in inches)				
4	Distance x (in)	Deflection y (in)	Slope z=dy/dx	Bending moment M	dz/dx=M/EI
5	0	**0.0000**	**-0.00539**	0	0
6	2	-0.0108	-0.00539	59667	1.00E-06
7	4	-0.0216	-0.00539	118667	2.00E-06
8	6	-0.0324	-0.00539	177000	2.98E-06
9	8	-0.0431	-0.00538	234667	3.95E-06
10	10	-0.0539	-0.00537	291667	4.91E-06
11	12	-0.0647	-0.00536	348000	5.86E-06
12	14	-0.0754	-0.00535	403667	6.80E-06
183	356	-0.0220	0.00551	118667	2.00E-06
184	358	-0.0110	0.00551	59667	1.00E-06
185	360	**0.0000**	0.00552	0	0

Figure 11-4. Simulation of beam deflection by the shooting method.
The final boundary values and the final value of the slope are shown in bold.
(folder 'Chapter 11 Examples', workbook 'ODE-BVP', worksheet 'Beam deflection (Euler)')

The calculated value of z for the required boundary value is shown in the third row of the table. The formula in cell H8 is

=H6-I6*(H7-H6)/(I7-I6)

If the problem is linear, the interpolated value of z obtained in this way will be the desired solution. The spreadsheet with final values is shown in Figure 11-4. A similar spreadsheet in which the y values were calculated using the Runge custom function can be seen on the CD-ROM.

This "shooting" procedure was performed manually—that is, successive trial values were entered into the spreadsheet, and the resulting values copied and pasted into the cells shown in Figure 11-3, in order to use interpolation to find the final value. You can obtain the same final result essentially in one step by using Goal Seek. After entering a trial value, z = 0, in cell C6, use Goal Seek to change cell C6 to make the target cell, B185, attain a value of zero.

The final results are shown in Figures 11-4 and 11-5. The maximum deflection, at the midpoint of the beam, is 0.6138 in, within the allowable deflection limit of 1/360 of the span. For comparison, the analytical expression for the deflection at the midpoint of the span, $5wL^4/384EI$, yields 0.6137 in.

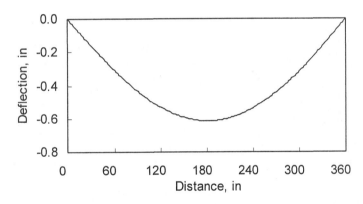

Figure 11-5. Beam deflection calculated by the shooting method.
(folder 'Chapter 11 Examples', workbook 'ODE-BVP', worksheet 'Beam deflection (Euler)')

Solving a Second-Order Ordinary Differential Equation by the Shooting Method and Euler's Method

Consider an unknown function $y = F(x)$ that obeys the second-order differential equation $y'' - y = 0$ and that is known to have boundary values of $y = 0$ at $x = 0$ and $y = 3.63$ at $x = 2$.

To solve the second-order differential equation

$$\frac{d^2y}{dx^2} - y = 0 \tag{11-6}$$

we express it as two first-order differential equations:

$$\frac{dz}{dx} - y = 0 \tag{11-7}$$

and

$$\frac{dy}{dx} = z \tag{11-8}$$

The initial calculation, using a trial value of $z = 0$, is shown in Figure 11-6.

	A	B	C	D	E	F
5	x	dz/dx=y	Δz	z=dy/dx	Δy	y
6	0.0			**1.000**		**0.0000**
7	0.1	0.100	0.000	1.000	0.100	0.1000
8	0.2	0.200	0.010	1.010	0.100	0.2000
9	0.3	0.301	0.020	1.030	0.101	0.3010
10	0.4	0.404	0.030	1.060	0.103	0.4040
11	0.5	0.510	0.040	1.101	0.106	0.5100
12	0.6	0.620	0.051	1.152	0.110	0.6201
24	1.8	2.705	0.244	2.855	0.261	2.7049
25	1.9	2.990	0.270	3.125	0.286	2.9904
26	2.0	3.303	0.299	3.425	0.313	**3.3030**

Figure 11-6. Preparing to solve the differential equation $y'' - y = 0$
by the shooting method. The initial boundary values
and the initial trial value of the derivative are in bold.
(folder 'Chapter 11 Examples', workbook 'ODE-BVP', worksheet 'y"-y=0 (Euler)')

As before, we will use Euler's method to develop an inaccurate but simple solution to the problem, then obtain a more accurate result by using the RK method. Euler's method formulas were used to calculate the values of y and z. The formulas used in cells C7 and D7 are, respectively

=B6*(A7-A6)

and

=D6+C7

The Euler's method calculation was performed in two steps in these two cells so as to make it convenient to convert to the RK calculation, as will be described in the following section.

Using an initial estimate of 1 for dy/dx, the boundary value at $x = 2.0$, in cell F34, is 3.3030. **Goal Seek** was used to find the value of z that produced the desired boundary value, $y = 3.63$. The final calculations are shown in Figure 11-7, together with the values calculated from the exact expression, $y = \sinh x$, and the percentage error.

	A	B	C	D	E	F	G	H
5	x	dz/dx=y	Δz	z=dy/dx	Δy	y	y(exact)	% error
6	0.0			1.099		0.0000	0.0000	
7	0.1	0.110	0.000	1.099	0.110	0.1099	0.1002	9.7
8	0.2	0.220	0.011	1.110	0.110	0.2198	0.2013	9.2
9	0.3	0.331	0.022	1.132	0.111	0.3308	0.3045	8.6
10	0.4	0.444	0.033	1.165	0.113	0.4440	0.4108	8.1
11	0.5	0.561	0.044	1.209	0.117	0.5605	0.5211	7.6
12	0.6	0.681	0.056	1.266	0.121	0.6815	0.6367	7.0
24	1.8	2.973	0.269	3.138	0.287	2.9727	2.9422	1.0
25	1.9	3.287	0.297	3.435	0.314	3.2865	3.2682	0.6
26	2.0	3.630	0.329	3.764	0.343	3.6300	3.6269	0.1

Figure 11-7. Final values for the solution of the differential equation $y'' - y = 0$ by the shooting method, using Euler's method to calculate y' and y. (folder 'Chapter 11 Examples', workbook 'ODE-BVP', worksheet 'y"-y=0 (Euler)')

In this example, the errors resulting from the use of Euler's method to perform the calculations are rather large, in some cases as large as 10%. A convenient way to reduce the level of error in the calculations is to use Euler's method with a smaller Δx. For the preceding problem, when a Δx value of 0.01 is used instead of 0.1 (281 rows of calculation instead of 29), the maximum error is 1% instead of the 10% seen in Figure 11-7.

Solving a Second-Order Ordinary Differential Equation by the Shooting Method and the RK Method

Using the Runge-Kutta method should produce much smaller errors than does Euler's method. Figure 11-8 shows the application of the RK method to the preceding problem, the solution of the differential equation $y'' - y = 0$. Four columns, B:F, were inserted and labeled TZ1...TZ4, for the four RK terms used to calculate z. Similarly, four columns were inserted for the calculation of y. As in Figure 11-7, the values in bold are the two boundary values (in cells G6 and L6) and the target value (cell L34). Columns B through G contain the series of

	A	B	C	D	E	F	G	H	I	J	K	L	M	N
5	x	dz/dx=y	TZ1	TZ2	TZ3	TZ4	z=dy/dx	TY1	TY2	TY3	TY4	y	y(exact)	% error
6	0.0	0.0000	0.000	0.000	0.000	0.000	**0.997**	0.100	0.105	0.105	0.110	**0.0000**	0.0000	
7	0.1	0.1049	0.010	0.011	0.011	0.012	0.997	0.100	0.105	0.105	0.110	0.1049	0.1002	4.7
8	0.2	0.2097	0.021	0.022	0.022	0.023	1.008	0.101	0.106	0.106	0.111	0.2097	0.2013	4.2
9	0.3	0.3158	0.032	0.033	0.033	0.035	1.030	0.103	0.108	0.108	0.114	0.3158	0.3045	3.7
10	0.4	0.4241	0.042	0.045	0.045	0.047	1.063	0.106	0.112	0.112	0.118	0.4241	0.4108	3.3
11	0.5	0.5360	0.054	0.056	0.056	0.059	1.108	0.111	0.116	0.117	0.122	0.5360	0.5211	2.9
12	0.6	0.6525	0.065	0.069	0.069	0.072	1.164	0.116	0.122	0.123	0.129	0.6525	0.6367	2.5
13	0.7	0.7750	0.077	0.081	0.082	0.086	1.233	0.123	0.129	0.130	0.136	0.7750	0.7586	2.2
14	0.8	0.9047	0.090	0.095	0.095	0.100	1.315	0.131	0.138	0.138	0.145	0.9047	0.8881	1.9
15	0.9	1.0429	0.104	0.110	0.110	0.115	1.410	0.141	0.148	0.148	0.156	1.0429	1.0265	1.6
16	1.0	1.1912	0.119	0.125	0.125	0.132	1.519	0.152	0.160	0.160	0.168	1.1912	1.1752	1.4
17	1.1	1.3510	0.135	0.142	0.142	0.149	1.645	0.164	0.173	0.173	0.182	1.3510	1.3356	1.1
18	1.2	1.5239	0.152	0.160	0.160	0.168	1.787	0.179	0.188	0.188	0.197	1.5239	1.5095	1.0
19	1.3	1.7118	0.171	0.180	0.180	0.189	1.947	0.195	0.204	0.205	0.215	1.7118	1.6984	0.8
20	1.4	1.9166	0.192	0.201	0.202	0.212	2.127	0.213	0.223	0.224	0.235	1.9166	1.9043	0.6
21	1.5	2.1403	0.214	0.225	0.225	0.237	2.329	0.233	0.245	0.245	0.257	2.1403	2.1293	0.5
22	1.6	2.3852	0.239	0.250	0.251	0.264	2.554	0.255	0.268	0.269	0.282	2.3852	2.3756	0.4
23	1.7	2.6538	0.265	0.279	0.279	0.293	2.805	0.280	0.294	0.295	0.310	2.6538	2.6456	0.3
24	1.8	2.9488	0.295	0.310	0.310	0.326	3.084	0.308	0.324	0.325	0.341	2.9488	2.9422	0.2
25	1.9	3.2731	0.327	0.344	0.344	0.362	3.394	0.339	0.356	0.357	0.375	3.2731	3.2682	0.2
26	2.0	3.6300					3.738					**3.6300**	3.6269	0.1

Figure 11-8. Final values for the solution of the differential equation $y'' - y = 0$ by the shooting method, using the RK method to calculate y' and y. (folder 'Chapter 11 Examples', workbook 'ODE-BVP', worksheet 'y''-y=0 (RK)')

RK formulas to calculate z, columns H through M a similar series to calculate y. The RK formulas in cells C7 through G7 are, respectively

=B6*(A7-A6)

=(B6+C7/2)*(A7-A6)

=(B6+D7/2)*(A7-A6)

=(B6+E7)*(A7-A6)

=G6+(C7+2*D7+2*E7+F7)/6

As expected, application of the RK method reduces the errors significantly. The results from the more precise calculation are shown in Figure 11-9. Every fifth data point has been plotted.

Even better accuracy can be obtained by using the RK method with a smaller Δx. When a Δx value of 0.01 is used instead of 0.1, the maximum error is 0.25%

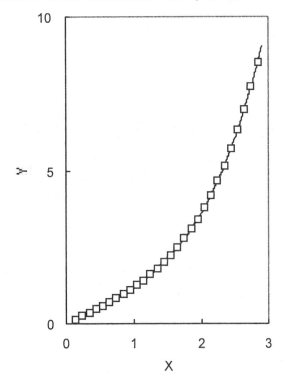

Figure 11-9. Solution of the differential equation $y'' - y = 0$ by the shooting method, using the RK method to calculate y' and y. Maximum error is ca. 1%.
(folder 'Chapter 11 Examples', workbook 'ODE-BVP', worksheet 'y"-y=0 (RK)')

Finite-Difference Methods

As described in the following, approximating the derivative of a function by a finite difference quotient will allow us to reduce a boundary-value problem to a system of simultaneous equations that can be solved by methods that have been discussed in Chapter 9. Problems that are difficult or impossible to solve by the shooting method may sometimes be solved by the finite-difference method.

Consider a two-point boundary value problem, where y is known at the ends of the range and the expression for the second derivative y'' is given. For a differential equation of the general form

$$y'' + ay = bx + c \tag{11-9}$$

where $a = F(x)$, we can replace the second derivative y'' by the central difference formula

$$y'' = \frac{y_{i+1} - 2y_i + y_{i-1}}{h^2} \tag{11-10}$$

where $h = \Delta x$ (equation 11-10 assumes equally spaced x values) to obtain

$$\frac{y_{i+1} - 2y_i + y_{i-1}}{h^2} + ay_i = bx_i + c \tag{11-11}$$

where x_i and y_i represent the point at which the derivative is calculated. Rearranging equation 11-11 yields

$$y_{i+1} + (h^2a - 2)y_i + y_{i-1} = h^2(bx_i + c) \tag{11-12}$$

We now divide the interval between the two boundary values into n equal parts to yield n simultaneous equations obtained from equation 11-12. The procedure is best illustrated by an example.

Solving a Second-Order Ordinary Differential Equation by the Finite-Difference Method

We wish to solve the boundary value problem

$$y'' - \left(0.15 - \frac{x}{2.3}\right)y = x \tag{11-13}$$

with boundary values $y = 2$ at $x = 1$ and $y = -1$ at $x = 3$. The differential equation is of the general form of equation 11-9 with $a = -(0.15 - x/2.3)$, $b = 1$ and $c = 0$. For this simple example, we will subdivide the x interval, $x = 1$ to $x = 3$, into ten subintervals; thus $h = 0.2$ and the x values defining the subintervals (sometimes called the *mesh points*) are $x_1 = 1.0$, $x_2 = 1.2$, ..., $x_{11} = 3.0$. We can now write an equation of the form

$$y_{i-1} + \left((0.2)^2 \left(-0.15 + \frac{x_i}{2.3} \right) - 2 \right) y_i + y_{i+1} = (0.2)^2 x_i \qquad (11\text{-}14)$$

for each subinterval. Since y is known at the ends of the interval, we need to write only nine simultaneous equations (e.g., at $x_2 = 1.2$):

$$y_1 + ((0.2)^2(-0.15 + x_2/2.3) - 2)y_2 + y_3 = (0.2)^2 x_2 \qquad (11\text{-}15)$$

$$2 - 1.985y_2 + y_3 = 0.048 \qquad (11\text{-}15a)$$

$$1.985y_2 + y_3 = -1.952 \qquad (11\text{-}15b)$$

at $x_3 = 1.4$:

$$y_2 - (2 - (0.15 - x_3/2.3)(0.2)^2)y_3 + y_4 = (0.2)^2 x_3 \qquad (11\text{-}16)$$

$$y_2 - 1.982y_3 + y_4 = 0.056 \qquad (11\text{-}16a)$$

and at $x_{10} = 2.8$:

$$y_9 - (2 - (0.15 - x_{10}/2.3)(0.2)^2)y_{10} + y_{11} = (0.2)^2 x_{10} \qquad (11\text{-}17)$$

$$y_9 - 1.957y_{10} - 1 = 0.112 \qquad (11\text{-}17a)$$

$$y_9 - 1.957y_{10} = 1.112 \qquad (11\text{-}17b)$$

These simultaneous equations can be expressed in matrix form:

$$
\begin{bmatrix}
-1.985 & 1 & 0 & 0 & 0 & 0 & 0 & 0 & 0 \\
1 & -1.982 & 1 & 0 & 0 & 0 & 0 & 0 & 0 \\
0 & 1 & -1.978 & 1 & 0 & 0 & 0 & 0 & 0 \\
0 & 0 & 1 & -1.975 & 1 & 0 & 0 & 0 & 0 \\
0 & 0 & 0 & 1 & -1.971 & 1 & 0 & 0 & 0 \\
0 & 0 & 0 & 0 & 1 & -1.968 & 1 & 0 & 0 \\
0 & 0 & 0 & 0 & 0 & 1 & -1.964 & 1 & 0 \\
0 & 0 & 0 & 0 & 0 & 0 & 1 & -1.961 & 1 \\
0 & 0 & 0 & 0 & 0 & 0 & 0 & 1 & -1.957
\end{bmatrix}
\begin{bmatrix}
x_2 \\ x_3 \\ x_4 \\ x_5 \\ x_6 \\ x_7 \\ x_8 \\ x_9 \\ x_{10}
\end{bmatrix}
=
\begin{bmatrix}
-1.952 \\ 0.056 \\ 0.064 \\ 0.072 \\ 0.080 \\ 0.088 \\ 0.096 \\ 0.104 \\ 1.112
\end{bmatrix}
$$

and can be solved by any of the methods described in Chapter 9.

The elements of the coefficients matrix and the constants vector can be generated easily by means of the spreadsheet layout illustrated in Figure 11-10. The formulas in cells C9 and F9 are, respectively,

=-(p-x/q)

=-(2-a*h^2)

It is important to remember that the formulas for the first and last terms of the constants vector are different. The formula in cells G10:G16 is

=h^2*bb*x+h^2*cc

while the formulas in cells G9 and G17 are, respectively,

=h^2*bb*x+h^2*cc-B8

and

=h^2*bb*x+h^2*cc-B16.

Be careful not to **Fill Down** the wrong formula when constructing a worksheet.

	A	B	C	D	E	F	G
1			BVP by Finite-Difference Method				
2			General formula: y" + ay = bx + c				
3			Example: y" - (0.15-x/2.3)y = x				
4		p =	0.15				
5		q =	2.3	h =	0.2		
6	x	y	a	b	c	Matrix terms	Constant s
7	1.0	2					
8	1.2		0.3717	1	0	-1.985	-1.952
9	1.4		0.4587	1	0	-1.982	0.056
10	1.6		0.5457	1	0	-1.978	0.064
11	1.8		0.6326	1	0	-1.975	0.072
12	2.0		0.7196	1	0	-1.971	0.080
13	2.2		0.8065	1	0	-1.968	0.088
14	2.4		0.8935	1	0	-1.964	0.096
15	2.6		0.9804	1	0	-1.961	0.104
16	2.8		1.0674	1	0	-1.957	1.112
17	3.0	-1					

Figure 11-10. Portion of the spreadsheet to solve the second-order differential equation $y'' - (0.15 - x/2.3)y = x$ by using the finite-difference method.
(folder 'Chapter 11 Examples', workbook 'ODE-BVP', worksheet 'Finite Difference 1')

The coefficients matrix (Figure 11-11) was assembled from the values in columns F and G by entering the formula

=IF(ROW()-top=COLUMN()-left,INDIRECT("F"&ROW()),IF(ABS((ROW()-top)
   -(COLUMN()-left))=1,1,0))

in cell I9 and filling the formula into the 9 × 9 matrix of cells I8:Q16 to produce the matrix shown in Figure 11-11. The cell I9 was assigned the name TopCell and the following named formulas were entered by using **Insert→Name→ Define…**

left: =COLUMN(TopCell)

top: =ROW(TopCell)

	I	J	K	L	M	N	O	P	Q
6				Cofficients matrix					
7									
8	-1.985	1	0	0	0	0	0	0	0
9	1	-1.982	1	0	0	0	0	0	0
10	0	1	-1.978	1	0	0	0	0	0
11	0	0	1	-1.975	1	0	0	0	0
12	0	0	0	1	-1.971	1	0	0	0
13	0	0	0	0	1	-1.968	1	0	0
14	0	0	0	0	0	1	-1.964	1	0
15	0	0	0	0	0	0	1	-1.961	1
16	0	0	0	0	0	0	0	1	-1.957

Figure 11-11. Coefficients matrix to solve the second-order differential equation $y" - (0.15 - x/2.3)y = x$ by using the finite-difference method. The matrix is generated from the matrix terms in column F of Figure 11-10, then **Fill Right**.
(folder 'Chapter 11 Examples', workbook 'ODE-BVP', worksheet 'Finite Difference 1')

The solution vector was produced by the array formula

{=MMULT(MINVERSE(I9:Q17),G9:G17)}

	R
6	Results
7	2.0
8	1.360
9	0.748
10	0.178
11	-0.332
12	-0.762
13	-1.089
14	-1.294
15	-1.356
16	-1.261
17	-1.0

Figure 11-12. Results vector for the second-order differential equation $y" - (0.15 - x/2.3)y = x$ solved by using the finite-difference method.
(folder 'Chapter 11 Examples', workbook 'ODE-BVP', worksheet 'Finite Difference 1')

Solving a Second-Order Ordinary Differential Equation by the Finite-Difference Method: Another Example

In preceding sections, we used Euler's method and the Runge-Kutta method to solve the second-order differential equation $y'' - y = 0$ by the shooting method. This differential equation can be solved readily by using the finite-difference method.

By comparison with equation 11-9, we see that a = -1, b = 0, c = 0. The elements of the coefficients matrix and the constants vector, calculated as before, are shown in Figure 11-13.

	A	B	C	D	E	F	G
1			BVP by Finite-Difference Method				
2			General formula: y" + ay = bx + c				
3			y"-y=0				
4			Exact y= sinh(x)				
5	h =	0.3					
6	x	y	a	b	c	Matrix terms	Constants
7	0.1	0.1002					
8	0.4		-1	0	0	-2.09	-0.1002
9	0.7		-1	0	0	-2.09	0.0000
10	1.0		-1	0	0	-2.09	0.0000
11	1.3		-1	0	0	-2.09	0.0000
12	1.6		-1	0	0	-2.09	0.0000
13	1.9		-1	0	0	-2.09	0.0000
14	2.2		-1	0	0	-2.09	0.0000
15	2.5		-1	0	0	-2.09	0.0000
16	2.8		-1	0	0	-2.09	-11.0765
17	3.1	11.0765					

Figure 11-13. Portion of the spreadsheet to solve the second-order differential equation $y'' - y = 0$ by using the finite-difference method.
(folder 'Chapter 11 Examples', workbook 'ODE-BVP', worksheet 'Finite Difference 2')

The errors in the finite-difference method are proportional to $1/h^2$, so decreasing the interval from $h = 0.3$ to $h = 0.1$ reduces the errors by approximately one order of magnitude.

In order to simplify the construction of the coefficients matrix, you can use the spreadsheet layout shown in Figure 11-14. The formula in cell I7, which has been assigned the name top, is

=IF(ROW()-ROW(top)=COLUMN()-COLUMN(top),INDIRECT("F"&ROW()),
IF(ABS((ROW()-ROW(top))-(COLUMN()-COLUMN(top)))=1,1,0))

	H	I	J	K	L	M	N	O	P	Q
6										
7										
8		-2.09	1	0	0	0	0	0	0	0
9		1	-2.09	1	0	0	0	0	0	0
10		0	1	-2.09	1	0	0	0	0	0
11		0	0	1	-2.09	1	0	0	0	0
12		0	0	0	1	-2.09	1	0	0	0
13		0	0	0	0	1	-2.09	1	0	0
14		0	0	0	0	0	1	-2.09	1	0
15		0	0	0	0	0	0	1	-2.09	1
16		0	0	0	0	0	0	0	1	-2.09
17										

Figure 11-14. Coefficients matrix to solve the second-order differential equation
$$y'' - y = 0.$$
(folder 'Chapter 11 Examples', workbook 'ODE-BVP', worksheet 'Finite Difference 2')

To create the spreadsheet, do the following:
- Enter the desired range of x values in column A. This is best done by inserting rows within the range of x values, so as to preserve the formulas in the last row.
- Enter the boundary values of y in the first and last rows.
- Enter values or expressions for the coefficients a, b and c in cells C13, D13 and E13, and **Fill Down**.
- Select cell I7 and **Fill Down**, then **Fill Right**, to create the coefficients matrix.
- Select the cell containing the formula for the results vector and Fill Down. Enter the formula by pressing CONTROL+SHIFT+ENTER.

The results vector is shown in Figure 11-15 and a plot of the results in Figure 11-16.

	R	S	T
6	Results	y(exact)	% error
7	0.1002	0.1002	
8	0.4133	0.4108	0.6
9	0.7637	0.7586	0.7
10	1.1828	1.1752	0.6
11	1.7083	1.6984	0.6
12	2.3876	2.3756	0.5
13	3.2817	3.2682	0.4
14	4.4712	4.4571	0.3
15	6.0632	6.0502	0.2
16	8.2008	8.1919	0.1
17	11.0765	11.0765	

Figure 11-15. Results vector from the solution of the differential equation
$y'' - y = 0$ by the finite-difference method.
(folder 'Chapter 11 Examples', workbook 'ODE-BVP', worksheet 'Finite Difference 2')

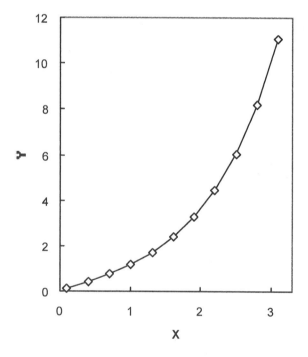

Figure 11-16. Solution of the differential equation $y'' - y = 0$
by the finite-difference method.
(folder 'Chapter 11 Examples', workbook 'ODE-BVP', worksheet 'Finite Difference 2')

A Limitation on the Finite-Difference Method

As with other methods, decreasing the size of the x increment will increase the accuracy of the calculations. But be aware that there are size limitations for Excel's MMULT and MINVERSE matrix functions: the size of the array must not exceed 52 columns by 52 rows.

Problems

Answers to the following problems are found in the folder "Ch. 11 (BVP)" in the "Problems & Solutions" folder on the CD.

1. Repeat the beam deflection example at the beginning of this chapter, using the Runge-Kutta method instead of Euler's method. Use **Goal Seek...** to solve the problem. What is the maximum beam deflection?

2. Modify the beam deflection example at the beginning of this chapter, so that 200 rows of calculation are performed, and the length of the beam L is a variable. Use **Goal Seek...** to solve the problem. What is the maximum beam deflection for a 400-in beam, the other parameters (w, E, I) remaining constant?

3. Use the shooting method and **Goal Seek...** to solve
$$y'' = x + (1-x^2)y$$
where $y(1) = 2$ and $y(3) = 0$. Use the Runge-Kutta method to calculate y.

4. Use the shooting method and **Goal Seek...** to solve
$$2y'' - xy' + 3y = 3$$
where $y(0) = 1$ and $y(1) = -6$. Use the Euler method to calculate y and y'.

5. Use the shooting method and **Goal Seek...** to solve
$$y'' - xy' + 3y = 0$$
where $y(0) = 1$ and $y(10) = 257$. Use the Euler method to calculate y and y'.

6. Use the shooting method and **Goal Seek...** to solve
$$y'' + xy' - 3y = 0$$
where $y(-3) = -9$ and $y(7) = 91$. Use the Euler method to calculate y and y'.

7. Repeat problem 3 using the Runge-Kutta method to calculate y and y'.

Chapter 12

Partial
Differential Equations

For a function $F(x,y)$ that depends on more than one independent variable, the partial derivative of the function with respect to a particular variable is the derivative of the function with respect to that variable while holding the other variables constant. For a function of two independent variables x and y, the partial derivatives are $\partial F(x,y)/\partial x$ (y held constant) and $\partial F(x,y)/\partial y$ (x held constant). There are three second-order partial derivatives for the function $F(x,y)$: $\partial^2 F(x,y)/\partial x^2$, $\partial^2 F(x,y)/\partial x \partial y$ and $d^2 F(x,y)/\partial y^2$.

Many physical systems are described by equations involving partial differential equations (PDEs). In this chapter, discussion will be limited to linear second-order partial differential equations in two independent variables. Typical examples include the variation of a property in two spatial dimensions, or the variation of a property as a function of time and distance.

Elliptic, Parabolic and Hyperbolic Partial Differential Equations

A general form of the partial differential equation (up to the second order) is

$$a\frac{\partial^2 F(x,y)}{\partial x^2} + b\frac{\partial^2 F(x,y)}{\partial x \partial y} + c\frac{\partial^2 F(x,y)}{\partial y^2} + d\frac{\partial F(x,y)}{\partial x} + e\frac{\partial F(x,y)}{\partial y} + f = 0$$

(12-1)

where the coefficients $a \ldots f$ are functions of x and y. Of course, a particular differential equation may be much simpler than equation 12-1. Depending on the values of the coefficients a, b and c, a partial differential equation is classified as elliptic, parabolic, or hyperbolic. A partial differential equation is elliptic if $b^2 - 4ac < 0$, parabolic if $b^2 - 4ac = 0$, hyperbolic if $b^2 - 4ac > 0$.

In many physical models, x represents space and y represents time. The partial differential equation known as Laplace's equation (equation 12-2) is an example of an elliptic partial differential equation.

$$\frac{\partial^2 F(x,y)}{\partial x^2} + \frac{\partial^2 F(x,y)}{\partial y^2} = 0 \qquad (12\text{-}2)$$

Elliptic equations are often used to describe the steady-state value of a function in two dimensions. Parabolic partial differential equations are often used to describe how a quantity varies with respect to both distance and time. The one-dimensional thermal diffusion equation

$$\frac{dT}{dt} = \kappa \frac{\partial^2 T}{\partial x^2} \qquad (12\text{-}3)$$

describing the temperature $T = F(x,t)$ at position x and time t in a material with thermal diffusion coefficient κ is an example of a parabolic equation ($a = b = 0$, $c = \kappa$, thus $b^2 - 4ac = 0$). A similar equation, Fick's Second Law, describes the diffusion of molecules or ions in solution, diffusion of dopant atoms into a semiconductor, and so on.

Hyperbolic partial differential equations, involving the second derivative with respect to time, are used to describe oscillatory systems. The wave equation in one dimension,

$$\frac{\partial^2 y}{\partial t^2} = k \frac{\partial^2 y}{\partial x^2} \qquad (12\text{-}4)$$

describes the vibration of a violin string. Equation 12-4 is an example of a hyperbolic partial differential equation ($a = -k$, $b = 0$, $c = 1$, thus $b^2 - 4ac = 4k$). Other applications include the vibration of structural members or the transmission of sound waves.

In the previous chapter, some general methods were described that could be applied to any system of ordinary differential equations. In contrast, different methods of solution are required in order to solve partial differential equations of these three different types. The following sections will illustrate the different methods for solving elliptic, parabolic and hyperbolic partial differential equations.

Elliptic Partial Differential Equations

Elliptic equations describe the value of a function in two spatial dimensions. Elliptic partial differential equations have boundary conditions which are specified around a closed boundary, while hyperbolic and parabolic partial differential equations have at least one open boundary. Since the values are specified around a closed boundary, the equation describes a steady-state condition.

Solving Elliptic Partial Differential Equations: Replacing Derivatives with Finite Differences

In Chapter 6 we used the following approximation for a derivative

$$\frac{dF(x)}{dx} = \frac{F(x+h)-F(x)}{h} \tag{12-5}$$

where h was a suitably small value. Equation 12-5 is the forward difference equation. The corresponding backward difference equation is

$$\frac{dF(x)}{dx} = \frac{F(x)-F(x-h)}{h} \tag{12-6}$$

For a partial derivative involving two independent variables, the finite difference equation will involve suitable small differences in both x and y. We will use h and k to represent these differences. The forward and backward difference equations corresponding to 12-5 and 12-6 are

$$\frac{dF(x,y)}{dx} = \frac{F(x+h,y)-F(x,y)}{h} \tag{12-7}$$

$$\frac{dF(x,y)}{dx} = \frac{F(x,y)-F(x-h,y)}{h} \tag{12-8}$$

and, for the partial derivative

$$\frac{\partial^2 F(x,y)}{\partial x^2} = \frac{\dfrac{dF(x+h,y)}{dx} - \dfrac{dF(x,y)}{dx}}{h} \tag{12-9}$$

Since we have used the forward difference equation 12-9 to calculate the partial derivative, we can use backward differences for dF/dx in order to eliminate bias. The result is

$$\frac{\partial^2 F(x,y)}{\partial x^2} = \frac{F(x+h,y)-2F(x,y)+F(x-h,y)}{h^2} \tag{12-10}$$

and in a similar fashion,

$$\frac{\partial^2 F(x,y)}{\partial y^2} = \frac{F(x,y+k)-2F(x,y)+F(x,y-k)}{k^2} \tag{12-11}$$

and

$$\frac{\partial^2 F(x,y)}{\partial x \partial y} = \frac{F(x+h,y+k)-2F(x,y)+F(x-h,y-k)}{hk} \tag{12-12}$$

Thus, for example, Laplace's equation (12-2) is rewritten as

$$\frac{F(x+h,y)-2F(x,y)+F(x-h,y)}{h^2}+\frac{F(x,y+k)-2F(x,y)+F(x,y-k)}{k^2}=0$$

(12-13)

Our approach for solving these problems will be to subdivide the region of interest into a lattice of mesh size $h \times k$ and write the difference equations that correspond to the lattice points, to obtain values of the function at each lattice point. For the general lattice point x_i, y_i the derivative expression is

$$\frac{F(x_{i+1},y_i)-2F(x_i,y_i)+F(x_{i-1},y_i)}{h^2}+\frac{F(x_i,y_{i+1})-2F(x_i,y_i)+F(x_i,y_{i-1})}{k^2}=0$$

(12-14)

If $h = k$, equation 12-14 simplifies to

$$F(x_{i+1},y_i)+F(x_i,y_{i+1})-4F(x_i,y_i)+F(x_i,y_{i-1})+F(x_{i-1},y_i)=0$$

(12-15)

from which we obtain equation 12-16

$$F(x_i,y_i)=\frac{F(x_{i+1},y_i)+F(x_i,y_{i+1})+F(x_i,y_{i-1})+F(x_{i-1},y_i)}{4}$$ (12-16)

For the case where $h \neq k$, an expression for $F(x,y)$ can readily be obtained from equation 12-14.

Note that four lattice points are involved in the calculation of $F(x,y)$ by equation 12-16, as represented in Figure 12-1. This representation is sometimes referred to as the *stencil* of the method.

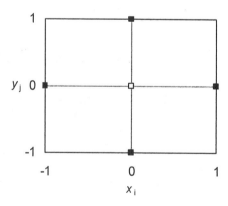

Figure 12-1. Stencil of the finite difference method for the solution of an elliptic PDE. The points shown as solid squares represent previously calculated values of the function; the open square represents the value to be calculated.

Methods for the solution of equation 12-16 can best be illustrated by reference to a concrete example.

An Example: Temperature Distribution in a Heated Metal Plate

A typical example of an elliptic partial differential equation involves the solution of a steady-state heat-flow problem. For example, if a thin steel plate, 10×10 cm, has one of the edges held at 100°C and the other three edges at 0°C, what are the steady-state temperatures within the plate? For simplicity, we assume that heat is not lost through the faces of the plate.

We subdivide the plate by means of a grid with $h = k = 0.5$ cm, thus creating a lattice of size 20×20. At equilibrium, heat flows in the x-axis direction into a lattice element at a rate proportional to the temperature of the adjoining element in the x-axis, and flows out of the element at a rate proportional to the temperature of the element. The same is true in the y-axis direction. This model gives rise to an elliptic partial differential equation of the form of equation 12-2. The time and the thermal conductivity k of the material do not enter into the equation.

We will use equation 12-16 to calculate the temperature at each lattice point; the temperature at a lattice point is the average of the temperatures of the four surrounding lattice points. Thus we have generated a system of 400 simultaneous linear equations in 400 unknowns. Although most of the terms in a given equation are zero, the problem is still unmanageable. However, we can solve the system by an iterative method, as described below.

Figure 12-2 shows part of the spreadsheet used to solve the system; each cell of the 20×20 array corresponds to a lattice point. The formula in cell B6 is

    =(B5+A6+C6+B7)/4

You can **Fill Down** the formula into 20 rows and then **Fill Right** into 20 columns to create the 20×20 array.

Since cell B6 refers to cell B7 and B7 similarly refers to B6, we have created a circular reference, a formula that refers to itself, either directly or indirectly. In fact, the spreadsheet contains a large number of circular references. A circular reference is usually an error; Excel displays the "Cannot resolve circular references" error message and puts a zero in the cell. In this case, however, the circular reference is intentional. We can make Excel recalculate the value in each cell, using the result of the previous iteration.

	A	B	C	D	E	F	G	H	I	J	K	L	M	N	O	P
5	0	0	0	0	0	0	0	0	0	0	0	0	0	0	0	0
6	0	0.25	0.49	0.72	0.94	1.1	1.3	1.4	2	2	2	2	2	2	1.4	1.3
7	0	0.50	1.0	1.5	2	2	3	3	3	3	3	3	3	3	3	3
8	0	0.77	2	2	3	3	4	4	5	5	5	5	5	5	4	4
9	0	1.1	2	3	4	5	5	6	7	7	7	7	7	7	6	5
10	0	1.4	3	4	5	6	7	8	8	9	9	9	9	8	8	7
11	0	2	3	5	6	8	9	10	10	11	11	11	11	10	10	9
12	0	2	4	6	8	9	11	12	13	13	14	14	13	13	12	11
13	0	3	5	7	9	11	13	14	15	16	16	16	16	15	14	13
14	0	3	6	9	11	14	16	17	18	19	20	20	19	18	17	16
15	0	4	7	10	13	16	18	20	22	23	23	23	23	22	20	18
16	0	4	9	12	16	19	22	24	25	26	27	27	26	25	24	22
17	0	5	10	15	19	23	26	28	30	31	31	31	31	30	28	26
18	0	6	12	18	22	27	30	33	35	36	37	37	36	35	33	30
19	0	8	15	21	27	31	35	38	40	42	42	42	42	40	38	35
20	0	9	18	25	32	37	41	44	46	48	49	49	48	46	44	41
21	0	12	22	31	38	44	48	51	54	55	56	56	55	54	51	48
22	0	15	28	38	46	52	56	59	62	63	64	64	63	62	59	56
23	0	20	36	48	56	62	66	68	70	71	72	72	71	70	68	66
24	0	30	49	61	68	73	76	78	80	81	81	81	81	80	78	76
25	0	50	69	78	83	86	88	89	90	90	90	90	90	90	89	88
26	100	100	100	100	100	100	100	100	100	100	100	100	100	100	100	100

Figure 12-2. Solving an elliptic PDE using intentional circular references. The worksheet shows part of the 20 × 20 array of lattice points representing the temperature distribution in a metal plate; the gray cells represent the temperature at the edges of the plate.
(folder 'Chapter 12 (PDE) Examples, workbook 'Elliptic PDE', sheet 'Temp in a Plate')

To "turn on" iteration, choose **Tools→Options→Calculation** and check the iteration box. Unless you change the default settings for iteration, Microsoft Excel stops calculating after 100 iterations or after all values in the circular reference change by less than 0.001 between iterations, whichever comes first. When you press OK the iterative circular reference calculations will begin.

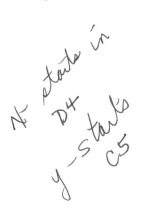

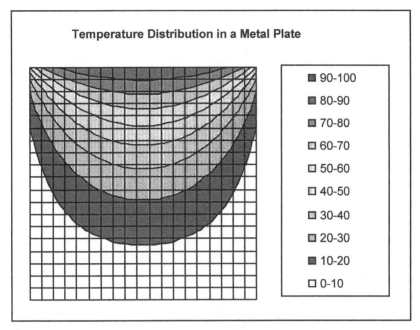

Figure 12-3. Temperature distribution in a metal plate.
(folder 'Chapter 12 (PDE) Examples, workbook 'Elliptic PDE', sheet 'Temp in a Plate')

Parabolic Partial Differential Equations

The previous example showed the steady-state distribution of temperature within a metal plate. We will now examine how temperature changes with time. This so-called heat equation is an example of a parabolic partial differential equation.

Consider the flow of heat within a metal rod of length L, one end of which is held at a known high temperature, the other end at a lower temperature. Heat will flow from the hot end to the cooler end. We want to calculate the temperature along the length of the rod as a function of time. We'll assume that the rod is perfectly insulated, so that heat loss through the sides can be neglected.

Consider a small element dx along the length of the rod. Heat is flowing from the hot end ($x = 0$) to the cooler end ($x = L$). The rate of heat flow into the element at the point x is given by

$$-\kappa A \frac{dT}{dx} \tag{12-17}$$

where κ is the coefficient of thermal conductivity (cal s^{-1} cm^{-1} deg^{-1}), A is the cross-sectional area of the rod (cm^2) and dT/dx is the temperature gradient. The minus sign is required because temperature gradients are negative (heat flows from a higher temperature to a lower). The material of which the rod is made has heat capacity c (cal g^{-1} deg^{-1}) and density ρ (g cm^{-3}).

The heat flow (cal s^{-1}) out of the volume element, at point $x + dx$, is given by

$$-\kappa A\left(\frac{dT}{dx} + \frac{d}{dx}\left(\frac{dT}{dx}\right)dx\right) \qquad (12\text{-}18)$$

The rate of increase of heat stored in the element Adx is given by

$$c\rho(Adx)\frac{dT}{dt} \qquad (12\text{-}19)$$

From equations 12-17 and 12-18, the rate of increase of heat stored in the element Adx is $H_{in} - H_{out}$, and this is equal to the expression in 12-19

$$-\kappa A\frac{dT}{dx} - \left(-\kappa A\left(\frac{dT}{dx} + \frac{d}{dx}\left(\frac{dT}{dx}\right)dx\right)\right) = c\rho(Adx)\frac{dT}{dt} \qquad (12\text{-}20)$$

which can be simplified to

$$\kappa\left(\frac{\partial^2 T}{\partial x^2}\right) = c\rho\frac{dT}{dt} \qquad (12\text{-}21)$$

or

$$\frac{\partial^2 T}{\partial x^2} - \frac{c\rho}{\kappa}\frac{dT}{dt} = 0 \qquad (12\text{-}21a)$$

an example of a parabolic partial differential equation.

There are several methods for the solution of parabolic partial differential equations. Two common methods are the explicit method and the Crank-Nicholson method. In either method, we will replace partial derivatives by finite differences, as we did in the example of the parabolic partial differential equation.

Solving Parabolic Partial Differential Equations: The Explicit Method

Using equation 12-21 as an example and writing it in the form

$$\frac{\partial^2 F}{\partial x^2} + k\frac{dF}{dy} = 0 \qquad (12\text{-}22)$$

we can replace derivatives by finite differences, using the central difference formula for $\partial^2 F/\partial x^2$

$$\frac{\partial^2 F}{\partial x^2}(i, j) = \frac{F_{i+1,j} - 2F_{i,j} + F_{i-1,j}}{(\Delta x)^2} \tag{12-23}$$

and the forward difference formula for dF/dy

$$\frac{dF}{dy}(i, j) = \frac{F_{i,j+1} - F_{i,j}}{\Delta y} \tag{12-24}$$

When these are substituted into equation 12-22, we obtain equation 12-25, where $r = \Delta y/(k(\Delta x)^2)$. (Using forward and central differences simplifies the expression.)

$$F_{i,j+1} = r(F_{i+1,j} + F_{i-1,j}) + (1 - r)F_{i,j} \tag{12-25}$$

Or, when i represents distance x and j represents time t,

$$F_{x,t+1} = r(F_{x+1,t} + F_{x-1,t}) + (1 - r)F_{x,t} \tag{12-25a}$$

Equation 12-25a permits us to calculate the value of the function at time t_{+1} based on values at time t. This is illustrated graphically by the stencil of the method.

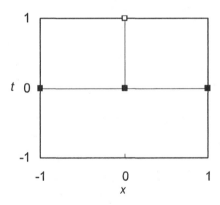

Figure 12-4. Stencil of the explicit method for the solution of a parabolic PDE.
The points shown as solid squares represent previously calculated values
of the function; the open square represents the value to be calculated.

An alternative to the use of equation 12-25 is to choose Δx and Δy such that $r = 0.5$ (e.g., for a given value of Δx, $\Delta y = k(\Delta x)^2/2$), so that equation 12-25 is simplified to

$$F_{i,j+1} = \frac{F_{i+1,j} + F_{i-1,j}}{2} \tag{12-26}$$

An Example: Heat Conduction in a Brass Rod

Consider an insulated 10-cm brass rod, initially at a temperature of 0°C. One end of the rod is heated to 100°C. Equation 12-20 describes the heat flow in the rod as a function of time. (For simplicity, we assume that there is no heat loss through the sides of the rod.) For brass, the coefficient of thermal conductivity k is 0.26 cal s^{-1} cm^{-1} deg^{-1}, the heat capacity c is 0.094 cal g^{-1} deg^{-1} and the density ρ is 8.4 g cm^{-3}. From these values, the coefficient k in equation 12-22 is 3.04 s cm^{-2}. Figure 12-5 shows part of the spreadsheet used to calculate the temperature along the rod, in 1-second and 1-cm intervals. The table extends to t = 100 seconds (row 113).

	A	B	C	D	E	F	G	H	I	J	K	L	M	N
1			Time-dependent Temperature Distribution in a Brass Rod											
2			(Temperature values in bold are constant)											
3			length, cm									10		
4			heat capacity of brass, cal/g/deg									0.1	(hcap)	
5			thermal conductivity of brass, cal/sec/cm/deg									0.3	(k)	
6			density of brass, g/cm3									8.4	(rho)	
7			Coefficient e in general PDE, =k/(hcap*rho)									0.3	(e)	
8			Δx									1	(Dx)	
9			Δt									1	(Dt)	
10			f=e*Dt/(Dx^2)									0.3	(f)	
11							Distance x (cm)							
12			0	1	2	3	4	5	6	7	8	9	10	
13		0	100	0	0	0	0	0	0	0	0	0	0	
14		1	100	32.9	0.0	0.0	0.0	0.0	0.0	0.0	0.0	0.0	0	
15		2	100	44.2	10.8	0.0	0.0	0.0	0.0	0.0	0.0	0.0	0	
16		3	100	51.6	18.2	3.6	0.0	0.0	0.0	0.0	0.0	0.0	0	
17		4	100	56.5	24.4	7.2	1.2	0.0	0.0	0.0	0.0	0.0	0	
18		5	100	60.3	29.3	10.9	2.8	0.4	0.0	0.0	0.0	0.0	0	
19		6	100	63.2	33.4	14.3	4.7	1.0	0.1	0.0	0.0	0.0	0	
20		7	100	65.5	36.9	17.4	6.6	1.9	0.4	0.0	0.0	0.0	0	
21		8	100	67.5	39.9	20.3	8.6	3.0	0.8	0.1	0.0	0.0	0	
22		9	100	69.1	42.5	22.9	10.6	4.1	1.3	0.3	0.1	0.0	0	
23		10	100	70.5	44.8	25.3	12.5	5.3	1.9	0.5	0.1	0.0	0	

Figure 12-5. Calculation of heat flow in a brass rod.
The text in cells M4:M10 are the names assigned to the cells L4:L10.
(folder 'Chapter 12 (PDE) Examples, workbook 'Parabolic PDE', sheet 'Temp distribution')

Cells K3:K9 contain constants used in the calculations; these cells were assigned the names shown in parentheses in column M. The formulas in cells K6, K7, K8 and K9 are, respectively

=k/(hcap*rho)   (coefficient k in general PDE, equation 12-22)

=D12-C12 (Δx)

=B14-B13 (Δt)

=e*Dt/(Dx^2)   (f)

[In the spreadsheet, the range name f was used for the parameter r in equation 12-26, since r can't be used as a name in Excel.]

The values in cells on the edges of the table of temperatures (column C and column M) are the constant temperature values at the ends of the rod; the values in row 13 are the initial temperature of the interior of the rod. The formula in the remaining cells in the body of the temperature table (D14:L113) is based on equation 12-22. For example, the formula in cell D14 is

=f*(C13+E13)+(1-2*f)*D13

Experience has shown that the factor f must be less than 1/2 in order to avoid instability in the calculations. For a given problem, this requires adjustment of both Δx and Δt.

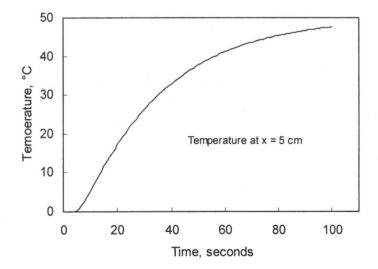

Figure 12-6. Temperature vs. time in a brass rod.
(folder 'Chapter 12 (PDE) Examples, workbook 'Parabolic PDE', sheet 'Temp distribution')

Solving Parabolic Partial Differential Equations: The Crank-Nicholson or Implicit Method

In the explicit method, we used a central difference formula for the second derivative and a forward difference formula for the first derivative (equations 12-24 and 12-25). A variant of equation 12-26 that makes the approximations to both derivatives central differences is known as the Crank-Nicholson formula

$$-rF_{i-1,j+1} + (2+2r)F_{i,j+1} - rF_{i+1,j+1} = rF_{i-1,j} + (2-2r)F_{i,j} + rF_{i+1,j}$$

(12-27)

or, if i represents distance x and j represents time t,

$$-rF_{x-1,t+1} + (2+2r)F_{x,t+1} - rF_{x+1,t+1} = rF_{x-1,t} + (2-2r)F_{x,t} + rF_{x+1,t}$$

(12-27a)

where $r = \Delta y/(k(\Delta x)^2)$. Choosing specific values for r and Δx determines the increment Δy. For $r = 1$, equation 12-27a simplifies to equation 12-28.

$$-F_{x-1,t+1} + 4F_{x,t+1} - F_{x+1,t+1} = F_{x-1,t} + F_{x+1,t}$$ (12-28)

Equation 12-27a or 12-28 shows that $F_{x,t+1}$ is a function of yet-to-be-calculated values at t_{+1} ($F_{x-1,t+1}$ and $F_{x+1,t+1}$) in addition to known values at time t (the quantities on the right-hand side of the equation). This is illustrated by the stencil of the method shown in Figure 12-7. Equation 12-27a results in a set of simultaneous equations at each time step. Again, the solution procedure is best illustrated by means of an example.

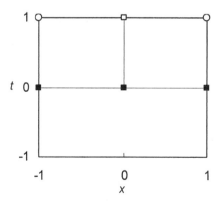

Figure 12-7. Stencil of the implicit method for the solution of a parabolic PDE. The points shown as solid squares represent previously calculated values of the function; the open circles represent unknown values in adjacent positions; the open square represents the value to be calculated.

An Example: Vapor Diffusion in a Tube

An air-filled tube 20 cm long allows water vapor to diffuse from a source (liquid water) to a drying chamber, where the vapors are dissipated. Initially the tube is capped so that the vapor cannot escape. The temperature of the tube is held at 30°C. The equilibrium vapor pressure of water at this temperature is 31.8 mm Hg; thus the vapor pressure inside the tube is 31.8 mm Hg. When the cap is removed, the vapor will diffuse toward the drying chamber, where the water vapor pressure is zero. We wish to model the vapor pressure along the length of the tube as a function of time.

The diffusion equation is

$$\frac{dp}{dt} = D\frac{\partial^2 p}{\partial x^2} \tag{12-29}$$

where p is the vapor pressure and D is the diffusion coefficient in units of cm^2 s^{-1}. For water vapor, $D = 0.115$ cm^2 s^{-1} at 30°C.

We subdivide the length of the tube into uniform subintervals and calculate the value of the function (here the vapor pressure p) at each interior point. Choosing $\Delta x = 4$ yields four x values where the function value needs to be evaluated (at $x = 4, 8, 12$ and 16 cm) and two boundary values where it is known (at $x = 0$ and 20). Also, using $\Delta x = 4$ and $r = 1$ sets $\Delta t = 139$ seconds.

Using equation 12-28 yields four simultaneous equations in four unknowns, thus:

for $x = 4, t = 139$: $\quad -p_{0,139} + 4p_{4,139} - p_{8,139} = p_{0,0} + p_{8,0}$

$\qquad\qquad\qquad\qquad -31.8 + 4p_{4,139} - p_{8,139} = 31.8 + 31.8$

$\qquad\qquad\qquad\qquad\quad\; 0 + 4p_{4,139} - p_{8,139} = 95.4$

for $x = 8, t = 139$: $\quad -p_{4,139} + 4p_{8,139} - p_{12,139} = p_{4,0} + p_{12,0}$

$\qquad\qquad\qquad\qquad -p_{4,139} + 4p_{8,139} - p_{12,139} = 63.6$

for $x = 12, t = 139$: $\;\; -p_{8,139} + 4p_{12,139} - p_{16,139} = p_{8,0} + p_{16,0}$

$\qquad\qquad\qquad\qquad -p_{8,139} + 4p_{12,139} - p_{16,139} = 63.6$

for $x = 16, t = 139$: $\;\; -p_{12,139} + 4p_{16,139} - p_{20,139} = p_{12,0} + p_{20,0}$

$\qquad\qquad\qquad\qquad -p_{12,139} + 4p_{16,139} - 0 = 31.8 + 0$

$\qquad\qquad\qquad\qquad -p_{12,139} + 4p_{16,139} - 0 = 31.8$

For $r = 1$, the values of the coefficients for the four simultaneous equations are shown in the spreadsheet in Figure 12-8. They are designated c1, c2, c3 and c4 in the table. These coefficients will have different values if a different value of r is chosen. The constants (the values of the right-hand side of the four equations) are also shown in Figure 12-8. The formulas in cells I15:L15 are

=C15+E15+C15

=D15+F15

=E15+G15

=F15+H15+H15

	A	B	C	D	E	F	G	H	I	J	K	L
1				**Time-Dependent Diffusion of Water Vapor**								
2				(calculated by the Crank-Nicholson method)								
3				Vapor pressure of water at 30°C = 31.8 mm Hg								
4		Diffusion coefficient at 30°C, cm/sec2							0.115	(D)		
5		Dx, cm							4	(Dx)		
6		Dt=Dx^2/D							139.1	(Dt)		
7		f							1	(f)		
8		coefficients:	c1	c2	c3	c4						
9			4	-1	0	0						
10			-1	4	-1	0						
11			0	-1	4	-1						
12			0	0	-1	4						
13				**Distance x (cm)**								
14			0	4	8	12	16	20		constants		
15	time t (sec)	0	31.8	31.8	31.8	31.8	31.8	0.0	95.4	63.6	63.6	31.8
16		139	31.8	31.5	30.6	27.2	14.8	0.0	94.2	58.7	45.3	27.2
17		278	31.8	30.4	27.6	21.3	12.1	0.0	91.2	51.7	39.7	21.3
18		417	31.8	29.0	24.8	18.6	10.0	0.0	88.4	47.7	34.8	18.6
19		557	31.8	27.9	23.1	16.7	8.8	0.0	86.7	44.5	31.9	16.7
20		696	31.8	27.1	21.8	15.4	8.0	0.0	85.4	42.5	29.8	15.4
21		835	31.8	26.6	20.9	14.5	7.5	0.0	84.5	41.1	28.4	14.5
22		974	31.8	26.2	20.3	14.0	7.1	0.0	83.9	40.2	27.4	14.0
23		1113	31.8	26.0	19.9	13.6	6.9	0.0				

Figure 12-8. A convenient spreadsheet layout for solving a parabolic PDE by the Crank-Nicholson method. The coefficients matrix is aligned directly above the table of values and the table of constants directly to the right.
(folder 'Chapter 12 (PDE) Examples, workbook 'Parabolic PDE', sheet 'Crank-Nicholson 1')

The set of simultaneous equations can be solved by methods described in Chapter 9. In this case the solution was found by the matrix inversion method; the array formula in cells D19:G19 is

{=MMULT(I15:L15,MINVERSE($D$9:$G$12))}

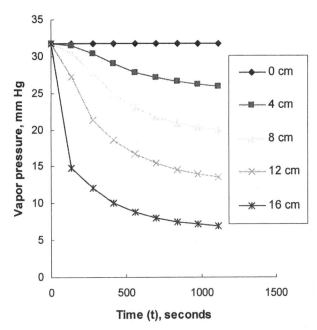

Figure 12-9. Chart of the results produced by the spreadsheet in Figure 12-8.
(folder 'Chapter 12 (PDE) Examples, workbook 'Parabolic PDE', sheet 'Crank-Nicholson 1')

A plot of the results, shown in Figure 12-9, indicates that a smaller increment of t is required.

In the preceding example, the parameter r was set equal to 1, which simplifies the equations but also determines the values of t that were used in the calculations. In most cases it will probably be desirable to solve the system at specified values of t. Choosing specific values for Δx and Δt determines the value of r. The following example, using the same data as Example 12-3, illustrates this.

Vapor Diffusion in a Tube Revisited

This example uses formulas that permit the construction of a more general model. In Figure 12-10, the following cells or ranges were defined: D: $G$4; Dx: $G$5; Dt: $G$6; f: $G$7; coefficients: $D$9:$G$12; constants: $J$15:$M$26; values: $C$15:$H$27. The formulas in cells G5:G7 are, respectively,

=D14-C14

=B16-B15

=(D*Dt)/Dx^2

	A	B	C	D	E	F	G	H
1		**Time-Dependent Diffusion of Water Vapor(2)**						
2		(calculated by the Crank-Nicholson method)						
3								
4		Diffusion coefficient at 30°C, cm/sec^2					0.115	
5		Dx, cm					4	
6		Dt=Dx^2/D					50	
7		f					0.3594	
8				c1	c2	c3	c4	
9		coefficients		2.7188	-0.3594	0.0000	0.0000	
10				-0.3594	2.7188	-0.3594	0.0000	
11				0.0000	-0.3594	2.7188	-0.3594	
12				0.0000	0.0000	-0.3594	2.7188	
13				**Distance x (cm)**				
14			0	4	8	12	16	20
15		0	**31.8**	**31.8**	**31.8**	**31.8**	**31.8**	**0.0**
16		50	**31.8**	31.8	31.6	30.6	23.2	**0.0**
17		100	**31.8**	31.7	31.1	28.3	18.7	**0.0**
18		150	**31.8**	31.4	30.2	26.0	16.0	**0.0**
19		200	**31.8**	31.1	29.1	24.1	14.2	**0.0**
20		250	**31.8**	30.6	28.0	22.5	12.8	**0.0**
21		300	**31.8**	30.1	27.0	21.1	11.8	**0.0**
22		350	**31.8**	29.6	26.0	20.0	11.0	**0.0**
23		400	**31.8**	29.1	25.2	19.0	10.3	**0.0**
24		450	**31.8**	28.7	24.4	18.2	9.8	**0.0**
25		500	**31.8**	28.3	23.8	17.5	9.3	**0.0**
26		550	**31.8**	27.9	23.2	16.8	8.9	**0.0**
27		600	**31.8**	27.6	22.6	16.3	8.6	**0.0**

(the B column label "time t (sec)" runs vertically alongside rows 19–22)

Figure 12-10. A convenient spreadsheet layout for solving a parabolic PDE by the Crank-Nicholson method. The coefficients matrix is aligned directly above the table of values and the table of constants is directly to the right.
(folder 'Chapter 12 (PDE) Examples, workbook 'Parabolic PDE', sheet 'Crank-Nicholson 2')

In the coefficients table, the formulas =2+2*f, =-f or 0, were entered in the appropriate cells to create the table.

The constants table employs a single formula:

=f*TableValue1+(2-2*f)*TableValue2+f*TableValue3+IF(COLUMN()=MinCol,f*TableValue1,0)+IF(COLUMN()=MaxCol,f*TableValue3,0)

where TableValue1, TableValue2 and TableValue3 correspond to the function values on the right-hand side of the general equation 12-27a; the IF function terms add the appropriate boundary value terms to the first and last constant terms (see the four simultaneous equations following equation 12-29). The preceding Excel formula uses the following named formulas (they can be examined by choosing **Insert** → **Name** → **Define**):

ValuesTableCol	=COLUMN()-7
TableValue1	=INDIRECT("RC"& ValuesTableCol,0)
TableValue2	=INDIRECT("RC"& ValuesTableCol +1,0)
TableValue3	=INDIRECT("RC"& ValuesTableCol +2,0)
MaxCol	=MAX(COLUMN(constants))
MinCol	=MIN(COLUMN(constants))

For readers unfamiliar with the INDIRECT function, INDIRECT(*ref_text, a1*) returns a reference specified by a text string. The optional argument a1 specifies what reference style is used: if a1 is TRUE or omitted, the reference is in A1-style; if a1 is FALSE the reference is in R1C1-style.

The ValuesTableCol formula returns the column number of the values table that corresponds to the column in the constants table. This column number is used in the TableValue1, TableValue2 and TableValue3 formulas to return the appropriate value from the table of values. (The number 7 in the formula might have to be changed if columns in the spreadsheet were rearranged.) The MaxCol and MinCol formulas are used in the IF function in the formula in the constants table so as to add the boundary value terms to the first and last constant terms.

Vapor Diffusion in a Tube (Again)

This example, using the same data, illustrates the use of a smaller grid size. The spreadsheet ('Crank-Nicholson 3'), not shown here, can be examined on the accompanying CD-ROM. The x-increment is 2 cm, thus creating a table of values that is 11 columns wide, including the boundary values, and requiring a 9 × 9 matrix of coefficients.

The spreadsheet employs a single formula for all cells of the coefficients table:

=IF(CoeffTableRow=CoeffTableCol,2+2*f,IF(ABS(CoeffTableRow-CoeffTableCol)=1,-f,0))

The formula uses the following named formulas

CoeffTableCol	=COLUMN()-MIN(COLUMN(coefficients))
CoeffTableRow	=ROW()-MIN(ROW(coefficients))

Thus a Crank-Nicholson calculation can be set up on a spreadsheet using a single formula to create the coefficients table, a (different) single formula to create the constants table, and a single formula for the values table.

The results using the smaller grid size are shown in the following chart.

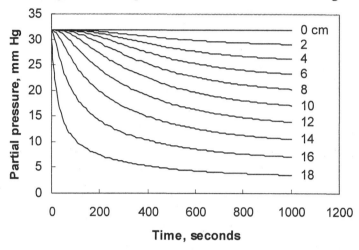

Figure 12-11. Chart of the results produced by the spreadsheet shown in Figure 12-10. (folder 'Chapter 12 (PDE) Examples, workbook 'Parabolic PDE', sheet 'Crank-Nicholson 3')

A Crank-Nicholson Custom Function

Using a smaller increment for Δt improves the accuracy of the calculations. It may be desirable to employ a variable value for Δt, so as to use smaller Δt near the beginning and use larger Δt where the function is not changing rapidly. This obviously can't be done with the spreadsheets in the preceding examples, since Δt determines the value of r and thus the values in the coefficients matrix. The following VBA code implements the Crank-Nicholson method. The partial differential equation must be of the form shown in equation 12-29, that is, $a\partial^2 C / \partial x^2 - \partial C / \partial y = 0$. The syntax of the function is CrankNicholson(***coeff, delta_x, delta_t, prev_values***). *Coeff* is the coefficient a in the above partial differential equation. *Delta_x* is the size of the x-increment, which must be constant. *Delta_y* is the size of the y-increment, which can vary. *Prev_values* is the range of function values, including the endpoint values, in the preceding row. The function returns an array of values in a row; the user must select the appropriate range of cells for the results, then press CTRL+SHIFT+ENTER (Windows) or CONTROL+SHIFT+RETURN (Macintosh) to enter the formula

```vba
Option Explicit
Option Base 1
Function CrankNicholson(coeff, delta_x, delta_t, prev_values)
'Solves a parabolic PDE by the Crank-Nicholson method.

Dim I As Integer, J As Integer, N As Integer
Dim F As Double
Dim CoeffMatrix() As Double, ConstantsVector() As Double

N = prev_values.Count
ReDim CoeffMatrix(N - 2, N - 2), ConstantsVector(N - 2, 1)
F = coeff * delta_t / delta_x ^ 2

'Create coefficients matrix.  This is an N x N matrix.
For I = 1 To N - 2
For J = 1 To N - 2
  Select Case J
  Case I
      CoeffMatrix(I, J) = 2 + 2 * F
  Case I - 1
      CoeffMatrix(I, J) = -F
  Case I + 1
      CoeffMatrix(I, J) = -F
  Case Else
      CoeffMatrix(I, J) = 0
  End Select
Next J, I

'Create constants vector.  This is a COLUMN vector.
For J = 1 To N - 2
  ConstantsVector(J, 1) = F * prev_values(J) + (2 - 2 * F) * prev_values(J + 1) + F * _
  prev_values(J + 2)
Next J
ConstantsVector(1, 1) = ConstantsVector(1, 1) + F * _ prev_values(1)
ConstantsVector(N - 2, 1) = ConstantsVector(N - 2, 1) + F * prev_values(N)

'Return results as an array in a row, thus use Transpose.
CrankNicholson = Application.Transpose(Application. _
MMult(Application.MInverse(CoeffMatrix),ConstantsVector))

End Function
```

Figure 12-12. VBA function procedure to evaluate a PDE
by the Crank-Nicholson method.
(folder 'Chapter 12 (PDE) Examples, workbook 'Parabolic PDE', module 'Module1')

Vapor Diffusion in a Tube
Solved by Using a Custom Function

This example, using the same data as the preceding one, illustrates the use of the custom function. The spreadsheet, not shown here, can be examined on the accompanying CD-ROM. Unlike the preceding spreadsheets, tables of coefficients and constants are not required. The x-increment is 2 cm, thus creating a table of values that is 11 columns wide, including the boundary values. The function returns values identical to those shown in Figure 12-11.

Hyperbolic Partial Differential Equations

Hyperbolic second-order differential equations result from problems involving vibration processes, and are of the form

$$p\frac{\partial^2 F}{\partial x^2} = q\frac{\partial^2 y}{\partial x^2} \tag{12-30}$$

For example, the wave equation in one dimension

$$\frac{\partial^2 y}{\partial t^2} = \frac{Tg}{w}\frac{\partial^2 y}{\partial x^2} \tag{12-31}$$

describes the vibration (i.e., the lateral displacement y) of a string of length L, weight W, tension T and weight/unit length $w = W/L$, as a function of distance x along the length of the string.

Solving Hyperbolic Partial Differential Equations:
Replacing Derivatives with Finite Differences

Once again, we can solve the problem by replacing derivatives by finite differences.

$$\frac{F_{x,t+1} - 2F_{x,t} + F_{x,t-1}}{(\Delta t)^2} = \frac{Tg}{w}\left(\frac{F_{x+1,t} - 2F_{x,t} + F_{x-1,t}}{(\Delta x)^2}\right) \tag{12-32}$$

which, when rearranged, yields

$$F_{x,t+1} = \frac{Tg}{w}\frac{(\Delta t)^2}{(\Delta x)^2}(F_{x+1,t} + F_{x-1,t}) - F_{x,t-1} + 2\left(1 - \frac{Tg}{w}\frac{(\Delta t)^2}{(\Delta x)^2}\right)F_{x,t} \tag{12-33}$$

If we set $Tg(\Delta t)^2/w(\Delta x)^2 = 1$, equation 12-33 is simplified to equation 12-34. Interestingly, this simplified expression also yields the most accurate results.

$$F_{x,t+1} = F_{x+1,t} + F_{x-1,t} - F_{x,t-1} \tag{12-34}$$

When employing the simplified equation, the value of Δt is determined by the expression

$$\Delta t = \frac{\Delta x}{\sqrt{Tg/w}} \qquad (12\text{-}35)$$

Equation 12-34 calculates the value of the function at time t_{+1} from values at t and t_{-1}. Figure 12-13 shows the stencil of the method.

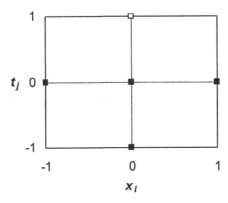

Figure 12-13. Stencil of the method for the solution of a hyperbolic PDE. The solid squares represent previously calculated values of the function; the open square represents the value to be calculated.

To begin the calculations (i.e., to calculate the value of the function at t_1), equation 12-34 requires values of the function at $t_0 = 0$ and also a value at t_{-1}. We can get a value for the function at t_{-1} by making use of the fact that the function is periodic. If the initial value of the function is zero, we can use the expression 12-36 for the first row of the calculation, and 12-34 afterwards.

$$F_{x,1} = \frac{F_{x+1,0} + F_{x-1,0}}{2} \qquad (12\text{-}36)$$

If the value of the function is not zero at $t = 0$, a different method of beginning the solution must be used.

An Example: Vibration of a String

A string 50 cm long and weighing 0.5 g is under a tension of 33 kg. Initially the mid-point of the string is displaced 0.5 cm from its equilibrium position and released. We want to calculate the displacement as a function of time at 5 cm intervals along the length of the string, using equation 12-34. From equation 12-35 the Δt must be 8.8×10^{-5} seconds.

The spreadsheet shown in Figure 12-14 illustrates the solution of the vibrating string problem. Column B contains time in increments of Δt from zero to 2.8×10^{-3} seconds (only part of the spreadsheet is shown). The first row of displacement values (row 12, values shown in bold on the spreadsheet) are the initial conditions. The values in the second row (row 13, values in italics) are calculated according to equation 12-36; the formula in cell D13 is

=(C12+E12)/2

Values in subsequent rows (rows 14-27 in Figure 12-14; rows 14-44 on the CD-ROM) are calculated according to equation 12-34; the formula in cell D14 is

=C13+E13-D12

	A	B	C	D	E	F	G	H	I	J	K	L	M
1		The Wave Equation: Vibration of a String											
2		length, cm								50			(L)
3		tension, g								33000			(T)
4		weight,g								0.5			(Wt)
5		weight per unit length, g/cm								0.01			(w)
6		gravitational constant, cm/sec2								980			(g)
7		Dx								5			(Dx)
8		Dt								8.79E-05			(Dt)
10							distance x, cm						
11			0	5	10	15	20	25	30	35	40	45	50
12		0	0	0.1	0.2	0.3	0.4	0.5	0.4	0.3	0.2	0.1	0
13		8.8E-05	0	0.1	0.2	0.3	0.4	0.4	0.4	0.3	0.2	0.1	0
14		1.8E-04	0	0.1	0.2	0.3	0.3	0.3	0.3	0.3	0.2	0.1	0
15		2.6E-04	0	0.1	0.2	0.2	0.2	0.2	0.2	0.2	0.2	0.1	0
16		3.5E-04	0	0.1	0.1	0.1	0.1	0.1	0.1	0.1	0.1	0.1	0
17		4.4E-04	0	0.0	0.0	0.0	0.0	0.0	0.0	0.0	0.0	0.0	0
18		5.3E-04	0	-0.1	-0.1	-0.1	-0.1	-0.1	-0.1	-0.1	-0.1	-0.1	0
19		6.2E-04	0	-0.1	-0.2	-0.2	-0.2	-0.2	-0.2	-0.2	-0.2	-0.1	0
20		7.0E-04	0	-0.1	-0.2	-0.3	-0.3	-0.3	-0.3	-0.3	-0.2	-0.1	0
21		7.9E-04	0	-0.1	-0.2	-0.3	-0.4	-0.4	-0.4	-0.3	-0.2	-0.1	0
22		8.8E-04	0	-0.1	-0.2	-0.3	-0.4	-0.5	-0.4	-0.3	-0.2	-0.1	0
23		9.7E-04	0	-0.1	-0.2	-0.3	-0.4	-0.4	-0.4	-0.3	-0.2	-0.1	0
24		1.1E-03	0	-0.1	-0.2	-0.3	-0.3	-0.3	-0.3	-0.3	-0.2	-0.1	0
25		1.1E-03	0	-0.1	-0.2	-0.2	-0.2	-0.2	-0.2	-0.2	-0.2	-0.1	0
26		1.2E-03	0	-0.1	-0.1	-0.1	-0.1	-0.1	-0.1	-0.1	-0.1	-0.1	0
27		1.3E-03	0	0.0	0.0	0.0	0.0	0.0	0.0	0.0	0.0	0.0	0

Figure 12-14. A spreadsheet layout for solving a hyperbolic PDE.
(folder 'Chapter 12 (PDE) Examples', workbook 'Hyperbolic PDE', sheet 'Sheet1')

If you examine the values in the table, you will see that 20 time increments constitute a complete cycle of vibration. This vibration time, 0.001758 seconds, corresponds to a frequency of 569 s^{-1}, and agrees exactly with the value calculated by the formula

$$f = \frac{1}{2L}\sqrt{Tg/w} \qquad (12\text{-}37)$$

The above procedure can be expanded to model vibrations in two space dimensions.

$$\frac{\partial^2 F}{\partial t^2} = a\left(\frac{\partial^2 F}{\partial x^2} + \frac{\partial^2 F}{\partial y^2}\right) \qquad (12\text{-}38)$$

Problems

Data for, and answers to, the following problems are found in the folder "Ch. 12 (Partial Differential Equations) problems" in the "Problems & Solutions" folder on the CD.

1. Repeat the example of temperature distribution in a metal plate, where two adjacent edges are at 0°C and where the temperatures of the other two edges increase from zero, in increments of 10°C, to 200°C at the corner diagonally opposite the two edges at zero.

2. Revise the example of temperature distribution in a metal plate to model the temperature in a conduit where the outside edges of the 20 × 20 matrix are at 0°C and the interior channel (a 10 × 10 matrix centered inside the 20 × 20 matrix) is at 200°C.

Chapter 13

Linear Regression and Curve Fitting

"Curve fitting" is frequently used in scientific or engineering applications to obtain the coefficients of a mathematical model that describes experimental data. In Chapter 5 we saw how to obtain the equation of a curve that passes exactly through a set of data points. This is the process of interpolation and requires (for example) four coefficients to describe a curve that passes through four data points. But what if, instead of four data points, we have 4000 data points? It would be ludicrous to try to find the 4000-parameter equation that describes the curve that passes through all the data points. Instead, we would like to find a relatively simple mathematical relationship that does not necessarily pass through data points but is a good fit to the data set as a whole. The "best fit" of a curve to a set of data points is considered to be found when the sum of squares of the deviations of the experimental points from the calculated curve is a minimum. This procedure is known as least-squares curve fitting or, more generally, as regression analysis. Excel provides several ways to obtain regression coefficients; these are described in the following sections.

Linear Regression

Linear regression is not limited to the case of finding the least-squares slope and intercept of a straight line. Linear regression methods can be applied to any function that is *linear in the coefficients*[*]. Many functions that produce curved x–y plots are linear in the coefficients, including power series, for example,

$$y = a + bx + cx^2 + dx^3 \qquad (13\text{-}1)$$

and some functions containing exponentials, such as

---

[*] Mathematically, a function that is linear in the coefficients is one for which *the partial derivatives of the function with respect to the coefficients do not contain coefficients*. For example, for the power series equation $y = a + bx + cx^2$, $\partial y/\partial a = 1$, $\partial y/\partial b = x$ and $\partial y/\partial c = x^2$.

$$y = ae^x \tag{13-2}$$

Least-Squares Fit to a Straight Line

Although it is relatively easy to draw a straight line with ruler and pencil through a series of points if they all fall on or near the line, it becomes more and more a matter of judgment if the data are scattered. The least-squares line of best fit minimizes the sum of the squares of the y deviations of individual points from the line. This statistical technique is called regression analysis. Regression analysis in the simplest form assumes that all deviations from the line are the result of error in the measurement of the dependent variable y.

Regression analysis uses the quantities defined below, where there are N measurements of x_i, y_i data pairs.

$$S_{xx} = \Sigma x_i^2 - (\Sigma x_i)^2/N \tag{13-3}$$

$$S_{yy} = \Sigma y_i^2 - (\Sigma y_i)^2/N \tag{13-4}$$

$$S_{xy} = \Sigma x_i y_i - \Sigma x_i \Sigma y_i/N \tag{13-5}$$

For a straight line $y = mx + b$, the least-squares slope and intercept are given by equations (13-6) and (13-7).

$$m = S_{xy}S_{xx} \tag{13-6}$$

$$b = (\Sigma y_i - m \, \Sigma x_i)/N \tag{13-7}$$

The *correlation coefficient*, R, is a measure of the correlation between x and y. If x and y are perfectly correlated (i.e., a perfect straight line), then $R = 1$. An R value of zero means that there is no correlation between x and y, and an R value of -1 means that there is a perfect negative correlation.

More commonly, R^2, the square of the correlation coefficient, given by equation (13-8), is used as the measure of correlation; it ranges from 0 (no correlation) to 1 (perfect correlation).

$$R^2 = \Sigma_{xy}^2/(S_{xx}\,S_{yy}) \tag{13-8}$$

R^2 can be used as a measure of the goodness of fit of data to (in this case) a straight line. A value of R^2 of less than 0.9 corresponds to a rather poor fit of data to a straight line.

Excel provides worksheet functions to calculate the least-squares slope, intercept and R^2 of the straight line $y = mx + b$.

Least-Squares Fit to a Straight Line
Using the Worksheet Functions
SLOPE, INTERCEPT and RSQ

Figure 13-1 shows the phase diagram of methane hydrate, one of a class of compounds known as clathrate hydrates. Methane hydrate, an ice-like solid, consists of methane molecules trapped in a crystalline lattice of water molecules; each unit cell of the crystal lattice contains 46 water molecules and up to 8 gas molecules. The figure shows that the solid phase forms under conditions of high pressure and relatively low temperature. Previously, information about the formation of methane hydrate was important in the natural gas transmission business because the solid can clog valves. More recently, the discovery of methane hydrate deposits on the ocean floor has led to estimates that they contain enough natural gas to provide an energy source for the next several hundred years, if they can be accessed.

The data of Figure 13-1 conforms to an exponential curve. It can be shown that the vapor pressure varies with the absolute temperature according to the Clausius-Clapeyron equation (13-9):

$$\ln P = -A\frac{1}{T} + B \qquad (13\text{-}9)$$

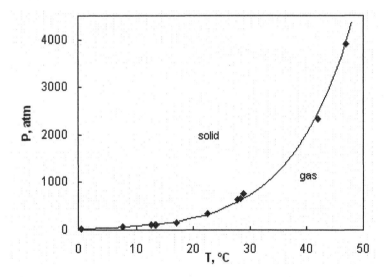

Figure 13-1. Methane hydrate phase diagram.
The line is the least-squares fit to the data points.
(folder 'Chapter 13 Examples', workbook 'Methane Hydrate', sheet 'Finished chart')

	A	B	C	D	E	F
1	**Methane Hydrate Phase Diagram Data**				**Data for Clausius-Clapeyron Plot**	
2	T, K	T, °C	P, atm		1/T	ln P
3	273.7	0.5	27		0.00365	3.31
4	280.9	7.7	58		0.00356	4.06
5	285.9	12.7	97		0.00350	4.57
6	286.5	13.3	105		0.00349	4.65
7	286.7	13.5	107		0.00349	4.67
8	290.2	17.0	157		0.00345	5.06
9	295.7	22.5	335		0.00338	5.82
10	301.0	27.8	640		0.00332	6.46
11	301.6	28.4	645		0.00332	6.47
12	302.0	28.8	765		0.00331	6.64
13	315.1	41.9	2344		0.00317	7.76
14	320.1	46.9	3918		0.00312	8.27

Figure 13-2. Portion of spreadsheet for Clausius-Clapeyron plot for methane hydrate.
(folder 'Chapter 13 Examples', workbook 'Methane Hydrate', sheet 'Phase diagram data')

When the data of Figure 13-2 is plotted in the form ln P vs. $1/T$ where T is in Kelvin, Figure 13-3 is obtained. The line is the least-squares best-fit line, obtained as follows.

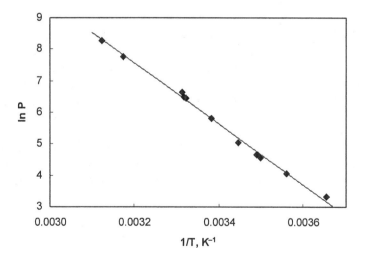

Figure 13-3. Clausius-Clapeyron plot (ln P vs. $1/T$) for methane hydrate.
(folder 'Chapter 13 Examples', workbook 'Methane Hydrate', sheet 'Phase diagram data')

The SLOPE, INTERCEPT and RSQ worksheet functions were used to obtain the least-squares best fit coefficients of the data, plus R^2, the coefficient of determination.   The syntax of the SLOPE function is SLOPE(**known_y's, known_x's**); the arguments of INTERCEPT and RSQ are the same as for the SLOPE function. The values are shown in Figure 13-4.

	E	F
16	slope =	-9705
17	intercept =	38.61
18	R^2 =	0.9959

Figure 13-4. Slope, intercept and R^2 of the plot of ln P vs. $1/T$ for methane hydrate. (folder 'Chapter 13 Examples', workbook 'Methane Hydrate', sheet 'Phase diagram data')

The formulas in cells F16, F17 and F18 are

=SLOPE(F3:F14,E3:E14)

=INTERCEPT(F3:F14,E3:E14)

=RSQ(F3:F14,E3:E14).

The least-squares line shown in Figure 13-1 was calculated using the regression coefficients A and B found for equation 13-9.

Multiple Linear Regression

Multiple linear regression fits data to a model that defines y as a function of two or more independent x variables. For example, you might want to fit the yield of a biological fermentation product as a function of temperature (T), pressure of CO_2 gas (P) in the fermenter and fermentation time (t), for example,

$$y = a \cdot T + b \cdot P + c \cdot t + d \qquad (13\text{-}10)$$

using data from a series of fermentation runs with different conditions of temperature, pressure and time. Or the dependent variable y could be a function of several independent variables, each of which is a function of a single original independent variable, for example,

$$y = a[\text{H}^+]^3 + b[\text{H}^+]^2 + c[\text{H}^+] + d \qquad (13\text{-}11)$$

Although equation 13-11 is a nonlinear function (a cubic equation), it is linear in the coefficients and therefore linear regression can be used to obtain the regression coefficients a, b, c and d of an equation such as 13-11. Excel provides at least three ways to perform linear regression: by adding a Trendline to a chart, by using the Regression tool in the Analysis ToolPak, or by using the worksheet function LINEST. LINEST (for <u>lin</u>ear <u>est</u>imation) is the most versatile of the three, so we will begin with it.

The worksheet function LINEST returns the coefficients of multiple linear regression. As a first illustration, we will use LINEST to obtain the slope and intercept of the least-squares straight line through the data points of Figure 13-2.

Least-Squares Fit to a Straight Line Using LINEST

Although you may find LINEST a bit confusing at first (the help description for most functions occupies a page or less, while the printed help for LINEST is seven pages), you will soon "get the hang of it" and will find that it is much to be preferred over the other methods that Excel provides for doing least-squares curve fitting.

The general form of the linear equation that can be handled by LINEST is

$$y = m_1x_1 + m_2x_2 + m_3x_3 + \cdots + b \qquad (13-12)$$

LINEST returns the array of regression coefficients m_n, ..., m_2, m_1, b. The syntax is LINEST(***known_ys***, *known_xs*, *const_logical*, *stats_logical*). If *const_logical* is TRUE or omitted, the regression coefficients include an intercept b; if *const_logical* is FALSE, the fit does not include the intercept b. If *stats_logical* is TRUE, LINEST returns an array of regression statistics in addition to the regression coefficients m_n, ..., m_1 and b. The layout of the array of returned values is shown in Figure 13-5. A one-, two-, three-, four-, or five-row array may be selected.

m(n)	m(n-1)	...	m(2)	m(1)	b
std.dev(n)	std.dev(n-1)	...	std.dev(2)	std.dev(1)	std.dev(b)
r^2	std.dev(y)				
F	df				
SS(regression)	SS(resid)				

Figure 13-5. Layout of regression results and statistics returned by LINEST.

LINEST is an array function; to use it, you must do the following:

- Select a range of cells of appropriate dimensions for the results. For this example we will select a range two columns wide and five rows deep. The selection is two columns wide because we are returning two regression coefficients, m and b, and five rows deep because that's the number of rows of statistical information returned by LINEST. You don't need to always select five rows for the results; often three rows are sufficient, in order to obtain the coefficients, their standard deviations, and the R^2 value.

- Type the LINEST formula with its arguments, in this example =LINEST(F3:F14,E3:E14,TRUE,TRUE). You can use the following "shorthand" for the logical arguments const and stats: FALSE can be represented by 0 and TRUE by any nonzero value, as in the formula =LINEST(F3:F14,E3:E14,1,1).

- Enter the formula by using CONTROL+SHIFT+ENTER.

When you "array-enter" a formula, Excel puts braces around the formula, as shown below:

{=LINEST(F3:F14,E3:E14,1,1)}

	H	I
2	Data from LINEST	
3	m	b
4	-9705	38.6
5	196	0.7
6	0.9959	0.1011
7	2454	10
8	25.1	0.1021

Figure 13-6. Regression results and statistics returned by LINEST
for the methane hydrate phase diagram data.
(folder 'Chapter 13 Examples', workbook 'Methane Hydrate', sheet 'Phase diagram data')

You do not type the braces; if you did, the result would not be recognized by Excel as a formula.

When the LINEST function is applied to the data in columns E and F of Figure 13-2, the results shown in Figure 13-6 are obtained.

As you can see, LINEST returns a large amount of useful statistical information simply by entering a single formula: the regression coefficients, their standard deviations, the R^2 value, plus several other statistical quantities. You must, however, be familiar with the layout of regression results and statistics shown in Figure 13-5 (also shown in Excel's On-Line Help for the LINEST worksheet function) in order to know what value each cell contains.

Multiple Linear Regression Using LINEST

Now that we've gained some familiarity with LINEST, let's apply it to an example of multiple linear regression. The data table in Figure 13-7 lists the freezing points of solutions of ethylene glycol. We want to be able to obtain the freezing point of a solution of ethylene glycol with wt% that is intermediate between the data values given in the table.

	A	B
1	Wt% Ethylene Glycol	Freezing Point, °F
2	0.0	32.0
3	5.0	29.4
4	10.0	26.2
5	15.0	22.2
6	20.0	17.9
7	25.0	12.7
8	30.0	6.7
9	35.0	-0.2
10	40.0	-8.1
11	45.0	-17.5
12	50.0	-28.9
13	55.0	-42.0
14	60.0	-54.9

Figure 13-7. Freezing point of ethylene glycol-water solutions.
(folder 'Chapter 13 Examples', workbook 'Dowtherm data', sheet 'Using Trendline')

Instead of using one of the interpolation techniques described in Chapter 5, we would like to have a single fitting function that handles the whole range of data. In the previous example, theory (the Clausius-Clapeyron equation) demanded that the data be fitted to the function ln $P = -A/T + B$, but in the present case we are free to choose any empirical fitting function that works.

Figure 13-8 shows that a plot of the freezing point as a function of wt% ethylene glycol is not a straight line, so the equation $y = a + bx$ will not be a good choice. What about the next higher power series: $y = a + bx + cx^2$? This is the equation of a parabola, and we can see that the curve in Figure 13-8 doesn't behave like a parabola. What about a cubic equation: $y = a + bx + cx^2 x + dx^3$? A cubic fitting function probably will do a good job. We'll fit our freezing point data to a cubic equation:

$$T = a \cdot W^3 + b \cdot W^2 + c \cdot W + d \qquad (13\text{-}13)$$

One of the requirements of LINEST when fitting the dependent variable y to multiple independent variables x_1, x_2, ... is that there must be a separate column of values for each independent variable (in our case W, W^2 and W^3). So the first thing we must do is insert two columns to the right of column A and enter formulas to calculate W^2 and W^3, as shown in Figure 13-9.

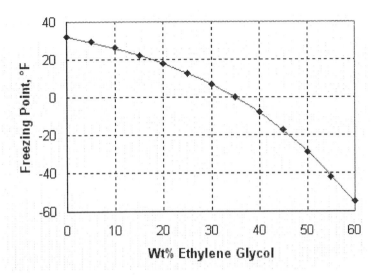

Figure 13-8. Fitting freezing point of ethylene glycol-water solutions by a power series. The line through the data points was calculated using the power-series coefficients in Table 13-10. (folder 'Chapter 13 Examples', workbook 'Dowtherm data', sheet 'Using LINEST')

Second, select a block of cells appropriate for the results that will be returned by LINEST. Since we are fitting the data to a cubic equation ($a + bx + cx^2 x + dx^3$), we need to select a range four columns wide (one column for each of the

	A	B	C	D	E	F
1	Wt% Ethylene Glycol	W^2	W^3	Freezing Point, °F	°F (calc)	diff °F
2	0.0	0.0	0.0	32.0	32.1	0.1
3	5.0	25.0	125.0	29.4	29.3	0.1
4	10.0	100.0	1000.0	26.2	26.0	0.2
5	15.0	225.0	3375.0	22.2	22.3	0.1
6	20.0	400.0	8000.0	17.9	18.0	0.1
7	25.0	625.0	15625.0	12.7	12.8	0.1
8	30.0	900.0	27000.0	6.7	6.8	0.1
9	35.0	1225.0	42875.0	-0.2	-0.2	0.0
10	40.0	1600.0	64000.0	-8.1	-8.4	0.3
11	45.0	2025.0	91125.0	-17.5	-17.9	0.4
12	50.0	2500.0	125000.0	-28.9	-28.8	0.1
13	55.0	3025.0	166375.0	-42.0	-41.2	0.8
14	60.0	3600.0	216000.0	-54.9	-55.3	0.4

Figure 13-9. Fitting freezing point of ethylene glycol-water solutions by a power series. The values in column D were calculated using the regression coefficients in Table 13-10. (folder 'Chapter 13 Examples', workbook 'Dowtherm data', sheet 'Using LINEST')

four regression coefficients) and up to five rows deep (LINEST can return five rows of regression statistics, as illustrated in Figure 13-5). If you want to see the curve-fitting coefficients, their standard deviations and the R^2 value, you need only select a range that is three rows deep.

Third, enter the LINEST formula with its arguments:

=LINEST(D2:D14,A2:C14,1,1)

Finally, enter the array function by pressing CONTROL+SHIFT+ENTER (Windows) or CONTROL+SHIFT+RETURN (Macintosh).

The results returned by LINEST are shown in Figure 13-10. At first you may find them a little confusing, since they aren't labeled. Refer to the layout of the results shown in Figure 13-5 to understand what value is contained in each cell. The first row contains the regression coefficients, the second row contains their standard deviations, and the third row contains the R^2 value in cell A20 and the SE(y) value (the standard error of the y-estimate, sometimes referred to as the RMSD, root-mean-square deviation) in cell B20.

One feature of the LINEST results that can initially be confusing is that, as shown in Figure 13-5, the regression coefficients b, m_1, m_2, m_3,... progress from right to left (in cells D18 C18, B18, A18 in Figure 13-10) while the corresponding independent variables x_1, x_2, x_3, ... progress from left to right (in columns A, B and C of Figure 13-9). Nonetheless, it's my opinion that using LINEST is by far the best way to do linear regression in Excel.

	A	B	C	D
18	-0.00017	-0.00495	-0.538589	32.09863
19	2.01E-05	0.001834	0.04619	0.307011
20	0.999878	0.359817	#N/A	#N/A
21	24656.24	9	#N/A	#N/A
22	9576.627	1.165217	#N/A	#N/A

Figure 13-10. Least-squares coefficients of a power series
for freezing point of ethylene glycol-water solutions.
(folder 'Chapter 13 Examples', workbook 'Dowtherm data', sheet 'Using LINEST')

Once you've obtained the regression coefficients by using LINEST, it's a simple matter to calculate the freezing point of a solution of any wt% ethylene glycol. Assigning the names aa, bb, cc, dd for the regression coefficients in cells A18:D18 and W for the wt% ethylene glycol values in column A, respectively, is a good idea. The formula

=aa*W^3+bb*W^2+cc*W+dd

was used to calculate the values in column E of Figure 13-9.

Handling Noncontiguous Ranges of *known_x's* in LINEST

One of the few limitations of LINEST is that the range of *known_x's* must be a contiguous selection (e.g., $A\$2:\$C\$13$ in Figure 13-9). Occasionally, you may wish to perform multiple linear regression where the *known_x's* are not in adjacent rows, and it may not be convenient to rearrange the spreadsheet so as to obtain a contiguous range of *known_x's*. You can use the custom function Arr to combine separate ranges into a single array. For example, if the ranges of independent variables x_1, x_2 and x_3 were in the ranges A2:A13, C2:C13 and E2:E13, respectively, and the dependent variable y in F2:F13, the LINEST expression would be

=LINEST(F2:F13, Arr(A2:A13, C2:C13,E2:E13),1,1)

A LINEST Shortcut

Here's a shortcut that eliminates the need to create the columns of W^2 and W^3 in Figure 13-10. If you've read Chapter 4, "Number Series," and understand array constants, you'll understand how the formula

{=LINEST(D2:D14,A2:A14^{1,2,3},1,1)}

creates an array of the values of the independent variable W raised to the first, second and third powers. Unlike the braces that are automatically placed around an array formula when you enter it by using CONTROL+SHIFT+ENTER, you must type the braces around the values of the array constant.

You can examine that part of the formula by highlighting A2:A14^{1,2,3} in the formula bar and pressing F9; you'll see the result displayed in the formula bar (only a portion of it is shown here):

{0,0,0;5,25,125;10,100,1000;15,225,3375;20,400,8000;...}

Note that successive array elements in a row are separated by commas, and rows of elements are separated by semicolons.

The formula, which must be entered by using CONTROL+SHIFT+ENTER, returns the same values that are shown in Figure 13-10.

LINEST's Regression Statistics

Additional regression statistics are returned by LINEST in rows 3, 4 and 5 of the array. The mathematical relationships between the regression statistics are given in equations 13-14 to 13-19 (N = number of data points, k = number of regression coefficients to be determined):

$$df \text{ (degrees of freedom)} = N - k \qquad (13\text{-}14)$$

$$SS_{regression} = \sum(y_{mean} - y_{calc})^2 \qquad\qquad (13\text{-}15)$$

$$SS_{residuals} = \sum(y_{obsd} - y_{calc})^2 \qquad\qquad (13\text{-}16)$$

$$R^2 = 1 - \frac{SS_{resid}}{SS_{regression}} \qquad\qquad (13\text{-}17)$$

$$F = \frac{SS_{regression}}{SS_{resid} / df} \qquad\qquad (13\text{-}18)$$

$$SE(y) = \sqrt{\frac{SS_{resid}}{N - k}} \qquad\qquad (13\text{-}19)$$

The coefficient of determination, R^2 (or the correlation coefficient, R), is a measure of the goodness of fit of the data to (in this case) a straight line. If x and y are perfectly correlated (i.e., the difference between y_{obsd} and y_{calc} is zero), then $R^2 = 1$. In contrast, an R^2 value of zero means that there is no correlation between x and y. A value of R^2 of less than 0.9 corresponds to a rather poor fit of data to a straight line.

The $SE(y)$ parameter, the standard error of the y estimate, is sometimes referred to as the RMSD (root-mean-square deviation).

The F-statistic is used to determine whether the proposed relationship is significant (that is, whether y does in fact vary with respect to x). For most relationships observed in chemistry, a relationship will unquestionably exist. If it is necessary to determine whether the variation of y with x is statistically significant, or merely occurs by chance, you can consult a book on statistics.

Linear Regression Using Trendline

You can also fit a least-squares line to data points such as those shown in Figure 13-9 by adding a *trendline* to a chart. You can choose from a menu of mathematical functions—linear, logarithmic, polynomial, power, exponential— as curve-fitting functions.

To add a trendline, select the chart by clicking on it, then choose **Add Trendline...** from the **Chart** menu.

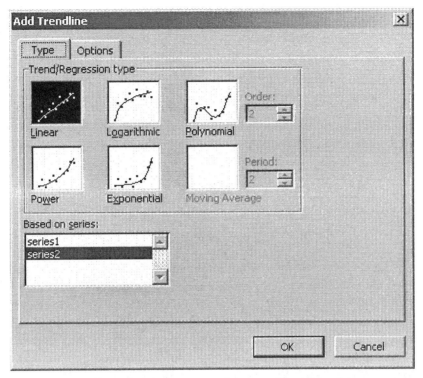

Figure 13-11. The Type tab of the Trendline dialog box.

If the chart has several data series, either select the desired data series before choosing **Add Trendline...** or choose the desired data series from the Based On Series box.

Choose the Type tab and then choose the appropriate fitting function from the gallery of functional forms. (Depending on the data in the series, the exponential, power or logarithmic choices may not be available.) If you choose the polynomial form, you can select the order of the polynomial by using the spinner. If you choose 3, for example, Excel will fit a polynomial of order three (i.e., a cubic equation) to the data points. The maximum order is a polynomial of order six.

Now choose the Options tab (Figure 13-12).

Check the boxes for Display Equation On Chart and Display R-squared Value On Chart; then press OK. Excel displays the trendline on the chart as a heavy solid line and the equation (with the least-squares coefficients) and R^2 value as text on the chart, as shown in Figure 13-13. You can change the appearance of the trendline by clicking on the trendline, then choosing **Selected Trendline...** from the **Format** menu.

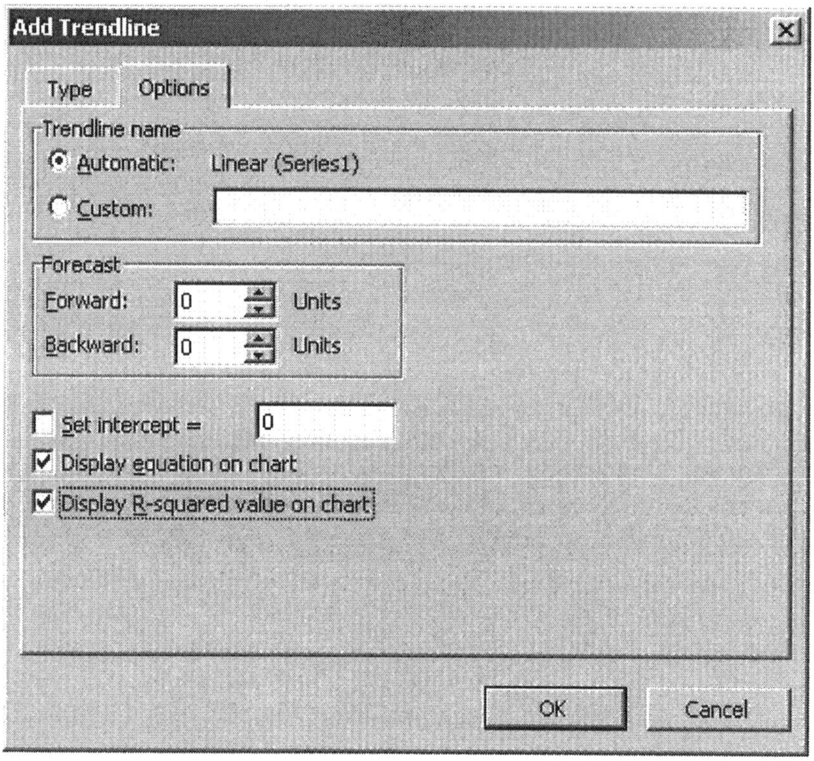

Figure 13-12. The Options tab of the Trendline dialog box.

If you want to use the coefficients for calculations, you'll have to copy them from the chart and paste them into worksheet cells. Usually the coefficients as displayed in the chart are not precise enough for calculations, but you can apply number formatting to the text to display more significant figures before copying the coefficients. Click once on the Trendline text to select it (a box indicates that the complete text has been selected), then choose **Selected Data Labels...** from the **Format** menu and choose the Number tab. Choose an appropriate number format (Scientific, for example), then press OK.

Alternatively, click on the Trendline text to select it and use the Increase Decimal toolbutton to display more figures.

Now **Copy** the individual coefficients of the Trendline equation and **Paste** them into spreadsheet cells.

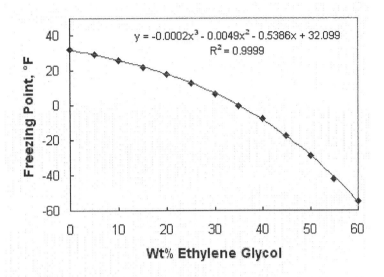

Figure 13-13. Least-squares coefficients of a power series
for freezing point of ethylene glycol-water solutions, obtained by using Trendline.
(folder 'Chapter 13 Examples', workbook 'Dowtherm data', sheet 'Using Trendline')

Limitations of Trendline

The Trendline dialog box offers only a limited menu of mathematical fitting functions: linear, polynomial, exponential, etc. And, in addition, the independent variables used in the regression must be mathematical functions of a single independent variable: x, x^2, x^3, etc. LINEST, on the other hand, can perform multiple linear regression with several different independent variables. For example, in a study of the yield of a biomolecule produced by fermentation, regression analysis using LINEST, on data produced by a number of experiments, could provide a relationship that relates the yield of product (the dependent variable) as a function of: fermentation time, temperature and pressure of CO_2 gas (the independent variables). In addition, only limited mathematical functions of the single x variable are available; you can fit a curve to a polynomial of the second degree ($y = ax^2 + bx + c$) for example, but not to the function $y = ax^2 + c$.

The most serious limitation of using Trendline to perform multiple linear regression is that the result is simply some text on a chart. You must then transfer the values of the regression coefficients from the chart to worksheet cells before you can use them, either by highlighting and copying individual sections of the trendline equation and pasting into the worksheet, or—horrors—manually typing the values.

After formatting to show a few more decimal places, for example,

y = -1.72727E-04x3 - 4.94605E-03x2 - 5.38589E-01x + 3.20986E+01

you are now ready to copy the values and paste them into your spreadsheet.

Importing Trendline Coefficients into a Spreadsheet by Using Worksheet Formulas

The following are the various Trendline fitting functions that are displayed in the Add Trendline dialog box directly into worksheet cells:

linear	$y = ax + b$
logarithmic	$y = a \ln(x) + b$
polynomial (e.g., order 3)	$y = ax^3 + bx^2 + cx + d$
power	$y = ax^b$
exponential	$y = ae^{bx}$

The linear, logarithmic and polynomial expressions are linear in the coefficients and can be handled by Excel's built-in linear regression code. Trendline uses linear transformation of the power and exponential functions to obtain the coefficients: the exponential expression is transformed to $\ln(y) = bx + \ln(a)$ and the power expression to $\ln(y) = b \ln(x) + \ln(a)$.

The following formulas allow you to get the coefficients of the various Trendline fitting functions directly into worksheet cells. The formulas use the results returned by LINEST, so there's really no reason not to use LINEST directly. But for those die-hards who insist on using Trendline, here are the relationships (in each formula, replace the arguments y_values and x_values with the appropriate range references):

linear	a	=INDEX(LINEST(y_values,x_values,1,0),1)
	b	=INDEX(LINEST(y_values,x_values,1,0),2)
logarithmic	a	=INDEX(LINEST(y_values,LN(x_values),1,0),1)
	b	=INDEX(LINEST(y_values,LN(x_values),1,0),2)
polynomial	a	=INDEX(LINEST(y_values,x_values^{1,2,3},1,0),1)
(e.g., order 3)	b	=INDEX(LINEST(y_values,x_values^{1,2,3},1,0),2)
	c	=INDEX(LINEST(y_values,x_values^{1,2,3},1,0),3)
	d	=INDEX(LINEST(y_values,x_values^{1,2,3},1,0),4)

power   *a*   =EXP(INDEX(LINEST(LN(y_values),LN(x_values),1,0),2))

             b   =INDEX(LINEST(LN(y_values),LN(x_values),1,0),1)

exponential *a*   =EXP(INDEX(LINEST(LN(y_values),x_values,1,0),2))

             b   =INDEX(LINEST(LN(y_values),x_values,1,0),1)

The formulas for polynomials of other orders should be apparent from the example given.

Even though LINEST is an array function and must be entered using CTRL+SHIFT+ENTER, you do not need to "array-enter" these formulas.

Note that the formulas for the regression coefficients *a* and *b* for linear, logarithmic and polynomial equations differ only in the value of the last argument (the *row_num* argument of INDEX).   The formulas for power and exponential are not identical.

The formula for RSQ for the linear equation is

=INDEX(LINEST(y_values,x_values,1,1),3,1)

and there are similar formulas for the other fitting functions.

Using the Regression Tool in Analysis Tools

Linear regression can also be performed using the Add-In package called the Analysis ToolPak.   If the Analysis ToolPak Add-In is installed, the **Data Analysis...** command will be present at the bottom of the **Tools** menu; if the **Data Analysis...** command is not present in the **Tools** menu, choose **Add-Ins...** from the **Tools** menu and check the box for Analysis ToolPak or Analysis ToolPak (VBA) to install it. Now when you click on the **Tools** menu you will see the **Data Analysis...** command.

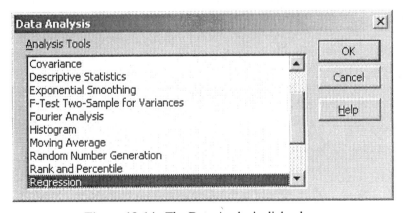

Figure 13-14. The Data Analysis dialog box.

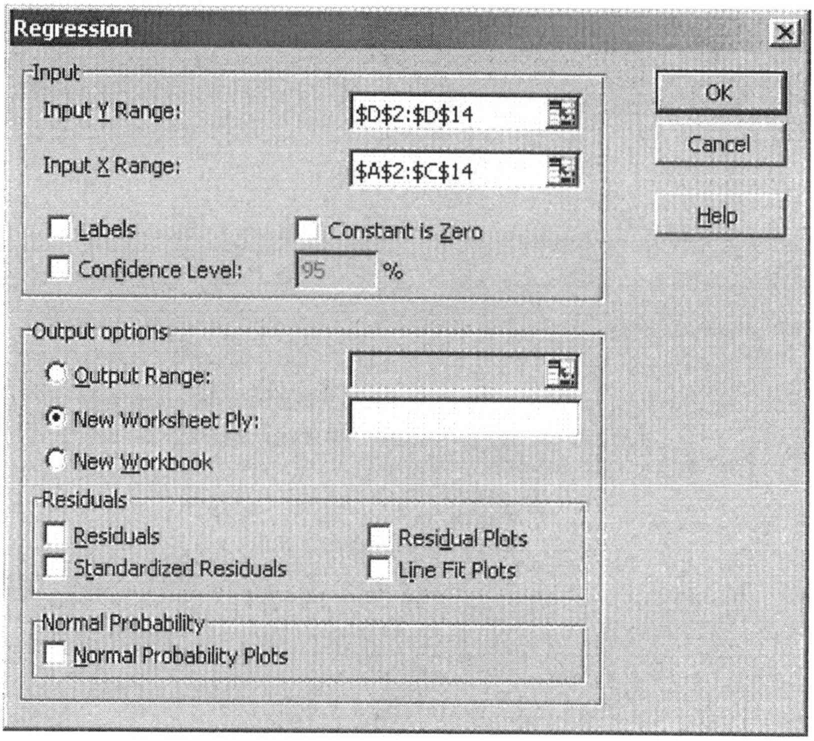

Figure 13-15. The Regression dialog box.

After you choose **Data Analysis...** from the **Tools** menu, choose Regression from the Analysis Tools list box. The Regression dialog box (Figure 13-15) will prompt you to enter the range of dependent variable (y) values and the range of independent variable (x) values, as well as whether the constant is zero, whether the first cell in each range is a label, and the confidence level desired in the output summary. Then select a range for the summary table. You need select only a single cell for this range; it will be the upper left corner of the range. You can also request a table of residuals and a normal probability plot. If you select a cell or range such that the summary table would over-write cells containing values, you will get a warning message.

In contrast to the results returned by LINEST, the output is clearly labeled, and additional statistical data are provided.

	A	B	C	D	E
1	SUMMARY OUTPUT				
3	*Regression Statistics*				
4	Multiple R	0.999939169			
5	R Square	0.999878342			
6	Adjusted R Square	0.999837789			
7	Standard Error	0.359817436			
8	Observations	13			
10	ANOVA				
11		*df*	*SS*	*MS*	*F*
12	Regression	3	9576.62709	3192.209	24656.244
13	Residual	9	1.165217283	0.1294686	
14	Total	12	9577.792308		
16		*Coefficients*	*Standard Error*	*t Stat*	*P-value*
17	Intercept	32.09862637	0.307011363	104.55192	3.4E-15
18	X Variable 1	-0.53858891	0.046189683	-11.660373	9.83E-07
19	X Variable 2	-0.00494605	0.001833799	-2.6971619	0.0245073
20	X Variable 3	-0.00017273	2.00596E-05	-8.6106907	1.224E-05

Figure 13-16. Regression statistics returned by the Regression tool.
(folder 'Chapter 13 Examples', workbook 'Dowtherm data', sheet 'Using Regression')

Limitations of the Regression Tool

Unlike Trendline, the Regression tool in **Data Analysis...** (the Analysis Toolpak) provides the coefficients and statistical parameters of linear regression as values in cells, ready to be used in calculations. And, they are presented in a nicely formatted table. The major limitation of the regression tool is that, unlike LINEST, it is not a function. With LINEST, the returned values are dynamically linked to the original data and are updated if the raw data is changed. If you use the Regression tool, the values are calculated from the raw data and entered into worksheet cells; they do not change if you change the input data.

Importing the Trendline Equation
from a Chart into a Worksheet

Scientists and engineers often use Excel's Trendline feature to obtain a least-squares fit to data in a chart. Trendline provides a limited gallery of mathematical fitting functions, including regular polynomials up to order six. The disadvantage of Trendline is that the trendline equation is merely a caption in the chart; to use it in the worksheet, the coefficients must be transferred manually by typing, or copying and pasting. The utility TrendlineToCell provided on the CD-ROM converts the Trendline equation to an Excel formula and transfers the formula to a selected cell on a worksheet. Figure 13-17 shows the VBA code.

```
Sub TrendlineToCell()
'Tranfers Trendline text to cell as formula.

'REMEMBER LOCATION OF CHART
If TypeName(ActiveSheet) = "Chart" Then
  ChartSheetName = ActiveSheet.Name
Else
  pointer = Application.Find("Chart", ActiveChart.Name)
  ChartObjectName = Mid(ActiveChart.Name, pointer, 100)
End If

'MAKE SURE A TRENDLINE IS SELECTED.
On Error GoTo BadSelection
'Selection.Name  e.g., "Text S3T1"
If Selection.Name Like "Text S*T*" Then
  pointer = Application.Find("T", Selection.Name, 3)
  SeriesNum = Val(Mid(Selection.Name, 7, pointer - 7))
  TrendlineNum = Val(Mid(Selection.Name, pointer + 1, 3))
Else
BadSelection:  MsgBox "You must select a Trendline label."
Exit Sub
End If
On Error GoTo 0

'CHANGE NUMBER FORMAT TEMPORARILY TO GET SUFFICIENT PRECISION
TLNumberFormat = Selection.NumberFormat
Selection.NumberFormat = "0.0000000000E+00"

'CONVERT TRENDLINE TEXT TO AN EXCEL FORMULA
'First, strip off y and R parts
TLText = Selection.Characters.Text
pointer = Application.Find("=", TLText)
TLText = Mid(TLText, pointer, 1024)
If Not (IsError(Application.Find("R", TLText))) Then
pointer = Application.Find("R", TLText)
TLText = Left(TLText, pointer - 2)
End If

'CONVERT DIFFERENT TYPES OF TRENDLINE EQUATION
Select Case ActiveChart.SeriesCollection(SeriesNum) _
  .Trendlines(TrendlineNum).Type
Case -4132 'Linear
    TLText = Application.Substitute(TLText, "x", "*x")
Case -4133 'Logarithmic
   TLText = Application.Substitute(TLText, "L", "*L")
Case 3 'Polynomial
   TLText = Application.Substitute(TLText, "x", "*x^")
   TLText = Application.Substitute(TLText, "x^ ", "x ")
Case 4 'Power
   TLText = Application.Substitute(TLText, "x", "*x^")
Case 5 'Exponential
   TLText = TLText & ")"
```

```
  TLText = Application.Substitute(TLText, "e", "*EXP(")
  TLText = Application.Substitute(TLText, "x", "*x")
End Select

'INPUT REFERENCES FOR FORMULA AND X
On Error GoTo CancelWasPressed
Set YAddress = Application.InputBox(prompt:= _
  "Select destination cell for formula.", Title:= _
  "COPY TRENDLINE TO CELL - STEP 1 OF 2 ", Type:=8)
  Y = YAddress.Address(external:=True)

Set XAddress = Application.InputBox(prompt:= _
  "Select cell for independent variable x.", Title:= _
  "COPY TRENDLINE TO CELL - STEP 2 OF 2 ", Type:=8)
  X = XAddress.Address
  X = Application.Substitute(X, "$", "")
TLText = Application.Substitute(TLText, "x", X)
Range(Y).Formula = TLText
CancelWasPressed: On Error GoTo 0

'RETURN TO TRENDLINE TEXT TO RESTORE ORIGINAL NUMBER FORMAT
If ChartSheetName <> "" Then
  Charts(ChartSheetName).Activate
  Charts(ChartSheetName).ChartArea.Select
Else
  ActiveSheet.ChartObjects(ChartObjectName).Activate
End If
ActiveChart.SeriesCollection(SeriesNum) _
  .Trendlines(TrendlineNum).DataLabel.Select
Selection.NumberFormat = TLNumberFormat

End Sub
```

Figure 13-17. VBA code for theTrendlineToCell utility.

The procedure is an Auto_Open macro; when you open the document, the procedure installs a new menu command, **Copy Trendline to Cell...**, in the **Tools** menu of the **Chart** menu bar (see Figure 13-18), then hides itself.

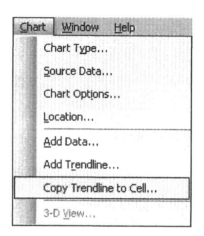

Figure 13-18. The new menu command in the **Chart** menu.

To use the utility, you first must select a Trendline equation in a chart. Then choose the **Copy Trendline to Cell...** command. Two dialog boxes direct you to, first, select the destination cell for the formula, and second, select the cell for the independent variable x. The utility converts a trendline equation such as

$$y = 3x^3 + 2.5x^2 - 5x - 11$$

into the corresponding Excel formula

$$= 3*A9^3 + 2.5*A9^2 - 5*A9 - 11$$

The utility can handle linear, logarithmic, polynomial, power and exponential Trendline equations.

Problems

Data for, and answers to, the following problems are found in the folder "Ch. 13 (Linear Regression)" in the "Problems & Solutions" folder on the CD.

1. The calibration curve data in Table 13-1 shows readings taken on a series of sodium standards, using a CIBA-Corning Model 410 flame photometer. The calibration line is noticeably curved.

x, ppm	y, reading
0	0
5	62
10	115
15	160
20	200
25	233

Table 13-1. Data for flame photometry calibration curve.

Fit the data to a cubic equation, $y = ax^3 + bx^2 + cx + d$.

2. If any of the coefficients found in problem 13-1 have unacceptably large standard errors, repeat the analysis using a different fitting function.

3. Fit the data In Table 13-2 (also available on the CD) to a power series function, $y = ax^b$, using (a) Trendline and (b) LINEST.

x	y	x	y
0.1	1.346	8	5.315
0.2	1.264	9	4.981
0.5	2.253	10	5.730
1	2.865	11	5.416
2	3.034	12	5.577
3	3.740	13	6.123
4	3.973	14	5.843
5	4.073	15	5.837
6	4.367	16	6.524
7	4.515		

Table 13-2. Data to be fitted with a power series.

4. Fit the data for freezing point of ethylene glycol by wt% shown in the following table (also found in the problems for Chapter 5) to a cubic fitting function and estimate the freezing points of 33.3 wt% and 42.3 wt% ethylene glycol.

Wt% Ethylene Glycol	Freezing Point, °F
0.0	32.0
5.0	29.4
10.0	26.2
15.0	22.2
20.0	17.9
25.0	12.7
30.0	6.7
35.0	-0.2
40.0	-8.1
45.0	-17.5
50.0	-28.9
55.0	-42.0
60.0	-54.9

Table 13-3. Heat transfer fluid freezing point data.

5. Table 13-4 (also found on the CD) gives the specific heat of water at various temperatures from 0°C to 100°C. Using LINEST, fit the data to a polynomial of order 5.

T,°C	cp, J/g	T,°C	cp, J/g
0	4.21588	50	4.17890
5	4.20040	55	4.18061
10	4.19040	60	4.18262
15	4.18400	65	4.18500
20	4.18011	70	4.18781
25	4.17781	75	4.19099
30	4.17672	80	4.19459
35	4.17639	85	4.19869
40	4.17680	90	4.20329
45	4.17768	95	4.20852
		100	4.21417

Table 13-4. Specific heat of water at various temperatures.

6. Power output (P) from a gas turbine engine was measured at several different throttle settings (T) and output shaft speeds (S). The data are shown in Table 13-5 and are also found on the CD-ROM. Use linear regression to obtain

the coefficients of a single equation $P = F(T,S)$ so that a controller can be programmed to command a load on the engine based on speed and throttle setting.

	A	B	C	D	E	F	G	H
5			Output Power (hp) as a Function of Shaft Speed and Throttle Setting					
6					Speed, rpm			
7			500	600	700	800	900	1000
8		0	60	83	123	149	184	237
9		1	75	105	140	193	237	305
10	Throttle	2	123	166	219	289	368	482
11		3	184	275	380	499	648	806
12		4	307	429	596	789	1016	1244
13		5	447	640	876	1157	1472	1823
14		6	613	894	1227	1621	2059	2541
15		7	824	1192	1630	2147	2734	3400

Table 13-5. Power output of a gas turbine engine
as a function of throttle setting and shaft speed.

Chapter 14

Nonlinear Regression Using the Solver

If you have read the preceding chapter on linear regression and are familiar with the use of LINEST, you should have no trouble recognizing a function that is linear in the coefficients. Some examples of functions that are linear in the coefficients are $y = a + bx + cx^2 + dx^3$ or $y = ae^x$.

However, if the function is one such as

$$y = e^{a + bx} \tag{14-1}$$

it is not linear in the coefficients. It should be obvious that it's not possible to apply LINEST to this equation; given a column of x values, you can't create a column of $e^{a + bx}$ when a and b are the "unknowns" you're trying to find.

Some nonlinear equations can be transformed into a linear form. Equation 14-1, for example, can be transformed by taking the logarithm to the base e of each side, to yield the equation

$$\ln y = a + bx \tag{14-2}$$

which is linear in the coefficients.

Some equations cannot be converted into a linear form and are said to be intrinsically nonlinear. Consider this example from the field of chemical reaction kinetics: a system of two consecutive first-order reactions (the reaction scheme $A \rightarrow B \rightarrow C$) where k_1 and k_2 are the rate constants for the reaction of species A to form the intermediate B and B to form the final product C, respectively. The equations for the concentrations of the species $[A]_t$, $[B]_t$ and $[C]_t$ in a reaction sequence of two consecutive first-order reactions can be found in almost any kinetics text. The expression for $[B]_t$ is

$$[B]_t = [A]_0 \frac{k_1}{k_2 - k_1} (e^{-k_1 t} - e^{-k_2 t}) \tag{14-3}$$

and a typical plot of $[B]_t$ vs. t looks like the one in Figure 14-1. Equation 14-3 is a classic example of an equation that is intrinsically nonlinear.

Nonlinear Least-Squares Curve Fitting

Unlike for linear regression, there are no analytical expressions to obtain the set of regression coefficients for a fitting function that is nonlinear in its coefficients. To perform nonlinear regression, we must essentially use trial-and-error to find the set of coefficients that minimize the sum of squares of differences between y_{calc} and y_{obsd}. For data such as in Figure 14-1, we could proceed in the following manner: using reasonable guesses for k_1 and k_2, calculate [B] at each time data point, then calculate the sum of squares of residuals, $SS_{residuals} = \Sigma([B]_{calc} - [B]_{expt})^2$. Our goal is to minimize this error-square sum.

We could do this in a true "trial-and-error" fashion, attempting to guess at a better set of k_1 and k_2 values, then repeating the calculation process to get a new (and hopefully smaller) value for the $SS_{residuals}$. Or we could attempt to be more systematic. Starting with our initial guesses for k_1 and k_2, we could create a two-dimensional array of starting values that bracket our guesses, as in Figure 14-2. (The initial guesses for k_1 and k_2 were 0.30 and 0.80, respectively and the array of starting values are 70%, 80%, 90%, 100%, 110%, 120% and 130% of the respective initial estimates.) Then, for each set of k_1 and k_2 values, we calculate the $SS_{residuals}$. The k_1 and k_1 values with the smallest error-square sum ($k_1 = 0.27$,

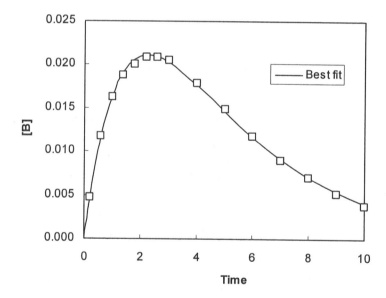

Figure 14-1. A typical plot of the concentration of species B for a system of two
consecutive first-order reactions (the reaction scheme A→B→C)

$k_1 = 0.64$ in Figure 14-2) become the new initial estimates and the process is repeated, using smaller bracketing values. Years ago this procedure, called "pit-mapping," was performed on early digital computers.

In essence we are mapping out the error surface, in a sort of topographic way, searching for the minimum. A typical error surface is shown in Figure 14-3 (the logarithm of the $SS_{residuals}$ has been plotted to make the minimum in the surface more obvious in the chart).

		Trial values of k_1						
		0.21	0.24	0.27	0.30	0.33	0.36	0.39
Trial values of k_2	0.56	1.5E-11	6.5E-12	5.5E-12	1.1E-11	2.1E-11	3.5E-11	5.3E-11
	0.64	2.0E-11	6.7E-12	7.2E-13	1.0E-12	6.4E-12	1.6E-11	2.9E-11
	0.72	3.4E-11	1.7E-11	7.8E-12	4.6E-12	6.3E-12	1.2E-11	2.1E-11
	0.80	5.2E-11	3.3E-11	2.1E-11	1.6E-11	1.5E-11	1.8E-11	2.4E-11
	0.88	7.2E-11	5.2E-11	3.9E-11	3.1E-11	2.8E-11	2.9E-11	3.3E-11
	0.96	9.3E-11	7.2E-11	5.7E-11	4.8E-11	4.4E-11	4.3E-11	4.5E-11
	1.04	1.1E-10	9.2E-11	7.7E-11	6.7E-11	6.1E-11	5.9E-11	6.0E-11

Figure 14-2. The error-square sums for an array of initial estimates. The minimum $SS_{residuals}$ value is in bold.

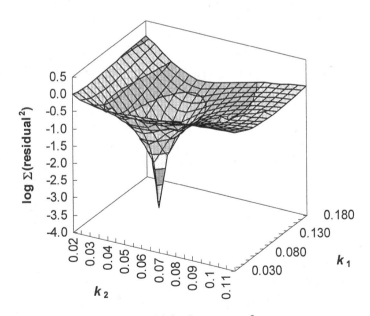

Figure 14-3. An error surface

A more efficient process, the *method of steepest descent*, starts with a single set of initial estimate values (a point on the error surface), determines the direction of downward curvature of the surface, and progresses down the surface in that direction until the minimum is reached (a modern implementation of this method is called the Marquardt-Levenberg algorithm). Fortunately, Excel provides a tool, the Solver, that can be used to perform this kind of minimization and thus makes nonlinear least-squares curve fitting a simple task.

Introducing the Solver

Like Goal Seek, the Solver can vary a *changing cell* to make a *target cell* have a certain value. But unlike Goal Seek, which can vary only a single changing cell, the Solver can vary the values of a number of changing cells.

The Solver is a general-purpose optimization package that can find a maximum, minimum or specified value of the target cell. The Solver code is a product of Frontline Systems Inc. (P.O. Box 4288, Incline Village, NV 89450; www.frontsys.com).

Microsoft's documentation makes no mention of the use of the Solver to perform least-squares curve fitting, but it is immediately obvious to almost any scientist that the Solver can be used to minimize the sum of squares of residuals (differences between y_{obsd} and y_{calc}) and thus perform least-squares curve fitting. The Solver can be used to perform either linear or nonlinear least-squares curve fitting.

How the Solver Works

The Solver uses the Generalized Reduced Gradient (GRG2) nonlinear optimization code developed by Leon Lasdon, University of Texas at Austin, and Allan Waren, Cleveland State University[*].

For each of the changing cells, the Solver evaluates the partial derivative of the objective function F (the target cell) with respect to the changing cell a_i, by means of the finite-difference method. The procedure works something like this: the Solver reads the value of each changing cell a_i in turn, modifies the value by a perturbation factor (the perturbation factor is approximately 10^{-8}), and writes the new value back to the worksheet cell. This causes the spreadsheet to recalculate, producing a new value of the objective. The Solver calculates the

---

[*] For linear and integer problems, the Solver uses the simplex method and branch-and-bound method, but these methods need not be discussed here. You can read more about the design and operation of the Solver in the following article (available online): "Design and Use of the Microsoft Excel Solver," Daniel Fylstra, Leon Lasdon, John Watson and Allan Waren, *Interfaces* 28, September 1998, pp. 29–55.

partial derivative $\partial F/\partial a_i$ according to equation 14-4 and then restores the changing cell to its original value and perturbs the next changing cell. The same method was used earlier in this book to calculate the first derivative of a function (see "Derivative of a Worksheet Formula Using the Finite-Difference Method" in Chapter 6).

$$\frac{\partial F}{\partial a_i} \approx \frac{\Delta F}{\Delta a_i} = \frac{F(a_i + \Delta a_i) - F(a_i)}{\Delta a_i} \tag{14-4}$$

The Solver uses a matrix of the partial derivatives to determine the gradient of the response surface, and thus how to change the values of the changing cells in order to approach the desired solution.

The use of finite differences to obtain the partial derivatives means that the Excel spreadsheet performs all of the intermediate calculations leading to the evaluation of the derivatives. Thus all of Excel's built-in worksheet functions, as well as any user-defined functions, are supported. The alternative, obtaining the derivatives analytically by symbolic differentiation of the spreadsheet formulas, would have been an impossible task.

Loading the Solver Add-In

The Solver is an Excel Add-in, a software program that is loaded only when needed. You'll find the Solver in the **Tools** menu; if it's not there, choose **Add-Ins...** from the **Tools** menu to display the Add-Ins dialog box, shown in Figure 14-4, check the box for Solver Add-In, then press OK.

Why Use the Solver for Nonlinear Regression?

A number of commercial statistical packages provide the capability to perform nonlinear least-squares curve fitting, so why use the Solver?

First, the Solver is used within the familiar Excel environment, so that you don't have to learn new commands and procedures.

Secondly, with commercial statistical packages you are generally restricted to using an equation chosen from a library of fitting functions provided within the program, whereas with the Solver you can fit data to any model (that is, any y_{calc} formula) you choose.

Finally, the Solver is part of Excel. It's free, so why not use it?

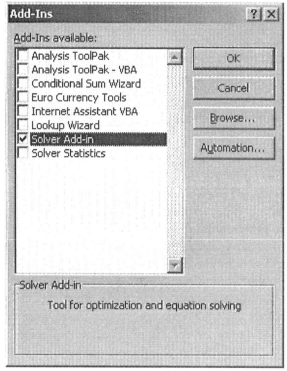

Figure 14-4. The Add-Ins dialog box.

Nonlinear Regression Using the Solver: An Example

To perform nonlinear least-squares curve fitting using the Solver, your spreadsheet model must contain a column of known y values and a column of calculated y values, so that the sum of squares of residuals can be calculated. The calculated y values must be spreadsheet formulas that depend on the curve fitting coefficients that will be varied by the Solver.

To illustrate the use of the Solver for nonlinear least-squares curve fitting, we'll use as an example the system of two consecutive first-order reactions (the reaction scheme A→B→C) where the species B is the observed variable. Equation 14-3 gives the expression for the concentration of species B as a function of time; as we have seen, $[B]_t$ depends on two rate constants, k_1 and k_2. In the experimental results that follow, species B was monitored by spectrophotometry (light absorption) and the relationship between the light absorbed (the absorbance) and the concentration of B is given by Beer's Law:

$$A = \varepsilon_B \times \text{(path length of light through the sample)} \times [B]$$

where ε_B is the molar absorptivity (a constant dependent on the chemical species and the wavelength, and thus a third unknown quantity in this example). Therefore three curve-fitting coefficients (k_1, k_2 and ε_B) must be varied in this example.   If two variable coefficients produce an error surface in three dimensions, as illustrated in Figure 14-3, then varying three coefficients requires that we work in four dimensions!

Figure 14-5 shows the spreadsheet that was used to produce the result shown in Figure 14-1. The experimental values of the dependent variable, A_{obsd}, are in column B, the concentration $[B]_t$ in column C, A_{calc} in column D and the square of the residual in column E.

	A	B	C	D	E	F
1	Consecutive First-Order Reactions (A → B → C)					
2	$[B]t = [A]_0 \cdot k_1 \cdot (EXP(-k_2 \cdot t) - EXP(-k_1 \cdot t))/(k_1 - k_2)$					
3	Only B absorbs light at the monitoring wavelength (243 nm). Path length 0.4 cm.					
4	Absorbance = molar absorptivity x path length x concentration $A = \varepsilon_B \times 0.4 \times [B]$					
5	Conc (mol/L)	4.00E-05	(C_A)	Rate constants:		
6	ε_A (cm L/mol)	0		k_1 (sec^{-1})	**0.500**	(k_1)
7	ε_B (cm L/mol)	**3.00E+03**	(E_B)	k_2 (sec^{-1})	**0.300**	(k_2)
8	ε_C (cm L/mol)	0				
9	**t, sec**	**A(obsd)**	**[B]**	**A(calc)**	∂^2	
10	0.0	0.0000	0.00E+00	0.0000	0.0E+00	
11	0.2	0.0047	3.69E-06	0.0044	7.2E-08	
12	0.6	0.0129	9.45E-06	0.0113	2.5E-06	
13	1.0	0.0163	1.34E-05	0.0161	3.4E-08	
14	1.4	0.0188	1.60E-05	0.0193	2.1E-07	
15	1.8	0.0201	1.76E-05	0.0211	1.1E-06	
16	2.2	0.0208	1.84E-05	0.0221	1.6E-06	
17	2.6	0.0208	1.86E-05	0.0223	2.3E-06	
18	3.0	0.0205	1.83E-05	0.0220	2.3E-06	
19	4.0	0.0178	1.66E-05	0.0199	4.4E-06	
20	5.0	0.0149	1.41E-05	0.0169	4.1E-06	
21	6.0	0.0118	1.16E-05	0.0139	4.2E-06	
22	7.0	0.0090	9.23E-06	0.0111	4.3E-06	
23	8.0	0.0070	7.24E-06	0.0087	2.9E-06	
24	9.0	0.0052	5.61E-06	0.0067	2.3E-06	
25	10.0	0.0038	4.30E-06	0.0052	1.9E-06	
26				(target)	**3.42E-05**	

Figure 14-5. The spreadsheet before optimization of coefficients by the Solver. The initial values of the three coefficients (the changing cells) and the current value of the objective (the target cell) are in bold.

The formulas in cells C10, D10 and E10 are, respectively,

=C_A*k_1*(EXP(-k_2*t)-EXP(-k_1*t))/(k_1-k_2)

=E_B*0.4*C10

=(B10-D10)^2

Range names were used in these formulas; the names assigned to cells are shown in parentheses in the cell to the right of each named cell.

The three changing cells ($E$6, $E$7 and $B$7) and the target cell ($E$26) are in bold. The initial values are guesses based on the appearance of the data in Figure 14-1. More specifically, the guesses were based on the rise time, decay time and maximum of the data, but if you experiment with the Solver you will see that much poorer guesses will almost always lead to the correct answer.

(A good way to get initial values for the changing cells is to create a chart of the data, then vary the coefficients in order to get an approximate fit of the calculated curve to the experimental data points.)

When the spreadsheet model has been set up, choose **Solver...** from the **Tools** menu. The Solver Parameters dialog box (Figure 14-6) will be displayed.

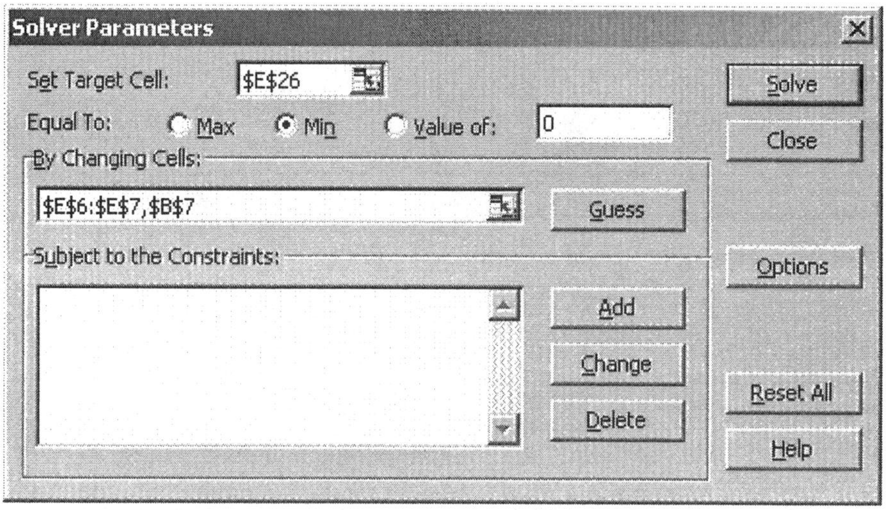

Figure 14-6. The Solver Parameters dialog box.

In the Set Target Cell box, type E26, or select cell E26 with the mouse. We want to minimize the sum of squares, so press the Min button. In the By Changing Cells box, enter E6:E7 and B7.

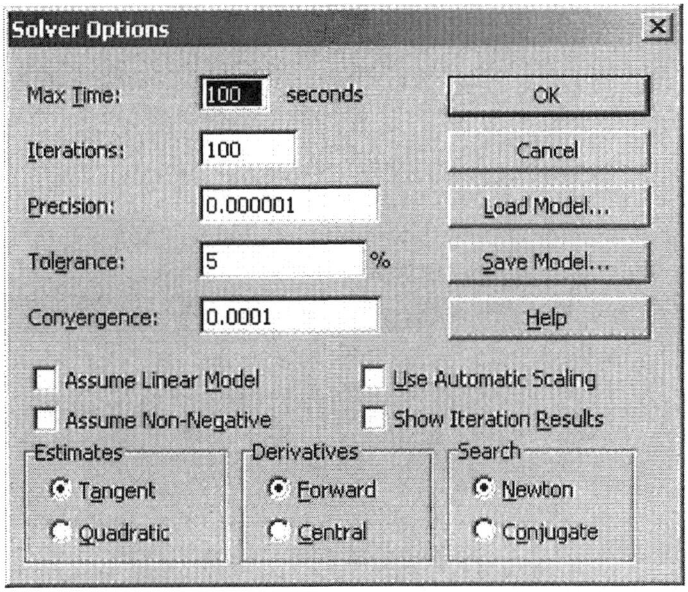

Figure 14-7. The Solver Options dialog box.

For reasons that will be explained in a subsequent section, press the Options button to display the Solver Options dialog box (Figure 14-7) and check the Use Automatic Scaling box.

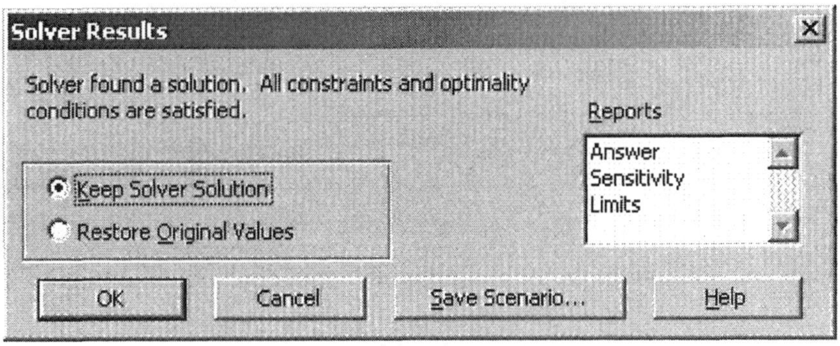

Figure 14-8. The Solver Results dialog box.

Press OK to exit from Solver Options and return to the Solver Parameters dialog box. Press the Solve button.

When the Solver finds a solution, the Solver Results dialog box is displayed (Figure 14-8). There are three reports that you can choose to print: Answer, Sensitivity and Limits, but none of these reports contain any information that we will use.

You have the option of accepting the Solver's solution or restoring the original values. Press the Keep Solver Solution button. The spreadsheet will be displayed with the final values of the changing and target cells (Figure 14-9).

	A	B	C	D	E	F
1	Consecutive First-Order Reactions (A → B → C)					
2	$[B]t = [A]_0 \cdot k_1 \cdot (EXP(-k_2 \cdot t) - EXP(-k_1 \cdot t))/(k_1 - k_2)$					
3	Only B absorbs light at the monitoring wavelength (243 nm). Path length 0.4 cm.					
4	Absorbance = molar absorptivity x path length x concentration $A = \varepsilon_B \times 0.4 \times [B]$					
5	Conc (mol/L)	4.00E-05	(C_A)	Rate constants:		
6	ε_A (cm L/mol)	0		k_1 (sec^{-1})	0.639	(k_1)
7	ε_B (cm L/mol)	2.53E+03	(E_B)	k_2 (sec^{-1})	0.285	(k_2)
8	ε_C (cm L/mol)	0				
9	t, sec	A(obsd)	[B]	A(calc)	∂^2	
10	0.0	0.0000	0.00E+00	0.0000	0.0E+00	
11	0.2	0.0047	4.66E-06	0.0047	8.5E-11	
12	0.6	0.0129	1.16E-05	0.0118	1.3E-06	
13	1.0	0.0163	1.62E-05	0.0164	2.6E-09	
14	1.4	0.0188	1.89E-05	0.0191	1.0E-07	
15	1.8	0.0201	2.04E-05	0.0206	2.2E-07	
16	2.2	0.0208	2.09E-05	0.0211	7.6E-08	
17	2.6	0.0208	2.07E-05	0.0209	1.2E-08	
18	3.0	0.0205	2.01E-05	0.0203	4.6E-08	
19	4.0	0.0178	1.75E-05	0.0177	2.1E-08	
20	5.0	0.0149	1.44E-05	0.0145	1.3E-07	
21	6.0	0.0118	1.15E-05	0.0116	3.9E-08	
22	7.0	0.0090	8.98E-06	0.0091	5.7E-09	
23	8.0	0.0070	6.94E-06	0.0070	8.7E-11	
24	9.0	0.0052	5.31E-06	0.0054	2.8E-08	
25	10.0	0.0038	4.04E-06	0.0041	8.2E-08	
26				(target)	2.06E-06	

Figure 14-9. The spreadsheet after optimization of coefficients by the Solver. The three coefficients (the changing cells) and the objective (the target cell) are in bold.

The Solver provides results that are essentially identical to those from commercial software packages. Any slight differences (usually *ca.* 0.001% or less) arise from the fact that, with all of these programs, the coefficients are found by a search method; the "final" values will differ depending on the convergence criteria used in each program. In fact, you would probably obtain slightly different results using the same program and the same data, if you started with different initial estimates of the coefficients.

Some Notes on Using the Solver

External References. The target cell and the changing cells must be on the active sheet. However, your model can involve external references to values in other worksheets or workbooks.

Discontinuous Functions. Discontinuous functions in your Solver model may cause problems. They can be either discontinuous mathematical functions such as TAN, which has a discontinuity at $\pi/2$, or worksheet functions that are inherently "discontinuous," such as IF, ABS, INT, ROUND, CHOOSE, LOOKUP, HLOOKUP, or VLOOKUP.

Initial Estimates. Since the Solver operates by a search routine, it will find a solution most rapidly and efficiently if the initial estimates that you provide are close to the final values. As mentioned previously, it is often useful to create a chart of the data that displays both y_{obsd} and y_{calc}, and then vary the parameters manually in order to find a good set of initial parameter estimates.

Global Minimum. To ensure that the Solver has found a *global minimum* rather than a *local minimum*, it's a good idea to obtain a solution using different sets of initial estimates.

"Unable to find a solution" When There Are a Large Number of Parameters. For a complicated model with a large number of adjustable coefficients, the Solver may not be able to converge to a reasonable solution. In such a case, it is sometimes helpful to perform initial Solver runs with subsets of the coefficients. For example, to fit a UV-visible spectrum with five Gaussian bands, and thus 15 adjustable coefficients, you could perform initial runs varying the coefficients for two or three of the bands at a time. When a reasonable fit has been found for the subsets, perform a final Solver run varying all of the coefficients.

Some Notes on the Solver Parameters Dialog Box

There are some additional controls in the Solver Parameters dialog box:

By Changing Cells. You can use names instead of cell references for individual cells or ranges in the By Changing Cells input box.

For ease of editing an extensive series of references in the By Changing Cells input box, press F2; you can then use the arrow keys to move within the box.

Constraints. With the Solver you can apply constraints to the solution. For example, you can specify that a parameter must be greater than or equal to zero, or that a parameter must be an integer. Although the ability to apply constraints to a solution may be tempting, it can sometimes lead to an incorrect solution. Don't introduce constraints (e.g., to force a parameter to be greater than or equal to zero) if you're using the Solver to obtain the least-squares best fit. The solution may not be the "global minimum" of the error-square sum, and the regression coefficients may be seriously in error.

Add, Change, Delete. The Add, Change and Delete buttons are used to apply constraints to the model. Since the use of constraints is to be avoided, these buttons are not of much interest.

Guess. Pressing the Guess button will enter references to all cells that are precedents of the target cell. In the example in Figure 14-9, pressing the Guess button enters the cell references $A$10:$B$25, $B$7, $B$5, $E$6:$E$7 (t values, E_B, C_A, k_1, k_2, respectively) in the By Changing Cells box. Obviously, some of these coefficients must not be allowed to vary. Avoid using the Guess button.

Reset All. The current Solver model is automatically saved with the worksheet. The Reset All button permits you to "erase" the current model and begin again.

Some Notes on the Solver Options Dialog Box

The Options button in the Solver Parameters dialog box displays the Solver Options dialog box (Figure 14-7) and allows you to control the way Solver attempts to reach a solution. The default values of the options are shown in Figure 14-7.

Max Time and Iterations. The Max Time and Iterations parameters determine when the Solver will return a solution or halt. If either Max Time or Iterations is exceeded before a solution has been reached, the Solver will pause and ask if you want to continue. For most simple problems, the default limits will not be exceeded. In any event, you don't need to adjust Max Time or Iterations, since if either parameter is exceeded, the Solver will pause and issue a "Continue anyway?" message.

Precision and Tolerance. Both the Precision and Tolerance options apply only to problems with constraints. The Precision parameter determines the amount by which a constraint can be violated. The Tolerance parameter is similar to the Precision parameter, but applies only to problems with integer solutions. Since adding constraints to a model that involves minimization of the error-square sum is not recommended, neither the Precision nor the Tolerance parameter is of use in nonlinear regression analysis.

Convergence. The Convergence parameter corresponds to the Maximum Change parameter in the Calculations tab of Excel's Options dialog box (see Chapter 8, Figure 17), but unlike the Maximum Change parameter, which is an absolute convergence limit, the Solver's Convergence parameter is relative; the Solver will stop iterating when the relative change in the target cell value is less than the number in the Convergence box for the last five iterations. Thus you don't have to scale the convergence limit to fit the problem, as you do when using **Goal Seek**....

Assume Linear Model. If the function is linear, checking the Assume Linear Model box will speed up the solution process. If the Assume Linear Model option is checked, the Solver performs a linearity test before proceeding; if the model fails this linearity test, the Solver returns the message "The conditions for Assume Linear Model are not satisfied."

Assume Non-Negative. Checking this box is equivalent to setting "greater than or equal to zero" constraints for each of the coefficients.

Use Automatic Scaling. For some models the Solver may refuse to converge satisfactorily. The Solver may fail to vary one or more changing cells or vary them by only an insignificant amount. This can occur when there is a large difference in magnitude between changing cells, for example, if you are varying two parameters, an equilibrium constant K, with magnitude 1×10^{10} and an NMR chemical shift δ, with magnitude 0.5, to fit data from an NMR "titration" (chemical shift as a function of pH). In such cases the Use Automatic Scaling option should be checked. In the example earlier in this chapter, you were instructed to check the Use Automatic Scaling box because there was a large difference between the parameters k_1 and k_2 (both on the order of 1) and the parameter E_B (on the order of 10^3). You may find it constructive to re-run this example using the original estimates (0.5, 0.3 and 3E+03) but with the Use Automatic Scaling box unchecked. You will find that the Solver varies k_1 and k_2 but does not appear to change E_B. But if you examine the value of E_B you will see that the value did change a very small amount. (When I ran this model, the value changed from 3000 to 2999.99999714051.)

Show Iteration Results. If the Show Iteration Results box is checked, the Solver will pause and display the result after each iteration. You may find it interesting to try this option when you are first learning to use the Solver.

If you create a model with a large number of cells to recalculate at each iteration, you may be able to observe the progress of the Solver in another way: after each iteration, the iteration number and the value of the target cell are displayed in the Status Bar at the bottom of the Excel worksheet. (The number format of the target cell in the Status Bar is the same as its format on the worksheet, so be sure to display enough decimal places on the worksheet so that you'll be able to see the progress of the iterations.) Also, for a large model that takes a long time to calculate, you can press ESC at any time to halt the iteration process and inspect the current results, and then continue.

Estimates, Derivatives and Search. These coefficients can be changed to optimize the solution process. The Search parameter specifies which gradient search method to use: the Newton method requires more memory but fewer iterations, while the Conjugate method requires less memory but more iterations. The Derivatives parameter specifies how the gradients for the search are calculated: the Central derivatives method requires more calculations (and will therefore be slower) but may be helpful if the Solver reports that it is unable to find a solution. The Estimates parameter determines the method by which new estimates of the coefficients are obtained from previous values; the Quadratic method may improve results if the system is highly nonlinear. For the majority of problems, you probably will not detect any difference in performance with any of these options.

Save Model... and Load Model.... The current Solver model is automatically saved with the worksheet. The Save Model... and Load Model... buttons permit you to save multiple Solver models. An additional 512 bytes are added to the workbook for each model that is saved.

When to Use Manual Scaling

The Use Automatic Scaling option is important for many problems, but so is manual scaling. Even when Use Automatic Scaling is in effect, the Solver may still be unable to find a solution. Automatic Scaling rescales the model based on values at the initial point. Objective and changing cells are scaled so their scaled values at the initial point are 1. But, if a value is less than 1E-05 at the initial point, that value is not scaled. Thus, even though you have checked the Use Automatic Scaling box, scaling may not be in effect. Therefore, you need to be aware of the need for manual scaling.

To apply manual scaling to the changing cells, modify one or more formulas so that the changing cells are all within three orders of magnitude or less of each other. For example, in the NMR titration example described in the previous paragraph, you could re-formulate the calculation so as to use log K instead of K. (Note that you can't apply a scaling factor directly to a changing cell, since it must be a number value that can be changed by the Solver; the scale factor must be incorporated into the target cell formula or into one of the intermediate formulas.)

In my experience, if the magnitude of the objective (the target cell) is very small (e.g., 1E-09), the Solver may assume that convergence has been reached and may not attempt to improve the solution[*]. Since many scientific problems can have values of the objective that are very small, manual scaling of the objective is extremely important. According to FrontLine Systems, "*The user should always be cautious when the final objective function is small and very cautious when the objection function is less than 1E–5 in absolute value. The best way to avoid scaling problems is to carefully choose the 'units' used in your model so that changing cells and target cell are all within a few orders of magnitude of each other, and preferably not less than 1 in absolute value.*"

You can apply a scale factor directly to the objective function. For example, an objective function formula such as

    =SUM(D4:D22)

that yields a sum-of-squares result with order of magnitude 1E–9 can simply be changed to the formula

    =1E09*SUM(D4:D22)

If you apply a scale factor to the objective, be sure to examine the objective after minimization. You may need to increase the magnitude of the scale factor and rerun the Solver.

Statistics of Nonlinear Regression

The only problem with the use of the Solver to perform least-squares regression is that, although you get the regression coefficients readily, the results aren't much use if you don't know their uncertainties as well. These aren't available from the Solver. The following illustrates how to obtain the standard deviations of the regression coefficients after obtaining the coefficients by using the Solver.

The standard deviation of the regression parameter a_i is given by equation 14-5.

$$\sigma_i = \sqrt{P_{ii}^{-1}}\ SE(y) \tag{14-5}$$

where P_{ii}^{-1} is the ith diagonal element of the inverse of the P_{ij} matrix

$$P_{ij} = \sum_{n=1}^{N} \frac{\partial F_n}{\partial a_i} \frac{\partial F_n}{\partial a_j} \tag{14-6}$$

---

[*] This can sometimes result in a situation where good initial estimates, which result in a very small value of the objective, do not lead to a solution, while for the same model, poorer initial estimates give a solution.

$\partial F_n/\partial a_i$ is the partial derivative of the function with respect to a_i evaluated at x_n. The above expressions can be found in some texts on nonlinear regression[*]. SE(y) is as defined in equation 13-19.

It's possible to carry out these calculations using a spreadsheet, but it's laborious and error-prone. A macro to perform the calculations is provided on the CD that accompanies this book.

The Solver Statistics Macro

The SolvStat Add-In returns regression statistics for regression coefficients obtained by using the Solver. The values returned are the standard deviations of the regression coefficients, plus the R^2 and SE(y) statistics

The add-in installs a new menu command, **Solver Statistics...**, in the **Tools** menu. If the Solver add-in has been loaded, the **Solver Statistics...** command will appear directly under the **Solver...** command in the **Tools** menu; if Solver is not installed, the **Solver Statistics...** command will appear at the bottom of the menu. See "Loading the Solver Add-In" earlier in this chapter for instruction on how to load the add-in. Both SolvStat.xls and SolvStat.xla versions are provided on the CD.

The macro calculates the $\partial F_n/\partial a_i$ terms for each data point by numerical differentiation, in the same way as in Chapter 6 (see the worksheet "Derivs by Sub Procedure"). This process is repeated for each of the k regression coefficients. Then the cross-products $(\partial F/\partial a_i)(\partial F/\partial a_j)$ are computed for each of the N data points and the $\Sigma(\partial F/\partial a_i)(\partial F/\partial a_j)$ terms obtained. The $\mathbf{P}_{ij}$ matrix of $\Sigma(\partial F/\partial a_i)(\partial F/\partial a_j)$ terms is constructed and inverted. The terms along the main diagonal of the inverse matrix are then used with equation 14-5 to calculate the standard deviations of the coefficients. This method may be applied to either linear or nonlinear systems.

When you choose the **Solver Statistics...** command, a sequence of four dialog boxes will be displayed, and you will be asked to select four cell ranges: (i) the y_{obsd} data, (ii) the y_{calc} data, (iii) the regression coefficients obtained by using the Solver and (iv) a 3R $\times$ nC range of cells to receive the statistical parameters. The Step 1 dialog box is shown in Figure 14-10. The y_{obsd} and y_{calc} values can be in row or column format. The Solver coefficients can be in non-adjacent cells.

---

[*] For example, K. J. Johnson, *Numerical Methods in Chemistry*; Marcel Dekker, Inc., New York, 1980, p. 278.

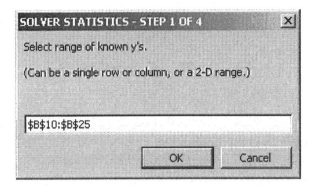

Figure 14-10. Step 1 of 4 of the Solver Statistics macro

The macro calculates the partial derivatives of the function, creates a matrix of sums of cross products, inverts the matrix and uses the diagonal elements to calculate the standard deviations.

If the SolvStat macro is used with the kinetics data of Figure 14-9, the regression coefficients shown in Figure 14-11 are returned. The array of values returned is in a format similar to that returned by LINEST: the regression coefficients are in row 5, the standard errors of the coefficients are in row 6 and the R^2 and SE(y) or RMSD parameter are in row 7.

	H	I	J
5	0.6381972	0.2856394	2528.05913
6	0.0477662	0.0191613	138.954138
7	0.9972227	0.0003983	

Figure 14-11. Regression statistics returned by the SolvStat macro.

The regression coefficients in row 5 are not calculated by the macro, but are the values returned by the Solver; they are provided simply to indicate which standard deviation is associated with which coefficient, since the Solver coefficients can be in nonadjacent cells.

Be Cautious When Using Linearized Forms of Nonlinear Equations

Some nonlinear relationships can be converted into a linear form, thus allowing you to use LINEST for curve fitting rather than applying the Solver. You should avoid this approach, because the curve fitting coefficients you obtain can be incorrect. An example will illustrate the problem.

In biochemistry, the reaction rate of an enzyme-catalyzed reaction of a substrate as a function of the concentration of the substrate is described by the Michaelis-Menten equation,

$$V = \frac{V_{\max}[\text{S}]}{K_m + [\text{S}]} \tag{14-7}$$

where V is the reaction velocity (typical units mmol/s), K_m is the Michaelis-Menten constant (typical units mM), $V_{\max}$ is the maximum reaction velocity and [S] is the substrate concentration. Some typical results are shown in Figure 14-10.

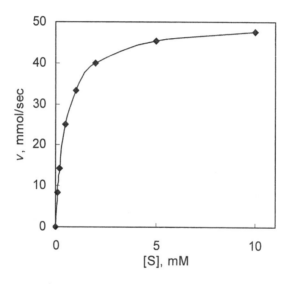

Figure 14-10. Michaelis-Menten enzyme kinetics.
The curve is calculated using equation 14-9 with $V_{\max}$ =50, K_m = 0.5.

Before desktop computers were available, researchers transformed curved relationships into straight-line relationships, so they could analyze their data with linear regression, or by means of pencil, ruler and graph paper. The Michaelis-Menten equation can be converted to a straight-line equation by taking the reciprocals of each side, as shown in equation 14-8.

$$\frac{1}{V} = \frac{K_m}{V_{\max}} \frac{1}{S} + \frac{1}{V_{\max}} \tag{14-8}$$

This treatment is called a double-reciprocal or Lineweaver-Burk plot. A Lineweaver-Burk plot of the data in Figure 14-10 is shown in Figure 14-11.

The parameters V_{max} and K_m can be obtained from the slope and intercept of the straight line (V_{max} = 1/intercept, K_m = intercept/slope).   However, the transformation process improperly weights data points during the analysis (very small values of V result in very large values of $1/V$, for example) and leads to incorrect values for the parameters.   In addition, relationships dealing with the propagation of error must be used to calculate the standard deviations of V_{max} and K_m from the standard deviations of slope and intercept.

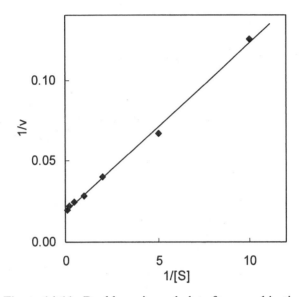

Figure 14-11. Double-reciprocal plot of enzyme kinetics.
The curve is calculated using equation 14-10 with $V_{max} = 50$, $K_m = 0.5$.

By contrast, when the Solver is used the data do not need to be transformed, y_{calc} is calculated directly from equation 14-7, the Solver returns the coefficients V_{max} and K_m, and SolvStat returns the standard deviations of V_{max} and K_m.

Problems

Data for, and answers to, the following problems are found in the folder "Ch. 14 (Nonlinear Regression)" in the "Problems & Solutions" folder on the CD.

1. **First Order Reaction.** The absorbance vs. time data in Table 14-1 was recorded for a chemical reaction. The reaction was believed to follow a first-order exponential decay:

$$A_t = A_0 e^{-kt}$$

Table 14-1. Absorbance vs. time data.

t, sec	A_{obsd}	t, sec	A_{obsd}
0	0.002000	10	0.000077
1	0.001441	11	0.000051
2	0.001070	12	0.000036
3	0.000739	13	0.000026
4	0.000542	14	0.000021
5	0.000367	15	0.000014
6	0.000263	16	0.000010
7	0.000200	17	0.000007
8	0.000140	18	0.000005
9	0.000100		

Determine the rate constant k using the Solver.

2. **Logistic Curve I.** The data in Table 14.2 can be described by a simple logistic curve

$$y = \frac{1}{1 + e^{-ax}}$$

Determine the constant a using the Solver.

Table 14-2. Data for simple logistic equation.

x	y	x	y
-8	0.0150	1	0.6198
-7	0.0338	2	0.7292
-6	0.0468	3	0.8177
-5	0.0712	4	0.8843
-4	0.1152	5	0.9206
-3	0.1850	6	0.9547
-2	0.2716	7	0.9706
-1	0.3775	8	0.9863
0	0.4972	10	0.6198

3. **Logistic Curve II.** The logistic function

$$y = \frac{a}{1 + e^{b+cx}} + d$$

takes into account offsets on the x-axis and the y-axis. Using the data in Table 14-3, determine the constants a, b, c and d using the Solver.

Table 14-3. Data for logistic equation.

x	y
-5	9.99
-3	9.96
-1	10.06
0	10.08
1	10.29
2	10.48
3	10.73
4	10.84
5	11.00
7	11.00
9	11.03
10	11.05

4. **Autocatalytic Reaction.** The data in Table 14-4 describes the time course of an autocatalytic reaction with two pathways: an uncatalyzed path ($A \rightarrow B$) and an autocatalytic path ($A \xrightarrow{B} B$). $[A]_0 = 0.0200$ mol L^{-1}. The rate law (the differential equation) is

$$-d[A]_t/dt = d[B]_t/dt = k_0[A]_t + k_1[A]_t[B]_t$$

Use any method from Chapter 10 to simulate the $[B] = F(t)$ data, then use the Solver to obtain k_0 and k_1.

Table 14-4. Rate data for an autocatalytic reaction.

t, sec	[B], mol L^{-1}	t, sec	[B], mol L^{-1}
0	0.0000	550	0.0149
50	0.0002	600	0.0161
100	0.0000	650	0.0175
150	0.0008	700	0.0190
200	0.0009	750	0.0188
250	0.0024	800	0.0196
300	0.0034	850	0.0198
350	0.0052	900	0.0201
400	0.0077	950	0.0199
450	0.0094	1000	0.0203
500	0.0127		

5. **van Deemter Equation.** Gas chromatography is an analytical technique that permits the separation and quantitation of complex mixtures. The mixture flows through a chromatographic column in a stream of carrier gas (usually helium), where the components separate and are detected. In the analysis of a sample of gasoline, for example, the components are separated based on their volatility, the lowest-boiling emerging from the separation column first. The degree of separation can be treated mathematically in the same way as for fractional distillation: a column can be considered to have a number of theoretical plates, just as a distillation tower in a refinery has actual "plates" for the separation of different petroleum products (naphtha, gasoline, diesel fuel, etc.). For gas chromatography, separation efficiency is usually expressed in terms of HETP (Height Equivalent to a Theoretical Plate), the column length divided by the number of theoretical plates. Separation efficiency is a function of the carrier gas flow rate v, as shown in the following figure. There is an optimum flow rate that provides the

smallest HETP; too fast and there is not sufficient time for equilibration, too slow and gaseous diffusion allows the components to re-mix.

The van Deemter Equation describes the relationship between HETP and carrier gas flow rate:

$$\text{HETP} = A + B/v + Cv$$

where v = carrier gas flow velocity. The data in Table 14-5 (also on the CD) shows measurements of HETP for a gas chromatographic column, using different flow rates.

Table 14-5. Gas chromatography data.

v, cm/sec	HETP, cm
0.9	0.64
1.5	0.51
3.0	0.42
4.2	0.47
5.6	0.55
7.0	0.63
8.0	0.69
9.0	0.75

Use the Solver to obtain the least-squares coefficients A, B and C for the van Deemter equation.

6. **NMR Titration.** The protonation constants K_1 and K_2 of a diprotic acid H_2A were determined by NMR titration. (Protonation constants, for example,

$$H^+ + L \leftrightharpoons HL \qquad\qquad K_1 = [HL] / [H^+] [L]$$

are used in this example because they simplify the equilibrium expressions The chemical shift δ of a hydrogen near the acidic sites was measured at a number of pH values over the range pH 1 to pH 11. The data are shown in the following Figure (data table and figure are on the CD that accompanies this book).

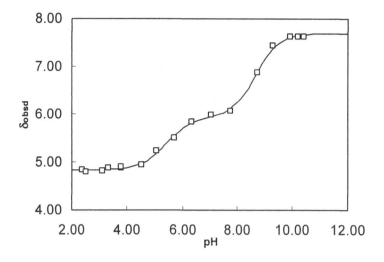

Figure 14-12. NMR titration.

At any pH value there are three acid-base species in solution: H_2A, HA^- and A^{2-}; the observed chemical shift is given by the expression

$$\delta_{calc} = \alpha_0 \delta_0 + \alpha_1 \delta_1 + \alpha_2 \delta_2$$

where α_j is the fraction of the species in the form containing j acidic hydrogens and α_j is the chemical shift of the species. The α values can be calculated using the expressions below:

$$\alpha_j = \frac{\beta_j [H^+]^j}{\Sigma \beta_j [H^+]^j}$$

$$\beta_j = K_1 K_2 \ldots K_j \quad (\beta_0 = 1)$$

e.g.,

$$\alpha_2 = \frac{K_1 K_2 [H^+]^2}{1 + K_1 [H^+] + K_1 K_2 [H^+]^2}$$

Use the Solver to determine K_1, K_2, δ_0, δ_1 and δ_2.

7. **2-D Regression.** Using the Power *vs.* Speed and Throttle setting data in problem 13-6, find the coefficients for the polynomial fitting equation

$$P = (aT^2 + bT + c) S^2 + (dT + e) S + f$$

8. **Deconvolution of a Spectrum I.** Use the data in Table 14-6 (also found on the CD in the worksheet "Deconvolution I") to deconvolute the spectrum. Close examination of the spectrum will reveal that it consists of four bands.

    Use a Gaussian band shape, i.e.,

    $$A_{calc} = A_{max} \exp\left(\frac{(x - \mu)^2}{s^2}\right)$$

    where A_{calc} is the calculated absorbance at a given wavelength, A_{max} is the absorbance at λ_{max}, x is the wavelength or frequency (nm or cm^{-1}), μ is the x at λ_{max} and s is an adjustable parameter related to, but not necessarily equal to, the standard deviation of the Gaussian distribution or to the bandwidth at half-height of the spectrum.

    Table 14-6. Spectrum of a nickel complex.

λ, nm	Absorbance	λ, nm	Absorbance	λ, nm	Absorbance
350	0.032	420	0.860	490	0.373
360	0.055	430	1.050	500	0.222
370	0.097	440	1.146	510	0.127
380	0.163	450	1.120	520	0.071
390	0.279	460	0.995	530	0.040
400	0.429	470	0.790	540	0.024
410	0.645	480	0.569	550	0.012

9. **Deconvolution of a Spectrum II.** Use the data in the worksheet "Deconvolution II" to deconvolute the spectrum of $K_3[Mn(CN)_6]$ in 2M KCN, shown in Figure 14-13. Use a Gaussian band shape. It should be clear from the figure that the spectrum contains multiple bands, perhaps five or more.

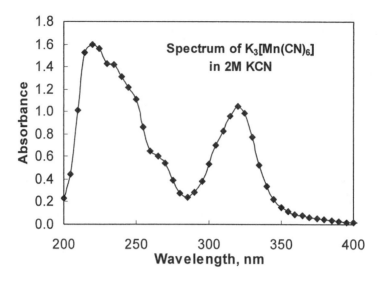

Figure 14-13. Spectrum of $K_3[Mn(CN)_6]$.

10. **Spectrum of a Mixture.** The UV-visible spectra of pure solutions of cobalt^{2+}, nickel^{2+} and copper^{2+} salts, and of a mixture of the three, are given on the CD-ROM over the wavelength range 350–820 nm. Instead of using absorbance readings at only three wavelengths to calculate the concentrations of the three salts in the mixture (as was done in problem 9-4), use the data at all 236 wavelength data points to calculate the three concentrations. Use the relationship $A = \varepsilon bc$, where ε, the molar absorptivity, is a dimensionless constant for a particular species at a particular wavelength, b is the light path length (1.00 cm in this experiment) and c is the molar concentration. For the mixture, $A_{obsd} = \varepsilon_{Co}C_{Co} + \varepsilon_{Ni}C_{Ni} + \varepsilon_{Cu}C_{Cu}$ at each wavelength.

Use the Solver Statistics macro to obtain the standard deviations of the three concentrations.

11. **Multiple-Wavelength Regression.** Dissociation of the second hydrogen ion of Tiron (1,2-dihydroxybenzene-3,5-disulfonate, H_2L) does not begin until the pH is raised above 10. The pK_{a2} of Tiron was determined spectrophotometrically by recording the spectrum at constant Tiron concentration and varying pH. The spectra are shown in the following figure; the absorbance readings (from 226 nm to 360 nm in 2-nm increments) at each pH value are tabulated on the CD that accompanies this text.

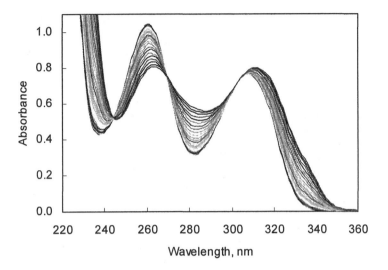

Figure 14-14. Spectra of Tiron at pH values between 10 and 12.

The equilibrium reaction being measured is (charges omitted for clarity)

$$HL \rightleftharpoons H^+ + L \qquad\qquad K_a = [H^+] [L]/[HL]$$

The dissociation of H_2L to HL^- is complete at pH values of 10 and higher, and can be neglected. The concentrations of L and HL are given by the following expressions:

$$[L] = L_T K_a /(K_a + [H^+])$$

$$[HL] = L_T [H+] /(K_a + [H^+])$$

where L_T is the total concentration of Tiron in the solution. The absorbance at a given wavelength is the sum of the contributions of the two species, that is,

$$A = \varepsilon_L[L] + \varepsilon_{HL}[HL]$$

where ε is the molar absorptivity of the species, a constant at a given wavelength.

Calculate the K_a value and the ε_L and ε_{HL} values at each wavelength, in one global minimization. (Excel's Solver can handle up to 200 changing cells, so we are pushing the limit here.) You will need to calculate the sum-of-squares-of-residuals for each wavelength, and minimize the "grand total" for all wavelengths. The Solver may have trouble "digesting" all this data. If so, use the Solver with data at a single wavelength to get the values of K_a, ε_L and ε_{HL}, then use these as starting value for a global minimization.

Chapter 15

Random Numbers and the Monte Carlo Method

The Monte Carlo method differs from the techniques we have considered in preceding chapters: instead of applying quantitative mathematical expressions to arrive at an answer, we approximate or simulate the process, repeat the calculation a large number of times using randomly selected inputs chosen within a suitable range, and then average the result or draw other statistical conclusions. The method can be lengthy and provide only an approximate answer, but it may be the only available way to arrive at an answer.

Monte Carlo methods have been used in economics, in nuclear physics and to model traffic patterns. We will look at two main types of application: Monte Carlo simulation and Monte Carlo integration.

Random Numbers in Excel

Since the Monte Carlo method involves the use of random numbers, we will begin by examining how random numbers are produced and used within Excel.

How Excel Generates Random Numbers

In Excel 2003, an improved random number generator was implemented. Earlier versions of Excel used a pseudo-random-number-generation algorithm whose performance on standard tests of randomness was not sufficient to satisfy the demand of power users who might require the generation of a million or more random numbers. For the majority of users, the older pseudo-random-number generator was satisfactory.

The earlier algorithm used the following iterative method to calculate pseudo-random numbers:

The first random number:

r = fractional part of $(9821 \times s + 0.211327)$

where $s = 0.5$, and successive random numbers:

r = fractional part of $(9821 \times s + 0.211327)$

where s = the previous random number

In an effort to increase the "randomness," Microsoft later provided a patch that caused r to be determined from the system clock (which added a further degree of randomness to the numbers generated). But because these pseudo-random numbers are produced by a mathematical algorithm, if a long sequence of them is produced, eventually the sequence will repeat itself. Statistical tests on series of random numbers produced by the earlier version of RAND revealed that the cycle before numbers started repeating was unacceptably short, in the vicinity of one million.

In the improved random number generator used in Excel 2003, three sets of random numbers are generated. Three of these random numbers are summed, and the fractional part of the sum is used as the random number. By this procedure, it is stated that more than 10^{13} numbers will be generated before the repetition begins.

The random-number algorithm in Excel 2003 was developed by B. A. Wichman and I. D. Hill ("Algorithm AS 183: An Efficient and Portable Pseudo-Random Number Generator," *Applied Statistics, 31*, 188–190, 1982; "Building a Random-Number Generator," *BYTE*, pp. 127–128, March 1987). This random number generator is also used in a software package that is provided by the U.S. Department of Health and Human Services. It has been shown to pass tests developed by NIST (National Institute of Standards and Technology).

Using Random Numbers in Excel

You can use random numbers in many ways, for example: to add "noise" to a signal generated by a formula, to select items randomly from a list, or to perform a simulation by using the Monte Carlo method. These and some other uses of random numbers will be described in following sections.

Excel provides several ways to generate random numbers. The worksheet function RAND returns a random real number greater than or equal to 0 and less than 1. RAND is a volatile function; that is, a new random number is returned every time the worksheet is calculated. You can test this, after entering =RAND() in a cell, by pressing F9 (Calculate Now) or by typing anything (even a space character) in a cell and pressing the Enter key. You will see that the value returned by the RAND function changes.

The fact that random numbers are recalculated every time you do just about anything on a spreadsheet can sometimes be problematic, especially if your spreadsheet contains large ranges of such numbers. In the old days of 133-MHz computers, there could be a delay of several seconds while the spreadsheet recalculated. Fortunately, that's not usually a problem with today's high-speed computers.

But when a random number is used as input into a calculation and the random number keeps changing, that can be a problem. If you want to use RAND to generate a random number but don't want the number to change every time the worksheet is calculated, you must convert the formula to its value. You can do this by entering the formula =RAND() in a cell, copying the cell, and then use Paste Special (Values). This will convert the contents of the cell from =RAND() to a value (e.g., 0.743487098126025). Alternatively, you can type the formula =RAND() in the formula bar, then press F9, then Enter.

Instead of using the RAND worksheet function, you can use the RANDBETWEEN function, one of the Engineering functions. If this function does not appear in the list of functions in the Insert Function dialog box, or returns the #NAME? error when you use it in a worksheet formula, you must load the Analysis ToolPak add-in. After you load the Add-In, you will see a new function category, Engineering functions, in the Insert Function dialog box. As well as this new function category (which provide capabilities for working with imaginary numbers, or for converting between binary, hexadecimal and decimal number systems, among others), there are a number of new functions which are dispersed in other function categories: the RANDBETWEEN function is located in the Math & Trig category. The complete list of Engineering functions can be found in Appendix 5.

If you load the older Add-In, Analysis ToolPak, the function appears in the function list in uppercase (e.g., RANDBETWEEN). If you load the newer Add-In, Analysis ToolPak-VBA, the function list contains both the older uppercase function names and the newer function names, in lowercase. This helps to distinguish between Excel's built-in worksheet functions, such as RAND, and the Add-In names, such as Randbetween.

RANDBETWEEN(*bottom,top*) returns an integer random number. Bottom is the smallest integer RANDBETWEEN will return, top is the largest. For example, the expression RANDBETWEEN(0,100) returns (e.g., 74).

To generate a random number between *bottom* and *top*, without loading the Analysis ToolPak, use

=RAND()*(*top* - *bottom*) + *bottom*.

For example, if *bottom* = 0 and *top* = 5, the returned result could be for example, 4.04608661978098.

To generate a random integer between *bottom* and *top*, use

=ROUND(RAND()*(*top* - *bottom*) + *bottom*,0)

For example, if *bottom* = 0 and *top* = 50, the returned result could be 27.

Since all of the above formulas include the RAND function, the returned result is volatile; that is, it changes each time the spreadsheet is modified.

Adding "Noise" to a Signal Generated by a Formula

One of the simplest uses for the RAND function is to add noise to a theoretical curve generated by means of a formula, so as to simulate a real signal. In other words, we want to modify our worksheet formula $F(x)$ by adding a random quantity δ. The δ must be scaled to produce a noise term of suitable magnitude and the δ terms must be equally distributed between positive and negative. Remember that RAND always returns a number greater than or equal to 0 and less than 1. There are several ways that you can add such a random quantity, for example,

(original worksheet formula) + scale_factor*(RAND()-0.5)

to produce a noise term of constant magnitude (scale_factor determines the magnitude of the noise term) or

(original worksheet formula)*(1 + scale_factor*(RAND()-0.5))

to produce a noise term of constant signal-to-noise ratio. Some people use the expression RAND()-RAND() instead of RAND()-0.5 to produce equal probability of positive or negative noise terms.

Figure 15-1 shows an example of a calculated curve with simulated experimental data points.

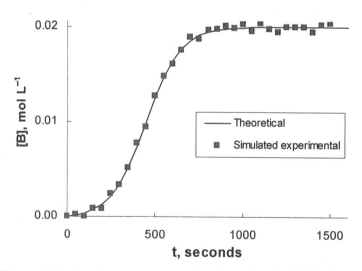

Figure 15-1. Experimental data simulated by using the RAND function.

Selecting Items Randomly from a List

You can use RAND to rearrange the values in a table so as to put them in random order, or to select a random sample from the table. There are two ways you can do this: either manually, using the **Sort** command, or by means of a formula. The former generates a randomized list that is "fixed"; that is, once randomized, the values in the list do not change. The latter method generates a list that will change each time the spreadsheet is recalculated. Clearly, there are advantages and disadvantages of either method.

To randomize manually, use =RAND() to generate a column of random numbers adjacent to (and most convenient, to the left of) the column of values to be randomized as shown in Figure 15-2.

	A	B
1	random #	Name
2	0.070428990	Agarwal, Brigitte
3	0.532482204	Ali, Le H
4	0.833901457	Alvarado, V
5	0.090748668	Amato, Andreas A
6	0.357788105	Antoine, Amy Louise
7	0.089596610	Atkinson, Sanya
8	0.801094843	Atwood, John
9	0.001795029	Barron, Johanna
10	0.210916288	Baumann, Carol
11	0.936376433	Beaubrun, Jeffrey
12	0.624696117	Beaudoin, Samir
13	0.505254770	Belfiore, Danielle M
14	0.599828277	Blee, Kangrok
15	0.578697880	Bleeker, David M
16	0.796914834	Blute, Roxanne M

Figure 15-2. A list of names before randomizing. Only part of the list is shown.
(folder 'Chapter 15 Examples', workbook 'Randomize', worksheet 'By Hand')

Then select the two columns and use the **Sort** command to Sort By the values in the column of random numbers. If the random number column is the leftmost column, you can use the Sort Ascending toolbutton ⟨A↓⟩. The randomized list is shown in Figure 15-3. To choose a random sample of N elements from the table, simply select, for example, the first N elements from the list.

	A	B
1	random #	Name
2	0.001795029	Barron, Johanna
3	0.002546605	Fournier, Elias T
4	0.005879847	O'Reilly, John
5	0.009157058	Dimattia, Tracey Ann
6	0.013827644	Underkoffler, Anne E
7	0.017823817	Lillis, Soyon
8	0.026750475	Ditolla, J Patrick
9	0.046036729	Eaton, Jennifer
10	0.056680621	Poon, Nicholas D

Figure 15-3. A list of names after randomizing. Only part of the list is shown.
(folder 'Chapter 15 Examples', workbook 'Randomize', worksheet 'By Hand')

To sort by means of a formula, begin with the two columns as in Figure 15-2. The names random and Database were assigned to the ranges A:A139 and B:B139, respectively; the range references can be used if desired. In cell C2, enter the formula

=SMALL(random,ROW()-1)

to sort the random numbers in ascending order. The expression ROW()-1 would have to be modified if the formula wasn't entered in row 2—for example, ROW()-10 if the first row of the table were in row 11. In cell D2 enter the formula

=MATCH(C2,random,0)

to return the relative position of the returned random number in cell C2. In cell E2 enter the formula

=INDEX(Database,D2)

to return the value at the same position in the array Database.

	A	B	C	D	E
1	random #	Database	sorted #	pos	Randomized
2	0.070428990	Agarwal, Brigitte	0.001795	8	Barron, Johanna
3	0.532482204	Ali, Le H	0.002547	50	Fournier, Elias T
4	0.833901457	Alvarado, V	0.00588	90	O'Reilly, John
5	0.090748668	Amato, Andreas A	0.009157	39	Dimattia, Tracey Ann
6	0.357788105	Antoine, Amy Louise	0.013828	124	Underkoffler, Anne E
7	0.089596610	Atkinson, Sanya	0.017824	78	Lillis, Soyon
8	0.801094843	Atwood, John	0.02675	40	Ditolla, J Patrick
9	0.001795029	Barron, Johanna	0.046037	45	Eaton, Jennifer
10	0.210916288	Baumann, Carol	0.056681	96	Poon, Nicholas D

Figure 15-4. A list of names randomized by using worksheet formulas.
(folder 'Chapter 15 Examples', workbook 'Randomize', worksheet 'By Formula')

The preceding formulas can be combined into a single "megaformula"

=INDEX(Database,MATCH(SMALL(random,ROW()-1),random,0))

to produce a more compact spreadsheet, as shown in Figure 15-5.

	A	B	C
1	random #	Database	Randomized
2	0.070428990	Agarwal, Brigitte	Barron, Johanna
3	0.532482204	Ali, Le H	Fournier, Elias T
4	0.833901457	Alvarado, V	O'Reilly, John
5	0.090748668	Amato, Andreas A	Dimattia, Tracey Ann
6	0.357788105	Antoine, Amy Louise	Underkoffler, Anne E
7	0.089596610	Atkinson, Sanya	Lillis, Soyon
8	0.801094843	Atwood, John	Ditolla, J Patrick
9	0.001795029	Barron, Johanna	Eaton, Jennifer
10	0.210916288	Baumann, Carol	Poon, Nicholas D

Figure 15-5. A list of names randomized by using a single "megaformula."
(folder 'Chapter 15 Examples', workbook 'Randomize', worksheet 'By Formula')

Random Sampling by Using Analysis Tools

If you have loaded the Analysis ToolPak Add-In (see earlier in this chapter), you will see that a command, **Data Analysis…**, appears at the bottom of the **Tools** menu. If it's not there, choose **Add-Ins…** from the **Tools** menu and check the box for Analysis ToolPak; this will install **Data Analysis…** in the **Tools** menu.

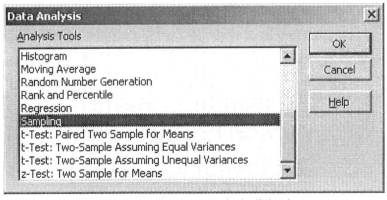

Figure 15-6. The Data Analysis dialog box.

The Data Analysis add-in provides a toolbox of statistical analysis tools, including Analysis of Variance, Correlation, Smoothing, Regression Analysis, Sampling and others; part of the list of statistical tools is shown in Figure 15-6.

The Sampling tool allows you to do either periodic or random sampling from a data array. To perform random sampling, choose Data Analysis from the Tools menu, choose Sampling from the list of tools, and press OK to display the Sampling dialog box.

The Sampling tool has one limitation: it will only accept numeric data. If you want to sort non-numeric data, like the list of names in our previous examples, you must add a column of integers 1, 2, 3... as shown in Figure 15-7. The column does not have to be adjacent, but in Figure 15-8 they have been entered in column A.

Then use the Sampling tool to perform random sampling on the values in this column. The input values in the Sampling dialog box are shown in Figure 15-8. In the example shown, the number of random samples is equal to the number of values in the original list, to randomize the complete list, but you could return a random sample of only 20, for example, if you wished.

	A	B	C	D
2	1	Agarwal, Brigitte	46	English, Katherine
3	2	Ali, Le H	87	Nhonguongsouthy, David
4	3	Alvarado, V	98	Prichard, Tammy N
5	4	Amato, Andreas A	51	Freyinger, Rehan
6	5	Antoine, Amy Louise	24	Chan, Kevin M
7	6	Atkinson, Sanya	33	Curtis, Cristine M
8	7	Atwood, John	51	Freyinger, Rehan
9	8	Barron, Johanna	72	Kyung, Jeffrey M
10	9	Baumann, Carol	40	Ditolla, J Patrick
11	10	Beaubrun, Jeffrey	80	MacNamara, Brad
12	11	Beaudoin, Samir	5	Antoine, Amy Louise
13	12	Belfiore, Danielle M	57	Habib, Farah
14	13	Blee, Kangrok	49	Forte, Joseph
15	14	Bleeker, David M	44	Drozdowski, Dennis
16	15	Blute, Roxanne M	110	Song, Mark A

Figure 15-7. A list of names randomized by using random sampling.
(folder 'Chapter 15 Examples', workbook 'Randomize', worksheet 'Sampling Tool')

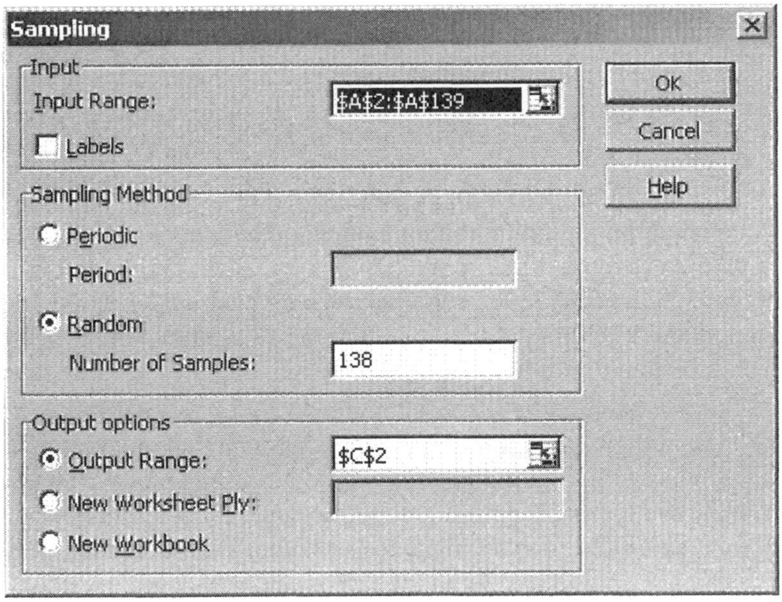

Figure 15-8.   The Sampling tool dialog box.

The randomly sampled integers, returned in column C, are then used with the INDEX worksheet function to return the corresponding text value from column B; the formula in cell D2 is

=INDEX(Name,C2)

Simulating a Normal Random Distribution of a Variable

You can create a table of random values having a normal distribution by using the NORMINV worksheet function. The syntax of the function is

NORMINV(***probability,mean,standard_dev***)

For example, to create a table of 10,000 random values having a normal distribution with mean 0 and standard deviation 1, enter the formula =NORMINV(RAND(), 0 , 1) in a cell and **Fill Down** into 10,000 cells. Figure 15-9 shows the distribution of these 10,000 values.

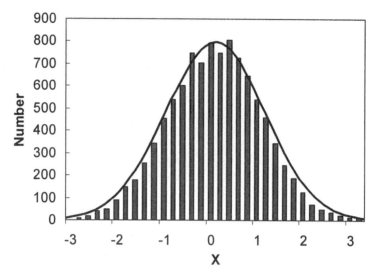

Figure 15-9.   10,000 random values with $\mu = 0$ and $\sigma = 1$,
created by using the NORMINV worksheet function.
The solid curve is the theoretical distribution.
(folder 'Chapter 15 Examples', workbook 'Randomize', worksheet 'Normal Distribution')

Monte Carlo Simulation

The Monte Carlo method is any technique of random sampling employed to approximate solutions to quantitative problems.   Often the system being simulated is clearly one that involves random processes, as, for example the Random Walk problem, sometimes described as the path a drunk takes as he staggers away from a telephone pole. If he takes N steps, each of length l, and each in a completely random direction, how far will he be from the telephone pole after the N steps? The problem can be solved algebraically (the answer is $d \approx l\sqrt{N}$), but it's apparent that a suitable answer can be obtained by using a random number to obtain an angle (the direction of each step relative to the one before), and thus the distance from the start point after each step. Figure 15-10 illustrates the result of such a calculation. Phenomena such as collisions of molecules in a gas, or neutron shielding, can be modeled similarly.

In other examples, the simulation appears little more than a game or diversion, but provides unexpected information. A classic example is the problem called Buffon's Needle, first proposed in 1777. A needle of length l is dropped on a sheet of paper with parallel rulings of spacing D. What is the probability of the needle crossing one of the lines? The surprising result is that the answer provides an estimate of the value of π.

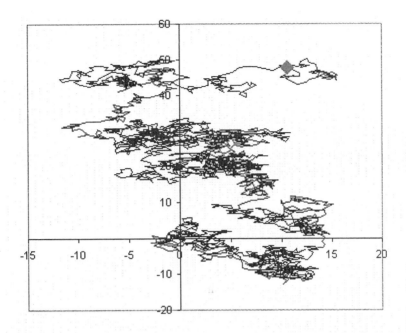

Figure 15-10. Random walk, 2000 steps of length 1.
The large diamond symbol is the position at the end of 2000 steps, a distance of 48.9
from the start point at 0,0. The "theoretical" distance $l\sqrt{N} = 44.7$.
(folder 'Chapter 15 Examples', workbook 'Random Walk', worksheet 'Random Walk')

We can solve the problem in the following way: (i) generate a random
number to calculate an angle θ, (ii) generate two more random numbers to obtain
the x and y coordinates of one end of the needle, (iii) from the coordinates of the
end, the length l of the needle and the angle θ, calculate the coordinates of the
other end of the needle, (iv) use these two pairs of coordinates to determine
whether either end of the needle crosses a gridline, (v) repeat the process N times,
counting the number of needles that cross a gridline. Figure 15-11 illustrates the
situation after 2000 needles of length $l = 2$ have been dropped on a sheet of paper
with ruling spacing $D = 2$ (the calculation is simplified when $l = D$). According
to statistical theory, the ratio N/N_c (N = total needles dropped, N_c = number of
needles that cross a line) is equal to $\pi/2$.

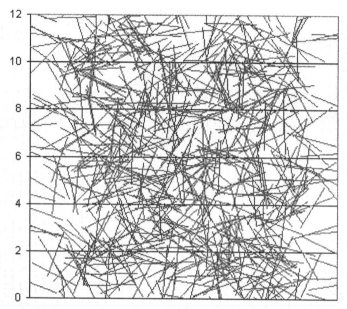

Figure 15-11. The Buffon's Needle experiment.
(folder 'Chapter 15 Examples', workbook 'Buffon's Needle', worksheet 'Calculation')

Since only the y coordinate of the end of the needle is used to determine whether the needle crosses a horizontal ruling, the spreadsheet shown in Figure 15-12 provides a simplified calculation. Only two horizontal rulings are assumed, at 0 and 1. Two random numbers are generated: one to specify the angle of the needle ($0 < \theta < 360$), the other to specify the y coordinate of the middle of the needle ($0 < y < 1$). Using these two values we calculate the y coordinate of the ends of the needle and determine whether it crosses either of the horizontal rulings. In the worksheet shown in Figure 15-12, the calculation was performed 2000 times (rows 5 through 2004) and the values in column H were summed.

The formulas used are

in cell A5:	=360*RAND()
in cell B5:	=RAND()
in cell C5:	=0.5*SIN(PI()*A5/180)
in cell D5:	=MIN(B5-C5,B5+C5)
in cell E5:	=MAX(B5-C5,B5+C5)
in cell F5:	=D5<=0
in cell G5:	=E5>=1
in cell H5:	=OR(F5,G5)*1

	A	B	C	D	E	F	G	H
4	angle, °	Y coord. of middle	vertical Y distance	Y coord. of lower end	Y coord. of upper end	crosses lower?	crosses upper?	Crossing
5	345.7	0.5477	-0.1233	0.4244	0.6710	FALSE	FALSE	0
6	158.7	0.4928	0.1817	0.3110	0.6745	FALSE	FALSE	0
7	20.6	0.2276	0.1761	0.0514	0.4037	FALSE	FALSE	0
8	201.7	0.4285	-0.1846	0.2439	0.6132	FALSE	FALSE	0
9	22.8	0.2548	0.1934	0.0614	0.4482	FALSE	FALSE	0
10	287.0	0.3133	-0.4781	-0.1648	0.7914	TRUE	FALSE	1
11	54.0	0.6497	0.4044	0.2453	1.0541	FALSE	TRUE	1
12	60.2	0.0564	0.4338	-0.3773	0.4902	TRUE	FALSE	1

Figure 15-12. Portion of table to calculate π by Buffon's Needle method. There are 2000 rows of calculation in the spreadsheet.
(folder 'Chapter 15 Examples', workbook 'Buffon's Needle', worksheet 'Calculation')

Figure 15-13 shows the result of recalculating the sheet 100 times, to provide a total of 200,000 calculations. As you can see, the calculation does not "converge" very efficiently. Compare the result with the evaluation of π by evaluation of a series (Chapter 4) or by integration of a function (Chapter 7); both methods are much more efficient.

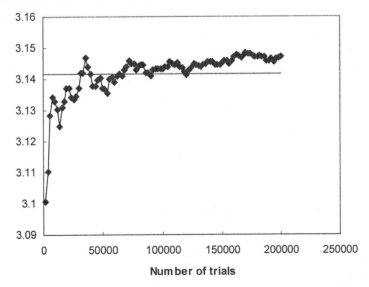

Figure 15-13. Approach of simulation result to the value π as the number of trials increases.
(folder 'Chapter 15 Examples', workbook 'Buffon's Needle', worksheet 'Many trials')

Monte Carlo Integration

The Monte Carlo method can be used to integrate a function that is difficult or impossible to evaluate by direct methods. Often the process of "integration" is the determination of the area of a figure. We'll illustrate the technique by determining the area of two figures: first, the area of a circle (from which we can evaluate π), and second, the area of an irregular figure.

The evaluation of π is a classic illustration of the determination of an area by the Monte Carlo method. Two random numbers in the range -1 to $+1$ are used to determine the coordinates of a point in the x, y plane. The number of points inside the circle, defined by the equation $x^2 + y^2 = 1$, divided by the total number of points, gives the ratio of the circle to the circumscribing square. Figure 15-14 illustrates such a calculation, using 4000 points.

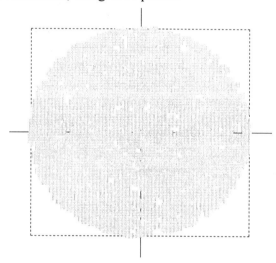

Figure 15-14. Estimation of π by using RAND.

This particular calculation gave 3.129 as the value of π.

The Area of an Irregular Polygon

When the preceding method is used to estimate the area of an irregular figure, we need a general method to determine whether a given point is inside or outside the figure. In the following, the figure must be a polygon, that is, a figure that can be described by a series of coordinates connected by straight lines. Since in an Excel chart, a curve can be approximated by a number of straight line segments, in theory a figure of any shape can be handled.

The standard method to determine whether a point lies inside or outside the figure is to draw a "ray" from the point extending out to infinity. In this example, illustrated in Figure 15-15, a "ray" is drawn vertically upwards from the point. If the ray crosses the boundary line(s) of the figure an odd number of times, the point lies inside the figure.

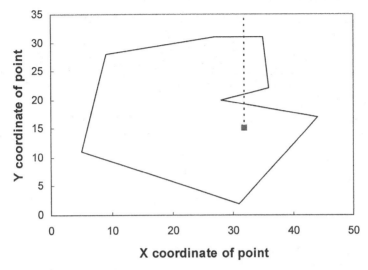

Figure 15-15. Determining whether a point lies inside or outside an irregular polygon.

The procedure to test whether a point x_A, y_A lies within the figure is as follows:

For each of the N edges that make up the figure:

(1) If the x coordinates of both ends of the edge lie to the left of x_A, then go to the next edge.

(2) If the x coordinates of both ends of the edge are to the right of x_A, then go to the next edge.

(3) If the y coordinates of both ends of the edge are below y_A, then go to the next edge.

(4) If none of the above is true, the y coordinates of one or both ends of the edge are above the point. Determine the y coordinate of the "crossing point" where the vertical ray and the edge cross, using the formula

$$y_C = y_L + \frac{y_R - y_L}{x_R - x_L}(x_A - x_L)$$

(5) If $y_C > y_A$, the ray crosses the edge of the polygon, so add one to the number of crossings found, and go to the next edge.

(6) When all N edges have been evaluated, if the number of crossings is odd, the point lies inside the figure.

This "inside or outside" calculation can be done either with worksheet formulas or with a VBA custom function. The following portion of a spreadsheet (Figure 15-16) illustrates the calculation using worksheet formulas.

	A	B	C	D	E	F
4			Does segment have...			
5	x	y	Both x to left?	Both x to right?	Both y below?	Yc-Ya positive?
6	27	31				
7	9	28	TRUE			
8	5	11	TRUE			
9	31	2	TRUE			
10	44	17	FALSE	FALSE	FALSE	FALSE
11	28	20	FALSE	FALSE	FALSE	TRUE
12	36	22	FALSE	FALSE	FALSE	TRUE
13	35	31	FALSE	TRUE		
14	27	31	FALSE	FALSE	FALSE	TRUE
15	(Coords in row above echo the first set of coords)					
16						
17	Enter coords here		Inside?			
18	x_a	y_a	(by formula)			
19	32	15	TRUE			
20						

Figure 15-16. Inside/outside determined by using worksheet formulas.
(folder 'Chapter 15 Examples', workbook 'Inside or Outside Figure', sheet 'Single Point Diagram')

Note that, in the table of coordinates of the line segments that describe the figure (A6:B14 in Figure 15-16), the coordinates of the initial point are repeated in line 15 so as to complete the figure. (This of course is also necessary to create a chart of the figure.) Thus the nine rows of points shown in Figure 15-16 describe eight line segments. That's why there are formulas in rows 7 through 14, but not in row 6. (It would be equally suitable to have formulas in rows 6 through 13 and not in row 14.)

The formulas in row 7 are:

in cell C7:   =AND($A$19>A6,$A$19>A7)

in cell D7:   =IF(C7=TRUE,"",AND($A$19<A6,$A$19<A7))

in cell E7:   =IF(OR(D7=TRUE,D7=""),"",AND($B$19>B6,$B$19>B7)) in cell F7:   =IF(E7=FALSE,(B6+(B7-B6)*($A$19-A6)/(A7-A6)-$B$19)>0,"")

and the formula in cell C19 (an array formula) is

{=MOD(SUM((F6:F14=TRUE)*1),2)<>0}

The following VBA code illustrates how to perform the "inside or outside" calculation by means of a custom function. The function takes four arguments: the range of *x* values describing the figure, the corresponding range of *y* values, the *x* coordinate of the point to be tested and the *y* coordinate of the point. The function returns TRUE if the point is inside the figure, otherwise FALSE.

```
Function Inside(x_values, y_values, x_point, y_point) As Boolean

Dim N As Integer, J As Integer, C As Integer
Dim YC As Double

N = x_values.Count
'Does figure have closure?
If x_values(1) <> x_values(N) Or y_values(1) <> y_values(N) Then Inside = _
  CVErr(xlErrValue): Exit Function
For J = 1 To N - 1
If x_values(J).Formula = "" Or y_values(J).Formula = "" Then Inside = _
  CVErr(xlErrValue): Exit Function 'Exit if cell is blank
'Both ends of segment to left of point?
If x_point >= x_values(J) And x_point > x_values(J + 1) Then GoTo EOL
'Both ends of segment to right of point?
If x_point <= x_values(J) And x_point < x_values(J + 1) Then GoTo EOL
'Both ends of segment below point ?
If y_point >= y_values(J) And y_point > y_values(J + 1) Then GoTo EOL
'If came here, one or both ends of the segment are above the point.
'Calculate the y coordinate where the "ray" crosses the segment.
YC = y_values(J + 1) + (y_values(J) - y_values(J + 1)) _
  * (x_point - x_values(J + 1)) / (x_values(J) - x_values(J + 1))
'if the crossing is above the point then add one to the count
If YC - y_point > 0 Then C = C + 1
EOL: Next J
Inside = C Mod 2
End Function
```

Figure 15-17. VBA code to determine inside/outside.
(folder 'Chapter 15 Examples', workbook 'Inside or Outside Figure', module 'Module1')

Figure 15-19 illustrates the use of the custom function to estimate the area of an irregular polygon such as the one shown in Figure 15-18. The values in cells $A$6:$B$14 specify the vertices of the polygon. The formulas in cells A17 and B17 use the RAND function to specify the *x* and *y* coordinates of a point within the area bounded by $x = 0$ to $x = 50$ and $y = 0$ to $y = 35$; the formulas are, respectively,

=50*RAND()

and

=35*RAND()

and the formula in C17 contains the custom function

=Inside($A$6:$A$14,$B$6:$B$14,A17,B17)

The formulas were filled down to fill 2000 cells. The formulas to calculate the area are:

in cell D7:   =COUNTA($C$17:$C$2016)   (total number of points)
in cell E7:   {=SUM(($C$17:$C$2016)*1)} (number of points inside polygon)
in cell E9:   =E7/D7   (fraction of points inside)
in cell D11:   =35*50   (area of the "box")
in cell E11:   =E9*D11   (area of polygon)

To plot only the points that lie within the polygon, the formula

=IF($C17,A17,"")

in cell D17 and the formula

=IF($C17,B17,"")

in cell E17 would seem to be suitable. These formulas, when filled down, yield the spreadsheet shown in Figure 15-19. But null-string values are plotted as zeros in a chart, so the chart doesn't turn out the way we want. Instead we use the NA() worksheet function; cells containing #NA! values are not plotted.

=IF($C17,A17,NA())

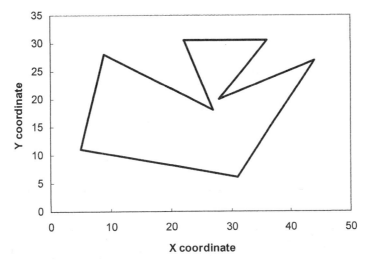

Figure 15-18. Estimating the area of an irregular polygon.

	A	B	C	D	E
5	X	Y		Calculation of area	
6	27	18		# points	# inside
7	9	28		2000	623
8	5	11			fraction
9	31	6			0.3115
10	44	27		total area	area
11	28	20		1750	545.1
12	36	30.5			
13	22	30.5			
14	27	18	(This row echoes the first set of coords)		
15	(2000 random points between x = 0 and x = 50, y = 0 and y = 35)				
16	Xa	Ya	Inside?	X and Y for plotting point	
17	31.54968765	19.50260778	TRUE	31.54968765	19.50260778
18	43.10121712	16.55383516	FALSE		
19	32.67162151	19.80326911	TRUE	32.67162151	19.80326911
20	36.71470616	15.93267943	TRUE	36.71470616	15.93267943
21	36.90754745	16.47652055	TRUE	36.90754745	16.47652055
22	44.32583965	27.69863231	FALSE		
23	7.71297725	24.09107738	FALSE		
24	27.96293313	17.55974824	TRUE	27.96293313	17.55974824
25	25.192141	31.28774952	FALSE		

Figure 15-19. Spreadsheet to estimate the area of the irregular polygon of Figure 15-18.
There are 2000 rows of inside/outside calculation in the spreadsheet.
(folder 'Chapter 15 Examples', workbook 'Inside or Outside Figure', sheet 'Area by Custom Function')

Now the blank cells, pleasing to the eye in the table but disastrous when used in a chart, are replaced by #NA! values, unpleasing in the table but perfect when used in a chart. To make the #NA! values "disappear," you can use Conditional Formatting. The conditional formatting formula applied to the cells in column D, beginning in cell D17, is =ISERROR(D17), which, when TRUE, sets the font color of the text in the cell to white, thus making the #NA! value invisible. A similar format was applied to the values in column E, beginning in cell E17. You can see the error values if you select the range of cells, as shown in Figure 15-20.

The data in $D$17:$E$2016, when added to the chart as a new series, shows the inside points, as illustrated in Figure 15-21.

	A	B	C	D	E
5	X	Y		Calculation of area	
6	27	18		# points	# inside
7	9	28		2000	623
8	5	11			fraction
9	31	6			0.3115
10	44	27		total area	area
11	28	20		1750	545.1
12	36	30.5			
13	22	30.5			
14	27		18 (This row echoes the first set of coords)		
15	(2000 random points between x = 0 and x = 50, y = 0 and y = 35)				
16	Xa	Ya	Inside?	X and Y for plotting point	
17	31.54968765	19.50260778	TRUE	31.54968765	19.50260778
18	43.10121712	16.55383516	FALSE	#N/A	#N/A
19	32.67162151	19.80326911	TRUE	32.67162151	19.80326911
20	36.71470616	15.93267943	TRUE	36.71470616	15.93267943
21	36.90754745	16.47652055	TRUE	36.90754745	16.47652055
22	44.32583965	27.69863231	FALSE	#N/A	#N/A
23	7.71297725	24.09107738	FALSE	#N/A	#N/A

Figure 15-20. Spreadsheet layout to estimate the area of an irregular polygon and to plot the random points within the polygon.
(folder 'Chapter 15 Examples', workbook 'Inside or Outside Figure', sheet 'Area by Custom Function')

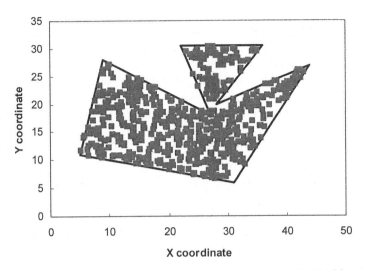

Figure 15-21. Estimating the area of an irregular polygon, with, the "inside" random points shown.
(folder 'Chapter 15 Examples', workbook 'Inside or Outside Figure', sheet 'Area by Custom Function')

Problems

Data for, and answers to, the following problems are found in the folder "Ch. 15 (Random Numbers & Monte Carlo)" in the "Problems & Solutions" folder on the CD.

1. **Estimation of π.** The equation of a circle is $x^2 + y^2 = r^2$. Evaluate π by determining the area of a circle of radius r circumscribed by a square of side $2r$. π is the ratio of the area of the circle to that of the square. Generate a pair of random numbers to use as the x and y coordinates. If the distance of the point from the origin is less than or equal to r, it is within the circle. Repeat this N times, evaluating N_C, the number of points that fall within the circle. The ratio N_C/N should be a reasonable estimate of π.

2. **Male Children.** A king wishes to increase the number of males in his kingdom. He decrees that all women in his kingdom may have as many children as they wish, as long as they are boys. As soon as a woman has a female baby, she must stop bearing children. If this decree is followed, what will be the ratio of boys to girls in the kingdom?

3. **Traffic Model.** Create a simple model of traffic patterns at a stoplight. Use one row of a spreadsheet to represent a unit of time, say 5 seconds. Use a random number to decide whether a car arrives at the intersection in a particular time unit. Vary the traffic density (probability) and traffic light timing; observe the effect on congestion at the stoplight.

4. **Traveling Salesman.** Given a number of cities and the costs of traveling from any city to any other city, what is the cheapest round-trip route that visits each city?

5. **Choose Once.** Using spreadsheet formulas only, create a list of unique integers (e.g., 1–15) in random order.

6. **Deck of Cards.** Using spreadsheet formulas only, simulate the shuffling of a deck of 52 cards.

7. **Frequency of Occurrence of Digits.** Create 1000 random numbers and determine the frequency of occurrence of the numbers 0 through 9 in the first digit.

8. **Frequency of Occurrence of Digits II.** Create two columns, each containing 1000 random numbers, RN1 and RN2. Determine the frequency of occurrence in the first significant digit of the numbers 1 through 9 in the product RN1 × RN2. Repeat for the product RN1 × RN2 × RN3.

Appendices

Appendix 1
Selected VBA Keywords

This listing of VBA objects, properties, methods, functions and other keywords will be useful when creating your own VBA procedures. The list is not exhaustive, but contains mainly those keywords that are used in the procedures shown in this book.

For each VBA keyword, the required syntax is given, along with some comments on the required and optional arguments, one or more examples and a list of related keywords. See Excel's On-Line Help for further information.

Abs Function
Returns the absolute value of a number.
Syntax: **Abs**(*number*)
Example: **Abs**(-7.3) returns 7.3
See also: **Sgn**

Activate Method
Activates an object.
*Syntax: object.***Activate**
Object can be **Chart, Worksheet** or **Window**.
Example: **Workbooks**("BOOK1.XLS").**Worksheets**("Sheet1").**Activate**
See also: **Select**

ActiveCell Property
Returns the active cell of the active window. Read-only.
Syntax: **ActiveCell** and **Application.ActiveCell** are equivalent.
See also: **Activate, Select**

ActiveSheet Property
Returns the active sheet of the active workbook. Read-only.
*Syntax: object.***ActiveSheet**
Object can be **Application, Window** or **Workbook**.
Example: **Application.ActiveSheet.Name** returns the name of the active sheet of the active workbook. Returns **None** if no sheet is active.
See also: **Activate, Select**

Address Property
Returns a reference, as text
*Syntax: object.***Address** *(rowAbsolute,columnAbsolute, referenceStyle, external, relativeTo)*

All arguments are optional. If *rowAbsolute* or *columnAbsolute* are **True** or omitted, returns that part of the address as an absolute reference. *ReferenceStyle* can be xlA1 or xlR1C1. If external is **True**, returns an external reference. See On-Line Help for information about the *relativeTo* argument.
See also: **Offset**

And Operator
Logical operator. (expression1 **And** expression2) evaluates to **True** if both expression1 and expression2 are **True**. Also can be used to perform bitwise comparison of two numerical values: (13 **And** 6) evaluates to 4. (13 = 00001101, 6 = 00000110, 4 = 00000100).
See also: **Or, Not, Xor**

Application Object
Represents the Microsoft Excel application.

Array Function
Returns a **Variant** containing an array.
Syntax: **Array** (*arglist*)
Example: **Array** (*31,28,31,30,31,30,31,31,30,31,30,31*)
See also: **Dim**

As Keyword
Used with **Dim** to specify the data type of a variable.

Asc Function
Returns the numeric code for the first character of text.
Syntax: **Asc**(*character*)
Example: **Asc** ("A") returns 65.
See also: **Chr**

Atn Function
Returns the angle corresponding to a tangent value.
Syntax: **Atn**(*number*)
Number can be in the range $-\infty$ to $+\infty$. The returned angle is in radians, in the range $-\pi/2$ to $+\pi/2$ ($-90°$ to $90°$). To convert the result to degrees, multiply by $180/\pi$.
Example: **Atn**(1) returns 0.785388573 or 45 degrees.
See also: **Cos, Sin, Tan**

Bold Property
Returns **True** if the font is Bold. Sets the Bold font. Read-write.
Syntax: *object*.**Bold**
Object must be **Font**.
Example: **Range**("A1:E1").**Font.Bold = True** makes the cells bold.
See also: **Italic**

Boolean Data Type
Use to declare a variable's type as **Boolean** (**True** or **False**), either in a **Dim** statement, or in a **Sub** or **Function** statement. Two bytes required per variable. When number values are converted to Boolean values, 0 becomes **False** and all other values become **True**. When Boolean values are converted to numbers, **False** becomes 0 and **True** becomes −1.
See also: **Dim, As, Double, Integer, String, Variant**

Call Command
Transfers control to a **Sub** procedure.
Syntax: **Call** *name (argument1, ...)*
Name is the name of the procedure. *Argument1*, etc., are the names assigned to the arguments passed to the procedure. **Call** is optional; if omitted, the parentheses around the argument list must also be omitted.
Example: **Call** Task1(argument1,argument2)
See also: **Sub, Function**

Case Keyword
See: **Select Case**

Cells Method
Returns a single cell by specifying the row and column.
Syntax: *object.***Cells***(row, column)*
Object is optional; if not specified, **Cells** refers to the active sheet.
Example: **Cells**(2,1).**Value** = 5 enters the value 5 in cell A2.
See also: **Range**

Characters Object
Represents characters in any object containing text. Use the **Characters** object to format characters within a text string.
Syntax: *expression.***Characters***(start, length)*
Example: **Selection.Characters(Start:=x, Length:=1).Font.Subscript = True**

Clear Method
Clears formulas and formatting from a range of cells.
Syntax: *object.***Clear**
Object can be **Range** (or **ChartArea**).
Example: **Range**("A1:C10").**Clear**
See also: **ClearContents, ClearFormats** in Excel's On-Line Help.

Close Method
Closes a window, workbook or workbooks.
Syntax: For workbooks, use *object.***Close**. For a workbook or window, use *object.***Close***(SaveChangesLogical, FileName)*.
Object can be **Window, Workbook** or **Workbooks**. If *SaveChangesLogical* is **False**,

does not save changes; if omitted, displays a "Save Changes?" dialog box.
Example: **Workbooks**("BOOK1.XLS").**Close**
See also: **Open, Save, SaveAs**

Column Property
Returns a number corresponding to the first column in the range. Read-only.
*Syntax: object.***Column**
Object must be **Range.**
See also: **Columns, Row, Rows**
Columns Method
Returns a **Range** object that represents a single column or multiple columns
*Syntax: object.***Columns**(*index*)
Object can be **Worksheet** or **Range.** *Index* is the name or number (column A = 1,
etc.) of the column.
Example: **Selection.Columns.Count** returns the number of columns in the selection.
See also: **Range, Rows**

ColumnWidth Property
Returns or sets the width of all columns in the range. If columns in the range
have different widths, returns **Null.**
Example: **Worksheets**("Sheet1").**Columns**("C").**ColumnWidth** = 30
See also: **RowHeight**

ConvertFormula Method
Converts cell references between A1-style and R1C1-style, and between absolute
and relative. On-Line Help states that *Formula* must begin with an equal sign, but
references in a string that does not begin with an equal sign are also converted.
Syntax: **expression.ConvertFormula(***Formula, FromReferenceStyle,*
*ToReferenceStyle, ToAbsolute, RelativeTo***)**
Example:
FormulaString = **Application.ConvertFormula**(FormulaString, **xlA1, xlA1, xlAbsolute**)
See also: **Address**

Copy Method
Copies the selected object to the Clipboard or to another location.
*Syntax: object.***Copy**(*destination*)
Object can be **Range, Worksheet, Chart** and many other objects. *Destination* specifies
the range where the copy will be pasted. If omitted, copy goes to the Clipboard.
Example: **Worksheets**("Sheet1").**Range**("A1:C50").**Copy**
See also: **Cut, Paste**

Cos Function
Returns the cosine of an angle.
Syntax: **Cos**(*number*)
Number is the angle in radians; it can be in the range $-\infty$ to $+\infty$. To convert an angle
in degrees to one in radians, multiply by $\pi/180$. Returns a value between -1 and 1.
See also: **Atn, Sin, Tan**

Count Property
Returns the number of items in the collection. Read-only.
Syntax: object.**Count**
Object can be any collection.
Example: The statement N = array.**Count** counts the number of values in the range
array.

Cut Method
Cuts the selected object and pastes to the Clipboard or to another location.
Syntax: object.**Cut**(*destination*)
Object can be **Range, Worksheet, Chart** or one of many other objects. *Destination*
specifies the range where the copy will be pasted. If omitted, copy goes to the
Clipboard.
Example: **Worksheets**("Sheet1").**Range**("A1:C50").**Cut**
See also: **Copy, Paste**

CVErr Function
Returns a Variant containing an error value specified by the user.
Syntax: **CVErr**(*number*)
CVErr can return either Excel's built-in worksheet error values, or a user-defined
error value.   The values of *number* for built-in worksheet error values are
xlErrDiv0, xlErrNA, xlErrName, xlErrNull, xlErrNum, xlErrRef, xlErrValue.
See also: **IsError**

Delete Method
Deletes the selected object.
Syntax: object.**Delete**(*SHIFT*)
Object can be **Range, Worksheet, Chart** and many other objects. *SHIFT* specifies
how to SHIFT cells when a range is deleted from a worksheet (xlToLeft or xlUp).
Can also use *SHIFT* = 1 or 2, respectively. If *SHIFT* is omitted, Excel moves
the cells without displaying the "SHIFT Cells?" dialog box.
Example: **Worksheets**("Sheet12").**Range**("A1:A10").**Delete** (xlToLeft) deletes the
indicated range and SHIFTs cells to left.

Dim Keyword
Declares an array and allocates storage for it.
Syntax: **Dim** *variable (subscripts)*
Variable is the name assigned to the array. *Subscripts* are the size dimensions of
the array; an array can have up to 60 size dimensions. Each size dimension has a
default lower value of zero; a single number for a size dimension is taken as the
upper limit. Use *lower* **To** *upper* to specify a range that does not begin at zero.
Use **Dim** with empty parentheses to specify an array whose size dimensions are
defined within a procedure by means of the **ReDim** statement.
Example: **Dim** Matrix (5,5) **As Double** creates a 6×6 array of double-precision
variables.
See also: **ReDim**

Do...Loop Command

Delineates a block of statements to be repeated.

Syntax: The beginning of the loop is delineated by **Do** or **Do Until** *condition* or **Do While** *condition*. The end of the loop is delineated by **Loop** or **Loop Until** *condition* or **Loop While** *condition*. *Condition* must evaluate to **True** or **False.**

Example: See examples of **Do...Loop** structures in Chapter 2.

See also: **Exit, For, Next, Wend, While**

Double Data Type

Use to declare a variable's type as double-precision floating-point (15 significant digits), either in a **Dim** statement, or in a **Sub** or **Function** statement. Eight bytes required per variable.

Example: **Dim** tolerance **As Double**

See also: **Dim, As, Boolean, Integer, String, Variant**

Else Keyword

Optional part of **If...Then** structure.

Elself Keyword

Optional part of **If...Then** structure.

End Command

Terminates a procedure or block.

Syntax: **End** terminates a procedure. **End Function** is required to terminate a **Function** procedure. **End If** is required to terminate a block **If** structure. **End Select** is required to terminate a **Select Case** structure. **End Sub** is required to terminate a **Sub** procedure. **End With** is required to terminate a **With** structure.

Example: See examples under **Select Case.**

See also: **Exit, Function, If, Then, Else, Select Case, Sub, With**

Endlf Keyword

Optional part of **If...Then** structure.

Err Function

Returns a run-time error number. Use in error-handling routine to determine the error and take appropriate corrective action.

Example: **If Err.Number = 13 Then**
                (code for corrective action here)
                Resume pt1
                End If

See also: **Error, On Error, Resume**

Evaluate Method

Converts a name or formula to a value.

Syntax: **Evaluate**(expression)

Expression must be a string, maximum length 255 characters. An initial equal

sign is not necessary.
Example: F$ = "2*3"
                 MsgBox Evaluate(F$)
See also: **Formula**

Exit Command
Exits a **Do...**, **For...**, **Function...** or **Sub...** structure.
Syntax: **Exit Do, Exit For, Exit Function, Exit Sub**
From a **Do** or **For** loop, control is transferred to the statement following the **Loop** or **Next** statement, or, in the case of nested loops, to the loop that is one level above the loop containing the **Exit** statement. From a **Function** or **Sub** procedure, control is transferred to the statement following the one that called the procedure.
Example: See examples of **Exit** procedures in Chapter 2.
See also: **Do, For...Next, Function, Stop, Sub**

Exp Function
Returns *e* raised to a power.
Syntax: **Exp**(*number*)
Returns the value of *e* raised to the power *number*.
See also: **Log**

False Keyword
Use the keywords **True** or **False** to assign the value **True** or **False** to Boolean (logical) variables.
When other numeric data types are converted to Boolean values, 0 becomes **False** while all other values become **True**. When Boolean values are converted to other data types, **False** becomes 0 while **True** becomes –1.
Example: **If** SubFlag = **False Then**...
See also: **True**

FillDown Method
Copies the contents and format(s) of the top cell(s) of a specified range into the remaining rows.
Syntax: object.**FillDown**
Object must be **Range**.
Example: **Worksheets**("Sheet12").**Range**("A1:A10").**FillDown**
See also: **FillLeft, FillRight, FillUp** in Excel's On-Line Help.

FillRight Method
Copies the contents and format(s) of the leftmost cell(s) of a specified range into the remaining columns.
Syntax: object.**FillDown**
Object must be **Range**.
Example: **Worksheets**("Sheet12").**Range**("A1:A10").**FillRight**
See also: **FillDown, FillLeft, FillUp** in Excel's On-Line Help.

Fix Function
Truncates a number to an integer.
Syntax: **Fix**(*number*)
If *number* is negative, **Fix** returns the first negative integer greater than or equal to *number*.
Example: **Fix**(-2.5) returns –2.
See also: **Int**

Font Property
Returns the font of the object. Read-only.
*Syntax: object.***Font**
Example: ActiveCell.Font.Bold = **True** makes the characters in the active cell bold.
See also: **FontStyle**

FontStyle Property
Returns or sets the font of the object. Read-write.
*Syntax: object.***FontStyle**
Example: **Range**("A1:E1").**Font.FontStyle** = "Bold"
See also: **Font**

For...Next Command
Delineates a block of statements to be repeated.
Syntax: **For** *counter* = *start* **To** *end* **Step** *increment*
                         (statements)
                         Next *counter*
Step *increment* is optional; if not included, the default value 1 is used. *Increment* can be negative, in which case *start* should be greater than *end*.
Example: See examples of **For...Next** procedures in Chapter 2.
See also: **Do...Loop, Exit, For Each...Next, While...Wend**

For Each...Next Command
Delineates a block of statements to be repeated.
Syntax: **For Each** *element* **In** *group*
                         (statements)
                         Next *element*
Group must be a collection or array. *Element* is the name assigned to the variable used to step through the collection or array. *Group* must be a collection or array.
Example: See examples of **For Each...Next** procedures in Chapter 2.
See also: **Do...Loop, Exit, For...Next, While...Wend**

Format Function
Formats a value according to a formatting code expression.
Syntax: **Format**(*expression,formattext*)
Expression is usually a number, although strings can also be formatted. *Formattext* is a built-in or custom format. Additional information can be found in *Microsoft*

Excel/Visual Basic Reference, or VBA On-Line Help.
Example: **Format**(TelNumber,"(###) ###-####") formats the value TelNumber in the form of a telephone number.

Formula Property
Returns or sets the formula in a cell.
If a cell contains a value, returns the value; if the cell contains the formula, returns the formula as a string.
See also: **Text, Value**

Function Keyword
Marks the beginning of a **Function** procedure.
Syntax: **Function** *name argument1, ...*
Name is the name of the variable whose value is passed back to the caller. *Argument1*, etc., are the names assigned to the arguments passed from the caller to the procedure.
Example: See examples of **Function** procedures in Chapter 2.
See also: **Call, Sub**
GoTo Command
Unconditional branch within a procedure.
Syntax: **GoTo** *label*
Label can be a name or a line number.

If...Then...Else...End If Command
Delineates a block of conditional statements.
Syntax: **If** *condition* **Then** ... **Else** ... **End If**
The statement can be all on one line (e.g., **If** *condition* **Then** *statement*). Alternatively, a block **If** structure can be used, in which case the first line consists of **If** *condition* **Then**; the end of the structure is delineated by **End If**. *Condition* must evaluate to **True** or **False**. The ellipsis following **Then** and **Else** can represent a single statement or several statements separated by colons; these are executed if *condition* is **True** or **False**, respectively.
Examples: If Char = "." **Then GoTo** 2000
                If (Char >= "0" **And** Char <= "9") **Then**
                (statements)
                End If
See also: **ElseIf, End**

InputBox Function
Displays an input dialog box and waits for user input.
Syntax: **InputBox**(*prompt,title,default,xpos,ypos,helpfile,context*)
See *Microsoft Excel/Visual Basic Reference* or On-Line Help for details.
See also: **InputBox** Method, **MsgBox**

InputBox Method
Displays an input dialog box and waits for user input.
*Syntax: object.***InputBox**(*prompt,title,default,left,top,helpfile,context, type*)
Object must be **Application**. The **InputBox** method has the additional *type* argument that allows the input of a reference. See *Microsoft Excel/Visual Basic Reference* or On-Line Help for details.
See also: **InputBox** Function, **MsgBox**

Insert Method
Inserts a range of cells in a worksheet.
*Syntax: object.***Insert**(*SHIFT*)
Object is a **Range** object. *SHIFT* specifies how to SHIFT cells when a range is inserted in a worksheet (xlToRight or xlDown). Can also use *SHIFT* = 1 or 2, respectively. If *SHIFT* is omitted, the "SHIFT Cells?" dialog box is not displayed.
Examples: **Worksheets**("Sheet12").**Range**("A1:A10").**Insert** (1) inserts the indicated range and SHIFTs cells to right.
Worksheets("Sheet1").**Columns**(4).**Insert** inserts a new column to the left of column D.
See also: **Delete**

Instr Function
Returns a number specifying the position of the first occurrence of one string within another. Returns zero if the search string is not found.
Syntax: **InStr**(*start, string_to_search, string_to_look_for, compare*)
Optional *start* specifies the start position for the search. If omitted, search begins at position 1. Optional *compare* determines the type of comparison. See On-Line Help for details.
Example: **InStr**(*1*,NameText,"!"*)* finds the first occurrence of the "!" character within the string contained in the variable NameText.

Int Function
Rounds a number to an integer.
Syntax: **Int**(*number*)
If *number* is negative, **Int** returns the first negative integer less than or equal to *number*.
Example: **Int**(-2.5) returns −3.
See also: **Fix**

Integer Data Type
Use to declare a variable's type as **Integer**, either in a **Dim** statement, or in a **Sub** or **Function** statement. Two bytes required per variable.
Example: **Dim** J **As Integer**
See also: **Dim, As, Boolean, Double, String, Variant**

Intersect Method
Returns a **Range** object that represents the intersection of two ranges.
Syntax: **Intersect** (*range1, range2*)
See also: **Union, Areas, Caller**

IsArray Function
Returns **True** if the variable is an array.
Syntax: **IsArray**(*name*)
See also: other **Is** functions

IsDate Function
Returns **True** if the expression can be converted to a date.
Syntax: **IsDate**(*expression*)
See also: other **Is** functions

IsEmpty Function
Returns **True** if the variable has been initialized.
Syntax: **IsEmpty**(*expression*)
See also: other **Is** functions

IsMissing Function
Returns **True** if an optional argument has not been passed to a procedure.
Syntax: **IsMissing**(*name*)
See also: other **Is** functions

IsNull Function
Returns **True** if the expression is null (i.e., contains no valid data).
Syntax: **IsNull**(*expression*)
See also: other **Is** functions

IsNumeric Function
Returns **True** if the expression can be evaluated to a number.
Syntax: **IsNumeric**(*expression*)
See also: other **Is** functions

Italic Property
Returns **True** if the font is Italic. Sets the Italic font. Read-write.
Syntax: *object*.**Italic**
Object must be **Font**.
Example: **Range("A1:E1").Font.Italic = True** makes the cells italic.
See also: **Bold**

LBound Function
Returns the lower limit of an array dimension.
Syntax: **LBound**(*array,dimension*)
Array is the name of the array. *Dimension* is an integer (1, 2, 3, etc.) specifying the

dimension to be returned; if omitted, the value 1 is used.
Example: If the array table was dimensioned using the statement **Dim** table (1 **To** 3, 1000), **LBound**(table,1) returns 1, **LBound**(table,2) returns 0.
See also: **Dim, UBound**

LCase Function
Converts a string into lowercase letters.
Syntax: **LCase**(*string*)
See also: **UCase**

LTrim Function
Returns a string without leading spaces.
Syntax: **LTrim**(*string*)
See also: **RTrim**

Left Function
Returns the leftmost characters of a string.
Syntax: **Left**(*string,number*)
If *number* is zero, a null string is returned. If *number* is greater than the number of characters in *string*, the entire string is returned.
Example: **Left**("CHEMISTRY",4) returns CHEM
See also: **Len, Mid, Right**

Len Function
Returns the length (number of characters) in a string.
Syntax: **Len**(*string*)
Example: **Len**("CHEMISTRY") returns 9.
See also: **Left, Mid, Right**

Log Function
Returns the natural (base-*e*) logarithm of a number.
Syntax: **Log**(*number*)
Number must be a value or expression greater than zero. VBA does not provide base-10 logarithms; use **Log**(value)/**Log**(10).
See also: **Exp**

MacroOptions Method
Sets options in the Macro Options dialog box.
Syntax: **Application.MacroOptions**(*macro, description, hasMenu, menuText, hasShortcutKey, shortcutKey, category, statusbar, helpContext, helpFile*)

macro is the name of the macro. *description* is the description that appears in the dialog box. *category* is the function category that the macro appears in: Financial, 1; Date & Time, 2; Math & Trig, 3; Statistical, 4; Lookup & Reference, 5;

Database, 6; Text, 7; Logical, 8; Information, 9; User Defined, 14; Engineering, 15.
Example: **Application.MacroOptions** macro:="FtoC", Description:= "Converts Fahrenheit temperature to Celsius", Category:=3
provides a description for the macro FtoC and assigns it to the Math & Trig category.

Mid Function
Returns the specified number of characters from a text string, beginning at the specified position.
Syntax: **Mid**(*string,start,number*)
If *start* is greater than the number of characters in *string*, returns a null string. If *number* is omitted, all characters from *start* to the end of the string are returned.
Example: **Mid**("H2SO4",2,1) returns 2.
See also: **Left, Len, Right**

Mod Operator
Returns the remainder resulting from the division of two numbers.
Syntax: *result* = *number1* **Mod** *number2*

MsgBox Function
Displays a message box.
Syntax: **MsgBox**(***prompt***,*buttons,title,helpfile,context*)
See *Microsoft Excel/Visual Basic Reference* or On-Line Help for details.
See also: **InputBox**

Name Property
Returns or sets the name of an object.
Example: SeriesName = **Selection.Name** assigns the name of the selected chart series to the variable SeriesName.
See also: **NameLocal, Names**

Next Keyword
Delineates the end of a **For...Next** or **For Each...Next** block of statements.
Not Operator
Logical operator. Performs logical negation: **True** becomes **False**, **False** becomes **True**.
See also: **And, Or**

Now Function
Returns the current date and time.
Syntax: **Now**
See also: other date and time functions.

NumberFormat Property
Returns or sets the number format code of a cell.
Example: **Range("A1:A10").NumberFormat=** "0.00" sets the number format of the specified range of cells.
See also: **GoSub, GoTo, Return, Select Case**

On...GoTo Command
Branches to one of several specified lines, depending on the value of an expression.
Syntax: **On** *expression* **GoTo** *label1, ...*
See explanation under **On...GoSub** command.
Example: See examples of **On...GoTo** procedures in Chapter 2.
See also: **GoSub, GoTo, Return, Select Case**

On Error GoTo Command
Enables an error-handling routine and specifies the action to be taken in event of an error.
Examples: **On Error GoTo** *line* (enables the error-handling routine at the specified location in the procedure)
On Error Resume Next (execution resumes with the statement immediately following the statement that caused the error)
On Error GoTo 0 (disables any enabled error handler in the current procedure)

Open Method
Opens a workbook.
*Syntax: object.***Open**(*filename, ...*)
Object must be **Workbooks**. *Filename* is required. See On-Line Help for the remaining arguments.
Example: **Workbooks.Open**("SOLVSTAT.XLS")
See also: **Close, Save, SaveAs**

Option Base Keyword
Use at module level to declare lower bound for an array.
Can be **Option Base** 0 or 1. The statement can appear only once in a module and must precede all **Dim** or equivalent declaration.
See also: **Dim, LBound, ReDim**

Option Explicit Statement
Use at module level to force explicit declaration of all variables in that module.
See also: **Option Base, Option Compare**

Optional Keyword
Indicates that an argument in a function is not required. All arguments following the **Optional** keyword must be optional. All optional arguments are **Variant**.

Syntax: **Function** name(*argument1,...* **Optional** *argument*)
See also: **Function, ParamArray**

Or Operator
Logical operator. (expression1 **Or** expression2) evaluates to **True** if either expression1 or expression2 is **True**. Also can be used to perform bitwise comparison of two numerical values: (13 **Or** 6) evaluates to 15. (13 = 00001101, 6 = 00000110, 15 = 00001111).
See also: **Or, Not, Xor**

ParamArray Keyword
Allows the use of an indefinite number of arguments for a function. The argument becomes an array of **Variant** elements. The array has lower array index of zero, even if **Option Base 1** is declared.
Syntax: **Function** name(*argument1,...* **ParamArray** *argument*() **As Variant**)
Example: **Function** test (**ParamArray** rng() **As Variant**)
See also: **Dim, Function, Variant**

Paste Method
Pastes the contents of the Clipboard onto a worksheet.
*Syntax: object.***Paste**(*destination*)
Object must be **Worksheet.** There are other **Paste** methods, with different syntax, for **Chart** and many other objects. *Destination* specifies the range where the copy will be pasted. If omitted, copy is pasted to the current selection.
Example: **Worksheets**("Sheet1")**.Range**("A1:C50")**.Copy**
        ActiveSheet.Paste
See also: **Copy, Cut**

Preserve Command
Preserves data in an existing array when using **ReDim.**

Private Command
Indicates that the procedure is available only to procedures in the same module.

Public Command
Indicates that the procedure is available to all other procedures.

Quit Method
Quits Microsoft Excel.
*Syntax: object.***Quit**
Object must be **Application**.
Example: **Application.Quit**
See also: **Close, Save**
Range Method
Returns a **Range** object that represents a cell or range of cells.
*Syntax: object.***Range**(*reference*)
Object is required if it is **Worksheet**. *Reference* must be an A1-style reference, in

quotes, or the name of the reference.
Example: **Worksheets**("Sheet12").**Range**("A1").**Value** = 5
See also: **Cells**

ReDim Keyword
Allocates or re-allocates dynamic array storage.
Syntax: **ReDim** *variable (subscripts)*
For discussion of *variable* and *subscripts*, see comments under the entry for **Dim**.
You can use **ReDim** repeatedly to change the number of elements in an array, or
the number or dimensions.
Example: **Dim** Matrix()
               (statements)
               ReDim Matrix (5,5)
               (statements)
               ReDim Matrix (15,25)
See also: **Dim**

Resume Command
Resumes execution after an error-handling routine is finished.
Examples: **Resume 0**
              Resume Next (execution resumes with the statement immediately
              following the statement that caused the error)
              Resume *label* (Execution resumes at the specified location in the
              procedure)
See *also:* **On Error GoTo**

Return Command
Delineates the end of a subroutine within a procedure.

Right Function
Returns the rightmost characters of a string.
Syntax: **Right**(*string,number*)
If *number* is zero, a null string is returned. If *number* is greater than the number of
characters in *string*, the entire string is returned.
Example: **Right**(303585842,4) returns 5842.
See also: **Left, Len, Mid**

Rnd Function
Returns a random number between 0 and 1.
Syntax: **Rnd**

Row Property
Returns a number corresponding to the first row in the range. Read-only.
*Syntax: object.***Row**
Object must be **Range**.
Example: **If ActiveCell.Row = 10 Then ActiveCell.Interior.ColorIndex = 27**

changes the interior color of the active cell to yellow if it is in row 10.
See also: **Column, Columns, Rows**

RowHeight Property
Returns or sets the height of all rows in the range.
Example: **Worksheets**("Sheet1").**Rows**(1).**RowHeight** = 15
See also: **ColumnWidth**

Rows Method
Returns a **Range** object that represents a single row or multiple rows.
*Syntax: object.***Rows**(*index*)
Object can be **Worksheet** or **Range**. *Index* is the name or number of the row.
Example: **Selection.Rows.Count** returns the number of rows in the selection.
See also: **Columns, Range**

RTrim Function
Returns a string without trailing spaces.
Syntax: **RTrim**(*string*)
See also: **LTrim, Trim**

Save Method
Saves changes to active workbook.
*Syntax: object.***Save**(*filename*)
Object must be **Workbook**. If *filename* is omitted, uses a default name.
Example: **ActiveWorkbook.Save**
See also: **Close, Open, SaveAs**

SaveAs Method
Saves changes to active workbook or other document with a different filename.
*Syntax: object.***SaveAs**(*filename, ...*)
Object can be **Worksheet, Workbook, Chart** or other document types.   See
Microsoft Excel/Visual Basic Reference or On-Line Help for details.
Example: NewChart.**SaveAs**("New Chart")
See also: **Close, Open, Save**

Select Method
Selects an object.
*Syntax: object.***Select**
Object can be **Chart, Worksheet** or one of many other objects.
Example: **Range**("A1:C50").**Select**
See also: **Activate**

Select Case Command
Executes one of several blocks of statements, depending on the value of an
expression.
Syntax: **Select Case** *expression*
              Case *expression1*

      (statements)
      Case expression2
      (statements)
      End Select

You can also use the **To** keyword in *expression*, e.g., **Case** "A" **To** "M". *Expression* can also be a logical expression. Use **Case Else** (not required) to handle all cases not covered by the preceding **Case** statements.

Example: See examples of **Select Case** procedures in Chapter 2.
See also: **If...Then...Else, On...GoSub, On...GoTo**

Selection Property
Returns the selected object. The object returned depends on the type of selection.
See also: **Activate, ActiveCell, Select**

Set Command
Assigns an object reference to a variable.
See also: **Dim, ReDim**

Sgn Function
Returns the sign of a number.
Syntax: **Sgn**(*number*)
Returns 1, 0 or -1 if *number* is positive, zero or negative, respectively.
Example: **Sgn**(-7.3) returns -1.
See also: **Abs**

Sin Function
Returns the sine of an angle.
Syntax: **Sin**(*number*)
Number is the angle in radians; it can be in the range $-\infty$ to $+\infty$. To convert an angle in degrees to one in radians, multiply by $\pi/180$. Returns a value between -1 and 1.
See also: **Atn, Cos, Tan**

Sort Method
Sorts a range of cells.
Syntax: *object*.**Sort**(*sortkey1,order1,sortkey2,order2, ...*)
Object must be **Range**. See *Microsoft Excel/Visual Basic Reference* or On-Line Help for details.

Sqr Function
Returns the square root of a number.
Syntax: **Sqr**(*number*)
Number must be greater than or equal to zero.

Step Keyword
Stops execution, but does not close files or clear variables.
See also: **End**

Stop Command

Stops execution, but does not close files or clear variables.

See also: **End**

Str Function

Converts a number to a string.

Syntax: **Str**(*number*)

A leading space is reserved for the sign of the number; if the number is positive, the string will contain a leading space.

See also: **Format**

String Data Type

Use to declare a variable's type as **String**, either in a **Dim** statement, or in a **Sub** or **Function** statement. One byte/character required per variable.

Example: **Dim J As Integer**

See also: **Dim, As, Boolean, Double, String, Variant**

Sub Keyword

Marks the beginning of a **Sub** procedure.

Syntax: **Sub** *name (argument1, ...)*

Name is the name of the procedure. *Argument1*, etc., are the names assigned to the arguments passed from the caller to the procedure. The end of the procedure is delineated by **End Sub**

Example: See examples of **Sub** procedures in Chapter 2.

See also: **Call, Function**

Tan Function

Returns the tangent of an angle.

Syntax: **Tan**(*number*)

Number is the angle in radians; it can be in the range $-\infty$ to $+\infty$. To convert an angle in degrees to one in radians, multiply by $\pi/180$. Returns a value between $-\infty$ and $+\infty$.

See also: **Atn, Cos, Sin**

Text Property

Returns or sets the text associated with an object.

The text can be associated with a chart, button, textbox, control or range. For all except range, this property is read-write, but for a range, it is read-only.

Example: **Worksheets**("Sheet1").**Buttons**(1).**Text** = "Undo"

See also: **Formula, Value**

Trim Function

Returns a string without leading or trailing spaces.

Syntax: **Trim**(*string*)

See also: **LTrim, RTrim**

True Keyword

Use the keywords **True** or **False** to assign the value **True** or **False** to Boolean (logical) variables.

When other numeric data types are converted to Boolean values, 0 becomes **False** while all other values become **True**. When Boolean values are converted to other data types, **False** becomes 0 while **True** becomes −1.

Example: If FirstFlag = **True Then GoTo** 2000

UBound Function

Returns the upper limit of an array dimension.

Syntax: UBound(*array, dimension*)

Array is the name of the array. *Dimension* is an integer (1, 2, 3, etc.) specifying the dimension to be returned; if omitted, the value 1 is used.

Example: If the array table was dimensioned using the statement **Dim** table (1 **To** 3, 1000), **UBound**(table,3) returns 1, **UBound**(table,2) returns 1000.

See also: Dim, LBound

UCase Function

Converts a string into upper case letters.

Syntax: UCase(*string*)

See also: LCase

Union Method

Returns a **Range** object that represents the union of two or more ranges, i.e., performs the same function as the comma character in the worksheet expression SUM(A1, B2, C3).

Syntax: Union (*range1, range2*)

See also: Intersect, Areas, Caller

Until Command

Optional part of **Do...Loop** structure.

Syntax: See explanation under **Do...Loop**.

Val Function

Converts a string to a number.

Syntax: Val(*string*)

Val stops at the first non-numeric character other than the period.

Example: Val("21 Lawrence Avenue") returns 21.

See also: Str

Value Property

Returns the value of an object.

Syntax: object.Value

If *object* is **Range**, returns or sets the value(s) of the cell(s). Read-write.

If **Range** contains more than one cell, returns an array of values.

Example: **Worksheets**("Sheet12").**Range**("A1").**Value** = "Volume, mL"

Variant Data Type

Use to declare a variable's type as **Variant**, either in a **Dim** statement, or in a **Sub** or **Function** statement. **Variant** is the default data type, so usually not required. It is required when using the **ParamArray** keyword. Sixteen bytes + one byte/character required per variable.

Example: **Function** test **(ParamArray** rng() **As Variant)**
See also: **Dim, As, Boolean, Double, Integer, String**

Wend Command

Delineates the end of a **While...Wend** procedure.

Syntax: See explanation under **Do...Loop.**
See also: **Do...Loop, While...Wend**

While...Wend Command

Executes a series of statements as long as a specified condition is true.

Syntax: See explanation under **Do...Loop.**
See also: **Do...Loop, Wend**

With...End With command

Delineates a block of statements to be executed on a single object.

Syntax: **With** *object*
              (statements)
              End With
See also: **Do...Loop, While...Wend**

XOr Operator

Exclusive Or operator.

Use to perform bitwise comparison of two numerical values: (13 **XOr** 6) evaluates to 11. (13 = 00001101, 6 = 00000110, 11 = 00001011).

See also: **Or, Not, Or**

Appendix 2

Shortcut Keys for VBA

Shortcut keys for running and debugging code

Halt execution	ESC
Run	F5
Step through code	F8
Toggle breakpoint	F9
Toggle between Visual Basic Editor and Excel	ALT+F11
Step into	F8
Step over	SHIFT+F8
Run to cursor	CTRL+F8
Clear all breakpoints	CTRL +SHIFT+F9
Display Quick Watch window	SHIFT+F9

Shortcut keys for working in the code window

View Code window	F7
Jump to beginning of module	CTRL +HOME
Jump to end of module	CTRL +END
Undo	CTRL +Z
Delete current line	CTRL +Y
Indent	TAB
Remove tab indent	SHIFT+TAB
Print	CTRL +P
Paste	CTRL +V
Delete	DEL or DELETE
Find	CTRL +F
Find Next	SHIFT+F4

Find Previous	SHIFT+F3
Replace	CTRL +H
Display Project Explorer window	CTRL +R
Display Properties window	F4
List Properties/Methods	CTRL +J
List Constants	CTRL +SHIFT+J

Appendix 3

Custom Functions Help File

MIndex

Returns a horizontal 2-element array containing the row and column numbers of a specified value in an array.

Syntax

MIndex(*lookup_value, array_,* match_type)

lookup_value   the value you use to find the value you want in *array_*

*array_*   a contiguous range of cells containing possible lookup values

match_type   the number -1, 0, or 1, that specifies the value found in *array_*

Remarks

- The arguments *lookup_value, array_* and *match_type* can be either references or names.
- If *match_type* is 0 or omitted, returns the position of the value that is exactly equal to lookup_value, or #N/A.
- If *match_type* is 1, returns the position of the largest value that is less than or equal to lookup_value.
- If *match_type* is –1, returns the position of the smallest value that is greater than or equal to lookup_value.
- *array_* must contain only numbers. If any cells contain text or error values, MIndex returns the #VALUE! error value. Empty cells are treated as zero.
- The MIndex function is an array function. To return the array, you must select a horizontal range of two cells, enter the function and then press CONTROL+SHIFT+ENTER (Windows) or COMMAND+RETURN or CONTROL+SHIFT+RETURN (Macintosh).

Example

If the range A contains the values {13,0,–1;5,12,22;–5,0,1}, the expression MIndex(MAX(A),A) returns the values {2,3}; the expression MIndex(7,A) returns the values {#N/A,#N/A}.

If the range B contains the values {2,11,–1;4,–1,7;–3,1,13}, the expression MIndex(MIN(B),B) returns the values {3,1}; the expression MIndex(0,B–1) returns the values {3,2}.

MIdent

Creates an identity matrix of a specified size.

Syntax
MIdent(*size***)**

size   optional argument specifying the size of the matrix to be created

Remarks
- The function can be used in a formula or used to fill a selection.
- When used to fill a selection, the *size* argument is not required. If selection is not square, returns #REF! error.
- The MIdent function is an array function. To return the array that results when a range of *N* rows by *N* columns is selected, enter =MIdent() and then press CONTROL+SHIFT+ENTER (Windows) or COMMAND+RETURN or CONTROL+SHIFT+RETURN (Macintosh).

Example
The expression MIdent(4) returns {1,0,0,0;0,1,0,0;0,0,1,0;0,0,0,1}.

Arr

Combines individual 1-D arrays into a 2-D array.

Syntax
Arr(*range1***,** *range2*...**)**

range1, *range2*...   1 to 29 ranges that you want to combine into a single array

Remarks
- The arguments *range1, range2,...* can be either references to ranges of cells or named ranges.
- All individual arrays must be "vertical" and must have same number of rows.
- The Arr function is an array function. To return the array that results when individual ranges with a total combined width of *N* columns, each with M rows, you must select a range of cells *N* columns by M rows, enter the function and then press CONTROL+SHIFT+ENTER (Windows) or COMMAND+RETURN or CONTROL+SHIFT+RETURN (Macintosh).

Example
The expression Arr(A4:A13,C4:D13) returns an array three columns wide and ten rows deep.

InterpL

Performs linear interpolation in a table of x- and y-values. Returns the interpolated y-value corresponding to a specified x-value.

Syntax

InterpL(*lookup_value, known_x´s, known_y´s*)

lookup_value   the x-value for which you want to find the interpolated y-value

known_x's   the range of x-values in the table (independent variable)

known_y's   the range of y-values in the table (dependent variable)

Remarks

- The argument *lookup_value* can be either a number or a reference to a cell that contains a number.
- The arguments *known_x's* and *known_y's* can be either a reference to a range of cells or a named range.
- The function cannot handle implicit references; that is, a name or range reference cannot be used for a range of lookup values.
- The table of x- and y-values must be arranged in ascending order of x-values.
- The table of x- and y-values can be either either horizontal or vertical.
- The function cannot be used for extrapolation. A lookup value that is either greater than or less than the range of x-values returns #REF!.
- The linear interpolation formula is:

$$y_x = y_0 + \frac{(x - x_0)}{(x_1 - x_0)}(y_1 - y_0)$$

where x is the lookup value and x_0 and x_1 are the values in the table that bracket the lookup value; x_0 is the value in the table that is equal to or less than *lookup_value*.

Example

The expression InterpL(33.3,$A$3:$A$47,$B$3:$B$47) where $A$3:$A$47 is the range containing the independent or x-values and $B$3:$B$47 is the range containing the dependent or y-values.

See Also

InterpC, InterpC2

InterpC

Performs cubic interpolation in a table of x- and y-values, using the LaGrange 4th-order polynomial. Returns the interpolated y-value corresponding to a specified x-value.

Syntax

InterpC(*lookup_value, known_x´s, known_y´s*)

lookup_value the x-value for which you want to find the corresponding y-value by cubic interpolation

known_x's   the range of x-values in the table (independent variable)

known_y's   the range of y-values in the table (dependent variable)

Remarks

- *lookup_value* can be either a number or a reference to a cell that contains a number.
- The function cannot handle implicit references; that is, a name or range reference cannot be used for a range of lookup values.
- The values in the table of x- and y-values must be numbers.
- The table of x- and y-values must be arranged in ascending order of x-values.
- The table of x- and y-values can be either either horizontal or vertical.
- The function cannot be used for extrapolation. A lookup value that is either greater than or less than the range of x-values returns #REF!.
- Cubic interpolation uses the values of four adjacent table entries, e.g., at x_0, x_1, x_2 and x_3, to interpolate between x_1 and x_2. The interpolated value is calculated using the LaGrange 4th-order polynomial:

$$y_x = \frac{(x-x_2)(x-x_3)(x-x_4)}{(x_1-x_2)(x_1-x_3)(x_1-x_4)}y_1 + \frac{(x-x_1)(x-x_3)(x-x_4)}{(x_2-x_1)(x_2-x_3)(x_2-x_4)}y_2$$
$$+ \frac{(x-x_1)(x-x_2)(x-x_4)}{(x_3-x_1)(x_3-x_2)(x_3-x_4)}y_3 + \frac{(x-x_1)(x-x_2)(x-x_3)}{(x_4-x_1)(x_4-x_2)(x_4-x_3)}y_4$$

where x is the lookup value and x_1, x_2, x_3 and x_4 are the four values from the table that bracket *lookup_value* (see Chapter 5 for further details).

Example

=InterpC(33.3,$A$3:$A$47,$B$3:$B$47) where $A$3:$A$47 is the range containing the independent or x-values and $B$3:$B$47 is the range containing the dependent or y-values.

See Also

InterpL, InterpC2

InterpC2

Performs cubic interpolation in a 2-way table of x-, y- and z-values. x and y are the independent variable, z is the dependent variable. Returns the interpolated z-value corresponding to a specified x-value.

Syntax:

InterpC2 (*x_lookup, y_lookup, known_x´s, known_y's, known_z's*)

x_lookup	the x-value for which you want to find the interpolated z-value
y_lookup	the y-value for which you want to find the interpolated z-value
known_x's	the set of x-values in the table (independent values)
known_y's	the set of y-values in the table (independent values)
known_z's	the set of z-values in the table (dependent values)

Remarks

- *x_lookup* and *y_lookup* can be either numbers or references to a cell that contains a number.
- The function cannot handle implicit references; that is, a name or range reference cannot be used for a range of lookup values.
- The values in the table of x- , y- and z-values must be numbers.
- The table must be arranged in ascending order of both x-values and y-values.
- The function cannot be used for extrapolation. An *x_lookup* value that is either greater than or less than the range of x-values, or a *y_lookup* value that is either greater than or less than the range of y-values returns #REF!.
- The function uses the LaGrange 4th-order polynomial. See InterpC for details.

Example

= InterpC2(K7,L7,$A$4:$A$29,$B$3:$I$3,$B$4:$I$29) where K7 is a reference to the *x_lookup* value, L7 is a reference to the *y_lookup* value, $A$4:$A$29 is the range containing the independent x-values, $B$3:$I$3 is the range containing the independent y-values and $B$4:$I$29 is the range containing the dependent or z-values.

See Also

InterpC, InterpL

dydx

Returns the first derivative of a function $y = F(x)$, represented by a formula in a cell, at a specified value of x. Returns #DIV/0! error value if $x = 0$, in which case use the optional argument *scale_factor*.

Syntax

dydx(*expression, variable,* *scale_factor*)

expression   reference to a cell containing a formula (the function $F(x)$ to be differentiated)

variable   cell reference corresponding to the independent variable x in the function $F(x)$

scale_factor   optional argument to be used when x is zero

Remarks

- The argument *expression* can be either a reference to a cell that contains a formula, or a name.
- The argument *reference* can be either a reference to a cell, or a name.
- Use the optional argument *scale_factor* to specify a suitable value of x to be used to calculate Δx. For example, if the function requires values of x in the range -1×10^5 to 1×10^5, use 1E-5 for *scale_factor*.
- The optional argument *scale_factor* can be either a number or a formula, or a reference to a cell that contains a number or formula, or a name.
- The function cannot handle implicit references; that is, a name or range reference cannot be used for a range of values.
- The workbook can be set to either R1C1- or A1-style.

Limitations

- None of the precedent cells of the argument *expression* may contain references to the argument *reference*.
- The function cannot handle implicit references; that is, a name or range reference cannot be used for a range of values.

Example

If cell C2 contains the formula =SIN(B2) and cell B2 contains the value 1, the formula =dydx(C2,B2) returns the value 0.5403023062. The correct value is cos (1) = 0.5403023059 (5.8×10^{-8} % error).

See Also

d2ydx2

d2ydx2

Returns the second derivative of a function $y = F(x)$, represented by a formula in a cell, at a specified value of x. Returns #DIV/0! error value if $x = 0$, in which case use the optional argument *scale_factor*.

Syntax

d2ydx2(*expression*, *variable*, *scale_factor***)**

expression	reference to a cell containing a formula (the function $F(x)$ to be differentiated)
variable	cell reference corresponding to the independent variable x in the function $F(x)$
scale_factor	optional argument to be used when x is zero

Remarks

- The argument *expression* can be either a reference to a cell that contains a formula, or a name.

- The argument *variable* can be either a reference to a cell, or a name.

- Use the optional argument *scale_factor* to specify a suitable value of x to be used to calculate Δx. For example, if the function requires values of x in the range -1×10^5 to 1×10^5, use 1E-5 for *scale_factor*.

- The optional argument *scale_factor* can be either a number or a formula, or a reference to a cell that contains a number or formula, or a name.

- The workbook can be set to either R1C1- or A1-style.

- Errors (difference between returned value and correct value, when the latter can be calculated using a calculus formula) are typically of the order of 10^{-6} to 10^{-8}.

Limitations

- None of the precedent cells of the argument *expression* may contain references to the argument *reference*.

- The function cannot handle implicit references; that is, a name or range reference cannot be used for a range of values.

Example

If cell C2 contains the formula =SIN(B2) and cell B2 contains the value 1, the formula =d2ydx2(C2,B2) returns the value –0.841470981782962. The correct value is cos $(1+\pi/2) = -0.841470984807897$ (3.6×10^{-7} % error).

See Also

dydx

CurvArea

Returns the area under a curve defined by a table of x- and y-values.

Syntax

CurvArea(*x_values, y_values*)

x_values   the range of x-values in the table (independent variable)

y_values   the range of y-values in the table (dependent variable)

Remarks

- The arguments *x_values* and *y_values* can be either a reference to a range of cells or a named range.

- Errors (difference between returned value and correct value, when the latter can be calculated using a formula) will depend on the number of "panels" in the table.

Example

CurvArea($A$5:$A$30,$C$5:$C$30) where the ranges $A$5:$A$30 and $C$5:$C$30 refer to a table of x- and y-values, respectively, defining a curve.

See Also

Integrate, IntegrateS, IntegrateT

IntegrateT

Returns the integral (the area under the curve) of an expression between specified limits. The area is calculated by using the trapezoidal approximation.

Syntax

IntegrateT(*expression, variable, from_lower, to_upper*)

expression   reference to a cell containing a formula (the integrand, the function $F(x)$ to be integrated)

variable   cell reference corresponding to x, the variable of integration

from_lower   the lower limit of integration

to_upper   the upper limit of integration

Remarks

- The argument *expression* can be either a reference to a cell that contains a formula, or a name.
- The argument *variable* can be either a reference to a cell, or a name.
- The arguments *from_lower* and *to_upper* can be either a number, a reference to a cell containing a number, a formula or a name.
- Errors (difference between returned value and correct value, when the latter can be calculated using a calculus formula) are variable and depend on the expression being integrated.
- The area under the curve is divided into N "panels" of equal width H. The area of each panel is approximated as the area of a trapezoid of width H and heights $F(x)$ and $F(x+H)$. The formula for the trapezoidal approximation is

$$A = H\left[\frac{F(x) + F(x+H)}{2}\right]$$

Example

The formula =IntegrateT(C3,B3,D3,E3), where C3 contains =B3^3, the expression to be integrated, B3 is the variable of integration, D3 contains the value 0 and E3 the value 1, returns the area under the curve of $y = x^3$ between the limits 0 and 1.

Limitations

- None of the precedent cells of the argument *expression* may contain references to the argument *reference*.
- The function cannot handle implicit references; that is, a name or range reference cannot be used for a range of values.

See Also

CurvArea, Integrate, IntegrateS

IntegrateS

Returns the integral (the area under the curve) of an expression between specified limits. The area is calculated by using Simpson's 1/3 method.

Syntax

IntegrateS(*expression, variable, from_lower, to_upper*)

expression   reference to a cell containing a formula (the integrand, the function $F(x)$ to be integrated)

variable   cell reference corresponding to x, the variable of integration.

from_lower   the lower limit of integration

to_upper   the upper limit of integration

Remarks

- The argument *expression* can be either a reference to a cell that contains a formula, or a name.

- The argument *variable* can be either a reference to a cell, or a name.

- The arguments *from_lower* and *to_upper* can be either a number, a reference to a cell containing a number, a formula or a name.

- Errors (difference between returned value and correct value, when the latter can be calculated using a calculus formula) are variable and depend on the expression being integrated.

- The area under the curve is divided into N "panels" of equal width H. The formula for the area of each panel by Simpson's 1/3 rule is:

$$A = H\left[\frac{F(x) + 4F(x + H/2) + F(x + H)}{3}\right]$$

Limitations

- None of the precedent cells of the argument *expression* may contain references to the argument *reference*.

- The function cannot handle implicit references; that is, a name or range reference cannot be used for a range of values.

Example

The formula =IntegrateS(C3,B3,D3,E3), where C3 contains =B3^3, the expression to be integrated, B3 is the variable of integration, D3 contains the value 0 and E3 the value 1, returns the area under the curve of $y = x^3$ between the limits 0 and 1.

See Also

CurvArea, Integrate, IntegrateT

Integrate

Returns the integral (the area under the curve) of an expression between specified limits. The area is calculated by using a tenth-order LeGendre polynomial.

Syntax

Integrate(*expression, variable, from_lower, to_upper*)

expression	reference to a cell containing a formula (the integrand, the function $F(x)$ to be integrated)
variable	cell reference corresponding to x, the variable of integration
from_lower	the lower limit of integration
to_upper	the upper limit of integration

Remarks

- The argument *expression* can be either a reference to a cell that contains a formula, or a name.
- The argument *variable* can be either a reference to a cell, or a name.
- The arguments *from_lower* and *to_upper* can be either a number, a reference to a cell containing a number, a formula or a name.
- Errors (difference between returned value and correct value, when the latter can be calculated using a calculus formula) are variable and depend on the expression being integrated.

Limitations

- None of the precedent cells of the argument *expression* may contain references to the argument *reference*.
- The function cannot handle implicit references; that is, a name or range reference cannot be used for a range of values.

Example

=Integrate (C3,B3,D3,E3), where C3 contains the expression to be integrated, B3 is the variable of integration, D3 contains the value 0 and E3 the value 1, returns the area under the curve between the limits 0 and 1.

See Also

CurvArea, IntegrateS, IntegrateT

NewtRaph

Returns the value of the independent variable contained in *variable* necessary to make the formula contained in *expression* have the value zero.

Syntax

NewtRaph(*expression, variable,* *initial_value*)

Expression   reference to a cell containing a formula $F(x)$

Variable   cell reference corresponding to x, the variable to be changed

initial_value   optional argument specifying the initial estimate to be used in the Newton-Raphson procedure

Remarks

- The argument *expression* can be either a reference to a cell that contains a formula, or a name.   The formula must depend on variable.

- The argument *variable* must be a reference to a cell.

- The argument *initial_value* can be either a number, a reference to a cell containing a number, a reference to a cell containing a formula, or a name.

- The workbook can be set to either R1C1- or A1-style.

- Use the optional argument *initial_value* for functions that have more than one root, to control the value of the root that is returned.   For example, a cubic equation can have three real roots, i.e., three different x-values that make $y = 0$. The root that NewtRaph returns will depend on the trial value that you begin with.

Limitations

- None of the precedent cells of the argument *expression* may contain references to the argument *reference*.

- The function cannot handle implicit references; that is, a name or range reference cannot be used for a range of values.

Example

=NewtRaph(B3,A3), where B3 contains the worksheet formula =A3^2-0.000001*SQRT(A3)-0.0000000051 and A3, the independent variable, contains the value 1.2E-04, returns 0.00012814, a root of the function.

See Also

Bairstow, GoalSeek

Bairstow

Returns an array of the roots, both real and imaginary, of a regular polynomial of maximum order six. A regular polynomial is one that contains only integer powers of x.

Syntax

BairStow(*equation, variable*)

equation   reference to a cell containing the formula $F(x)$ of a regular polynomial

variable   cell reference corresponding to x, the independent variable

Remarks

- The argument *equation* can be either a reference to a cell that contains a formula, or a name.
- The argument *variable* must be a reference to a cell.
- The workbook can be set to either R1C1- or A1-style.
- The Bairstow function is an array function. To return the roots of a polynomial of order N, you must select a range of cells 2 columns by N rows, enter the function and then press CONTROL+SHIFT+ENTER (Windows) or COMMAND+RETURN or CONTROL+SHIFT+RETURN (Macintosh).
- The table of results contains the real part of the root in the first column, the imaginary part in the second column.

Limitations

- The function cannot handle implicit references; that is, a name or range reference cannot be used for a range of values.

See Also

NewtRaph, GoalSeek

GoalSeek

Returns the value of the independent variable x necessary to make the formula $F(x)$ have a specified value. The function uses the Newton-Raphson method.

Syntax

GoalSeek(*target_cell, changing_cell, objective_value,* initial_value)

target_cell   reference to a cell containing a formula $F(x)$.

changing_cell   cell reference corresponding to x, the variable to be changed.

objective_value the value to be returned by *target_cell*.

initial_value   optional argument specifying the initial estimate to be used in the Newton-Raphson procedure

Remarks

- The argument *target_cell* can be either a reference to a cell that contains a formula, or a name. The formula must depend on *changing_cell*.

- The argument *changing_cell* must be a reference to a cell.

- The argument *objective_value* can be either a number, a reference to a cell containing a number, a reference to a cell containing a formula, or a name.

- The argument *initial_value* can be either a number, a reference to a cell containing a number, a reference to a cell containing a formula, or a name. Use *initial_value* for functions that have more than one value of x that satisfies the relationship $F(x)$ = *objective_value*, to control the value of x that is returned.

- The workbook can be set to either R1C1- or A1-style.

- Microsoft does not provide a goal-seeking function, only **Goal Seek...** in the **Tools** menu. The **Goal Seek...** tool accepts only a fixed value as the objective, not a reference to a cell. In contrast, the GoalSeek function allows the user to use a cell reference as the objective. The cell can contain either a number or a formula. In addition, **Goal Seek...** is a **Sub** procedure that must be run each time the formula in the target cell or the objective value is changed. The GoalSeek function updates automatically when either the formula or the objective is changed.

- Note that, unlike **Goal Seek...**, the custom function does not change the value of *changing_cell* on which the cell containing *target_cell* depends. If you think that there is a possibility that an incorrect value could be returned, you should enter a copy of the formula in another cell, and make the formula depend on the value returned by GoalSeek, to confirm that the desired objective was found.

Limitations

- None of the precedent cells of the argument *expression* may contain references to the argument *reference*.

- The function cannot handle implicit references; that is, a name or range reference cannot be used for a range of values.

Example

If cell B5 contains the formula = A5^2+8*A5-10 and cell A5 contains the value 0, the expression GoalSeek(B5,A5,210) returns 12.1327, a value of the independent variable that makes the formula have the value 210. Since the formula describes a parabola, there are two values of the independent variable that cause the formula to return the value 210. The expression GoalSeek(B5,A5,H,-20) returns -18.1327, the other value.

See Also

Bairstow, NewtRaph

Runge1

Performs fourth-order Runge-Kutta integration of an ordinary differential equation. Returns the value of the independent variable y at $x + \Delta x$, based on specified values of x and y at x, and a differential equation.

Syntax

Runge1(*x_variable, y_variable, deriv_formula, interval*)

x_variable	the value of x
y_variable	the value of y at x
deriv_formula	the differential equation $dy/dx = F(x\_variable, y\_variable)$
interval	Δx, the interval for the calculation

Remarks

- The argument *x_variable* can be a value, or a reference to a cell containing a value or a formula.
- The argument *y_variable* can be a value, or a reference to a cell containing a value or a formula.
- The argument *deriv_formula* can be a value, or a reference to a cell containing a value or a formula.
- The argument *interval* can be a value or a formula, or a reference to a cell containing a value or a formula.
- The workbook can be set to either R1C1- or A1-style.

Limitations

- None of the precedent cells of the argument *expression* may contain references to the argument *reference*.
- The function cannot handle implicit references; that is, a name or range reference cannot be used for a range of values.

See Also

Runge, Runge3

Runge3

Performs fourth-order Runge-Kutta integration of a system of N ordinary differential equations. Returns the values of the N independent variables y at $x + \Delta x$, based on specified values of x and the N independent variables y at x, and N differential equations.

Syntax

Runge3(*x_variable, y_variables, deriv_formulas, interval,* index)

x_variable	the value of x
y_variables	the array of y values at x
deriv_formulas	the array of differential equations $dy/dx = F(x\_variable, y\_variable)$, in the same order as *y_variables*
interval	Δx, the interval for the calculation
index	an optional argument specifying which one of the array of *y_variables* to be returned; if omitted, returns the complete array

Remarks

• The argument *x_variable* can be a value, or a reference to a cell containing a value or a formula.

• The argument *y_variables* can be an array of values, or of references to cells containing values or formulas.

• The argument *deriv_s* is an array of references to cells containing values or formulas. The array must be in the in the same order as *y_variables*.

• The argument *interval* can be a value or a formula, or a reference to a cell containing a value or a formula.

• The optional argument *index* can be a value or a formula, or a reference to a cell containing a value or a formula.

• The workbook can be set to either R1C1- or A1-style.

• The Runge3 function is an array function. If you omit the optional argument *index*, you must select a horizontal range of cells, enter the function and then press CONTROL+SHIFT+ENTER (Windows) or COMMAND+RETURN or CONTROL+SHIFT+RETURN (Macintosh).

Limitations

• None of the precedent cells of the argument *expression* may contain references to the argument *reference*.

• The function cannot handle implicit references; that is, a name or range reference cannot be used for a range of values.

See Also

Runge, Runge1

GaussElim

Solves a set of N linear equations in N unknowns by the Gaussian Elimination method. Returns the array of N unknowns, in either a row or a column, depending on the range selected by the user.

Syntax

GaussElim(*coeff_matrix,const_vector*)

coeff_matrix   a reference to an N row × N column array of coefficients

const_vector   a reference to an N row × 1 column array of constants

Remarks

- The *coeff_matrix* and the *const_vector* tables can contain values or formulas.
- The GaussElim function is an array function. You can select either a 1 row × N column horizontal range of cells or an N row × 1 column vertical range of cells, enter the function and then press CONTROL+SHIFT+ENTER (Windows) or COMMAND+RETURN or CONTROL+SHIFT+RETURN (Macintosh).

See Also

GaussJordan1, GaussJordan2, GaussSeidel, SimultEqNL

GaussJordan2

Solves a set of N linear equations in N unknowns by the Gaussian-Jordan method. Returns the array of N unknowns, in column format only.

Syntax

GaussJordan2(*coeff_matrix*,*const_vector*)

coeff_matrix   a reference to an N row × N column array of coefficients

const_vector   a reference to an N row × 1 column array of constants

Remarks

- The *coeff_matrix* and the *const_vector* tables can contain values or formulas.
- The GaussJordan2 function is an array function. You must select an N row × 1 column vertical range of cells, enter the function and then press CONTROL+SHIFT+ENTER (Windows) or COMMAND+RETURN or CONTROL+SHIFT+RETURN (Macintosh).

See Also

GaussElim, GaussJordan1, GaussSeidel, SimultEqNL

GaussJordan1

Identical to GauddJordan2 except returns a single specified element of the results array.

Syntax

GaussJordan1(*coeff_matrix*,*const_vector*, *value_index*)

coeff_matrix   a reference to an N row × N column array of coefficients

const_vector   a reference to an N row × 1 column array of constants

value_index   a value or a reference to a cell containing a value

Remarks

- The *coeff_matrix* and the *const_vector* tables can contain values or formulas.
- The GaussJordan1 function is an array function. You must select an N row × 1 column vertical range of cells, enter the function and then press CONTROL+SHIFT+ENTER (Windows) or COMMAND+RETURN or CONTROL+SHIFT+RETURN (Macintosh).

See Also

GaussElim, GaussJordan2, GaussSeidel, SimultEqNL

GaussSeidel

Solves a set of *N* linear equations in *N* unknowns by the Gaussian-Seidel method. Returns the array of *N* unknowns, in column format only.

Syntax

GaussSeidel(*coeff_matrix,const_vector*, *init_values*)

coeff_matrix   a reference to an *N* row × N column array of coefficients

const_vector   a reference to an *N* row × 1 column array of constants

init_values   a reference to an *N* row × 1 column array of initial values

Remarks

- The *coeff_matrix, const_vector* and *init_values* tables can contain values or formulas.
- The *optional init_values* may be helpful for large arrays.
- The GaussSeidel function is an array function. You must select an *N* row × 1 column vertical range of cells, enter the function and then press CONTROL+SHIFT+ENTER (Windows) or COMMAND+RETURN or CONTROL+SHIFT+RETURN (Macintosh).

See Also

GaussElim, GaussJordan1, GaussJordan2, SimultEqNL

SimultEqNL

Solves a set of *N* non-linear equations in *N* unknowns by Newton's iteration method. Returns the array of *N* unknowns, in column format only.

Syntax

SimultEqNL(*equations, variables, constants*)

equations   a reference to an *N* row × N column array of coefficients

variables   a reference to an *N* row × 1 column array of constants

constants   a reference to an *N* row × 1 column array of initial values

Remarks

- The *coeff_matrix, const_vector* and *init_values* tables can contain values or formulas.
- The *optional init_values* may be helpful for large arrays.
- The SimultEqNL function is an array function. You must select an *N* row × 1 column vertical range of cells, enter the function and then press CONTROL+SHIFT+ENTER (Windows) or COMMAND+RETURN or CONTROL+SHIFT+RETURN (Macintosh).

See Also

GaussElim, GaussJordan1, GaussJordan2

Appendix 4

Some Equations for Curve Fitting

This appendix describes a number of equation types that can be used for curve fitting. Some of the equation types can be handled by Excel's Trendline utility for charts; these cases are noted below.

Multiple Regression. Multiple regression fits data to a model that defines y as a function of two or more independent x variables. For example, you might want to fit the yield of a biological fermentation product as a function of temperature (T), pressure of CO_2 gas (P) in the fermenter and fermentation time (t)

$$y = a \cdot T + b \cdot P + c \cdot t + d \tag{A4-1}$$

using data from a series of fermentation experiments with different conditions of temperature, pressure and time.

Since you can't create a chart with three x-axes (e.g., T, P and t), you can't use Trendline for multiple regression.

Polynomial Regression. Polynomial regression fits data to a power series such as equation A4-2:

$$y = a + bx + cx^2 + dx^3 + \cdots \tag{A4-2}$$

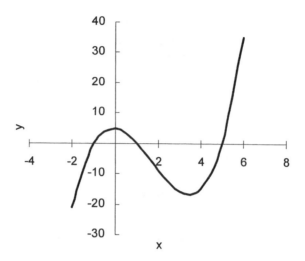

Figure A4-1. Polynomial of order 3.
The curve follows equation A4-2 with $a = 5$, $b = -1$, $c = -5$ and $d = 1$.

The Trendline type is Polynomial. The highest-order polynomial that Trendline can use as a fitting function is a regular polynomial of order six, i.e., $y = ax^6 + bx^5 + cx^4 + dx^3 + ex^2 + fx + g$.

LINEST is not limited to order six, and LINEST can also fit data using other polynomials such as $y = ax^2 + bx^{3/2} + cx + dx^{1/2} + e$.

Exponential Decrease.

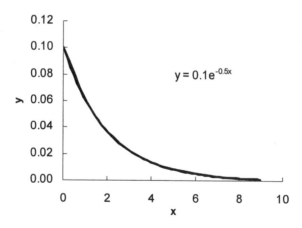

Figure A4-2. Exponential decrease to zero.
The curve follows equation A4-3 with $a = 0.1$ and $b = -0.5$.
The Trendline equation is shown on the chart.

Data with the behavior shown in Figure A4-2 can be fitted by the exponential equation

$$y = ae^{bx} \qquad \text{(A4-3)}$$

The sign of b is often negative (as in radioactive decay), giving rise to the decreasing behavior shown in Figure A4-2.

The linearized form of the equation is $\ln y = bx + \ln a$; the Trendline type is Exponential.

Exponential Growth.   If the sign of b in equation A4-3 is positive, the curvature is upwards, as in Figure A4-3.

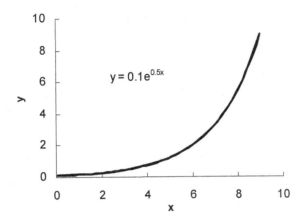

Figure A4-3. Exponential increase.
The curve follows equation A4-3 with $a = 0.1$ and $b = 0.5$.
The Trendline equation is shown on the chart.

Exponential Decrease or Increase Between Limits.   If the curve decreases exponentially to a nonzero limit, or rises exponentially to a limiting value as in Figure A4-4, the form of the equation is

$$y = ae^{bx} + c \qquad \text{(A4-4)}$$

Excel's Trendline cannot handle data of this type.

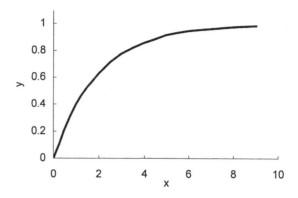

Figure A4-4. Exponential increase to a limit.
The curve follows equation A4-4 with $a = -1$, $b = -0.5$ and $c = 1$.

The linearized form of the equation is $\ln(y - c) = bx + \ln a$.

Double Exponential Decay to Zero. The sum of two exponentials (equation A4-5) gives rise to behavior similar to that shown in Figure A4-5. This type of behavior is observed, for example, in the radioactive decay of a mixture of two nuclides with different half-lives, one short-lived and the other relatively longer-lived.

$$y = ae^{-bt} + ce^{-dt} \tag{A4-5}$$

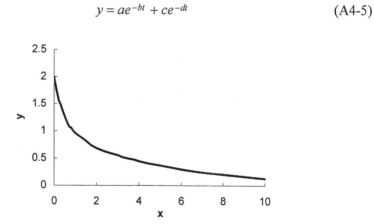

Figure A4-5. Double exponential decay.
The curve follows equation A4-5 with $a = 1$, $b = -2$, $c = 1$ and $d = -0.2$.

If the second term is subtracted rather than added, a variety of curve shapes are possible. Figures A4-6 and A4-7 illustrate two of the possible behaviors.

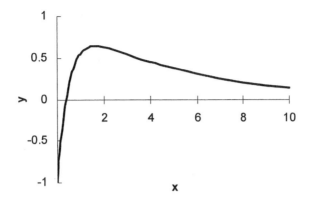

Figure A4-6. Double exponential decay.
The curve follows equation A4-5 with $a = 1$, $b = -0.2$, $c = -2$ and $d = -2$.

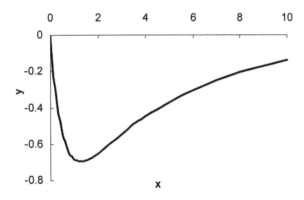

Figure A4-7. Double exponential decay.
The curve follows equation A4-5 with $a = 1$, $b = -2$, $c = -1$ and $d = -0.2$.

Equation A4-5 is intrinsically nonlinear (cannot be converted into a linear form).

Power. Data with the behavior shown in Figure A4-8 can be fitted by equation A4-6.

$$y = ax^b \qquad (A4\text{-}6)$$

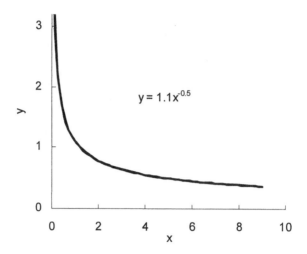

Figure A4-8. Power curve.

The curve follows equation A4-6 with $a = 1.1$, $b = -0.5$.
The Trendline equation is shown on the chart.

The linearized form of equation A4-6 is $\ln y = b \ln x + \ln a$; the Trendline form is Power.

Logarithmic.

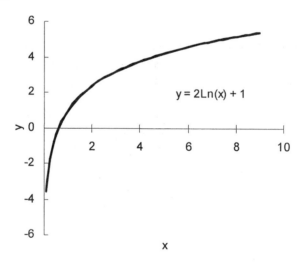

Figure A4-9. Logarithmic function.
The curve follows equation A4-7 with $a = 2$, $b = 1$.

Data with the behavior shown in Figure A4-9 can be fitted by the logarithmic equation A4-7.

$$y = a \ln x + b \tag{A4-7}$$

The Trendline type is Logarithmic.

"Plateau" Curve. A relationship of the form

$$y = \frac{ax}{b+x}$$ (A4-8)

exhibits the behavior shown in Figure A4-10.

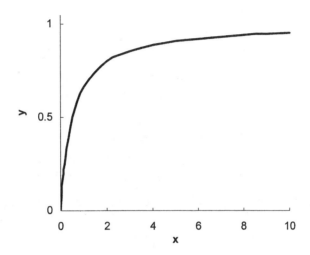

Figure A4-10. Plateau curve.
The curve follows equation A4-8 with $a = 1$, $b = 1$.

In biochemistry, this type of curve is encountered in a plot of reaction rate of an enzyme-catalyzed reaction of a substrate as a function of the concentration of the substrate, as in Figure A4-10. The behavior is described by the Michaelis-Menten equation,

$$V = \frac{V_{max}[S]}{K_m + [S]}$$ (A4-9)

where V is the reaction velocity (typical units mmol/s), K_m is the Michaelis-Menten constant (typical units mM), V_{max} is the maximum reaction velocity and [S] is the substrate concentration. Some typical results are shown in Figure A4-11.

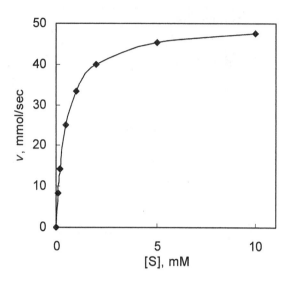

Figure A4-11. Michaelis-Menten enzyme kinetics.
The curve follows equation A4-9 with $V_{max} = 50$, $K_m = 0.5$.

Double Reciprocal Plot. The Michaelis-Menten equation can be converted to a straight line equation by taking the reciprocals of each side. This treatment is called a Lineweaver-Burk plot, a plot of the reciprocal of the enzymatic reaction velocity ($1/V$) versus the reciprocal of the substrate concentration ($1/[S]$).

$$\frac{1}{V} = \frac{K_m}{V_{max}} \frac{1}{S} + \frac{1}{V_{max}} \qquad (A4\text{-}10)$$

A double-reciprocal plot of the data of Figure A4-11 is shown in Figure A4-12. The parameters V_{max} and K_m can be obtained from the slope and intercept of the straight line (V_{max} = 1/intercept, K_m = intercept/slope). However, relationships dealing with the propagation of error must be used to calculate the standard deviations of V_{max} and K_m from the standard deviations of slope and intercept. By contrast, when the Solver is used the expression does not need to be rearranged, y_{calc} is calculated directly from equation A4-19, the Solver returns the coefficients V_{max} and K_m, and SolvStat.xls returns the standard deviations of V_{max} and K_m.

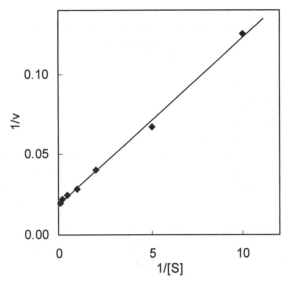

Figure A4-12. Double-reciprocal plot of enzyme kinetics. The curve follows equation A4-10 with $V_{max} = 50$, $K_m = 0.5$.

Logistic Function. The logistic equation or dose-response curve

$$y = \frac{1}{1 + e^{-ax}}$$ (A4-11)

produces an S-shaped curve like the one shown in Figure A4-13.

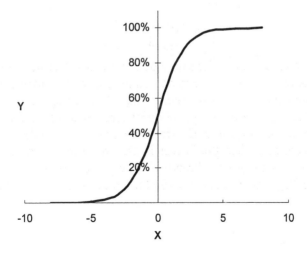

Figure A4-13. Simple logistic curve. The curve follows equation A4-11 with $a = 1$.

In the dose-response form of the equation, the y-axis (the response) is normalized to 100% and the x-axis (usually logarithmic) is normalized so that the midpoint (the half-maximum response or EC_{50}) occurs at $x = 0$.

Logistic Curve with Variable Slope. In equation A4-11, the coefficient a determines the slope of the rising part of the curve; in biochemistry a is referred to as the Hill slope. Figure A4-14 illustrates the effect of varying Hill slope. At the midpoint the slope is $a/4$.

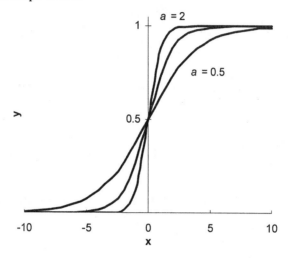

Figure A4-14. Variable slopes of logistic curve.
The three curves have $a = 0.5$, 1 and 2, respectively.

Logistic Curve with Additional Parameters. Equation A4-12 is the logistic equation with addition parameters that determine the height of the "plateau" and the offset of the mid-point from $x = 0$.

$$y = \frac{b}{c + e^{-ax}}$$
(A4-12)

The height of the plateau is equal to b/c.

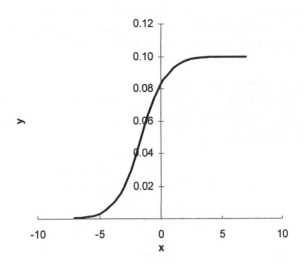

Figure A4-15. Logistic curve with additional variables.
The curve follows equation A4-12 with $a = 1$, $b = 0.5$ and $c = 5$.

Logistic Curve with Offset on the *y*-Axis. The logistic equation

$$y = \frac{a}{1 + e^{b+cx}} + d \qquad (A4\text{-}13)$$

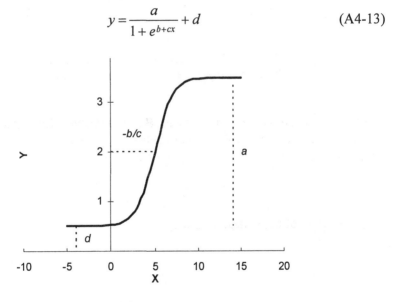

Figure A4-16. Logistic curve with offset on the *y*-axis.
The curve follows equation A4-13 with $a = 1$, $b = -2$, $c = 1$ and $d = -0.2$.

This equation takes into account the value of the plateau maximum and minimum (coefficients a and d, respectively), the offset on the *x*-axis, and the Hill slope.

Gaussian Curve. The Gaussian or normal error curve (equation A4-14)

$$y = \frac{\exp[-(x - \mu)^2 / 2\sigma^2]}{\sigma\sqrt{2\pi}}$$ (A4-14)

can be used to model UV-visible band shapes, usually in order to deconvolute a spectrum consisting of two or more overlapping bands. When used for deconvolution, a simplified form of the Gaussian formula can be used, for example

$$A = A_{max}e^{-[(x-m)/s]^2}$$ (A4-15)

where A is absorbance, x is the independent variable, either wavelength (e.g., nm), or, more commonly, 1/wavelength (e.g., cm^{-1}), and m is the value of x at A_{max}. The parameter s is related to the bandwidth at half-height.

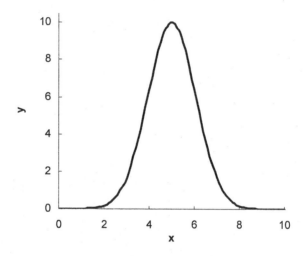

Figure A4-17. Gaussian curve.
The curve follows equation A4-15 with $A_{max} = 10$, $m = 5$ and $s = 1.5$.

Log vs. Reciprocal. The function

$$y = \exp\left(a - \frac{b}{x}\right)$$ (A4-16)

is often seen in the relationship of physical properties to temperature. The linearized form is $\ln y = -b/x + a$.

This equation form is encountered in the Clausius-Clapeyron equation

$$\ln P = \frac{-\Delta H_{vap}}{RT} + C$$ (A4-17)

which relates vapor pressure of a pure substance to temperature, and the Arrhenius equation

$$\ln k = \frac{-E_a}{RT} + \ln A \tag{A4-18}$$

which relates rate constant k of a reaction to temperature.

Trigonometric Functions. Excel's trigonometric functions require angles in radians. For an angle θ in degrees, use $\pi\theta/180$.

The function represented by equation A4-19

$$y = a \sin (bx + c) + d \tag{A4-19}$$

or its cosine equivalent produces a curve with the appearance of a "sine wave" centered around the x-axis if $d = 0$, or offset from the x-axis if $d \neq 0$.

Functions of the form

$$y = \sin ax + \sin bx \tag{A4-20}$$

and their cosine equivalents produce a "beat frequency" curve such as the one shown in Figure A4-17.

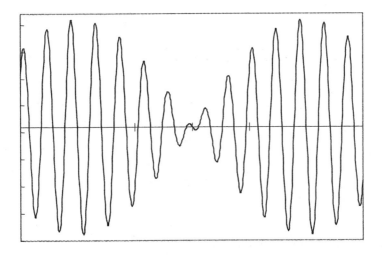

Figure A4-18. "Beat frequency" curve.
The curve follows equation A4-21 with $a = 1$, $b = 0.9$.

Equation A4-21 combines the parameters of equations A4-19 and A4-20.

$$y = a \sin (bx + c) + d \sin (ex + f) + g \tag{A4-21}$$

Appendix 5

Engineering and Other Functions

The following functions are available only if you have loaded the Analysis ToolPak. Most are listed in the Engineering category in the Insert Function dialog box.

BESSELI	Returns the modified Bessel function $In(x)$
BESSELJ	Returns the Bessel function $Jn(x)$
BESSELK	Returns the modified Bessel function $Kn(x)$
BESSELY	Returns the Bessel function $Yn(x)$
BIN2DEC	Converts a binary number to decimal
BIN2HEX	Converts a binary number to hexadecimal
BIN2OCT	Converts a binary number to octal
COMPLEX	Converts real and imaginary coefficients into a complex number
CONVERT	Converts a number from one measurement system to another
DEC2BIN	Converts a decimal number to binary
DEC2HEX	Converts a decimal number to hexadecimal
DEC2OCT	Converts a decimal number to octal
DELTA	Tests whether two values are equal
EDATE[1]	Returns the serial number of the date that is a specified number of months before or after the specified start date.
EOMONTH[1]	Returns the serial number of the last day of the month that is a specified number of months before or after the specified start date
ERF	Returns the error function
ERFC	Returns the complementary error function

FACTDOUBLE[3]	Returns the double factorial of a number. See On-Line Help for more information.
GCD[3]	Returns the greatest common divisor of 1 to 29 integers.
GESTEP	Tests whether a number is greater than a threshold value
HEX2BIN	Converts a hexadecimal number to binary
HEX2DEC	Converts a hexadecimal number to decimal
HEX2OCT	Converts a hexadecimal number to octal
IMABS	Returns the absolute value (modulus) of a complex number
IMAGINARY	Returns the imaginary coefficient of a complex number
IMARGUMENT	Returns the argument theta, an angle expressed in radians
IMCONJUGATE	Returns the complex conjugate of a complex number
IMCOS	Returns the cosine of a complex number in $x + yi$ or $x + yj$ text format.
IMDIV	Returns the quotient of two complex numbers
IMEXP	Returns the exponential of a complex number
IMLN	Returns the natural logarithm of a complex number
IMLOG10	Returns the base-10 logarithm of a complex number
IMLOG2	Returns the base-2 logarithm of a complex number
IMPOWER	Returns a complex number raised to an integer power
IMPRODUCT	Returns the product of 1 to 29 complex numbers
IMREAL	Returns the real part of a complex number
IMSIN	Returns the sine of a complex number
IMSQRT	Returns the square root of a complex number
IMSUB	Returns the difference of two complex numbers
IMSUM	Returns the sum of 1 to 29 complex numbers
ISEVEN[2]	Returns TRUE if number is even, or FALSE if number is odd
ISODD[2]	Returns TRUE if number is odd, or FALSE if number is even
LCM[3]	Returns the least common multiple of 1 to 29 integers.
MROUND[3]	Returns a number rounded to the desired multiple.
MULTNOMIAL[3]	Returns the ratio of the factorial of a sum of values to the product of factorials.
OCT2BIN	Converts an octal number to binary

OCT2DEC	Converts an octal number to decimal
OCT2HEX	Converts an octal number to hexadecimal
QUOTIENT[3]	Returns the integer portion of a division
RANDBETWEEN[3]	Returns a random integer between specified lower and upper limits
SERIESSUM[3]	Returns the sum of a power series. (See On-Line Help for more information)
SQRTPI[3]	Returns the square root of (number $* \pi$)
WEEKNUM[1]	Returns the week number (1–52) in the year
WORKDAY[1]	Returns the serial number of the date that is a specified number of workdays before or after the specified start date

[1] Listed in Date & Time category

[2] Listed in Information category

[3] Listed in Math & Trig category

Appendix 6
ASCII Codes

The following table lists the ASCII codes for some useful non-printing keyboard characters (codes 8, 9, 10, 13, 27), the keyboard characters (codes 32–127) and the "alternate character set" (codes 128–255). The alternate characters can be printed by holding down the ALT key while typing 0###, e.g., for ±, type ALT+0177.

8	backspace	10	line feed	27	escape
9	horizontal tab	13	carriage return		

32	(space)	64	@	96	`
33	!	65	A	97	a
34	"	66	B	98	b
35	#	67	C	99	c
36	$	68	D	100	d
37	%	69	E	101	e
38	&	70	F	102	f
39	'	71	G	103	g
40	(	72	H	104	h
41	)	73	I	105	i
42	*	74	J	106	j
43	+	75	K	107	k
44	,	76	L	108	l
45	-	77	M	109	m
46	.	78	N	110	n
47	/	79	O	111	o
48	0	80	P	112	p
49	1	81	Q	113	q
50	2	82	R	114	r
51	3	83	S	115	s
52	4	84	T	116	t
53	5	85	U	117	u
54	6	86	V	118	v
55	7	87	W	119	w
56	8	88	X	120	x
57	9	89	Y	121	y
58	:	90	Z	122	z
59	;	91	[	123	{
60	<	92	\	124	|
61	=	93	]	125	}
62	>	94	^	126	~
63	?	95	_	127	(bksp)

128	€	160		192	À	224	à
129	*(NP)**	161	¡	193	Á	225	á
130	,	162	¢	194	Â	226	â
131	ƒ	163	£	195	Ã	227	ã
132	„	164	¤	196	Ä	228	ä
133	…	165	¥	197	Å	229	å
134	†	166	¦	198	Æ	230	æ
135	‡	167	§	199	Ç	231	ç
136	ˆ	168	¨	200	È	232	è
137	‰	169	©	201	É	233	é
138	Š	170	ª	202	Ê	234	ê
139	‹	171	«	203	Ë	235	ë
140	Œ	172	¬	204	Ì	236	ì
141	*(NP)**	173	-	205	Í	237	í
142	Ž	174	®	206	Î	238	î
143	*(NP)**	175	¯	207	Ï	239	ï
144	*(NP)**	176	°	208	Ð	240	ð
145	'	177	±	209	Ñ	241	ñ
146	'	178	²	210	Ò	242	ò
147	"	179	³	211	Ó	243	ó
148	"	180	´	212	Ô	244	ô
149	•	181	µ	213	Õ	245	õ
150	–	182	¶	214	Ö	246	ö
151	—	183	·	215	×	247	÷
152	~	184	¸	216	Ø	248	ø
153	™	185	¹	217	Ù	249	ù
154	š	186	º	218	Ú	250	ú
155	›	187	»	219	Û	251	û
156	œ	188	¼	220	Ü	252	ü
157	*(NP)**	189	½	221	Ý	253	ý
158	ž	190	¾	222	Þ	254	þ
159	Ÿ	191	¿	223	ß	255	ÿ

*non-printing

Appendix 7

Bibliography

Ayyub, Bilal M. and Richard H. McCuen, *Numerical Methods for Engineers*, Prentice-Hall, 1996.

Bourg, David M., *Excel Scientific and Engineering Cookbook*, O'Reilly, 2006.

Chapra, Steven C. and Raymond P. Canale, *Numerical Methods for Engineers*, 4th ed., McGraw-Hill, 2002.

Cheney, Ward and David Kincaid, *Numerical Mathematics and Computing*, Brooks/Cole, 1985.

Gerald, Curtis F. and Patrick O. Wheatley, *Applied Numerical Analysis*, 3rd ed., Addison-Wesley, 1984.

Hecht, Harry G., *Mathematics in Chemistry*, Prentice-Hall, 1990.

Hoffman, Joe D., *Numerical Methods for Engineers and Scientists*, McGraw-Hill, 1992.

Johnson, K. Jeffrey, *Numerical Methods in Chemistry*, Marcel Dekker, 1980.

Kuo, Shan S., *Numerical Methods and Computers*, Addison-Wesley, 1965.

Press, William H., *et al.*, *Numerical Recipes in FORTRAN*, 2nd ed., Cambridge University Press, 1992.

Rao, S. S., *Applied Numerical Methods for Engineers and Scientists*, Prentice-Hall, 2002.

Rusling, J. F. and Kumosinski, T. F. *Nonlinear Computer Modeling of Chemical and Biochemical Data*, Academic Press, 1996.

Shoup, Terry E., *Numerical Methods for the Personal Computer*, Prentice-Hall, 1983.

Appendix 8

Answers and Comments for End-of-Chapter Problems

Chapter 3 Matrices

1. (a) inverse:

	G	H	I
2	-0.10278	0.188889	-0.01944
3	0.105556	0.022222	-0.06111
4	0.063889	-0.14444	0.147222

det = −360

(b) inverse:

	G	H	I
2	0.75	0.5	0.25
3	0.5	1	0.5
4	0.25	0.5	0.75

det = 4

(c) Inverse:

	G	H	I
2	2	-1	0
3	-1	2	-1
4	0	-1	2

det = 0.25

(d) Inverse:

	G	H	I
2	1	-1	-1.1E-16
3	0	-1	1
4	-1	3	-1

det = −1

2. (a) det = 0. If **A** is a square matrix and two of its rows are proportional or two of its columns are proportional, the determinant is zero.

(b) det = 1.55431E-15   (c) det = 6

Chapter 4 Number Series

1. (a) Sum of 24 terms = 2   (b) Sum of 100 terms = 1.6349839.
    (c) Sum of 24 terms = 1.71828182845899

2   0.632120558828558, one of the so-called incomplete gamma functions.

3. It's interesting to experiment with different values for a and x.

4. Answer: 1.5   5. Answer: 0.5

6. Summing the first 100 terms, the series sum is $\pi = 3.133787$ (0.2% error).

7.

	H	I	J
7	n	$2 \times S_n$	% error
8	65536	3.141581	1.2E-03

The formula in cell I8 is

{=2*PRODUCT((2*ROW(INDIRECT("1:"&H8)))^2/(2*ROW(INDIRECT("1:"&H8))-1)/(2*ROW(INDIRECT("1:"&H8))+1))}

8. The spreadsheet answer also incorporates the formula for the initial estimate (problem 9).

9. Here is one possible formula. The number is in cell C2; the initial estimate formula is

    =LEFT(C2,0.5*(LEN(C2)+1))

10. The series is described in Edward Kasner and James R. Newman, *Mathematics and the Imagination*, Simon & Schuster, 1940; Harper & Row, 1989. The sum (10 terms) is $\pi = 3.14159265359$ (9×10^{-14} % error).

Chapter 5 Interpolation

1. Interpolated values: 6.04, 0.59. The formula uses an external reference to refer to the data table on a different worksheet.

2. This problem requires you to "lookup" to the left. You can either use a linear interpolation formula using MATCH and INDEX, like the one illustrated in Figure 5-3, or reorganize the data table so that the freezing point data is on the left of the wt% data. The latter approach permits the use of cubic

interpolation. If you use this approach, you must sort the data table so that the x values are in ascending order. Answer: 34.9%.

3. Answers: 3.34231, 5.40473.

4. Answers: 1.52, 1.18.

5. Data from *J. Research National Bureau of Standards*, 68A, 489 (1964).
    Answers: 1.50173, 1.48727, 1.52508, 1.53731, #VALUE!

6. Depending on the behavior of the data, these interpolation methods can give values that are very close to the theoretical (if that is available) or values that are not so close. This example is one of the latter.

x	y(interp)	y(exact)	% error
1.81	4.512445	4.4887	0.53
3.11	-21.81015	-21.7016	-0.50
5.2	-74.35316	-75.2167	-1.15
5.4	-29.73034	-30.5699	-2.75

Chapter 6 Differentiation

1. I used worksheet formulas, as illustrated in Figures 6-2 and 6-4. The value of the first derivative is a maximum at $V = 20.00$ mL ($\Delta\text{pH}/\Delta V = 61.949$).

2. There are two end-points, one at $V = 7.16$ mL and the second at $V = 15.44$ mL. Since the data is real student data, there is some noise, which is accentuated in the first derivative and even more so in the second derivative.

3. I used worksheet formulas to calculate the various derivative formulas. As expected, the errors are smaller (several orders of magnitude, in this example) when using the four-point central derivative formula, compared to the two-point formula.

4. You can experiment with different coefficients for the cubic by changing the values on the worksheet.

5. I used the custom function for this problem. The optional *scale_factor* was required for the case where $x = 0$.

6. (a) $F'(x) = 0.11072$ at $x = -4$, 0 at $x = 0$.
    (b) $F'(x) = 9.0028E\text{-}07$ at $x = -4$.
    (c) $F'(x) = 0$ at $x = 0$, -0.5 at $x = 1$.
    (d) $F'(x) = 0$ at $x = 1$, -0.01176 at $x = 10$
    (e) $F'(x) = 0.00242$ at $x = 90$, $-2E\text{-}10$ at $x = 100$.

7. I used the custom function to calculate the first derivative. For $a = 1$, the mid-point slope was 0.25.

8. I used the custom functions dydx and d2ydx2 to calculate the first and second derivatives. Errors were all in the range 10^{-7} to 10^{-9}.

Chapter 7 Integration

1. Area = 2.4105 (approx.).

2. (a) Answer: $\dfrac{1}{1+n}$ (b) 0.746824133375978   (c) 2

    (d) $-\dfrac{\pi^2}{12}$ (e) $-\dfrac{\pi^2}{8}$ (f) -6 (g) 0.287682

3. Answer given in a table: 1.3506.

4. Answer: 5.864 (approx.), 5.877 (exact).

5. Answer: 2.711 (approx.), 2.721 (exact).

6. I chose x-increments of 0.2 and calculated the two curves from -2 to $+4$. Fortunately the two curves intersected at $x = -1$ and $x = 3$. The cells that were summed to obtain the area are in blue. Area = 10.640.

7. As in the preceding problem, I used x-increments of 0.2. This time it was necessary to use **Goal Seek...** to find the points where the two curves crossed. After using **Goal Seek**, the target cell (Y1-Y2) was deleted. The cells that were summed to obtain the area are in blue. Area = 4.822.

8. As in the preceding problem, **Goal Seek...** was used to find the two intersection points. Approximate answer 14900.

9. After evaluating the areas using a trial value of c, **Goal Seek...** was used to set the relationship *area bounded by y=4 – 2* area bounded by y = c* to zero. The changing cell and the target cell are shown on the spreadsheet. $c = 2.528$.

10. The same procedure was followed as in the preceding problem. $c = 8.68$

11. Answer $= 6.51413$ (approx.), $\pi^4/15 = 6.493939$ (exact).

12. (a) Answer: 1   (b) 1   (c) ½   (d) $\dfrac{1}{2}\sqrt{\dfrac{\pi}{a}}$ (e) $\sqrt{\pi}$

Chapter 8 Roots of Equations

1. To find the first time after $t = 0$ when the current reaches zero, you must begin with a value of t that will force Goal Seek to converge to the first $i = 0$ after $t = 0$. Using $t = 1$ is a good choice. $t = 1.576$ seconds.

2. Use **Goal Seek...** $D = 0.756$.

3. The spreadsheet shows a manual method, similar to the interval-halving method, and also uses Goal Seek. $[Ba^{2+}] = 1.28 \times 10^{-5}$ M.

4. The spreadsheet shows the graphical method and also uses Goal Seek. $S = 0.13$ mol/L.

5. Use Goal Seek with Y1-Y2 as target cell formula. Use two different initial values of x to get the two different x-values. Formulas are under the chart. Answer: $x = -5.857$ and $x = 12.494$.

6. Follow same procedure as in the preceding problem. For $h = 0.5$, $x = -0.87$ and $x = 0.87$. If you use the Goal Seek custom function, you can change the value of h and observe the intersections change.

7. This problem requires two successive uses of Goal Seek. The procedure is described on the spreadsheet..

8. $x = 0.288$, $[A] = 0.4858$ mol L^{-1}.
9. $x = 0.8598$, $[A] = 0.1402$ atm

11. I used **Goal Seek...** with the cell containing the formula MDETERM as the
target cell and the cell containing the (1,1) element of the matrix as the
changing cell. The cell value 0.25 gives a determinant value of zero. Two
elements of the matrix cannot be varied so as to give a zero value: the (1, 3)
element and the (3, 1) element.

Chapter 9 Simultaneous Equations

1.   Using the GaussElim function, $x_1 = 40.6752697$, $x_2 = -77.86744959$,
$x_3 = 3.111657335$, $x_4 = 10.63794438$.

2.   Using the GaussElim function, $I_1 = 1$, $I_2 = 0$, $I_3 = 1$.

3.   Using the GaussElim function, $x_1 = 0.621563612$, $x_2 = -5.5 \times 10^{-06}$,
$x_3 = 0.216058954$, $x_4 = 0.758779009$.

4. $[Co^{2+}] = 0.0533$, $[Ni^{2+}] = 0.1125$, $[Cu^{2+}] = 0.1022$ mol/L.

5.   (a) Not solvable. Row 3 is a multiple of row 1.

     (d) $x_1 = 1$, $x_2 = 0$, $x_3 = 3$, $x_4 = 2$.

6.   Using the GaussElim function, $x_1 = 29.746$, $x_2 = 19.991$, $x_3 = -20.487$,
$x_4 = -4.455$, $x_5 = -48.369$, $x_6 = -8.270$.

7.   Using the SimultEqNL custom function, $x = 0.707$, $y = 0.707$.

8.   Using the SimultEqNL custom function, $x = -1$, $y = 2$, $z = -1$

Chapter 10   ODEs with Initial Conditions

1. I used the Runge1 custom function. Set up the spreadsheet with three
columns: x, y, y'.

2. I used the Runge1 custom function. Set up the spreadsheet with three
columns: x, y, y'. The exact expression for y is given in the answer
spreadsheet.

3. Set up the spreadsheet with three columns: x, y, y'. I used the Runge1 custom function. The exact expression for y is given in the answer spreadsheet.

4. Set up the spreadsheet with five columns: t, x, y, x' y'. Plot x *vs.* y to visualize the trajectory. I used **Goal Seek** to find the value of t that makes $y = 0$.

5. Make a copy of the spreadsheet of problem 4 and modify it (I used the Runge1 custom function). The projectile struck the ground at $x = 31967$ m. Note that the velocity was identical to that when it left the muzzle.

6. It may be helpful to set up the problem using the Euler method first, without air drag, and then modify the spreadsheet to include air drag. Set up the spreadsheet with eight columns: t, x, y, x' y', x'', y'' and v.
If you experiment with different angles, it appears that an angle of about 30° gives the longest drive when air resistance is taken into account.
For calculations and interesting discussion on Mickey Mantle's "tape measure home run" of 565 feet, hit at Griffith Stadium on April 17, 1953, see Grant R. Fowles and George L. Cassiday, *Analytical Mechanics*, 7th ed., Brooks Cole.

7. Excel's SIN function requires angles in radians. It may be helpful to solve the problem using the Euler method first.

8. The problem requires using two Runge-Kutta or Euler calculations. It may be helpful to solve the problem using the Euler method first.

10. I used the Runge3 custom function to calculate the concentrations of A and B. Note that the exact expressions fail if [A] = [B]; thus I made [B] very slightly greater than [A].

11. I used names for the rate constants k_1, k_2, k_3 and k_4, to make the formulas clearer; I used the Runge3 custom function to calculate the concentrations of A, B and C.

Chapter 11   ODEs with Boundary Values

1. Set up the spreadsheet as in Figure 11-2. Use an initial value of zero for the slope. Then use **Goal Seek** to get the value of the slope (changing cell) that gives a value of zero for the deflection at the other end of the beam (target cell). Maximum deflection: 0.6138 in.

2. Use procedure as in problem 1. Maximum deflection: 0.9353 in at 200 in.

3. Set up spreadsheet as in Figure 10-17. This system is very sensitive to changes in y''; sometimes Goal Seek fails to converge. You may have to provide some manual guidance.

4. Set up spreadsheet as in problem 3.

5. Set up spreadsheet as in problem 3.

6. Set up spreadsheet as in problem 3.

Chapter 12   PDEs

1. Set up spreadsheet as in Figure 12-2.

2. Set up spreadsheet as in Figure 11-2, but with additional temperature constants as described in the problem.

Chapter 13   Linear Regression

1. Insert columns for x^2 and x^3, then use LINEST. Answer: $a = 0.00141 \pm 0.0005$, $b = -0.193 \pm 0.019$, $c = 13.28 \pm 0.19$, $d = 0.079 \pm 0.498$, $R^2 = 0.999986$.

2. The constant term d has a standard error much larger than its value; therefore it should be eliminated from the model. Fitting the data to $y = ax^3 + bx^2 + cx$ gives a slightly better R^2 value.

3. The answer spreadsheet shows the results from Trendline and also how to get the regression parameters of a power function using LINEST.

4. The LINEST formula in this example uses an array constant to produce the squared and cubed values of the known_x's. (Answers: 33.3 wt%, 2.3°F; 42.3 wt%, -12.6°F)

5. The LINEST formula in this example uses an array constant to produce the values of known_x's raised to the required powers. (Answers: 33.3 wt%, 2.3°F; 42.3 wt%, -12.6°F)

6. I first made a 3-D plot of the data. The shape of the surface (smooth upward curvature) suggested to me that the data vs. each independent variable could be a simple function, perhaps exponential or polynomial. I created XY plots of Power vs. Throttle and Power vs. Speed and experimented; quadratic or

cubic (polynomials of 2nd or 3rd order) fitted the data quite well. Using that information I used LINEST to find regression coefficients that fitted Power to Speed (S) for each value of Throttle (T) (the fitting function was $a \cdot S^2 + b \cdot S$). I then fitted the regression coefficients a and b individually vs. Throttle. (From charts, it appeared that a could be fitted using a 3-term function, b using a 2-term function.) The final fitting function was $(c \cdot T^2 + d \cdot T + e)S^2 + (f \cdot T + g)S$. The g term had a large standard error and perhaps could be eliminated or modified.

The final sheet in the workbook shows how the Solver (see following chapter) can be applied to the same data. Both the preceding 5-term fitting function and a 6-term fitting function, $(c \cdot T^2 + d \cdot T + e)S^2 + (f \cdot T + g)S + h$, were tried.

The preceding fitting function can be written in the following form:
$$c \cdot T^2 \cdot S^2 + d \cdot T \cdot S^2 + e \cdot S^2 + f \cdot T \cdot S + g \cdot S + h$$

Chapter 14   Nonlinear Regression and the Solver

1. Enter formula for A_{calc} (you'll need a cell for k, the changing cell). Enter formula for (residual)^2 and sum the squares of residuals (this is the target cell). Use the Solver to minimize the target. Answer: $k = 0.3290$.

2. Follow the same procedure as in problem 1. Answer: $a = 0.5005$.

3. Follow the same procedure as in problem 1, except that there are four changing cells. Answer: $a = 1.0644246$, $b = 1.8495246$, $c = -0.8966248$, $d = 9.97124864$.

4. The answer spreadsheet has been set up with headings for using the Runge3 custom function. The workbook contains a "Data for Problem" sheet and the complete problem.

5. Follow the same procedure as in problem 1, except that there are three changing cells. Answers I got were $A = 0.10119$, $B = 5.1337$, $C = 0.0117922$.

6. This example requires scaling. The data for the exercise and the answer spreadsheet are in different workbooks.

8. The workbook contains a worksheet with the raw data, plus two worksheets with solutions. You can compare the use of wavelength vs. wavenumber as the independent variable in deconvoluting UV-visible spectra. Although it is generally considered that an independent variable that is proportional to energy (e.g., wavenumber) is the correct independent variable to use, in this

example a better fit is found when using wavelength as the independent variable.

On the sheet "Deconvolution using wavenumber," wavelength (nm, 1×10^{-9} m) is converted into wavenumber (cm^{-1}) by using the relationship wavenumber = 10000/wavelength.

9. The data for the exercise and the answer spreadsheet are in different workbooks. The spectrum contains a number of bands. I have not yet obtained a satisfactory solution.

10. Using the spectra of the pure species, calculate the ε for each of the three species, cobalt, nickel and copper, at each wavelength. Then, at each wavelength, use the relationship

$$A_{obsd} = \varepsilon_{Co}C_{Co} + \varepsilon_{Ni}C_{Ni} + \varepsilon_{Cu}C_{Cu}$$

You now have 236 equations with only three unknowns. Use the Solver to find the three unknowns. The answers are slightly different from the results found in Chapter 9.

11. The equations in the problem lead to the following worksheet formula for the absorbance:

    =TL*(K*eL+H*eHL)/(K+H)

(Names were used for all cell references in this worksheet.) The changing cells are the log K value and the ε_L and ε_{HL} values, one pair for each column of absorbance values at a particular wavelength.

Since the data table is large, it was most convenient to have the experimental absorbance values on one sheet and the calculated values on another.

The SUMSQ worksheet function was used to calculate the sum of squares of residuals for each column.

I used the Solver on the absorbance values at 260 nm first, to get a value of log$K$ (changing cells and target cell for this calculation are in red). I then used these as starting values for the global refinement. Convergence was very slow.

12. The five changing cells have very different magnitudes (values were estimated from the data table and/or the chart); three were of magnitude 10^{-3} and two were of magnitude 1. Using the Solver in the usual way did not give a reasonable solution (see the sheet "First Trial"). Checking the Use Automatic Scaling box did not give a reasonable solution either (see "With Automatic Scaling"). Manual scaling was done as described in the worksheet "Manual+Automatic Scaling" and this led to an acceptable solution.

Chapter 15   Random Numbers and Monte Carlo

1. The answer spreadsheet contains two examples. The first uses 32 points, and is intended mainly to illustrate the method. Random number formulas are used to generate a pair of *x, y* coordinates in columns A and B. The formula in column C uses an IF statement to determine whether the point is inside the circle; if inside, the formula returns the *y* coordinate, otherwise the cell is blank.

    The second example uses 4000 points and is used to create the chart. The formula in column G returns the *y* coordinate if the point is inside the circle; if not the cell returns #N/A. A cell containing #N/A is not plotted in a chart.

    π is the number of points within the circle divided by the total number of points.

2. A random number is used to specify whether a child is male (>0.5) or female. The simulation shown uses 100 mothers and a maximum of 10 children per mother. The "series" is terminated when the first "F" is generated. (Very occasionally 10 children is not sufficient to end the series.) It's fairly clear from the results from 100 mothers that the proportion is 50:50, but a macro button has been provided that sums the results of 100 recalculations.

    When I first encountered this problem many years ago, I sat down and derived an analytical expression for the result, but right now I can't reproduce it.

3. Constructing a spreadsheet to simulate the traffic pattern is left to the reader.

4. The Traveling Salesman problem is usually formulated as follows: a salesman must travel to a number of cities, visiting each one only once and finally returning to the city of origin. The problem is to minimize the distance traveled. It's obvious that this problem has many real-world applications, so an algorithm for a general solution would be very useful. But this seemingly simple problem is actually essentially impossible to solve for all but the simplest of cases.

    The straightforward approach would be to determine the distance between each city and to calculate the total distance of all possible routes. Thus, for example, if only five cities are to be considered, there are five cities at which to begin; having chosen one of the five, there are four possible destinations, etc. The total number of possible routes is 5! = 120. But as *N*, the number of cities increases, *N*!, the number of possible routes, quickly increases to a number so large as to be make the solution impossible even with today's computers. Obviously, an approach that will simplify the problem is required. One strategy is to always travel to the city that is closest (of the ones not yet visited, of course). Strategies such as this may not provide the perfect solution but may at least provide a useful one. This method is illustrated on the sheet "Method 1."

Another approach has been to use the Monte Carlo method, illustrated on the sheet "Method 2."

5. You can't use the expression 15*RAND(), since this has the possibility of returning the same number more than once. The same is true of the expression RANDBETWEEN(1,15). The same deficiency occurs with the Sampling Tool in **Tools→Data Analysis...**. If you specify, for example, five random numbers from the list of integers 1, 2, 3, 4, 5 you could get the result 2, 5, 2, 1, 3.
    The only way to do this (that I can think of) is to create a two-column table with the integers 1–15 and 15 random numbers using RAND() and sort the table manually in ascending or descending order, in the same was as the example shown in Figure 15-2. You can also sort the list by using a formula, as shown in Figure 15-5.

6. This problem is similar to the previous one (you could just create a list of the integers 1–52 in random order), except that it opens up the possibility of displaying the 52 values as numbers 1–13 in the four suits: clubs, diamonds, hearts, spades. The workbook shows several ways to display the results. The symbols for the four suits are in the Symbol font; Conditional Formatting was used to provide the red color for the diamonds and hearts.

7. This workbook requires the RANDBETWEEN worksheet function. Some code has been provided so that if the Analysis ToolPak is not loaded, a **Sub** procedure in the sheet ThisWorkbook loads the Add-In.

8. The surprising result of this simulation shows that about 30% of all numbers obtained from real numerical data start with the digit 1. This has been termed Benford's Law.
    Newcomb (1881) observed that the first pages of tables of logarithms were more worn and dirty than later pages, suggesting that numbers with a low first digit occurred in calculations more often than ones with a high first digit. (The counter-argument, of course, is that people start at the beginning of the table and page through until they reach the page they need.)
    Benford (1938) determined the distributions of leading digits in data sets taken from a wide variety of sources, including molecular weights of compounds, surface area of rivers, and street addresses. He found the following distribution: 1, 30.6%; 2, 18.5%; 3, 12.4%; 4, 9.4%; 5, 8.0%; 6, 6.4%; 7, 5.1%; 8, 4.9%; 9, 4.7%
    Hill (1996) showed that, for a variety of statistical data, the first digit is D with the probability $\log_{10}(1+1/D)$.
    Benford's law is more than a numerical curiosity; it has practical applications for the design of computers and for detection of fraudulent data. Benford's law was used as a plot device in the episode, "The Running Man" (2006), of the CBS television crime drama NUMB3RS.

Index